RABUN COUNTY, GEORGIA, NEWSPAPERS, 1894 – 1899

Compiled by Dawn Watson

BONE DIGGERS PRESS
CLAYTON, GA

In Memoriam
Linda Ledford Watson
1948 – 2009

Funding assistance for publication of the hard cover edition provided by the R. J. Taylor, Jr. Foundation, Atlanta, Ga.

Hard cover edition: ISBN 978-0-9852701-1-7
Paperback edition: ISBN 978-1-943465-70-5

Hard cover edition printed by McNaughton & Gunn, Inc., Saline, Michigan.

For purchasing information, contact:
info@bonediggerspress.com

TABLE OF CONTENTS

PREFACE

This compilation contains local news, legal items, and advertisements extracted from periodicals published for the benefit of the citizens of Rabun County, Georgia, from 1894 through 1899. Only three newspapers fitting this description are known to have extant issues:

- *The Clayton Argus*, published in 1894, with two extant issues;
- *The Tallulah Falls Spray*, published from at least 1896 and into 1898, with extant issues from 1897 and 1898;
- *The Clayton Tribune*, published beginning in 1898, with at least portions of extant issues available from 1899 to the present.

No periodicals are currently known to have been published within the bounds of Rabun County before 1894. There were, however, several newspapers published from the 1890s forward. *The Clayton Telegraph* was published by A. B. Sams in Clayton circa 1898. Similarly, *Echoes from Tallulah Falls*, edited by Walter Hunnicutt and managed by William Berrie, was published for at least a short time in 1899, and possibly into 1900. Neither of these newspapers is known to have extant issues.

There are many missing issues of *The Clayton Tribune* within each year until around 1930. Through 1905, no issues are known to be extant for the years 1898, 1900, 1901, and 1904.

Information on the locations of print issues and microfilm can be found at the beginning of the section for each newspaper. The microfilm was produced by the University of Georgia's Georgia Newspaper Project. UGA's main library in Athens contains one of the largest collections of Georgia newspapers on microfilm.

Several problems were encountered while compiling items from *The Clayton Tribune*. These are addressed in detail at the beginning of the section for that newspaper.

METHODOLOGY

The contents of this volume are arranged chronologically by the newspaper's starting date, and then by extant issue, earliest to latest.

Local items were included in their entirety whenever possible, if brief, and with pertinent details if not, where "local" is defined as anything directly affecting or pertaining to residents of Rabun and surrounding counties in Georgia, North Carolina, and South Carolina. Because many issues used as the basis of this work have not been microfilmed and, in most cases, are known to have only one extant copy per issue, nearly all local items were extracted in their entirety.

For advertisements, the name and nature (if not obvious from the name) of the business, its location, and the names of the proprietors or managers were retained, at the least. Advertisements and legal notices were included only once, generally for the first issue in which they appeared. This includes notices for the payment of debts, and notices intended to warn trespassers.

Mentions of non-local items were usually excluded as these are believed to have been published in and/or covered adequately by other newspapers from the same era.

Local community columns were treated as one item.

Most of the local community columns were submitted by correspondents via letters to the editor. These correspondents often used nicknames or pseudonyms that make it virtually impossible for modern-day readers to ascertain the identity of the writer. Unless the correspondent's full name was given in the original, his or her name was omitted entirely here.

Words were transcribed as given within the original, especially proper names. Spelling was incredibly fluid at that time. Many instances of apparent typographical errors represent the actual appearance of the word in the original record. This includes instances where words and letters were inadvertently omitted, reversed, or otherwise mislaid by the typesetter.

Some punctuation was added to improve clarity, uniformity, or readability, especially within lists. The formatting of items as they appeared in the original issues was generally not retained due to space considerations.

While every effort was made to accurately transcribe or abstract items from these newspapers, it is always advisable to refer back to the originals.

2022 PAPERBACK EDITION

No substantial changes were made to the hardbound edition when converting it to paperback, outside of necessary changes to the front matter and a shift of wording on funding in the acknowledgments.

ACKNOWLEDGMENTS

My deepest gratitude to the following:

My family, for their continuing support, but especially to Caleb and Richard, who patiently assisted with the production of this volume in whatever way they could.

The board and members-at-large of the Rabun County Historical Society, who graciously allowed access to their collection of newspapers. Special thanks to Mrs. M. E. Law who brought my attention to the society's newspaper collection and kindly discussed it with me.

The staff of the Rabun County Public Library in Clayton, GA, who have ever been helpful and supportive.

The staff, past and present, of the Probate Court in Clayton, GA.

The University of Georgia's Georgia Newspaper Project, which has continued to ferret out and preserve historical periodicals, and to the University of Georgia's library system for housing these important records.

Vivian Saffold Price and Linda Woodward Geiger, whose seminar on the various aspects of publishing, in general, and through the R. J. Taylor Jr. Foundation, specifically, was especially helpful. Vivian also delivered invaluable assistance in sorting out problems concerning the proper treatment of certain issues of *The Clayton Tribune* and answering further questions on the publication process, all of which was greatly appreciated.

The publication of the hardbound edition was made possible by a grant from the R. J. Taylor Jr. Foundation in Atlanta, GA, without whose help many volumes on Georgia's early records would not now be available to researchers. Thank you for your support and guidance, and for your assistance in making this publication possible.

ABBREVIATIONS

*	See page 53 for a full explanation.
‡	See page 53 for a full explanation.
[?]	Indicates a questionable transcription of the original.
[illegible]	Indicates an illegible entry or portion thereof.
[missing]	Indicates a missing entry or portion thereof.
[*sic*]	Spelling is correct. Because of the frequent misspellings and typesetting mistakes, this is used only with the most egregious errors.
C. S. C.	County School Commissioner; Clerk of the Superior Court
col.	Colored
Col.	Colonel
Gen.	General
Hon.	Honorable
J. S. C.	Judge of the Superior Court
Lieut.	Lieutenant
Messr(s).	Mister or Misters
Ord'y, Ordy.	County Ordinary
Prof.	Professor
R. C.	Rabun County
T. C.	Tax Collector
T. R.	Tax Receiver

THE CLAYTON ARGUS

AUGUST 3 AND 10, 1894

There are only two known extant issues for this newspaper: August 3 and 10, 1894. These issues are currently held in the University of Georgia's Hargrett Rare Book and Manuscript Collection. They have been microfilmed by UGA's Georgia Newspaper Project.

The Clayton Argus, Volume 1, Number 7, August 3, 1894

§   The Argus issued Weekly at $1 a Year. R. E. A. Hamby, Editor. Room 3, Court House, Clayton, Georgia. W. M. Fowler, Business Manager, Demorest, Georgia.

§   Burton Bubbles
The railroad strike is over at Burton and the president has withdrawn his troops and the Chicago of Rabun county is again quiet.

We have plenty of rain and crops are doing well at present.

Mr. W. L. Arendale is still wrestleing with disease. We hope he will soon recover.

Mrs. Henry Burrell appears to be some better.

Mr. H. C. Blalock paid us a very pleasant call on Sunday.

The hum of the thresher is heard in every direction and the grain is turning out well.

Prof. M. L. Powell opens school at Timpson to-day.

J. M. Tilly says some of the boys have gone crazy playing checkers at Burton.

We are glad to see Nin Ramey on his way to the Academy.

We have a letter from Dr. W. H. McClure, stating that he has been nominated by the democratic party for the senator of the 40th district without opposition. His letter also states that G. W. Johnson is his republican antagonist. Rabun will give the doctor a rousing vote.

Mr. C. E. Grant is again at Burton looking after some improvements on his wife's grave. Let's take a lesson by Mr. Grant's effort and improve the graves of our kindred.

Mr. Wm. Stonecypher and his daughter Lillie are visiting relatives in Franklin county this week.

More timber men from North Carolina this week. Mr. J. H. Derrick is buying timber for Mr. Webster, of Ohio.

If our populist candidate for representative will read the first article in the sixth section of the constitution of 1877 he will find a remedy for his care.

§   F. D. Hahnenkratt, Demorest, Georgia. Dealer in Real Estate. I always have bargains in Farm and City Property. I also have on hand some valuable Fruit Land.

§ Demorest Foundry and Machine Works. General Founders and Machinists, Demorest, Georgia. Call the attention of mill and machinery owners to our facilities for doing their work and repairs. Good work and low prices. Our foundry and pattern shop enables us to do repairs of all kinds in iron or brass with the least possible delay. We solicit correspondence with those who desire work in our line. Our specialties are castings and repairs on engines, saw-mills, cane-mills, gearings, grate bars, etc.

§ They All Do It! Do What? Complain of Hard Times! ... Safford & Dunlap, Dealers in Dry Goods, Hardware and Groceries. We also handle crockery, glassware, paints, oils, varnishes, etc. Call and see us. Demorest, Georgia.

§ The Bank of Demorest... Correspondents: Chase National Bank, New York. Lowry Banking Co., Atlanta. Board of Directors: A. A. Safford, W. H. VanHise, G. W. Dunlap, A. A. Campbell, J. M. Boutelle, A. Hampton. Officers: A. Hampton, President. W. H. VanHise, Vice-President. A. A. Campbell, Cashier.

§ Demorest Normal School. First Fall term opens August 6; Second fall term opens Oct. [illegible]. Departments in Pedagogy, Science, Literature, Music, Arts, Elocution. Thorough, Up with the Times. Progressive. Special Classes in Book-Keeping and Actual Business... Demorest, GA.

§ Job Printing. When you are in need of the Job Printer Send or Call on The Times, Demorest, GA...

§ The weather is beautiful and the crops are growing and looking fine.

§ Mr. Andy Garland, of Rabun valley gave town a visit a few days ago.

§ A. J. Duncan, of Cherchero gave us a pleasent call not long since. Dev is our famous Sunday school worker. He is secretary of the Rabun county Sunday School Association and is one of its most able and proficient workers.

§ Judge Bleckley visited the Falls last Friday and Saturday on business.

§ Rev. W. L. Singleton has been conducting a protracted meeting at the Methodist church. He has had quite a marked degree of success.

§ We were greatly pleased not long since by the gift of a basket of roasting ears and tomatoes from our popular hotel mistress, Mrs. Wm. Wall.

§ Col. John H. Addington, who lives three miles north from town and who has been quite sick for several months past is convalescent.

§ Rev. John S. Dickson baptised eleven on Scott's Creek last Sunday.

§   Prof. J. S. Ramey, of lower War Woman, called on his best girl in town last Saturday. Come again, Sport.

§   Marshal Godfry was in town on Monday. He gave us a call and a subscription.

§   A new shoe shop in town. W. A. Hunnicutt is making shoes and boots for W. E. Thompson, the tanner.

§   Subscribe for The Argus, it is your only county paper and gives you fresh news from all parts of Rabun county and elsewhere...

§   The Ordinary is constantly annoyed by someone asking for the keys to Col. John L. Asbury's office. Col. Asbury, it seems, has something in his office in which the public, or a part of it at least, is highly interested. Gentlemen, Mr. Asbury has his own keys and lives at Tallulah Falls or elsewhere.

§   Prof. John A. Green is taking an outing in North Carolina.

§   Rev. W. S. Whitmire held a protracted meeting on Scott's Creek last week which resulted in quite a number of accessions to the Stecoa Baptist church. Bro. Whitmire is a good man and one of the best revivalists in the country.

§   We are sorry to hear that Col. W. D. Young, Tallulah Falls' hotel king is accused by Receiver Lauraine of the Blue Ridge & Atlantic R. R. of violating his agreement to supply the railroad with water. Col. Young is a man who has not the reputation of violating contracts and agreements. Mr. Lauraine must remember that those washing showers are very destructive to viaducts and water ways. The colonel, too, ought to remember that the wheels of progress must not be stopped for lack of water.

§   The scene of battle seems to be changed from Chicago to Pine Mountain. We hear that one day last week a number of the boys met at or near the post office at Pine Mountain and by some means a dispute arose which precipitated a fight the result of which was knives. It is also stated that the boys had been taking on some tangle foot. We are sorry that so many of our young men participated in this useless habit of drinking. Boys, quit it, and you will certainly be glad of it.

§   While on a business trip to Chechero last Saturday we were invited by Mrs. F. A. Bleckley to visit the family cemetery, which invitation we cordially accepted, and of which we are by no means sorry. This sacred city of the dead which is on top of a high hill overlooking the family residence on one side and the Methodist church on the other, is the final resting place of the family and its nearest relatives and dearest friends. We were greatly impressed by the good condition in which this hallowed spot is kept. It is enclosed by a nice lattice fence and the grounds within are most beautifully laid off and most scrupulously clean. What prevents the citizens of Clayton from paying the same homage to their departed loved ones? Let us not omit this sacred duty longer.

§ He Replies to [Mr.] Fidus. Editor Argus:--I see in your valuable paper of the 27th inst. a reply to what I had said about the good people [of] this place being dissatisfied about there being two schools within a mile of each other, one at Tiger and the other at Shirley... D. Cub.

§ Pine Mountain

Mrs. N. A. Holden is visiting her old home near here.

Mr. Tobe White, of Clayton is spending a few days with friends over here. He and Mr. Bob spent Sunday with their best girls at Hail Ridge.

Misses Lena Bleckley, Mary Billingsley and Mr. Will Holden opened their schools near here last Monday with good attendance.

Messrs. John Billingsley and Thomas Mongold have plenty of melons ready for market. They claim to have the earliest here this [illegible].

[Illegible] little dispute seems to be [illegible] about the bridge between the road commissioners and the hands; the public is largely in sympathy with the hands of the road.

The post-office will change hands shortly to Miss Mary Billingsley as postmistress and Mr. David Hunter as assistant.

The farmers are all going hunting and giving up the farms to the rain.

§ Ordinary's Notices.

Georgia, Rabun County—Mrs. Lydia Coleman, widow of Thomas Coleman, deceased, has had a year's support set apart for herself out of the estate of her said deceased husband, and I will pass upon the same at 12 o'clock, M. on the first Monday in August, 1894. F. A. Blecklie, Ordinary R. C. This July 5, 1984.

§ Georgia, Rabun County—W. M. Darnell has in due form applied to the undersigned for permanent letters of administration on the estate of Harrison Darnell, late of said county, deceased, and I will pass upon the said application on the first Monday in August, 1894. Given under my hand and official signature, this, the fifth day of July, 1894. F. A. Bleckley, Ordinary, R. C.

§ Administrator's Sale. By virtue of an order of the Court of Ordinary of Rabun county, will be sold at the court house in Rabun county within the legal hours of sale on the first Tuesday in August, next, to the highest bidder for cash the following described lands: A part of lot No. 66, in the 13th district, of originally Habersham now Rabun county, it being the place where Melvin Horshaw resided at the time of his death, containing 100 acres more or less. Sold as the property of Melvin Horshaw, late of Rabun county, deceased, for the purpose of paying the debts and making distribution among the heirs. James M. Tilly, Administrator.

§ Rabun Sheriff's Sale.

Will be sold before the court house door in Rabun county, the first Tuesday in August, next, within the legal hours of sale, to the highest bidder for cash, the following described property to wit:

Part of lot of land No. 27, in the fourth land district of Rabun county, containing 25 acres, more or less, and bounded as follows: Adjoins the land of J. W. Smith on the east and south by the lands of Clarence Singleton on the north and west by the land of M. W. Swafford. Levied on as the property of William E. Singleton by virtue of a fi fa issued from the Superior court of Rabun county in favor of [officers] of court against said W. E. Singleton. A. L. Dillard, Sheriff Rabun Co. This July 2, 1894.

§   Will be sold on the first Tuesday in August next at the court house door in Rabun county, within the legal hours of sale to the highest bidder for cash the following described property, to-wit:

One third undivided interest in fractional lot of land No. 10 in the 5th land district of Rabun county, levied on and to be sold by virtue of an execution issued from the justice court of the 597th district, G. M., in favor of W. D. Young against Sarah E. White. Levied on as the property of Sarah E. White. July 3, 1894. A. L. Dillard, Sheriff.

§   Cullasaja Items

Cullasaja, N. C., July 25.—Mr. Frank C. Bidwell and wife are on a trip north.

H. S. Lucas has sold his interest in the corrundum mines here and at Laurel creek to Bidwell, Harwood & Co. The doctor is yet working a few hands on Screamer. John Stanfield is superintendent.

Mining is more active than it has been for some time past in Macon. Corrundum and mica mines are being opened all around. Mica is looking up both in price and quantity.

A. L. Beck and family are well pleased with their new home in North Carolina.

§   Newsy Bits from Stecoa Falls

The farmers of this section have completed their crops so now they can sweetly rest for a few months.

Mr. Wm. Cartey has his thrasher on Wolf Creek this week. We think has very near the same opinion as our friend Wall in regard to country life especially about threshing time. Bill "is to blacksmith" too.

There has been a protracted meeting at Bethel for several days past conducted by the pastor, Rev. J. S. Dickson. The church has been greatly revived and a number of conversions made.

Mr. John Donaldson spent a few days over in North Carolina last week. We imagine the girls over there are aware that John is still single.

There was a singing class at the school house Sunday afternoon, conducted by two of our Habersham county friends. They sang "and don't you forget it."

§   J. F. Earl's Notice.

All persons indebted to me by accounts must come and settle, either by cash or notes, as I have sold out my stock and am no longer in business. Last year's debts must be paid at once.

Thanking the public for past favors, I am yours truly, J. F. Earls, Masonic Bl'dg. Clayton, Ga.

§   Wall House. Mrs. Wm. Wall, Proprietress. Fare the best the country afford, and prices reasonable. Good, clean beds and nicely kept rooms. Beautiful and healthy location. In view of the famous Screamer and Blue Ridge mountains. Stables to accommodate the custom. Address Mrs. William Wall, Clayton, Ga.

§ J. D. Williams, M. D. Office at Residence. Special Attention to all Chronic Diseases. Teeth extracted without Pain. Demorest, Georgia.

§ Livery Stable. W. W. Nix, Proprietor. Buggies and Teams for Hire. Best accommodations for horses. Demorest, Ga.

§ Robt. E. A. Hamby, Room 3, Court House. Attorney and Counsellor at Law, Clayton, GA. Will practice in all the courts of the North Eastern circuit and elsewhere upon special contract. Collections a specialty.

§ Lake View Hotel, Demorest, Ga. One of the coolest and best kept hotels in northeast Georgia. Summer Boarders may get at this hotel pleasant rooms and good board at reasonable rates. Write for terms.

§ [Illegible] can get the same at 15 cents a gallon by leaving order and can with Safford & Dunlap.

§ We Guarantee to sell you a bicycle 25 per cent cheaper than you can buy same machine... Pianos... Sewing Machines... Buggies... The Times, Demorest, Ga.

§ D. J. Starkweather and Co., Demorest, Georgia. First rate assortment of first-class Shoes, Dry Goods, and Stationery...

§ Furniture. At the Factory opposite the railroad station. Goods Very Low. Suits $9 to $15. Oak furniture finished in all styles. Mill work for builders. H. Willet, Demorest, GA.

§ Blue Ridge & Atlantic. W. V. Lauraine, Receiver. Time Table No. 25 in Effect June 3, 1894. Going South. Stations. Tallulah Falls... Turnerville... Anandale... Clarksville... Demorest... Cornelia... Going North. Stations. Cornelia... [Illegible] Turnerville... Tallulah Falls...

The Clayton Argus, Volume 1, Number 8, 10 August 1894

§ Who lost some whiskey a few days back? The two marshals scoured the woods for some and came lugging it in late last Saturday evening.

§ Atlanta Artillery Anniversary.
  The Company Will Go to Tallulah Falls in a Special Car.
  The eighth anniversary of the organization of the Atlanta Artillery will be celebrated in fitting style by the members of that popular company on the 18th of August instead of on the 16th, as has been the custom heretofore.

The company will go to Tallulah Falls on that day in a special coach tendered them by the North East Georgia Chautauqua Association of Demorest, Ga...

After spending several hours at Tallulah, viewing the magnificent scenery surrounding the falls, the company will take the train for Demorest, where the artillerymen will be royally entertained by the people of that place.

A fine concert will be given in their honor, at the chautauqua.

Among the artists who will take part in the concert is Miss Marguerite Wuertz, who is so well and favorably known in Atlanta.

A grand naval battle will be given on the beautiful sheet of water known as Lake Demorest, after the concert...—Atlanta Constitution

§ R. E. Cannon, of Tiger, gave us a pleasant call a few days ago. He says he killed a big rattlesnake the other day.

§ We hear that Guss Billingsley and Wood Bryson, the chief sufferers in the riot at Pine Mountain in our last week's issue are getting considerably better. It was thought that Bryson was fatally wounded, but we are glad to hear that he was not.

§ North-East Georgia Chautauqua, Demorest, Ga. August 13 – 23, 1894.

Location: Eighty-two miles north of Atlanta on the Richmond & Danville and Blue Ridge & Atlantic R. R., changing cars at Cornelia Junction...

Principles: To maintain a Christian Summer Assembly for twelve days in August each year...

William Shaw, President and Supt.

§ J. F. Earls is having the fence rebuilt in front of his residence.

§ Prof. James E. Ledford is having quite a large school at the academy.

§ Ben and John Bleckley of the firm of Sylvester Bleckley Mercantile Co., Anderson, S. C., are spending a few days with their parents, Judge and Mrs. F. A. Bleckley of Checheroe.

§ Mr. Jno. R. Scruggs gave us a pleasant call and subscription last Saturday.

§ The bridge in Mrs. Bell's field on the Checheroe road over which so much unnecessary breath has been spent, will we hope, be built. The hands within the incorporation have been ordered by the council to begin operations Monday. Lets every body lend a helping hand. It will take us only a day or two to build the bridge and a highway that is long needed will be opened to the public.

§ Marshal Godfry presented us a fine cabbage head the other day. John says he thinks he can beat Jim Almon on cabbage.

§ Col. R. B. Ritchie, of Rabun Gap was on our streets Saturday. Mr. Ritchie is one of Rabun's best farmers and also a great advocate of popular education and has given much time and attention to the great cause. He served sixteen years on the county board of education and now stands ready to do anything possible for the better education of our youths.

§   The Sons of Rest are thoroughly organised with Squire Derrick as president, editor the Argus secretary and treasurer. Addresses by D. T. Duncan, recitation by John A. Green, who is now in North Carolina or elsewhere, and music by Lish Holcomb and Bill Tid. Meets every day except Sunday from 8 A. M. to 6 P. M. Good entertainment and plenty of fresh air.

§   Mrs. Sarah Martin and family of Dawson county are visiting relatives and friends in Rabun. Mrs. Martin is a sister of Hon. J. W. Green, of Rabun Valley.

§   Capt. Dillingham, who has been quite sick with a sore foot, is improving. The captain is near four score years old, but is remarkably active at that ripe old age.

§   Squire Derrick's court of August, which was held in the court house Friday was somewhat interesting. The squire imprisoned one of his constable for contempt of court, a thing that probably never happened before in a Rabun county Justice court.

§   Hon. W. C. Scruggs returned from the gubernatorial convention with a long democratic smile on his face. Bill says that if the convention meant anything that democratic success in Georgia is sure.

§   Several of our neighbors attended the Rabun county annual singing convention held at Boiling Springs, [at?] Persimmon, last Friday, Saturday, and Sunday.

§   Uncle Lewis Jones gave us a call a few days ago. Uncle Lewis is one of our best farmers and one of our most distinguished and popular citizens.

§   We see in the Anderson (S. C.) Intelligencer that Mr. W. R. Dillingham is one of the democratic candidates for city alderman, receiving the second highest number of votes[?] with a dozen or more of Anderson's most distinguished citizens in the field. Rush is one of Rabun's emigrants...

§   Fidus Replies to D. Cub. Editor Argus.—I see in your paper of the 3rd inst., a reply to what I had to say in regard to the schools at Shirley and Tiger... The general understanding in this section is that the Liberty school died a natural death... Fidus.

§   A Murder.
We understand that a murder has been committed in Persimmon district, but the particulars we have not secured. The story as learned is: Jack Hopper and his cousin Jasper and Mr. Kilby were returning from the singing convention at Boiling Spring, in Persimmon district. They were drinking and lay down by the roadside to rest. Kilby went to Mr. James, who lives near by, to look after a violin string. While up there he heard a noise and retuned with Mr. James and others. Jack was stabbed in the right side. Jasper was working with him and seemed not to be very badly hurt. Jasper says he and Jack went to sleep while Kilby was gone; he was awakened by

Jack's cries and on getting up saw a man running away from them. He asked Jack what was the matter and Jack said he was cut. Jasper went for Jack's folks, but got lost in the mountains as it was dark, and went home thinking Jack was not seriously wounded. Jack died at 10 o'clock that night. Jasper was arrested the next morning at home by Sheriff Dillard and lodged in jail. The boys were cousins and good friends, and Jasper persists that he is innocent.

§   Tiger News

Everything seems to be on rising ground here and most all the farmers have a splendid prospect for plenty of corn in the fall.

Mr. H. R. Cannon, of Tallulah Falls has purchased of V. C. Kerby the house and lot where he now lives also a business lot upon which he intends to erect a nice store house soon.

Our school is improving fast and our teacher, Mr. Head, is certainly a man in the right place.

Mr. S. S. Whitmire bought out V. C. Kerby's entire stock of merchandise and is doing a splendid business, considering the hard times.

V. C. Kerby will commence work on his new building in a few days, which he proposes to complete by the first of November.

If you want to sell your chickens and eggs come to Tiger. You can buy goods reasonable and if they don't suit you can get the cash.

The meeting at Bethel church closed last night, it has been going on some two weeks and resulted in many conversions.

The toots of the steam thresher has been heard on every side for the last few days and the rye crop has proved to be a good one.

We hope everybody will come out to Sabbath school Sunday. We must not let our literary school interfere with our Sabbath school. Surely anyone can give an hour to God once a week.

Mr. S. S. Burnett, with Gramling, Spaulding & Co., gave us a call one day this week. Mr. Burnett is a fine young man and is with one of the best shoe houses in Atlanta.

If you want blacksmithing done you can get it done and [illegible].

§   Asbestos works in Georgia.

An industry of far reaching importance has just been inaugurated in Georgia. Near Demorest, in White county, in the midst of extensive asbestos deposits, has been erected a plant for preparing the fiber for market. After several years of experimenting to secure proper machinery, the plant is now complete and has commenced operations with a daily output of from twenty-five to thirty tons of the finished material.

The Sal Mountain Asbestos Co., built the plant, which, to show the plentiful supply of the asbestos, is built upon a bed of the article... H. S. Benjamin is secretary of the company, and T. W. Hix, general manager.—Manufacturers' Record.

§   Clayton Directory.

County Officers. Hon. John M. Massengill, representative. Hon. Frank A. Bleckly, ordinary. J. L. Hamby, clerk of the Superior court. A. L. Dillard, sheriff. James L.

Dickson, tax receiver. Miles C. Canup, tax collector. Jeff C. Dickson, treasurer. Manley Johnson, coroner. M. M. Crawford, surveyor. Postmaster at Clayton: Jas. I. Langston. U. S. Commissioner: R. B. Dillard.

Masonic. Rabun Gap Lodge, F. A. M., No. 265. Regular meetings at 10 a. m., Friday before each full moon. Annual festival 23d inst. A full attendance is requested at all times.

Religious worship. BAPTIST—Rev. R. S. Sanders and W. S. Whitmire, pastors. Preaching at 11 a. m. every third Sunday. Sunday school at 3 and prayer-meeting at 7:30 p. m. every Sunday. METHODIST—Rev. W. L. Singleton, pastor; preaching at 11 a. m. every fourth Sunday. Sabbath school each Sabbath at 10 a. m. Prayer meeting at 7 p. m. Wednesday.

THE TALLULAH FALLS SPRAY

APRIL 8, 1897 – FEBRUARY 17, 1898

The Tallulah Falls Spray was first published on July 16, 1896, with known issues published into 1898. From that time period, most extant issues date from 1897 with a few dating from the very early part of 1898.

The July 1, 1897 issue of this newspaper has been microfilmed by the University of Georgia's Georgia Newspaper Project, and is available through them. The remaining issues abstracted below are held by the Rabun County Historical Society and are, as far as is known, not microfilmed. Unfortunately, there are issues missing from the range of those held by the Historical Society.

The Tallulah Falls Spray, Volume 1, Number 38, Thursday, April 8, 1897

§   Published Weekly by The Spray Publishing Co. J. B. Young, Walter Hunnicutt, Editors. Subscription $1.00 a year in advance. This paper is, by law, the official organ of Rabun county. Entered in the Post-Office at Tallulah Falls, Georgia as second-class mail matter.

§   Church Directory.
Tallulah Falls.
   M. E. Church. Rev. W. R. Stilwell, Pastor. Services every fourth Sunday at 8 o'clock p. m. Sabbath school at 4 o'clock p.m.
   Catholic Church. (St. Margaret's Chapel), Glenbrook. Rev. C. Schadewell and Rev. J. Kennedy, periodically.
   Baptist Church. Rev. D. C. Carter, Pastor. Services every fourth Sunday at 11 o'clock a. m. Sabbath school at 10 o'clock a. m. Rev. H. H. Harris second Saturday and Sunday.
   St. James Episcopal Chapel, not supplied at present.
Clayton Directory.
   Baptist Church. Rev. J. S. Dickson, pastor. Services every third Saturday and Sunday at 11 o'clock a. m. Sabbath school at 3 o'clock p. m.
   M. E. Church. Rev. D. C. Brown, Pastor. Services every fourth Sunday at 11 o'clock a. m. Sabbath school at 10 a. m.

§   Masonic.
   Rabun Gap Lodge No. 165 F. & A. M. meets at Clayton on Friday before the full moon in each month at 10 o'clock a. m.
   M. W. Swanford, W. M.
   F. A. Bleckley, Secretary.
   Tallulah Chapter, No. 68, Royal Arch Masons, meets at Clayton on Friday before the full moon in each month at 6 o'clock p. m.

D. T. Duncan, H. P.
R. S. Sanders, Secretary.

§   Tiger court, second Saturday in each month. Wiley Pitts, J. P.   H. B. Cannon, Notary Public.

§   Tallulah Falls, Georgia—A Place of Beauty.

Many have undertaken a description of the marvelous beauty and grandeur of Tallulah Falls, and I fear what I have to say will fall far short of the justice of the place. The grand handiwork of the Creator is illustrated here in the lofty mountains and dashing, splurging cataracts; we feel most sensibly our unworthiness, littleness, in gazing at such a vast panorama of loveliness. There is a fascinating charm about Tallulah that is at once felt.

Here, then, are a people to welcome a stranger. The Falls were once called Tenora (which signifies terrible.) They were afterwards named Tallulah for an Indian princess who fell over a precipice into a chasm.

A distinguished bishop prophesied that this section of Georgia was destined to become the grandest portion of the state. And why not, for its resources are of a superior kind. Here at Tallulah Falls water power is fine for mills and factories. It is in the line of the gold region...

Tallulah Falls is at present the terminus of the Blue Ridge and Atlantic railroad. The route has been surveyed to Knoxville, Tenn., and it is thought work will be resumed on the road very soon... West of Tallulah are Mount Echo, Hickory-nut mountain, Pidgeon and the Tallulah range, then on the north side is Mount Prosephine from which the scenery is magnificent and extended, Tunnel Hill and Currakee can be seen in a more entirely direction...

§   Chetcheroe Dots

The farmers at this place are farther behind in their work than I have ever known them to be at this season of the year. Owing to the continuous rainfall there has been but little plowing done in this section, but we are all in good heart and hope to see the sunshine soon.

We are still anxious and waiting to hear of some church calling for the county union meeting.

I hear that there has been a gold mine discovered on top of the mountain near Lem Wilkerson's, and hands now at work at it. Who knows but what Rabun contains as much gold as any county in the state of Georgia.

Watch out boys, it takes the people to give men offices.

William Long (our present Ordinary) has some good friends in this part of the country. He seems to be started out right, and is ready for business when called on.

§   Died in Stone Pile District.

On Thursday, April 1, 1897, just at the close of the day, Sanford Elard, one of Rabun county's handsome young men, just in the bloom of life, passed away. Sanford leaves a widowed mother and several brothers and sisters and many friends to mourn his death. Yes, it seems hard that one so young and handsome should be called away while in his youthful days, but we are to believe that the all-wise Creator chose last Thursday evening, just as the shades of night were deepening into darkness, to send the angel of death to bear away his departing spirit to eternal rest.

§   Notice.

Will be sold at the depot at Clarkesville, Ga., on Wednesday, April 21st, 1897, in accordance with the law:

74 Pcs. Mixed Oak Lumber, 6' by 10' by 10', for storage charges, same having been loaded on So. Ry. Car No. 48055, and remained thereon for a period of six months.

2 Bdles W. B. Baskets, 40 Bdles Baskets, 20 Bdles Corers, and 4 Bdles Handles; refused by consignee, J. M. Boutell, Demorest, Ga. Also, ½ Bbl. Cider; refused by consignee, C. Almond, Clarkesville, Ga.

Also, 1 Bdle. P. Bags; refused by consignee, J. B. Tomlinson, Demorest, Ga.

Also, 1 Box Hardware; refused by consignee, J. R. Anderson, Turnerville, Ga.

Also, 1 Pa. Signs, E. P. West & Co., Clarkesville, Ga.

W. V. Lauraine, Rec. B. R. & A. R. R. Co.

§   Legal Advertisements.

Georgia, Rabun County: Martin L. Dickerson, having in due form applied to the undersigned for guardianship of the person and property of William T. Dickerson, a person imbecile from old age, etc.

Notice is hereby given that his application will be heard at my office on the first Monday in May next.

Given under my hand and official signature this, 30th day of March, 1897. W. S. Long, Ordinary.

§   Georgia, Rabun County: The return of the appraisers setting apart twelve months' support to the widow of Thomas I. Ledbetter, deceased, having been filed in office, all persons concerned are cited to show cause by the 3d day of May, 1897, why said application for twelve months' support should not be granted.

This, March 30th, 1897. W. S. Long, Ordinary.

§   Georgia, Rabun County: At Chambers, April 1st, 1897—Samuel Taylor as executor of Cincinatus Taylor, having filed his petition for probate of Cincinatus Taylor's will in solemn form, and it appearing that citation should issue to be served personally on Jane Taylor, Mary Wellborn, Catharine Page, Jesse Taylor, Sarah J. Stancell, William Jiles, Nat Jiles, Andy Jiles, Rachel Lawin, Nancy Eller, Susan Littleton and Mary Burrell, ordered that the usual citation issue, to be served on them ten days before the May term of this court, and as John Taylor, Mary J. Brinkley, Martha Gaines, Gus Ledbetter and Susan Ledbetter not being residents of this state and their residence unknown, and can only be served by publication, that they be cited and made a party by publication once a week for four weeks in The Tallulah Falls Spray, a newspaper published at Tallulah Falls, State of Georgia, before the May term, 1897, of said Court of Ordinary, and that this order so published constitute such citation.

W. S. Long, Ordinary.

§   Georgia, Rabun County: Whereas W. E. Thompson, administrator of Peter Thompson, represents to the court in his petition, duly filed and entered on record, that he has fully administered Peter Thompson's estate, this is, therefore, to cite all persons concerned, heirs and creditors, to show cause, if any they can, why said administrator should not be discharged from his administration and receive letters of dismission on the first Monday in July, 1897. W. S. Long, Ordinary.

§   Through Rabun County—Tallulah Falls Briefs.

Mrs. H. R. Cannon and children have returned from Atlanta. Will spend the summer at Tallulah.

We hope the wet weather is over, so the farmers can till the [soil?] and other business can be carried out. Monday and Tuesday were two fine days. Last Sunday it rained without ceasing. The river was the fullest it has been for years. The falls were sending their spray to the top off the cliffs on either side.

§   In the Home of the Rhododendron. Glenbrook Cottage. A Dreamland of Romance. The Ideal Home for the Summer Months is Now Open for the Season of 1897... For Terms of Board, Room, etc., etc., apply to Mrs. M. A. Hunnicutt, Tallulah Falls, GA.

§   Everybody Should Visit The Emporium And examine our Stock before purchasing. We deal in almost everything, and have some bargains constantly arriving. Our aim is, to first underbuy and then undersell. Our motto is low prices and courtesy to customers. Taylor & Sweet, Proprietors, Tallulah Falls, Georgia.

§   J. W. Green is at Foddrell's old stand. Will handle Country Produce at the highest market price in exchange for Groceries. Also will handle Scott's High Grade Acid in exchange for corn at highest cash prices. Call and see me. J. W. Green, Turnerville, Georgia.

§   Two Papers for One. The Atlanta Weekly Journal and The Tallulah Falls Spray One Year $1.25...The Spray Publishing Co., Tallulah Falls, GA.

§   Call and See Us. We have a lot of bargains in General Merchandise. Highest prices paid for Country Produce. Greenwood & York, Dillard, Ga.

§   Charles E. Cannon, Tiger, GA., Dealer in General Merchandise. Will handle all kinds of country produce. Will run freight wagon two trips each week from Tiger to Tallulah Falls and return.

§   Want Column.

Notices in this column 3 cents per line each insertion.

WANTED—Everybody to know that Sweet & Taylor have just received a large lot of ready-made clothing and want to sell at once.

WANTED—Every business man in Rabun county to advertise in The Spray...

WANTED—R. W. Davidson's old customers to know that he is still at his old stand and ready to serve them.

WANTED—To sell a 4x5 photo outfit, price $7; makes 4x5 picture. Address Walter Hunnicutt, Tallulah Falls, Ga.

The Demorest Magazine of February is well illustrated and the reading matter is of great variety, very rich and highly moral, and I look for the March number to be better.

WANTED—All the readers of The Spray to read J. W. Green's advertisement in another column.

Six pounds soda 25 cents. Eighteen pounds rice $1.00. Six pounds good coffee $1.00. Other things in proportion. Greenwood & York, Dillard, Ga.

Want to Sell. One 4-horse power Frick engine, $200.00. One 10-horse power Frick engine, $500.00. One 30-horse power engine, $800.00. Will take lumber, shingles, horses, mules in exchange for this one. J. B. Young.

§   J. H. Shirley, Canon, GA., Repairs All Kinds of Machinery. Buys and Sells on Commission All Second-Hand Machinery. J. B. Young will act as his agent at Tallulah Falls. If you want to buy or sell, call on him.

§   Porter, Green & Free, Turnerville, Ga. When you come to Turnerville, Trade with us. We deal in General Merchandise And have Bargains for all. Give us a trial before you trade. We deal in All Country Produce. We solicit your patronage—will give you down weight and square measure.

§   J. B. Young, Carpenter and Builder, Tallulah Falls, GA. Specifications given on short notice.

§   Robt. E. A. Hamby, Attorney at Law, Clayton, Georgia. Collecting a specialty.

§   Blue Ridge Hotel, Clayton, GA. D. T. Duncan, Proprietor. Magnificent mountain scenery; finest water in the world; good accommodations; moderate rates.

§   Your Picture Enlarged Free.
Any person getting up a club of ten yearly subscribers for The Tallulah Falls Spray and sending us one of their small pictures [illegible] one of some relative or friend that you [illegible] like to have enlarged and nicely framed [illegible] 8x10 inches, and delivered free of [illegible] either at Tallulah Falls, Ga., or Clayton, Ga....
Address, The Spray Pub. Co., Tallulah Falls, Ga.

§   Blue Ridge and Atlantic Railroad. Time Table No. 37. In Effect September 8, 1896 11 A. M.... Tallulah Falls... Turnerville... Anandale... Clarkesville... Demorest... Cornelia... W. V. Lauraine, Receiver.

§   When You Want Photographs You will do well to call at the new studio of G. L. Matteson, Toccoa, Ga. We have been established here since October 1st, 1896, and our trade since then shows us that a permanent, well appointed gallery was really needed in this section of Georgia. We are [missing] to stay and have the best light and [missing] studio in North East Georgia. [Missing] make nothing but first-class work[?] in all styles. Shall be glad to see you[?] at any time. Geo. Matteson, Jr., Toccoa, Ga.

The Tallulah Falls Spray, Volume 1, Number 39, Thursday, April 15, 1897

§   Communicated.

Dear Spray:

I am in receipt of a letter from state school commissioner, in which he says that he has no intention of changing the place of holding the combined institute, and directing that all arrangements be made at once for holding the institute at Tallulah Falls. I am asking the county school commissioners of Hall, Habersham and White counties to meet me at Tallulah on Monday, the 19th inst., for the purpose of making the necessary arrangements. I hope to have the hearty co-operation of the people and hotel men of Tallulah in the effort to make the institute a grand success. Every teacher in our county should by all means attend this meeting...

We have in the above named counties, according to the last report of S. S. C., 213 teachers...

We hope to have the mayor and the hotel men meet with us on the 19th, so as to perfect our plans... Also, we would be very much pleased to have the railroad officials to meet with us and agree to give reduced rates on the B. A. R. R. for the benefit of the teachers south of us.

Respectfully, W. J. Neville, C. S. C. April 12, 1897.

§   Dillard News

Messrs. T. N. and J. M. Carter, of Westminster, S. C., have been in the valley since Saturday.

Mr. W. P. Garland, of Otto, N. C., was in our place Saturday.

Greenwood & York have a nice lot of dry goods to arrive this week.

Mr. S. V. Garland made a trip to Scaly, N. C., last week.

A. L. Dillard and Miss Minnie Beorest attended the marriage of Ed Mosely and Miss Penland, of Otto, N. C., last week.

We note that we are to soon have a new shoe house in the valley.

§   Tallulah Items

A new hotel is to be built in Tallulah.

Quite like the opening of the summer season at the Willard Cottage one or two days.

The publishers of The Spray intend to get up a large issue for the benefit of the summer season for the aid of the hotels about the first of May

Mr. W. R. Sweet is having a lot of tanbark gotten out.

Tallulah Falls is ahead in the tanbark season and Mr. R. W. Davidson takes the lead in bringing the first load of new bark.

§   Death of Lewis N. Jones.

He passed to the spirit world at 5 o'clock on the morning of the 9th inst., at the ripe age of 82 years. He was well known by the county and beloved by all. A faithful member of the Baptist church and the oldest F. A. M. belonging to Rabun Gap lodge. He leaves two daughters, Mrs. Wm. Roan and Mrs. J. B. Murray. By his death Rabun county has lost one of its most estimable citizens. He was respected by all who knew him. He was kind, warm-hearted and generous to a fault, and in his life he has left an example for young men and many older men to follow. While we mourn his loss we feel assured of his happiness in spirit life. To the relatives we extend our heartfelt sympathies in their grief.

§   Arrivals at the Willard Cottage. C. C. Chappel and wife, New York. Melville Hart, Toccoa. P. McFadden, Toccoa. V. W. Billings, Toccoa. C. P. Jordan, Toccoa. E. R. David, Toccoa. J. F. Pennington, Toccoa. G. L. Matison, Toccoa. G. T. Alerton, Toccoa. Mr. Ray, Indian River, Fla. John A. Reynolds, Baldwin. Mrs. M. P. Griggs, Clarkesville. Mr. A. P. Houston, Clarkesville.

§   A Card.
Dr. D. N. de Dubœay once again desires to state that in consequence of his own ill health, that he will not be able at present to respond to any sick calls. He will, however, gladly do his best to serve those who may call at his residence for medicine or advice.

§   Adminstrator's Sale.
Henry L. Wilson, Auctioneer.
Georgia, Fulton County—By virtue of an order of the court of ordinary of said county, granted at the April term, 1897, of said court, there will be sold before the Fulton county courthouse door in the [missing] of Atlanta, on the first Tuesday in May, 1897, within the legal hours of sale, the following described real property belonging to the estate of Henry Jackson, deceased, towit:
An undivided one-half interest in and to all that certain tract or parcel of land, lying and being in land lot 175, of the thirteenth district of originally Habersham, now Rabun county, described as follows: Commencing at the eastern line of lot 163, which separates it from lot 175, on the eastern slope of Hickory Nut mountain, at the point where the main path now used by residents and visitors of the town of Tallulah Falls in ascending the eastern slope of said mountain crosses said line, and running down said mountain to a large and prominent point of rocks on said path overlooking the village or town of Tallulah Falls, at the lower edge of bench or ledge of such mountain, in such manner that said path shall divide seventy-five acres of land as nearly in half, by running through the center thereof, as the conformation of the ground will permit, and also one undivided one-quarter interest in all that portion of said lot 175 other than the seventy-five acres aforesaid, which lies west of a line commencing on the original northwest line of said lot, which divides it from lot 174, where a street which has been laid off crosses the said line, thence along the southwest side of said street, coming eastward to the northwest corner of Woodall's lot, near the branch, thence along the south side of Clayton road towards the railroad station to Young's millpond branch, within 15 feet of said branch, thence on the west side of said branch to a street which has been laid off near Young's stables, thence along the west side of said street to within fifteen feet of said branch, thence up said branch, on the west side, and fifteen feet therefrom to the head of said branch, thence up the left hand hollow to the line which divides said lot 175 from lot 163; Together with all the rights, privileges, franchises and easements, and subject to all the covenants, warranties, conditions and charges to said land pertaining, as

contained in the deed of James M. Cartledge and W. D. Young to Henry Jackson and A. O. Bacon, dated October 14th, 1887, and recorded in clerk's office, Rabun superior court, in book "M," pages 75 to 78, inclusive.

Also, a one-half interest in and to that certain tract or parcel of land, lying and being in the thirteenth district of Habersham county, and being land lot 163 of said district. The same being part of Hickory Nut mountain, together with all the rights, members and appurtenances thereunto appertaining and belonging.

Terms, one-third cash, balance 6 and 12 months, 7 per cent interest.

§   American Gems.

Although not many precious stones of great value are found in the United States, yet as Mr. George F. Kunz shows in his recent report to the Geological Survey, they include diamonds, rubies and sapphires... Rubies are found in Macon County, North Carolina...

The Tallulah Falls Spray, Volume 1, Number 50, Thursday, April 22, 1897

§   Tallulah Falls Briefs.

Tallulah is beginning to have a few visitors and its rather early, too.

Our Sabbath school is well attended. Let everyone be on time promptly at 10 o'clock next Sunday.

The county school commissioners failed to meet on the 19th at this place.

The Spray needs some money just now. Let all those due us send it in at once.

There was a very mean, low-down trick played our town last Saturday night. Some of our pretty shade trees were broken down. It is reported that the town has some proof against the party that did it—we hope so.

§   Clayton Dots.

The Blue Ridge Hotel has entertained a party of New Yorkers this week.

Our merchants are having a fair trade. Old Clayton is sure to get her share.

Mr. D. T. Duncan and son made a trip to Tallulah Falls this week.

§   Chetcheroe Dots.

The farmers at this place are all in good heart, as this week has been pretty and fair. Next week will be the last week to plant corn, and Chetcheroe will be most ready, for this district is always up on everything.

The people here worked the road last Saturday.

Mr. A. J. Duncan and wife spent last Saturday night with Mr. John Scruggs of the Valley.

The Tallulah Falls Spray, Volume 1, Number 42, Thursday, May 6, 1897

§   Dots from Rabun Gap.

Mr. W. R. Coffee has begun to plant corn.

Mr. John Tanner went to Warwoman Saturday to see his new grandson at Mr.

John Wilson's.

About 300 head of stock, consisting of horses, cattle and hogs, were driven to the mountains from our valley Saturday.

David Lacount is doing some nice rock work for Mrs. Fish.

A singular case was tried at the mayor's court last Tuesday. The party fined was accused of saying that a certain young lady had the prettiest eyes he had ever seen. Our mayor imposed a fine of $2 and cost of suit. Be careful, boys, what you say and how you say it. Col. Parris of Clayton, and Col. Edwards of Clarkesville were the two attorneys at the trial.

There was quite a large attendance last Saturday at Tallulah. The B. & A. railroad gave our neighbors over at Clarkesville an excursion for the benefit of the Clarkesville Sunday school. Among the excursionists was Editor Bass, of The Advertiser, who, after the picnic, gave a short lecture to suit the occasion.

§   Clayton Dots.

Prof. O'Kelley's school at this place is moving along nicely. The attendance is small, but the professors instructions are very fine as shown by the pupils' progress.

Misses Leila Bleckley and Amanda Earl are visiting relatives in Walhalla, S. C.

W. J. Neville, C. S. C., of Rabun Gap, passed through en route to Hawkinsville to the state meeting of the C. S. C.

Mr. Sandy Cunningham, of Atlanta, a rising young attorney, is in the mountains fishing and hunting.

§   Boarding! W. T. York's House is in the edge of Tennessee Valley; fine views of the mountains, near Mud Creek Falls, five hour's drive from Tallulah Falls. Trout fishing—an ideal spot to spend the summer. Good board at reasonable rates. Apply to W. T. York, Rabun Gap, Rabun County, Ga.

§   Parties Wishing Board in Rabun county at private houses and at prices to suit the times, will find it in their interest to call on or write the undersigned. Two hours' drive from Tallulah Falls. Address: V. C. Kerby, Tiger, Ga.

The Tallulah Falls Spray, Volume 1, Number 43, Thursday, May 13, 1897

§   Memorial Resolutions Of Rabun Gap Lodge No. 265 F. and A. M. On the Death of Brother Lewis N. Jones.

Whereas, Brother Lewis N. Jones was born on 22d day of June, 1814; and,

Whereas, He was a member of this lodge of F. and A. M. and has remained a faithful and consistent member of the same since the beginning of his said membership; and,

Whereas, he has lived a pure, virtuous and upright life, a life exemplary in all its phases; and,

Whereas, God in His wisdom and mercy saw fit to call him from the walks of men on 8th day of April, 1897, at the ripe age of four score and two years, nine months and sixteen days; therefore be it

Resolved by this, Rabun Gap Lodge No. 265 F. and A. M., now in mourning. That after consigning our dear brother's body to the dust from whence it came, we commend his spirit to God, who gave it; and be it

Resolved, further, That the life our beloved brother led as a Mason, a citizen and a Christian be a model for each member of this lodge; and, be it

Resolved, further, That it is the prayer of this lodge that the blessings of God's mercy rest upon each individual member of the bereaved family of our departed brother; and, be it

Resolved, further, That a copy of these resolutions be furnished each to Mrs. M. F. Roane and Mrs. J. B. Murray, daughters of our dear departed brother; and, be it

Resolved, further, That these resolutions be spread on the minutes of this lodge; and, bet it

Resolved, further, That a copy of these resolutions be printed in The Tallulah Falls Spray, a newspaper published at Tallulah Falls, Ga.

D. T. Duncan, Chairman, J. L. Hamby, R. E. A. Hamby, Committee on Resolutions.

§   Tallulah Falls Briefs.

The county school commissioners met last Saturday at this place and have decided that the institute will be held at Tallulah Falls.

Miss Effie Duncan and Master Harry Duncan, of Clayton, visited Mrs. H. R. Cannon last week.

Several strangers visited our town this past week.

Mr. H. R. Cannon arrived in Tallulah last Tuesday.

§   Clayton Briefs.

Guests at Blue Ridge are pleasantly amused by the music of Mr. Richardson.

Mr. Cabe is making quite a general search for the mineral wealth of Rabun county.

Col. Parris and Hon. Rube Hamby have laid down the law long enough to plant gardens; farmer-lawyers, etc.

§   Chechero Dots.

The County Union meeting is now dead, but resting at Wolfcreek church. How is it that we don't hear from Tiger and Tallulah districts?

Mrs. Sarah Langston, of Clayton, spent last Saturday night with Mr. and Mrs. F. A. Bleckley, of this place.

§   Rabun Gap.

We are expecting Thomas King and others from Tallulah District next Saturday to sing for the children, as it is children's day. No people should ever get to old to be S. S. children. Every child from 100 years old down ought to be in S. S. if they can.

Some of the Valley folks are still on the sick list.

Friday was law day. We had Col. Parris, of Clayton, with us.

Mr. D. M. Green is having a new dwelling house built this summer.

Mr. Robt. Ritchie will start to Texas in June to engage in school teaching.

Dr. Wolf and son and others passed through the Valley Sunday morning going to White county in search of gold. They are from Silvey, N. C.

Some of the girls call at the postoffice very often since the school closed. Be careful, boys, don't disappoint them.

W. J. Neville, C. S. C., has just returned from Hawkinsville, where he says he met some of the greatest educators of the state of Georgia.

The Tallulah Falls Spray, Volume 1, Number 44, Thursday, May 20, 1897

§   Tallulah Falls Dots.

Dr. De Dulœay and wife returned from Clarkesville.

Mr. Lockhart has opened the soda fountain for this season.

There are four guests at Willard Cottage.

Tax receiver will be at Tallulah Falls the 27th inst. Don't forget to give in your taxes.

Mr. J. B. McCracken, of Fort Hill, S. C., is on a visit to his parents, Mr. and Mrs. Hyram McCracken, of this county.

A good sewing machine cheap for case. J. B. Young, Tallulah Falls.

§   Tennessee Valley.

The Children's day, Saturday, the 15th of May, was celebrated in good style at the M. E. S. in the Valley. Quite a large congregation assembled. The Sunday school exercises were conducted by Mr. John Howard, the superintendent.

The exercises were recitations and reading by the S. S. scholars and were very appropriately delivered, especially the five little girls.

The music by Mr. T. E. King and his class was one of the special features of the day.

There was a fine spread in the grove from the dinner baskets. The ladies brought for the children lots. I think the older ones enjoyed it fully as well.

The afternoon exercises were short. The speaker of the occasion, Rev. A. P. Foster, of North Carolina, delivered a very nice lecture, to be impromptu. This is a day that will long be remembered.

§   List of Grand Jurors for August Term.

The following is the list of grand jurors drawn for our August term, 1897:

John C. Hamby, Alfred E. Dickerson, John C. Howard, William J. Ramey, Balis C. Nicholson, Americus K. Allen, Virgil M. Lovell, Albert A. Darnell, George H. Lovell, William S. Price, James B. Bramblet, Drew M. Green, Virgil T. Stonecypher, James R. Ritchie, George W. Reed, Sr., John B. Young, A. L. Dillard, Patrick Colman, James F. Smith, James I. Fincannon, Columbus F. Garland, H. C. Blalock, Samuel Taylor, Sr., William P. McCrackin, Joseph L. Dickerson, L. N. Shearley, Joshua F. Earls, Cicero Blalock, William E. Powell, Augustus M. Wall.

§   Georgia, Rabun County.—W. H. Hicks vs. W. H. Hughes—In the Superior Court, February term, 1897—Rule Nisi to Foreclose Mortgage.

It appearing to the court by the W. H. Hicks that W. H. Hughes, on the 18th day of March, 1891, executed and delivered to J. F. Earls his certain mortgage notes on part of land lot No. 50 in the second land district of said county, more fully described in a deed from Z. Sweatman to W. H. Hughes, for the purpose of securing the payment of said mortgage notes of the same bearer and date as aforesaid, the notes and mortgages being in the same instrument, and that said mortgage together with the lien has been for value transferred by said Earls to Walter Hunnicutt and by said Hunnicutt to your petitioner, which notes the said W. H. Hughes refuses to pay—

It is, therefore, ordered, that the said W. H. Hughes pay into this court on or before the first day of the next term thereof the principal, interest and attorneys' fees due thereon and cost of this foreclosure, or in default the court will proceed as to justice may appertain; and it is further ordered, that this rule be published as required by law, or served three months before the next term of this court. This February 26th, 1897.

J. J. Kimsey, J. S. C.

Geo. P. Erwin, Attorney for Petitioner.

Georgia, Rabun County.—I, L. C. Hollifield, clerk of the Superior Court in and for said county, do certify that the above and foregoing is a true transcript from the minutes of Rabun Superior court at the February term, 1897.

Witness my hand and seal of office this 14th May, 1897.

L. C. Hollifield, C. S. C.

§   List of Traverse Jurors—August Term, 1897.

The following are the names of the traverse jurors for the August term, 1897:

H. B. Stonecypher, A. J. Hamby, James C. York, A. J. Billingsby, William R. Sweat, Bry F. Phillips, Sandy B. Willbanks, Andrew J. Grist, S. S. Whitmore, Virgil A. Benfield, John T. Long, William J. McCurry, Andrew J. Duncan, Jesse W. Smith, John Nix, James H. Williams, Julius W. Carver, Elijah B. Philyaw, James R. Stonecypher, James A. Hopper, David W. Rickman, John M. Willson, John W. Crumpleton, Allen J. Williams, Beryman H. Atkins, John D. Price, Andrew J. Burrell, William J. Evans, James N. Justice, Wm. E. Thompson, Frank D. Blackwell, James J. Greenwood, Isaac J. H. Hunnicutt, John M. Crisp, James M. Welch, Edmon C. Price.

The Tallulah Falls Spray, Volume 1, Number 45, Thursday, May 27, 1897

§   Tumbled Into Tallulah.

A Young Man Loses Life In Turbulent Whirl of Tempests.

W. Marshall Clower, a young commission man and broker of Atlanta, Ga., fell headlong into the turbulent waters of Tallulah Falls Thursday afternoon and was dashed to death in the mad whirlpools and on the rocks.

He was one of a party of excursionists who went up with the conductors to picnic at the falls. He was fishing a minute before he met his death.

A stiff breeze was blowing at the time. When at one of the highest points of the cliff the hat of Clower blew off toward the edge of the stream and in endeavoring to regain it he lost his balance and fell in a tumbled heap into the rapid flowing waters beneath.

§   Georgia, Rabun County.—To all whom it may concern: J. L. Hamby has in due form applied to the undersigned for permanent letters of administration on the estate of L. N. Jones, late of said county, deceased, and I will pass upon said application on the first Monday in July, 1897. Given under my hand and official signature this 26th day of May, 1897. W. S. Long, Ordinary of Rabun County.

The Tallulah Falls Spray, Volume 1, Number 47, Thursday, June 10, 1897

§   Tallulah Falls Briefs.

Bringing in the bark.

Frying chickens are scarce just now.

Mr. T. A. Robinson went to Atlanta this week on some important business.

Ordinary W. S. Long went to Gainesville last week.

Tallulah is expected to have a good crowd by the first of July.

The Willard House is entertaining several guests already.

We have a new enterprise opened up in our town in the way of a nice soda fount, where you can get ice cold drinks, coca cola, etc.

There has been a little unavoidable delay in getting out The Spray last week. It will not occur again soon we hope.

To our correspondents let us say that some of the locals reached us too late for publication for the week intended for, so we did not use them in our next issue as locals must be fresh to be appreciated. Always write in time for us to get your letter by Tuesday each week.

The Teachers' Institute will open on Monday, the 21st of June. At least 200 are expected. Preparations will be made to accommodate that many or more. Four days will be the length of the session.

Tanbark, it seems, is far more plentiful than it was ten years ago. Our merchants have already shipped between three and four hundred cords. This is quite a business and bark continues to come. The streets are crowded with wagons every day.

Why don't you subscribe for The Spray. Every new name added to our subscription list will help the paper, and by helping your county paper you will help yourself. If you receive a sample copy of The Tallulah Falls Spray it will be an invitation for you to subscribe. Don't wait until you chance to see the editor, but send your name along and $1.00 for the paper one year.

§   Clayton Dots.

Monday the County Board of Education met and settled the matter in regard to the school at Tallulah between H. C. Crumley and Garnette Williams. Both had out articles from the school. Williams withdrew his claims or articles, so the Board gave Crumley the school.

Crops are looking splendid around Clayton. Oats are extra fine. We saw some the other day over 5 ½ foot high.

§   Georgia—Rabun County—To all whom it may concern: P. A. Crane having in due form applied to the undersigned for the guardianship of the persons and property of Ella Crane, Asberry Crane and Jane Crane, minor children of Franklin Crane, late of said county, deceased, notice is hereby given that his application will be heard at my office on the first Monday in July next. Given under my hand and official signature, this 31st day of May, 1897. W. S. Long, Ordinary.

§   The Grand View Hotel and Willard House, Tallulah Falls, GA. The Niagara of the South. Will be Open June 10th, 1897.

The Switzerland of America. The view from the Grand View Park is unsurpassed anywhere in the world. Summer houses built upon the brink of the great chasm and sell secured, have been furnished with seats from which you can look down eight hundred feet almost perpendicular, where the river trails like a great serpent, and Bridal Veil Falls and many of the cascades are seen leaping below. Beautiful fountains on the grounds of the Grand View.

Amusements... A band is kept during the season. Fishing with hook and line and seine. There is a ten-pin alley at the Grand View, which is free to guests. A good livery stable is kept at Tallulah...

The Mineral Springs Have become famous in the last two seasons on account of their fine medicinal qualities, the analysis of which is here given. The Mineral Springs are in the Park of the Grand View Hotel, and are free to guests of Grand View and Willard House. A remarkable pure chalybeate.

Analysis: Carbonate of Iron 3 ½ grains to the imperial gallon. Carbonate of Magnesia. Sulphate of Lime. Carbonate of Soda. Chloride of Sodium... Piercy N. De Dubœay, M. D., F. R. C. S. England.

§   J. Hamp Vickery. W. J. Alford. "The Niagara of the South." The Leading Bar and Wine Cellar of Tallulah Where you will find at any time the Best of Drinks either Hot or Ice Cold. Any one who visits our place of business will find a Cordial Welcome and Ample Protection. Our Prices are as Cheap as the Quality of the Goods we keep will allow. Call and Be Convinced.

The Tallulah Falls Spray, Volume 1, Number 48, Thursday, June 24, 1897

§   Communicated. Atlanta, GA., June 16th, 1897.

Mr. Editor—Will you allow me space in your paper to return my sincere thanks, with those of my wife, to the noble-hearted men of your town and surrounding country for their untiring efforts to recover the body of my son, W. M. Clower who was accidentally drowned at Tallulah Falls. Without their assistance the object of my search might have never been found. I also desire to thank Capt. Lorraine, and his engineer, Capt. Johnson, of the Blue Ridge road for courtesies extended. And my family shall always hold them in grateful remembrance. May Heaven's richest blessing be upon each one of that party of unselfish men. I have been unable to send you this card sooner, which I regret. Very truly, T. W. Clower.

§   Persimmon Breeze.

Messrs. McElwain and Merritt have been in this locality buying walnut timber for the past week.

We sincerely regret to pen the death of Mrs. Mattie Keener, which occurred last Sunday morning at 2 o'clock. She leaves a loving husband and two children. She was a member of the Methodist church, a devoted Christian mother. Her husband, children and relatives have our sincere sympathy. While we mourn her loss, the same is her eternal gain.

Mr. George H. Thompson, who lives on Tallulah river, is erecting a new store house. He says, "Bring me all your chickens."

Messrs. J. C. Howard, C. J. Crunkleton and Miss Texie York are attending the Teachers' Institute at Tallulah Falls this week.

§   Tallulah Falls Briefs.

Concerning the Institute Next Week.

Dr. Merritte, of Clarkesville, is spending this week in Tallulah. If you have any dental work that needs doing don't fail to call on him.

Prof. Bradwell, of Athens, president of the Athens Normal school, arrived Wednesday at noon and gave a lecture for the benefit of the institute.

Prof. Albert Bell also came in Wednesday from Athens. Prof. Bell's many friends are glad to welcome him once more.

Miss Annie Gipson, a charming young lady from Beaty, N. C., is visiting friends and relatives in Tallulah this week. She will soon leave for Clayton and from there to the beautiful Tennessee valley, where her childhood days will be recalled to memory while she spends a few pleasant days with her relatives at the old Gipson homestead.

Tallulah is exceedingly lively this week. The teachers' institute is in session. There must be over one hundred teachers and as many visitors besides. The institute was organized at 2 o'clock Monday and has been mechanically moving on every since.

The Hill Bros'. orchestra came over Tuesday from Clarkesville. Their music can't be beat. Friday night they will give a concert in the Hall. Let all come out.

The hotels and boarding houses all have a good crowd.

Prof. Jennings and wife arrived in Tallulah Wednesday. They are en route to Highlands, N. C.

The photographer has been busy making groups for the institute all the week.

There are so many professors here this week we can't name them all, but among them are Prof. Kittle of White county, C. S. C.; Prof. Lyon of Habersham county, C. S. C. Owing to sickness Prof. W. J. Neville of Rabun county, C. S. C, is absent.

Prof. O'Kelley, principal of the Clayton High school, is here.

We will try to give you all the news of interest.

§   Clayton Dots.

Crops are growing fine.

Plenty of rain.

The farmers are nearly all done harvesting.

Corn crops are looking fine for this time of year.

We are sorry to hear of the death of Mr. Patten Queen.

Quite a crowd left this morning for Tallulah Falls to visit the institute.

The mining interest in Rabun is getting lively.

§   Robinson Hotel At Tallulah is within 100 yards of the beautiful rapids and 200 yards of the mammoth falls, is located between the postoffice and the depot, 100 yards from each. The Robinson Hotel is neatly furnished and keeps a good table. It is before the people that everybody that stops at the Robinson Hotel has a good time. It is before the people that the Robinson Hotel is the place to go spend the summer. It is before the people that the Robinson Hotel has the finest grove of shade trees in

Georgia and the coolest place in the mountains to sleep and have a good time. Rates reasonable. T. A. Robinson, Manager.

The Tallulah Falls Spray, Volume 1, Number 49, Thursday, July 1, 1897

§   The Grand View Hotel Burned.
One of Tallulah's Hotels Goes Up in Smoke on June 29th.
Fire was discovered about half past one a. m. by Miss Higgins, of Atlanta, the kitchen being in flames.
She was with her invalid mother on the second floor, whom she safely got into the Willard House.
She was awakened by the smoke in the room, and as soon as she discovered the fire she screamed and awoke some of the gentlemen in the hotel who gave the alarm.
Miss Higgins sustained considerable loss, it being over $400, probably more than any other guest stopping in the hotel. The hotel was insured, and was totally destroyed, with all furnishings and fixtures.
The guests in the hotel at the time were Mr. Howheansee, of Macon, Ga.; Mr. Keith, Columbus, Ga., Miss Evans, Hardensville, S. C.; Mrs. Higgins, Atlanta, Ga.
The value of the hotel was between $15,000 and $20,000; insurance, $8,000.

§   Tallulah Falls Briefs.
The citizens of Tallulah Falls were made sad when the alarm of fire sounded through the village Tuesday morning. Yes, the beautiful Grand View hotel was no more to be seen as the sun rose Tuesday morning, as fire had totally destroyed the building. The Willard house barely escaped being burned also, probably the heavy rain Monday evening had something to do with keeping the Willard from being caught, as the two houses stand within one hundred yards of one another.
We are unable this week to give you an account of the teachers' institute with resolutions, etc., but hope to next week.
Col. Rob. E. A. Hambey is on business in Atlanta this week.
Tallulah is quite lively this week, owing to the loss of the Grand View. The crowd at Tallulah will not be as large as has been expected. The Willard House can entertain about 50 or 75; hotel Robinson about 150; Glenbrook about 50 or 75; the Cliff House about 200.
Col. Howard Thomson of Gainesville, Ga., was in Tallulah this week.
Dr. de Dubuœay and wife are stopping in Clarkesville this week.

§   Clayton Items.
We are glad to see our teachers returning from the combined institute which closed at Tallulah Falls last Friday. All reports success.
We are sorry to hear of the late shooting affray, which took place on Warwoman last week. We are informed that it took place as follows: Sam Beck was on a "whiz" and during a temporary madness ran his family, consisting of his wife and a dozen children, off "the placc." While the family was "off," our fellow townsman, "Chub" Wall "called." About this time one of Beck's boys returned, and seeing his father pick up the ax, took refuge behind young Wall. Beck made for the boy and "Chub" told

him to stand back; Beck advanced with the ax drawn; "Chub" drew his revolver and fired. The ball glanced over Beck's left breast and entered his left arm. The wound is very impressive, but not necessarily fatal.

Colonels Paris and Ritchie visited the institute at the Falls last week.

Mr. J. F. Earls spent Saturday and Sunday last with "friends" in Warwoman and Moccasin.

§   Death. Mrs. Delia W. White, for ten years a resident of Tallulah Falls, departed this life June 20th. She was a devoted Christian and led a very exemplary life. She leaves one daughter. We mourn her loss, but our loss is her eternal gain.

The Tallulah Falls Spray, Volume 1, Number 50, Thursday, July 15, 1897

§   Tallulah Falls Briefs.

Mr. and Mrs. Rittenhouse Moore and family have arrived in Tallulah to spend the summer.

The camping parties are coming in every day.

The Spray needs money if it keeps going. Let everyone that is due us anything on subscriptions or advertising send it in at once.

Lightning knocked a few horses down at the church Sunday but no serious damage done.

Miss Bertha Scruggs has returned home from Toccoa, Ga., where she has been spending a few weeks with her cousin, Mrs. J. B. Whitmire.

Mr. David Garland lost a good mare Sunday morning.

Five revenue men visited our valley Saturday.

Messrs. W. E. Thompson and T. B. Carter are running a team sawmill on Betties Creek, sawing out a yard for W. J. McCurry. They have fine poplar timber.

§   Teachers at Tallulah Falls.

Tallulah Falls, GA., June 21st, 1897.

The teachers of Rabun, Habersham and White counties met in combined institute at Tallulah Falls Monday the 21st inst., to hold five days, County Commissioners L. L. Lyons of Habersham county and G. S. Kytle of White county presiding.

After engaging in prayer with Prof. J. E. H. Fry the institute went into permanent organization and elected A. H. Henderson, Jr., of White county secretary by acclamation. The chair then appointed a committee on resolutions, as follows:

L. H. Garland of Rabun county, J[?]. C. Howard of Habersham county and A. H. Henderson, Jr., of White county.

From three counties represented here were present about 75 teachers. Interesting programmes were arranged for each day. Professors A. E. Lashley and J. W. Smith of White county and Professors J. E. H. Fry and J. H. Shilling of Habersham county conducted the normal work for the week. On Wednesday of the institute week Capt. S. D. Bradwell of the State Normal school addressed the teachers on the subject of normal training for teachers, followed on Thursday by the Hon. G. R. Glenn, our efficient state school commissioner, who talked to the teachers in a very interesting and instructive way on the subject of progressive education.

The Institute was an enjoyable affair from beginning to end, besides being of lasting benefit to the teachers who attended.

Friday of the institute week was set aside for general discussion and hearing resolutions from the committee, etc....

6—Be it further resolved, That we express our thanks to the citizens of Tallulah Falls for their courtesies and the hospitable manner in which they have entertained the institute during this session, and especially to Messrs. Taylor and Sweet.

The Tallulah Falls Spray, Volume 1, Number 52, Thursday, July 29, 1897

§   Tallulah Falls Briefs.

There were six camping parties in town Tuesday. On Wednesday two more arrived. One was from Lavonia, Ga., four young men—Robert and Seab Weldon, Ardel Vickery and Ben Harris.

Mr. Rit Moore, Jr., left this week for Highlands, N. C., to spend a few weeks.

There will be a lecture given in St. James chapel Sunday, Aug. 1st, by Sister Mary Francis, of the Episcopal church, at 11 o'clock.

We will send The Youth's Advocate one year together with this paper for $1 paid in advance. The Spray Publishing Co., Tallulah Falls, Ga.

The Atlanta Weekly Constitution and this paper one year for 1.50 cash in advance.

§   Clayton Briefs.

Crops are fine around Clayton.

The Blue Ridge Hotel has entertained several strangers the past few weeks.

Rev. W. A. Simmons and wife arrived last Tuesday to spend a few pleasant days with Mr. and Mrs. W. S. Dover.

A party of four young men passed Clayton Wednesday en route to Highlands, N. C. They are from Lavonia, Ga.

§   Persimmon Breezes.

The farmers are about ready to echo the agricultural shout, "Done laying by."

Miss Mary Ray, of Shooting Creek, N. C., and Mrs. Dr. York, of Cornelia, Ga., are visiting Mrs. M. V. York.

The mining interest is at a low ebb at present. We hope that the lease and mining outfit will be sold in the near future. We hope that some financial and influential man will purchase and operate the same to perfection.

§   First Class Shoe Shop Near the Postoffice. Repairing done on short notice in first class style. All work guaranteed. John W. Woodall, Prop. Tallulah Falls, GA.

§   For Good Teams And Saddle Horses For any points in the mountains, call on or leave note at your hotel and they will be promptly filled. Stable, One Block South of Post Office, Tallulah Falls, Ga. J. D. Prather.

The Tallulah Falls Spray, Volume 1, Number 53, Thursday, August 5, 1897

§   First Class Barber Shop at the Robinson House. Work Done in Neat Style. Joe Jinkins, Prop.

§   Georgia, Rabun County.—Geo. M. Dillard, having in due form applied to the undersigned for the guardianship of the person and property of Rachel M. Dillard, a person imbecile from old age, etc. Notice is hereby given that his application will be heard at my office on the first Monday in September next. Given under my hand and official signature this July 30th, 1897. W. S. Long, Ordinary.

§   Georgia, Rabun County.—The return of the appraisers setting apart twelve months' support to the family of Robert L. Dillard, deceased, having been filed in my office, all persons concerned are cited to show cause by the 2nd day of September, 1897, why said application for twelve months' support should not be granted. This July 30th, 1897. W. S. Long, Ordinary.

§   Tallulah Falls Briefs.
The lecture given in St. James Chapel last Sunday was quite instructive.
Remember there is to be a lecture given in St. James chapel next Sunday at 11 o'clock to mothers and daughters.
Mr. H. R. Cannon came home last Saturday, and will spend a few pleasant weeks with his family.
L. P. Wall, Esq., of Chechero district, was in town Monday. Uncle Pearson says he likes The Tallulah Falls Spray very much.
The following names are registered at Glenn Brook: Mr. J. R. Taylor, Mr. W. B. Sweet, Tallulah Falls; Col. Robert G. Barnwell, Atlanta; Mr. Garner and family, Dade city, Fla.; Mr. and Mrs. Middlebrook, Savannah, Ga.; Mr. and Mrs. Roote, Florida; Mr. Phil Thomas, Florida; Mr. J. D. Prather, Tugaloo, Ga.
Mr. George Camp, of Carnesville, is spending a few days in Tallulah sight seeing.
The Spray is one year old; it has lived beyond many people's expectations. The first copy was issued July 16th, 1896. Some said The Spray would "spray" out before three months expired. Others said they would give it six months to go dead. Now, if our readers will only lend a helping hand, The Spray will exist another year...
Mr. John Wes Godfrey has been appointed deputy marshal for this district. John has carried off two of the Rabun boys, but was clever enough to bring them both back. Well, if we have to have revenue officials let's be thankful we have our own county men to fill the offices if possible.
Mr. D. T. Duncan and daughter, Miss Effie Duncan, are visiting Mr. and Mrs. H. R. Cannon this week.

§   Chechero Dots.
Crops are looking fine; plenty watermelons and peaches; only about one-half crop of late apples.
The timber men are cutting and shipping a lot of walnut logs from our district.
Mr. John Bleckley and wife are spending a few pleasant weeks with Judge F. A. Bleckley and family.

Chechero can't be beat for schools. Prof. Price's is getting on fine. Prof. Thos. Carven also has a good school and still, there is another, Prof. S. T. Taylor has a good school.

§   Died, in Warwoman district, Mrs. Martin Page, Saturday, 31st. She leaves a husband and children to mourn her loss.

§   Died, Aug. 1st, 1897, at Tiger, Ga., Mr. P. A. Dickson, after several days' illness with fever. He leaves father, mother, brother and sisters to mourn his loss. Our deepest sympathy is extended to the bereaved parents.

The Tallulah Falls Spray, Volume 2, Number 2, Thursday, August 12, 1897

§   Tallulah Falls Briefs.

Tallulah is quite lively. Hotels all entertain a good crowd, besides the company and excursion parties that are coming in each day.

Col. John O. Dean's guide of Tallulah Falls is going fast. The first one thousand will soon be gone. You will find them on sale at the photo gallery, 25 cents per copy.

Editor Owens, of the Free Press, was in Tallulah this week.

Dr. G. T. Key, Miss Annie Key, Norcross, Ga.; Col. J. A. Hunt, Mrs. J. A. Hunt, Mrs. P. G. Conelly, Master Mose and Lily Connelly, and Mrs. Clarence Dean, of Norcross, have been a jolly crowd at Tallulah the past week. They took part in our Sunday school last Sunday and named the cottage they stopped at Roll Jordan Roll. We like to have such people visit our town that can enjoy themselves and make others do so.

Mr. Beg and Miles Phillips was in town this week. They like The Spray.

Mr. Nathan Parker and wife of South Carolina and Mr. John Parker of White county have been visiting at Mr. Henry Parker's this week.

Mrs. and Miss Toccoa Prather of Tougaloo, Ga., are registered at Glenbrook Cottage this week.

Next Monday week is Clayton court.

Married, at Mount Rest, S. C., on Sunday last, Miss Mary Billingsley of Pine Mountain, Ga., to Mr. J. M. Baldwin of Walhalla, S. C.

§   Clayton Locals.

Dr. D. J. Henson and family have moved to our town and occupy the Beck house.

Crops are looking fine around Clayton.

Call and see new millinery at Mrs. J. L. Hensons, Clayton, Ga. Experienced milliners from Baltimore, have charge of trimmings and dressmaking. Satisfaction guaranteed; lowest prices.

Many camping parties have visited Clayton this summer. They like our crystal cold water and the refreshing mountain breezes.

The Tallulah Falls Spray, Volume 2, Number 3, Thursday, August 19, 1897

§   In Rabun County.

Rich Gold Mines Nearer Home Than Klondyke.

Well, the gold fever is raging in Alaska...

Well, our Northeast Georgia is not quite that rich in the yellow metal, but there is some very rich gold-bearing quartz in Rabun county.

In Persimmon district is the Moore mines that have been worked at for years on a small scale and have always paid expenses and a small margin over. Last year there was a small stamp mill put in operation in this mine. Its capacity for crushing was ten tons a day of the hard quartz. The average gold washed out was about 18 pennyweights to the ton of quartz. This was operated with only five or six hands. As the quartz of this mine is extremely hard—almost as hard as corundum—it is difficult to work with the old style machinery and some of the modern plans of working gold mines should be used. The vein at this mine is at least 30 feet wide, of this hard quartz, and is full of small particles of gold of the finest quality, and the vein extends through a large mountain. There is no doubt that large nuggets would be found at a depth of two or three hundred feet...

And there are the mines on the head of Tallulah river that have been worked at for years only in the old-fashioned way, with shovel and pan; and the Horse cove mine, only three miles from the Rabun county line, in the northeast corner of the county, where two men took out near $4,000 worth of gold nuggets only last year, and lost the vein and quit work, believing it had give out...

§   Tallulah Falls Briefs.

Next week is court week at Clayton.

The grand jury presentments will be published in The Spray the week after court.

M. D. Vandiver was in town Wednesday.

Subscribers to The Spray will receive sample copies of Thrice-a-Week World next week.

Mr. John B. Young will be at Clayton next week and will have a list of all accounts that is due The Spray. So let every one come prepared to meet such.

FOR SALE VERY CHEAP.—One good tin type gallery. Address or call on Walter Hunnicutt, Tallulah Falls, Ga.

§   Society Fads Around Tallulah.

A large party visited Sinking mountain last Wednesday. This mountain has been a wonder ever since it began to gradually disappear, but Aunt Fannie's big dinners are of greater curiosity to the visitor.

Mr. and Mrs. Rittenhouse Moore and friends have returned from Ashville, N. C., to their beautiful summer home at this place after a ten day's stay. They visited Clayton, Rabun Gap, Tennessee Valley and from there through Horse Cove to Highlands, N. C., from there to the Land of the Sky, the beautiful city of Ashville and many other places of interest.

Mayor Sweet has just returned from Atlanta after a short stay.

Last Tuesday a large party went to the top of Rock Mountain. The distant mountains in North Carolina seen from the summit of this mountain is grand beyond description.

Col. R. L. Moss and family have arrived and will enjoy the refreshing weeks.

The kodak is among the latest fads at Tallulah this summer. Almost everyone has one or more kodaks with them.

The bicycle plays its part also. Many use their bicycles to ride around the falls on but none have become expert enough to.

§   Dew Drops From Stonepile.

Mr. J. B. McCracken, of Clemson college, S. C., is visiting his father, Mr. Hiram McCracken, of Tiger district, who is very sick. The many friends sincerely wish to know of the father's recovery, but his recovery is very doubtful.

Miss Laura Dodson, of Stonepile, who has been sick for some time, seems to be improving.

Mr. Thomas Werley is no better.

Mr. Henry Dockins, we learn, is better.

Mr. Radway Taylor is said to be no better.

A new church house is building at Tiger.

Mr. V. C. Taylor, of Chechero, lost his new dwelling with all its contents on Friday night, 13th inst., by fire, while he and his family were spending the night with Mr. William Price, his father-in-law. It is, doubtless, the work of an incendiary. Loss, about $1,500, including $110 in cash and some notes.

We learn that Mr. Chub Wall, of Clayton, while on a visit to Stonepile a few nights ago, with Mr. Bob Denny, came across Mr. John Stansell and broke a bottle of beer over Stansell's head. Others were with them when the blow was given, but don't know the cause.

Miss Susie Ramey is progressing fine with her school at Tiger.

What has become of Georgia's burning negro?

When the new appropriation of $400,000 comes in, perhaps teachers can get a reasonable salary. It is hoped the school term will be cut down to four months, as the term of five months is too long for country schools.

The board of education, at a meeting held on the 7th inst., refused to locate the school at Holly Spring. There is, however, a school going on there, under the supervision of Professor O. Abbott, of South Carolina, with a view of demanding of the board their portion of the public funds.

The Tallulah Falls Spray, Volume 2, Number 4, Thursday, August 26, 1897

§   Tallulah Falls Briefs.

Mr. W. H. Duncan's many friends are glad to see him in Rabun once more. He is visiting his father's family in Clayton for a few days; then he will return to his business in Atlanta.

Tallulah has a good crowd just now, and the weather is fine, cool and nice.

Mr. W. R. Sweet's relative, Mr. Mitchell, of Atlanta, is paying him a visit this week.

Mr. George W. Docking has been on the sick list for a few days, but he is much better now.

Next week we will give you all the news, and also the garnd jury presentments.

§   Clayton News.

As this is court week and everybody busy, we can't give you much news.

Court opened Monday morning at 10 o'clock. There was quite a large attendance Monday. The bar was well represented.

Colonels Dean, Furly, Thompson, of Gainesville; Bowden, Erwin, Edwards, Crane, of Clarkesville; Judge Strickland, of Athens, and many others were here.

Colonel R. L. Moss, of Athens, was here also.

We will give you all the news next week.

The Tallulah Falls Spray, Volume 2, Number 5, Thursday, September 2, 1897

§   Tallulah Falls Briefs.

Rev. R. S. Sanders is in our town this week. He is teaching an art work for the purposes of decorating country homes. Several are taking lessons.

Mr. J. M. Turpin hauled over one hundred dollars' worth of tan bark to our town this summer.

Mr. W. H. Duncan is spending this week with Mr. H. R. Cannon and family.

The corn crop in Rabun county is splendid this time. The late apples are also plentiful.

The rye straw traffic is on the decline just now, market overrun.

The grand jurors presentments did not reach us in time for this week. We hope to be able to give them to our readers next week.

Don't forget the Sunday school is at 4 o'clock, p. m. every Sabbath in Powell Chapel. Let all come out.

We have added several new names to our subscription list in the last few days. Quite a number of our old subscribers have renewed their subscriptions for another year. This is quite encouraging to the publishers.

§   Dew Drops From Stonepile.

The community was saddened by the death of Mr. Hiram McCracken, which occurred on the 19th inst. By his death we lose one of Rabun's most hospitable men.

The superior court at Rabun parted two husbands and wives. We don't believe it is right for Georgia to give divorces to people of other states who come here for them.

Mr. J. B. McCracken has returned to his business at Clemson College, S. C.

The sick people of Stonepile are nearly all improving. Mr. Henry Dockins, we understand, is growing worse.

Rev. Mr. Saunders preached an interesting sermon at Tiger Sunday.

Miss Carrie Whitmire is getting along fine with her school at Camp Creek.

The gold standard, we understand, has reduced silver to 41 cents per hundred...

The niggers of Buffalo gave Mack an ovation the other day, which he recognized, appreciated and enjoyed. No doubt it was an honor to him.

We don't believe in paying revenue officers a salary. The country would flow with whisky; there would be no impediment to whisky making and no restraint from crime, except the superior court and opposition on the part of the churches; and the battle is already hard enough for them.

§   Chechero Dots.

It seems that the hot, dry weather has scorched the Chechero dots up, for they have not got down to The Spray lately.

To be sure, we are having some extremely hot weather.

Corn crops are a little short for want of rain, and you can tell that foddering time is near, by the ugly grin of the farmers.

There was a Negro association held in Chechero last fourth Sunday until Friday and Saturday before. This is the first colored association ever held in Rabun.

Chechero seems to have had her share of visitors for the last few days.

The wife and children of Mr. Gus Swaffard, of Atlanta, have been spending several weeks with Gus' father and mother, Mr. and Mrs. M. W. Swaffard.

Mr. John Bleckley and wife and Mr. Ben Bleckley, of Anderson, S. C.; Mrs. Dr. Bell, of Walhalla, S. C., and her daughter, and the children of Mr. Amos McCurry, of Greenville, S. C., have been visiting relatives in Rabun.

Clayton court lasted all week, then, it seems, it did not get through with the business.

You have the directory of the Clayton Baptist church incorrectly. Rev. W. S. Whitmire is the present pastor.

Rev. J. S. Dickson preached to a large and attentive audience at Big Chechero last Sunday. Prof. O'Kelly, of Athens, Ga., who is teaching at Clayton, was present. We would be glad to have him come again.

Miss Ina Coffee, who is teaching in the northern part of Rabun, spent Saturday and Sunday at home with her mother and father, in this district. She seems not to have partaken of the wild nature of her mountainous abode, but is still the same sweet girl.

We are sorry, indeed, of the death of our friend, Mr. Bartow Whitmire, of Toccoa, Ga. It was quite a shock to us all, as she had been raised among us, and had many friends to think of him. But we, as friends and relatives, must give him up as best we can do to help others who are yet permitted to live...

§   Georgia, Rabun County.—John F. Ritchie has in due form applied to the undersigned for permanent letters of administration on the estate of Geo. W. Kelly, late of said county, deceased, and I will pass upon said application on the first Monday in October, 1897. Given under my hand and official signature, this 25th day of August, 1897. W. S. Long, Ordinary Rabun County.

§   Georgia, Rabun County.—John F. Ritchie having in due form applied to the undersigned for guardianship of the persons and property of George Kelly, Thomas Kelly and Frank Kelly, minor children of Geo. W. Kelly, late of said county, deceased. Notice is hereby given that this application will be heard at my office on the first Monday in October next. Given under my hand and official signature, this 25th day of August, 1897. W. S. Long, Ordinary.

§   Georgia, Rabun County.—A. Shook, executor of the last will and testament of John Shook, applies to me for letters of dismission from said executorship, and I will pass upon his application on the first Monday in December next, at my office in Clayton, said county. Given under my hand and official signature. This August 25th 1897. W. S. Long, Ordinary.

§   Georgia, Rabun County.—A. S. Williams has in due form applied to the undersigned for permanent letters of administration on the estate of A. H. Williams, late of said county, deceased, and I will pass upon said application on the first Monday in October, 1897. Given under my hand and official signature, this the 26th day of August, 1897. W. S. Long, Ordinary Rabun County.

The Tallulah Falls Spray, Volume 2, Number 6, Thursday, September 9, 1897

§   Tallulah Briefs.

Things Seen and Heard About People You Know.

Mr. W. J. Nevill, C. S. C., was in Tallulah last week and gave a lecture at the school house.

There was quite a little riot at the Cliff House last Saturday night among the colored waiters. It ended in one of them getting pretty badly cut up with a razor.

On last Monday while Mr. B. H. Atkins, Tallulah's marshal, and Constable Pitts were trying to arrest a negro at the depot or on the leaving train as it was just departing, and the darkey was trying to dodge the officers by getting on the train, so both officers and darkey mounted the moving train. The negro saw he was getting in close quarters, so he jumped off and so did Marshal Atkins and Pitts, one on one side and one on the other, landing on their heads. So both are stove up but not seriously.

The beautiful services of the "Catholic church" were held last Sunday in the private chapel, (St. Margaretts) on the "Glenbrook" property. The Rev. Father Bazin, assisted by the Rev. Father Davide, officiated. The alter, almost hidden in lovely floral offerings, presented a most beautiful picture. An interesting feature of the occasion was the baptism and christening of the heiress and daughter of the "house of Glenbrook" Madam and Dr. Percy de Duboeay's idolized daughter, and who now bears the name of Margaret Leicester, so named after the deceased, but never to be forgotten, mother of the doctor, and after the doctor's wife. May every blessing follow the little child through its pilgrimage on earth and into the ultimate world beyond.

On next Sunday Rev. H. H. Harris will begin a protracted meeting at Powel's chapel.

Mr. J. R. Taylor went to Sinking Mountain last Sunday.

Mrs. D. T. Duncan and her daughter, Miss Eppee, are[?] spending this week with Mr. and Mrs. H. R. Cannon.

We do not understand why we have not been furnished with a copy of the grand jury presentments for The Spray. It seems that we should have been furnished with a copy, as we print them free of charge.

Hon. Carter Tate, our popular congressman, was in Clayton court week, and received a warm welcome from a host of old friends. His friends have declared him a candidate for re-election.

Mrs. James Dockins is visiting at Mr. and Mrs. G. B. Dockins this week. Her son, Mr. Dockins, is quite sick.

Mr. H. R. Cannon left yesterday for Atlanta.

The fiction offered in Demorest's for September is exceptionally good, not only in plot and literary style, but in the unique character of the illustrations. The drawings by Abby E. Underwood, in R. C. V. Meyers' story "A Woman of Fashion," are in her quaintest and most attractive style.

If you want a beautiful picture of Mud Creek Falls in Tennessee valley, send 35c to Walter Hunnicutt, Tallulah Falls, Ga. Size of picture 6 ½ x 8 ½ inches, mounted on 8 x 10 card. Mailed postage prepaid.

"The Richest College in America" has its story most interestingly set forth by word and picture in the September number of Demorest's Magazine...

§   Communicated.

Clemson College, S. C. Sept. 2, 1897.

Editor of The Spray:

Dear Sir—Kindly allow me space in your paper to extend my thanks to the people for their kindness shown my father in his sickness, and I hope the Lord will bless them.

I am yours truly, J. B. McCrackin.

§   Refugees From infected points will be welcomed at Tallulah Falls, Ga.

Two thousand feet above sea level, in the cool breezes of the Blue Ridge, the dread yellow jack cannot exist.

Hotel accommodations for 500 people. W. R. Sweet, Mayor.

§   Georgia, Rabun County.—The return of the appraisers setting apart twelve months' support to the family of Robert L. Dillard, deceased, having been filed in my office, all persons concerned are cited to show cause by the 2nd day of September, 1897, why said application for twelve months' support should not be granted. This July 30th, 1897. W. S. Long, Ordinary.

§   I. A. M'Curry, Contractor and Builder. For estimate of work call on or write me at Rabun Gap, GA.

The Tallulah Falls Spray, Volume 2, Number 7, Thursday, September 16, 1897

§   Tallulah Falls Briefs.

Tallulah has been blessed all this week with a protracted meeting. Rev. H. H. Harris and Rev. Dave Carter have preached to quite an interested audience twice each day since last Saturday. We are certain there is need of reform in our immediate community. This place has often been called "Beautiful Tallulah," and this name is very appropriate, but will be much more so when Christ is accepted to come into the hearts of our citizens, for the Savior can do more to make things beautiful than all earthly power.

Miss Lelah Rembert, of Savannah, Ga., is the charming guest of Miss M. L. Rembert this week.

Mrs. R. Moore and family left Wednesday last.

Mr. J. B. Murry of Clayton was in Tallulah last week.

Mr. John Green, Sr., and Mr. Benn Thomas of Tennessee Valley were in town this week.

We are glad to see Mr. J. W. Harvey able to come to town once more. Mr. Harvey has almost supplied our town with fresh vegetables for the last ten years.

Col. W. S. Parris was in town this week on his way to Clarkesville court.

We print you 200 envelopes for 50 cents and 200 letter heads to match them for 60 cents cash with the order; if to be sent by mail, 10 cents for postage extra.

Book of 100 blank notes 35 cents, 50 blank notes 20 cents. Spray Pub. Co., Tallulah Falls, Ga.

We want a correspondent from each district in the county.

The Tallulah Falls Spray, Volume 2, Number 8, Thursday, September 23, 1897

§   Turpen Not Guilty.

He Was Tried Last Week for Murder at Walhalla, S. C.

Communicated to The Spray.

Mr. Jas. H. Turpen, who was tried at Walhalla, S. C., last week for killing Rollie Dunn, was found not guilty. It will be remembered that Jas. Turpen had gone to church at Damascus, S. C., on the second Sunday in June, four miles from where he stayed in that state, and on his return home had stopped in at Hascal Homes'. While there Rollie Dunn, who had threatened several times to kill Turpen, made his appearance.

Soon after Dunn arrived he called Turpen out, knocked him down and began to beat him with his fist. After he had bruised him considerably in the face, some one made him quit, telling him he was too large to fight so small a boy as Turpen. Dunn then took out a knife, which was already open in his pocket, and started at Turpen, striking at him furiously.

Turpen backed eleven steps, begging Dunn, as he had from the beginning, not to have any row. Seeing there was no chance to avoid a fight, Turpen took out his knife, opened it, and the two ran together, locked up with their left arms, and the terrible work began. Only a minute, and Turpen had received a stab in the left shoulder joint and a horrible gash in the left side. Dunn had received three cuts. Dunn quit then; Turpen quit and they both walked into the yard. Dunn sat down by the house and Turpen by a stump. Dunn died immediately. Turpen fell into insensibility and was awakened after midnight and put under arrest.

Last week at the trial, the above facts were proven, and the jury had been gone thirty minutes when they returned with a verdict of "not guilty." They then rushed to Turpen to congratulate him. They and the anxious waiting gentlemen and ladies crowded upon him and almost smothered him with tears and hand-shaking of congratulations. Dunn was Oconee county's desperado and weighed 170 pounds. Turpen was a boy of 130 pounds weight, who was raised in Rabun county, Ga., and went to South Carolina two years ago.

§   Things Seen and Heard Around Tallulah.

Among the charming visitors of Tallulah this week were Miss Dancie Taylor, of Stone Pile, and Miss Mary Davidson, of Habersham county.

Mr. J. F. Robinson, of our town, is, through his energy, proving what can be done around Tallulah in the way of farming. He has opened up several acres of land at the old side track, about one mile from Tallulah. He will make four or five hundred bushels of corn this time, and his cabbage, potatoes and onions cannot be beat. He has onions that will measure 4 ¾ inches across. This shows what might be done.

Don't forget that next Saturday and Sunday there will be a preaching at Powel's Chapel. On Sunday morning five converts are to be baptized. Rev. D. L. Carter will administer the baptism.

Mr. E. A. Dorsey was in Tallulah Wednesday with some fine apples. We would be glad to see him come again.

§   Clayton Items.

U. S. Marshal J. W. Godfrey is capturing and carrying off a number of our boys.

Rev. D. C. Brown returned to our town last Saturday from Clarkesville, where he had been to get him a wife. The bride was a Miss Sallie Church and Bro. Brown says he joined the church and she joined the conference. They have our best wishes and we hope them a long, prosperous union.

Brer' Duncan, of the Blue Ridge hotel, has a broad smile on. He has been swapping horses lately.

Miss Katie Bell, of Walhalla, S. C., and Miss Zoa Bleckley, of Anderson, S. C., are visiting their aunt, Mrs. Emily Wall, this week.

The protracted meeting that has been in progress at the "Pine" on Scott's creek, resulted in about forty conversions, twenty-four of whom joined the church.

The presiding elder, Rev. E. R. Cook, was in town last Saturday. He held a quarterly meeting at Tiger Saturday and Sunday.

J. L. Hamby has moved his store to the Whitmire old stand which he has recently purchased.

Sam Mitchell has sub-rented his mail route from Clayton to Tallulah Falls to J. B. Murray.

§   Dew Drops From Stonepile.

Prof. S. T. Taylor has vacated his school at Wolf Creek for fodder and is now exhibiting his familiar smiles among his many friends of Stonepile.

Miss Laura Dodson, who has been sick so long, was improving in health until last Thursday, when she grew worse. Dr. P. N. deDuboeay made a visit to her last Saturday. Her many friends are anxious for her recovery.

Rev. Mr. Brown, our efficient circuit preacher, who is an allround church man, passed through Stonepile last Saturday a benedict. He belongs to the M. E. church; he went to Clarksville and on last Tuesday married a pretty Miss Church, who belongs to the church; and last Saturday they were on their way to church. The bride and groom have our best wishes.

The quarterly meeting began at Ivy Hill last Saturday.

Miss Annie Flor of Demorest, has been visiting Miss Drucie Taylor for a few days.

§   Yellow Gold.

A new gold find just across the line between Rabun county, Ga., and Oconee county, S. C. The ore proves very rich. The mine is on Mr. Martin Pitt's land, also other lands adjoining. A company is being formed to work the mine.

The Tallulah Falls Spray, Volume 2, Number 10, Thursday, October 7, 1897

§   Church Directory...
Clayton Directory.
Baptist Church. Rev. W. S. Whitmire, pastor...

§   Cliff House Closed at Tallulah.

On last Thursday the Cliff House closed, after a successful season. This speaks well for Tallulah as a summer resort, owing to the house not being opened until late. Other summer resorts had quite a crowd of guests before the Cliff was let.

Messrs. Gresham and Moss have proven beyond a doubt what can be done at Tallulah. The Cliff house was opened about the first of June, closed first of October and entertained quite a nice crowd from the first week to the last week it was open.

We are informed that Gresham & Moss will advertise and open the Cliff in 1898 at least two months earlier than it was opened this season.

§   Briefs Gathered From Throughout Rabun County.

There has been quite a religious revival at Old Tiger for the past week.

Mr. Jesse C. Dover left Clayton Tuesday to attend Medical college at Atlanta.

There are two or three photographers making some large views of Tallulah Falls this week.

Mr. Alex L. Roan was in Tallulah this week.

Col. R. E. A. Hanbey is attending U. S. Court in Atlanta this week.

Mr. J. W. Godfrey passed Tallulah this week with more prisoners. Boys, watch out for John, for he is always on the hunt.

§   Chambers.

Cleveland, GA., Sept. 23, 1897.

It appearing that the business of the court requires it,

It is therefore ordered that a special term of Rabun superior court be held, commencing at 9 o'clock a. m. on the third Monday in February, 1898, being the week next preceding the regular court. This court to be held for the purpose of disposing of civil cases, and also criminal cases, if necessary.

The traverse jurors who compose the regular panels of traverse jurors for the August term, 1897, are hereby ordered to give their attendance on said special term.

The first week will be devoted to civil and the second week to criminal cases.

All parties and attorneys and witnesses in civil cases must give their attendance on said special term the first week where they have been heretofore subpœnaed to attend the said superior court without a new summons for that purpose.

Let this order be placed on the minutes of said court and let the clerk have true copies published or circulated in the county, provided it can be done without cost to said county.

J. J. Kimsey, J. S. C.

§   Georgia, Rabun County.—Whereas B. R. Dillard, administrator of J. B. Dillard, represents to the court that he has fully administered J. B. Dillard's estate. This is therefore to cite all persons concerned to show cause, if any they can, why said administrator should not be discharged from his administration and receive letters of dismission on the first Monday in January, 1898. This Oct. 4th, 1897. W. S. Long, Ordinary.

§   Georgia, Rabun County.—A. S. Williams, administrator of A. H. Williams, deceased, has in due form applied to the undersigned for leave to sell the lands belonging to the estate of said deceased and said application will be heard on the first Monday in November next. This 4th day of October, 1897. W. S. Long, Ordinary.

§   Georgia, Rabun County.—John H. Ritchie, having in due form applied to the undersigned for the guardianship of the person and property of Belle Kelly, a person of unsound mind, etc. Notice is hereby given that his application will be heard at my office on the first Monday in November next. Given under my hand and official signature. This Oct. 4th, 1897. W. S. Long, Ordinary.

§   Georgia, Rabun County.—The return of the appraisers setting apart twelve months support to the family of Hiram McCrackin, deceased, having been filed in my office, all persons concerned are cited to show cause by the 1st day of November, 1897, why said application for twelve months support should not be granted. This September 29th, 1897. W. S. Long, Ordinary.

§   Georgia, Rabun County.—The return of the appraisers setting apart twelve months support to the family of George W. Kelly, deceased, having been filed in my office, all persons concerned are cited to show cause by the 1st day of November, 1897, why said application for twelve months support should not be granted. This September 29th, 1897. W. S. Long, Ordinary.

The Tallulah Falls Spray, Volume 2, Number 11, Thursday, October 14, 1897

§   We will probably have another religious revival at Tallulah this week. Our Clarkesville friends will be over to lead for us. Our town needs more divine strength.

§   We are glad to say that Mr. J. B. Dockins, who has been down with fever is able to be up again.

§   Mr. H. R. Cannon and family are visiting relatives at Clayton this week.

§   Dr. Green and Miss Lizzie Duncan of Clayton visited our town last week.

§   Glenbrook still entertains a few strangers.

The Tallulah Falls Spray, Volume 2, Number 12, Thursday, October 21, 1897

§   Prosperity Throughout the Length and Breadth of Rabun County—Things Seen and Heard.

Prosperity seems to be in our county just now. The chestnut crop is fine. Already many market wagons, loaded with chestnuts, apples and cabbage, have made from two to three trips to market and we have been told by several that they got an average good price for their load. Of course the late apple crop will be exhausted long before Christmas as there is not a large crop. There must be a good many dried apples, as the early crop was good.

Irish potatoes, owing to the drouth, is cut short, so is onion, which is bringing a good price to be so early.

§   The leading article in Demorest's Magazine for November tells the story of "A Winter in an Oasis"...

§   Mr. J. M. Phillips has just opened up a new store in our town. He is located at the Sweet old stand.

§   It seems that everything goes by twos.

§   Mr. H. R. Cannon has gone to Atlanta to buy goods, and will soon open up another store in Tallulah.

§   Mr. R. W. Davidson has just received a car load of salt.

§   Miss Manoah Atkins is fast improving. She has had typhoid fever.

§   Colonel Edwards of Clarksville dined with Dr. P. N. deDubeouy last week.

§   Mr. A. C. Godfrey has been appointed postmaster at Tallulah Falls to succeed Mr. J. R. Taylor. Mr. Taylor has made us a good postmaster and many regret to give him up. He was oppointed under the Democratic administration. Mr. Godfrey was recently appointed and will hold the office under the McKinley administration. We feel sure that he will make us a good postmaster. He was postmaster seven years ago at this place and gave splendid satisfaction. The office will be removed from the Emporium to the J. F. Robinson old stand.

§   Mrs. J. L. Henson will succeed Mr. J. I. Langston at Clayton as postmistress.

§   Call at Sweet's old stand for your groceries. We keep the best flour. J. M. Phillips.
When you come to Tallulah Falls call on J. M. Phillips before you do your trading and examine his goods.

§   Notice.

This is to give notice that the following local bills will be introduced at the coming session of the next legislature:

"A bill to be entitled an Act, to prohibit seining, trapping, etc., in Tallulah river and all its tributaries in Rabun county, Georgia.

Also "a bill to be entitled an Act, to amend the charter of the town of Clayton, in Rabun county, Georgia, and for other purposes."

Robt. E. A. Hamby, Representative of Rabun County.

The Tallulah Falls Spray, Volume 2, Number 13, Thursday, October 28, 1897

§   Tallulah Falls Briefs.

Ex-Ordinary F. A. Bleckley was in Tallulah last week on his way to Macon to attend the Grand Lodge.

Col. R. E. A. Hamby, our representative, left last week to help improve our laws.

Tallulah is going to be the upper market in the future for your produce.

Mr. John W. Godfrey, our vigilant and busy U. S. marshal, found spare time to visit his brother-in-law, W. F. Brown in Spartanburg, S. C., last week.

Some of our Tallulah boys are talking of being off very soon for Klondike. Boys, there is gold under the Rabun soil yet. Wait a little and help develop it.

Says the Dover News: President Kirkly, General Boon and General Council Williams will be at Anderson, S. C., Nov. 4th in the interest of the Black Diamond railroad. Matters are in such a shape in that state that it will not take long to secure a franchise through her borders. The Black Diamond railroad will start in the west and go through Rabun Gap to Port Royal, S. C.

§   Rabun Gap Items.

The weather is cool and pleasant in the valley now.

The cattle trade seems to be quieted down some.

Apple hauling is a very common employment with the farmers.

W. J. McCurry lost a good work steer while hauling lumber to Clayton the 22d inst. He fell dead under the yoke.

Rev. J. S. Dickson is running a meeting at the Baptist church. Our valley needs something. A good case of religion would help us.

Mrs. R. B. Ritchie has been very sick for several days.

Capt. L. M. Beaurt and family went to Highlands, N. C., last week.

Miss Beulah Green and Miss Lizzie Page visited Toccoa, Ga., and returned well pleased with the city.

Professor Bell and Miss Neal are doing good work at their school at this place.

Some of our church members are a little careless about driving their teams and wagons on Sunday. You know what the Lord says about such in Exodus xx, 8 – 11.

Messrs. Powell and Nevels are contemplating making some improvements on their mill.

§ Special Notice—Read Carefully.

We want $1.00 in advance for The Spray this year from all our readers that can possibly spare it; and to all that are due us for last year will send it in at once...

§ Communicated.

Rabun Gap, GA, Oct. 25, 1897.

Editor Spray: I have been frequently asked lately about the time teachers would receive pay for the last quarter, or for the quarter ending 30th of September.

I wish to say through The Spray that it will be about the 1st of November. Some of the counties of the state will have to wait longer, but our county having drawn but little for the first and second quarters, there is enough funds in the treasury and standing to our credit to pay off all our indebtedness. Truly yours,

W. J. Neville, C. S. C.

§ Strayed or Stolen.

Tiger, GA., Rabun County.

Strayed off from my place one work oxen, about six years old, dark brindle color with some white on his hips and about his flanks; ear marks, a swallow-fork and under-bit in the right ear and a slope on the left ear and 2 letters on his right horn, "H. A." Any information concerning whereabouts will be gladly received at Vandviere, Ga. H. B. Cannon.

§ The United States has no particular rank among nations as a producer of precious stones, and yet within its limits nearly all the varieties have been found... Cowee Valley in North Carolina furnishes rubies, and those [illegible] in developing the district believe they have found a veritable ruby-bearing deposit similar to that of Burmah...

§ J. M. Phillips, Dealer in General Merchandise. Will buy all your Grain and Produce. Call and see us before you trade elsewhere. Tallulah Falls, GA.

The Tallulah Falls Spray, Volume 2, Number 14, Thursday, November 4, 1897

§ Tallulah Falls Briefs.

It seemed that last Saturday was young ladies' day at Tallulah Falls.

Prof. H. J. Pearce, accompanied by about 75 young ladies from the Gainesville Female seminary of Gainesville came up and enjoyed the evening sight-seeing around the falls.

Miss Susie Ramy, one of Rabun county's accomplished young lady teachers, was also in Tallulah last Saturday.

Mr. H. R. Cannon has just opened up the largest stock of piece goods that has ever been seen in our town at any one time before. The stock comprises all styles and grades of dress goods.

Marshal Atkins set a net last Monday night and caught four young men suspected of breaking shade trees in our town. Two of them were found guilty and Mayor Sweet gave them $10 and cost. The two guilty ones were Essey and Joe Sherley.

We will send you The Spray on trial for 6 months for 35 cents, paid in advance. This offer will hold good for 30 days. We extend the same offer to our old subscribers. All that want to send us 35 cents, in advance, for 6 months, or 70 cents for 12 months, if sent in within 30 days from the date of this paper can do so. Let every reader of The Spray show this to their friends and help us to double our subscription list.

§   Notice.

Agreeably to an order of the court of ordinary of Rabun county will be sold at auction at the courthouse door of said county, on the first Tuesday in December next, within the legal hours of sale the following property to-wit: Part of lot of land number 21, in the 4th land district of Rabun county, and containing four hundred acres more or less, sold as the property of A. H. Williams, late of said county, deceased. Terms, twelve months time with note and approved security. This first day of November, 1897. A. S. Williams, Administrator.

§   The "Bazar," H. R. Cannon, Esq., Proprietor. This elegant commissary of splendid merchandise is now open to public patronage, containing the largest, the most beautiful and the cheapest stock of goods ever offered to the people of Northeast Georgia.

Imported Dress Goods. Embracing the finest material, patterns and combinations unsurpassed for ladies and children's dresses. Double width and double value.

Calicoes. In glorious colors, surpassing the gorgeous rainbow in brilliancy and beauty.

Notions. A line so complete and perfect, that nothing is left to the imagination.

Shoes. To meet the taste of ladies, gentlemen and children. Suitable, indeed, to walk "dem golden streets of Paradise." Fall and winter shoes a specialty.

Hardware—A General Line. Our staple family groceries you are invited to inspect. Fresh, bright and good—wonderful value for the money.

Why travel friend, away so far? Come, trade a little now with me. Just call in at the "Grand Bazar," You'll find a friend in H. R. C.

The Tallulah Falls Spray, Volume 2, Number 19, Thursday, December 9, 1897

§   Tallulah Falls Briefs.

There has been very little said about who will be mayor of our town in 1898. Some have been thinking, we guess, well, its time now that the people center on some good man, and let's not run more than half a dozen for this honorary office.

And what about our school for next year? It's high time to be thinking the matter over, as first-class teachers—the kind of business teacher that it takes to govern a first-class school—are scarce, and such teachers are now making arrangements where they will teach for next year, and if we wait we can be certain of last choice. Now is the time to get first choice.

I want to buy all kinds of fur skins; will pay fair prices for them. J. M. Phillips, Tallulah Falls, Ga.

....Dr. J. H. McLean's Liver and Kidney Balm... Price $1 a bottle. For sale by H. R. Cannon.

J. M. Phillips will buy all kinds of fur, skins, such as mink, o'possum, coon, fox, polecat, black house cat, otter, musk rat and most any kind caught in this country.

§   Georgia, Rabun County.—B. F. Smith, guardian of Walton Wall, applies to me for letters of dismission from said guardianship, and I will pass upon his application on the first Monday in January next, at my office in Clayton, said county. Given under my hand and official signature, this 6th day of December, 1897.   W. S. Long, Ordinary.

§   When You visit Clarksville, Ga., be sure and call on Barron & Hix, Dealers in all kinds of confectioneries. Hot chocolates a specialty.

The Tallulah Falls Spray, Volume 2, Number 20, Thursday, December 16, 1897

§   Market Prices Revised Up to Date...

§   Clayton Locals.
Prof. O'Kelley's school closed last Friday. The exercises were both entertaining and instructive. Now let every one help to make the school in 1898 the best that Clayton has ever had.

We think it will be a great improvement to have our school house enlarged and it won't cost much. Let all help.

§   Notice.
We have bought a complete stock of Christmas novelties, comprising a nice line of Chinese and Japanese dolls, toys, Christmas cards, etc., which we will sell at a sacrifice. We have a few dozen taffeta and serge silk umbrellas for 50 cents each worth two dollars. Also a line of overcoats for $2.25 and $2.50 worth three times that amount. Buy before they are gone. Taylor & Sweet.

§   Tallulah Falls Briefs.
We have just been informed that the school fund checks will be furnished our county school commissioner, Mr. W. J. Nevill, on the 18th, so it will not be many days until the Rabun county teachers will receive their school money.

Our streets are being put in good order just now.

Yes, let's have a nice Christmas tree, and let every one that can, give liberally to help get it up, and if you can't give but one nickle, give it cheerfully.

We are sorry to know that Mr. J. R. Taylor is in bed sick. Hope to see him at his place of business soon.

Dr. P. N. deDubeary is enlarging Glenn Brook cottage.

§   Rabun Gap.
Mr. J. A. Hopper made a working Saturday to cover his house. We covered one side, then made away with a lot of his winterjohns, as hard as they were.

D. P. Lacount has finished D. M. Green's rock work.

We are glad to have the editor of The Spray with us for a few days, although he made some ugly impressions in our valley. Of course he is a photographer. He failed to get Miss Neal's picture in the school group. The school closed Wednesday.

Prof. Albert Bell is visiting our valley. We were glad to have him with us Sunday in prayer meeting.

T. N. Carter & Co. are filling up their store with goods at Dillard, Ga., one mile from this office.

Mrs. R. B. Ritchie is improving in health. She has been very sick for some time.

I. A. McCurry is building a dwelling for David Garland.

Miss Ida Scruggs is teaching school at the Martin schoolhouse where Mr. H. Garland began to teach.

The Christmas tree will be at the Baptist church this time. The M. E. Sunday school will join in with them.

§   Wolf Creek Lookouts.

Quite an interesting crowd went from Wolf Creek to the city of Clayton last Tuesday to the sale.

We understand that a lively crowd of hunters caught a large fox last Saturday after a race of about five hours. The crowd consisted of M. L. Jones, J. V. Page, E. M. Jones, M. A. Jones, E. H. Williams, J. C. Flanigan. The boys will try it again about Christmas, we guess.

We understand that Mr. G. [?]. Smith and Mr. E. A. Dorsey have gone to market. We wish the boys good luck and a safe return.

The school at Wolf Creek will close next Friday. They will probably make a lively thing of it.

Christmas is coming. You may look[?] out—the serenaders will be around till you can't rest; the Christmas bells will ring. Look careful; they will be here before you know it.

The wedding bells have been ringing on Wolf Creek for the last month, and will probably ring again in a few days.

The Jones & Moore merchandise business will probably take a rise, as Mr. Moore had a fine heir added to his family a few days ago.

§   All Kinds of Job Work Neatly Done at The Spray Office... The Spray Publishing Co. Tallulah Falls, GA. Send stamp for samples.

The Tallulah Falls Spray, Volume 2, Number 22, Thursday, December 30, 1897

§   Rabun Mission. Geo. P. Gary, Pastor in Charge.
Bethel, first Sunday, 10 a. m. and Saturday before.
Lipscomb, first Sunday, 3 p. m.
Ledford's Store, first Sunday night.
Tallulah Falls, second Sunday, 11 a. m.
Antioch, third Sunday, 10 a. m., and Saturday before.

Spruce Pine, third Sunday, at 3 p. m.

Blue Ridge, third Sunday night.

Wolf Fork, fourth Sunday, 11 a. m.

Betty's Creek, fourth Sunday, 3 p. m.

Note—The first quarterly meeting for the Rabun mission will be held at Antioch church Feb. 5 – 6 (Saturday and Sunday). Let the official members and others friendly to the work be present.

§   Communicated.

Dillard, GA., Dec. 27th, 1897.

Last Wednesday Mr. Emery Keener of our valley went to North Carolina after a Miss Holebrooks, and so it is Mrs. Huldy Keener now, as they were married. One of her sisters accompanied the bride and groom back to Georgia, where she was made a Mrs. Oliver, as she and Mr. Charlie Oliver were joined heart and hand in matrimony.

Our valley had a nice Christmas tree at the Baptist church Christmas day.

Capt. L. M. Beavert has been on the sick list for several days.

There was a big turkey dinner enjoyed at Mr. J. W. Godfrey's Christmas day.

Mr. Jessie McCurry and family went to Clayton to enjoy a Christmas dinner with Wall.

Last Thursday was sale day at the residence of B. R. Dillars, being the guardian sale of Rachel Dillard.

During Christmas some of the Macon bachelors were in charge of our Rabun girls.

Mr. R. L. Ritchie has returned from Texas and is spending Christmas at his father's.

Eula Dillard.

§   Tallulah Falls Briefs.

During the Christmas holidays our town has enjoyed a peaceful quietude, notwithstanding our young folks and older ones have had a good time. There was a nice Christmas tree in Powel's Chapel given for the benefit of the little folks on Christmas eve. Messrs. Tim and Dan Hix and Mr. Alford Dyre entertained the crowd during the occasion with appropriate music.

Mrs. W. D. Young gave the children a candy pulling Christmas day p. m., which was highly enjoyed.

Rev. Dave Carter preached in Powel's Chapel Saturday and Sunday at 11 o'clock and gave a Sunday school lecture at 10 o'clock Sunday morning.

Col. A. J. Ritchie, who has a law office in Athens, spent Monday night in Tallulah. He was on his way to the beautiful Tennessee Valley, to spend a few days with his father and family.

Col. Rob E. A. Hambry has been in Atlanta a few days trying to secure a pardon for Will Hopkins.

We are glad to hear the Mr. Cartny Davidson, who has typhoid fever is slowly improving.

Miss Susie Rainey, one of Rabun county's young lady teachers, is visiting in Tallulah this week.

Mr. J. F. Godfrey of Chechero has a fine hog. It measures six feet in circumference, five foot 8 inches in length, and weighs 400 pounds and only a little over one year old. Who can beat this?

§   Notice. We have just received a great bargain in men's hats, and can offer them for less than half of value... Taylor & Sweet.

The Tallulah Falls Spray, Volume 2, Number 23, Thursday, January 6, 1898

§   Tallulah Falls Briefs.
Mr. A. J. Ritchie returned to Athens this week.
Miss Susie Ramey will begin her school next Monday at this place.
Rev. Geo. P. Gary will preach at Powel's Chapel next Sunday at 11 o'clock. It is hoped by the citizens of Tallulah that he will be a resident of our town this year.
Mr. H. B. Cannon will have in a carload of acid this week, so if you have not bought call and see him before buying elsewhere. His price will be as cheap as you can get it anywhere.
The revenue officers made a big raid the other day in this county and J. W. Godfrey and other prominent officers made a big haul the other day in this county. They arrested George Benfield and got two coppers in one house and also arrested Lafathe Frady. He was accused of shooting at the officers. He is now in Gainesville jail.
An Irish peddler was found three miles from Tallulah Falls frozen to death. He was in Tallulah last Friday and obtained a pack of goods and inquired the pathway leading up the river from this place. He had been drinking and we did not learn his name.

§   A. J. Ritchie—Attorney at Law, Atlanta, Ga.

The Tallulah Falls Spray, Volume 2, Number 24, Thursday, January 13, 1898

§   Tallulah Falls Briefs.
Everything is quiet around Tallulah just now.
The school opened Monday with a good attendance.
The name of the young man that was frozen to death a week ago was Barney McIntyre[?]. His brother, accompanied by the Catholic priest, came to Tallulah last Monday to claim the remains of the unfortunate young man.

§   Communicated.
Burton, GA., Jan. 5, 1898.
Mr. Editor—Some of Mr. Collector Rucker's deputies have been capering around in Tallulah district, had some of the boys are scared, and, we understand, got some copper and destroyed a lot of beer and mash.
Last Friday, Dec. 31st, was general moving day. Among others we note H. J. Camp, H. C. Blalock, D. M. Trady, S. M. Arrendale, H. N. Burrell, J. M. Marsengill

and Prof. R. N. Dover all changed homes on that day, but all remained within our district, except Mr. Camp, who goes to Troy, Habersham county, where he will continue to stand behind the counter and ask "anything else?"

We are sorry to hear that Mr. A. J. Powell is very sick.

Several children are sick with scarlatina.

Mud! Mud!! Mud!!!

§   Clayton Dots.

Prof. O'Kelley's school opened last Monday morning with a large attendance.

The municipal election was held here last Monday for elective officers for 1898: Mayor, J. E. Derrick; councilmen, D. T. Duncan, Dr. W. J. Green and J. F. Dickson.

The United States revenue officers arrested Lester Queen and Will Ledbetter last week.

§   A $2,000 Word!

This paper announces, in connection with The Atlanta Weekly Constitution, a new offer in which everyone may have a chance to supply the missing word in this sentence:

"At First It Was Considered By The '_____' As A Good Omen."

This sentence is taken from a well-known publication. The word is a familiar one, and may readily suggest itself.

Contest began Jan. 1—Ends March 1, '98.

To enter the contest you must subscribe for The Atlanta Constitution In Connection With The Tallulah Falls Spray, At The Extremely Low Price Of $1.50...

The Tallulah Falls Spray, Volume 2, Number 27, Thursday, February 3, 1898

§   Tallulah Falls Sprays.

Prospects for this year at Tallulah are rather flattering. We learn that the Cliff house has been let and will be opened up early.

Mr. and Mrs. W. D. Young have rented the Robinson house and will run it in connection with the Willard house in the coming season, and of course they will have a good crowd.

Glenn Brook is being enlarged and will be able to entertain quite a number more than it had last season.

We still hear talk of the new hotel being built, but can't say how soon.

George P. Gary will preach at Powell's chapel the first Sunday in February and Saturday before.

The Blue Ridge and Atlantic railroad is in excellent condition. All the trestles have been rebuilt and many new crossties have been put in. Everything is in good order.

Our merchants are having a splendid trade this season, far better than usual. They are busy buying and shipping all kinds of grain and produce. We suppose one good reason of the unusual good trade the merchants are having is on account of the splendid new road leading from the Falls to the poll bridge. It makes no difference how much it rains or how muddy you find our common country roads, you always find this road firm and dry, as it is built on a scientific plan. It is high up on the side of the ridges and winds around almost on a level, and was surveyed out in such a way that it is impossible for it to get boggy. Too much credit cannot be said for our ex-ordinary, F. A. Bleckley. Of course at the beginning of the building of this road everybody grumbled at the very idea of securing the services of an expert surveyor to lay out this road, but nearly all will admit now that his good judgment has been worth a great deal to our country, after all.

§   Communicated.
Tiger, GA., Jan. 31, 1898.
It's been snowing and rather cold, but not so cold as to stop Mr. H. C. McCrackin and his little people from going to school. Mr. McCrackin is one of Tiger's up-to-date young men, and has a nice school at old Tiger. And we regret to know that Mr. H. C. Ramey, of our district, has left for South Carolina, where he will go into business. We wish him worlds of success. Yes, and Mr. Dud McCrackin and family, of Tiger, have moved from his farm to the village of Tallulah Falls, where he will be general salesman in Mr. H. R. Cannon's store.

§   Georgia, Rabun County.—George W. Lovell has in due form applied to the undersigned for permanent letters of administration on the estate of W. B. Lovell, late of said county, deceased, and I will pass upon said application on the first Monday in March, 1898. Given under my hand and official signature this 31st day of January, 1898. W. S. Long, Ordinary Rabun County.

§   Notice.
Notice is hereby given that after the first day of March, 1898, the advertising connected with the Ordinary's office of Rabun county will be done in the Clayton Tribune instead of the Tallulah Falls Spray. This January 31st, 1898. W. S. Long, Ordinary.

§   Real Estate For Sale.
One small farm, two and one half miles from Tallulah Falls. There is about 300 acres; has a grist mill and dwelling house; is in a common state of cultivation, suited for dairy and poultry farm. Can be bought for one hundred and sixty dollars. Write or call on Walter Hunnicutt, Agent, Tallulah Falls, Ga.

§   Notice. We have another line of those cheap hats and umbrellas, and can supply [missing] other lots. Any of these will cost twice the money elsewhere... Taylor & Sweet.

The Tallulah Falls Spray, Volume 2, Number 29, Thursday, February 17, 1898

§   County Officers.
Clerk Superior Court—L. C. Hollifield. Ordinary—W. S. Long. Sheriff—J. B. Dockins. Tax Collector—J. F. Smith. Tax Receiver—M. M. Kell. County Treasurer—W. E. Thompson. County School Commissioner—W. J. Nevill.

§   Valedictory.

With this issue The Tallulah Falls Spray passes into the hands of Col. T. A. Robinson.

We thank the people for their liberal patronage in the past. We trust the people will continue their patronage.

Confident are we that under the new management the paper will merit your support.

Very respectfully, Walter Hunnicutt.

§   Spray Locals.

It is reported that smallpox has made its appearance in Habersham county.

Mr. T. H. Hunnicutt of Red Hill, Franklin county, was in the city last Wednesday.

Our Sunday school under the management of Superintendent Atkins is well attended.

Rev. Roy R. Sibley, pastor in charge of the Clayton circuit was in Tallulah on the 8th inst.

Geo. P. Gary preached last Sunday morning in the hall over Sweet and Taylor's store. A good congregation was present. After services a Methodist church was organized.

Walter Hunnicutt made a business trip to Franklin county last Saturday.

Services at the Baptist church 4th Sunday and Saturday before by the pastor.

Our school, under the management of Miss Susie Ramie, is now doing good work—a good number of pupils are in attendance.

§   Tiger Topics.

Rev. George Seay is now selling Bibles. If you need a good one see him.

Miss Elsie Ramey has returned from a visit to Mrs. Bob Deneys.

Walter Taylor has returned from a trip to Toccoa.

Rev. Mr. Ella will preach at Tiger's Baptist church Friday night before the fourth Sunday.

Mr. Sport Ramie of Tiger is teaching school in "Germany."

Col. Robt. Hamby made an appreciated speech to our school last Friday, and here we will state that we are having a good school, and in the person of Prof. H. C. McCrackin we have a good teacher.

Mr. J. H. Hunnicutt has returned from a visit to North Carolina.

We are glad to see Mr. Bell McCrackin, of South Carolina, in old Rabun once more.

§   ...Dr. J. H. McLean's Volcanic Oil Liniment... Price 25c, 50, and $1 a bottle. For sale by H. R. Cannon.

§   State of Georgia, Rabun County—This is to notify all persons that they are hereby forbidden to feed, harbor or entertain my wards, George R. Hallifield, Walter Hallifield and Rallie N. Hallifield, ages 16, 13 and 11 years old. George R. Hallifield and Walter Hallifield have left their home on February 4th, 1898. Any person knowing of their whereabouts will do me the favor of notifying me at Tiger, Ga. This February 7, 1898. Charles Smith, Guardian for above named wards.

§   J. H. Williams, Worker in Wood and Iron Is prepared to repair your Wagons, Buggies and Farming Tools on short notice, at reasonable figures. Call on him. Tallulah Falls, GA.

THE CLAYTON TRIBUNE

JANUARY 6 TO DECEMBER 28, 1899

The Clayton Tribune was first published in January, 1898. It was published continuously until 1918, when it was merged with *The Clarkesville Advertiser* and renamed *The Tri-County Advertiser*. *The Clayton Tribune* was revived in 1924, and has been continuously published to the present day. Many early issues are now missing, even for years where a large number of issues have been located, as with 1899. There are no known extant issues at all for the years 1898, 1900, 1901, and 1904, the very earliest days of the paper.

The following issues from 1899 are available on microfilm through the University of Georgia's Georgia Newspaper Project: June 22 and 29; July 6, 13, and 27; August 3, 10, 17, and 24; September 14 and 21; October 5, 12, 19, and 26; November 23 and 30; and December 7 (incorrectly dated as "~~30~~ 28" on the paper), 21, and 28.

Portions of the remaining extant issues from 1899 were salvaged by the Rabun County Historical Society from issues too fragile to maintain. In some cases, only a few items from each issue could be kept. All salvageable items were cut out and photocopied together along with the date of the issue's publication, and are available as a file copy at the Historical Society. The issue number was not retained by the Historical Society for some issues. Such issues are marked here by the symbol *.

There were some problems encountered while transcribing items from the salvaged issues. Several items from the January 20 issue were inadvertently, but very clearly, photocopied with items from the next issue, dated January 26, in the Rabun County Historical Society's files; similarly for the issues dated March 16 and 23; for the April 20 and 27 issues; and for the May 4 and 11 issues, the latter being particularly problematic. Items from these issues have been placed here with their appropriate issue, wherever it was possible to determine what items belonged under which date. All items that were corrected in this way are marked in a conspicuous place (at the end of the title for longer entries, and at the end of the entry for shorter ones) by the symbol ‡.

Be aware that while due diligence was employed to verify dates independently whenever possible, some items from these issues as transcribed herein may have been incorrectly placed under the wrong date. It was often difficult to ascertain dates one way or another, and as no original issues survive, there was often no way to tell except by context. It may also be the case that other instances of inadvertent mixing of papers while photocopying may have occurred, but were not caught during the compilation of this volume. Readers are advised to independently verify items pertinent to their research.

The Clayton Tribune, Volume 1, Number 50, Friday, January 6, 1899

§   Woman's Column.

All comminications for this column are refered to Miss Pearl Cannon, Rabun Gap, Ga.

I promised to tell you something more about the Jubilee, but Christmas followed it so closely that the "Peace Jubilee" is already a thing of the past. You remember that several men who were heroes in the Spanish-American war were to visit Atlanta then. Well, they were here, each accompanied by some member of his family.

Gen. Shafter and the famous hero of Merrimac, Lieut. Hobson, and others responded to the invitation of the Jubilee committe. But the one distinguished guest who received more attention than anyone, unless it was the president, was little Joe Wheeler. All through the parade he was wildly cheered by the crowds on the sidewalks. I was not fortunate enough to see the floral parade but heard many speak of its beauty. The first prize for the carriage judged to have the prettiest decorations was awarded to Mrs. Tompkins.

These celebrations in honor of peace have been held both North and South and many have enjoyed them, but we are having a universal jubilee now.

This is Christmas eve and from the noise of fire-crackers and tin horns on the streets you would think that the question of war had not been settled and that the Spaniards were storming Atlanta. But it's only the young folks having a good time as only boys can...

Pearl Cannon

§   Notice.

C. E. & W. R. Cannon will pay good prices for all kinds of raw furs and want to buy all they can get immediately such as wild cat, fox, opossum, house cat, skunk and etc.

§   A New Store. J. M. York wants his friends to come and look at His Stock of Goods; He Has a Well Selected Stock of Staple and Fancy Groceries. Good Coffee at 9ct for $1.00. Sugar 18 pounds for $1.00. Good Flour 60 cents for 25 lbs. We buy your produce. J. M. York, Clayton, Ga.

§   The Wall House. Strictly First-Class. Elevated Location. Beautiful Scenery. Spring and well water. Clean Beds. The best furnished table and[?] the most delightful stopping place in the mountains.

§   Old Time Quilting.

Away back in the 40's, when times were good and people were more neighborly and honest, is the time I will talk about. There are a few left yet that were young then who know that what I write is true. In those days there were not many people in the county—a few roads, mostly trails. Such things as we have now were never heard of then—such as organs, buggies, stores, fine clothes and such were not known. I remember Uncle Bill K----, of the Valley, had some boys and girls, all grown up. Well, they gave a quilting and Log Rolling. The whole country went, some rode mules, some went in ox carts, some walked, but we all got there by time to do a full day's work. The girls went to quilting, the old women went to smacking their lips telling of old times, and the middle aged women went to cooking dinner. The boys and young men went to rolling logs and trying their strength, the old men to taking their bitters and smoking their pipes and telling of their manhood in days past. After a while Miss Jane K, a pretty black haired girl of sixteen, clumb up on the fence and gave three loud, long blows on the horn. All knew what was meant by that and it was answered by a long, hearty whoop from the new ground by the boys and then a long race by the boys and then a long race for the house by the young ones followed. Then it was "Howdy Jane, Sue, Rosy, Polly, Bill, Jack, Joe, Virge, Mart, Sam and John" with none of the young Misters and Misses put to it as there are now. Then dinner was called, the old folks ate first, and what a dinner and such cooking! Back bone pie and stew with Irish potatoes, good white cabbage, well cooked, turnips, corn bread, fat rye biscuits with stewed turkey, fried chicken, butter, buttermilk, sweet milk, store coffee, honey and too many other good things to talk about. Oh Lord, it makes tears come in my eyes to think of it. Times were good then, while the old folks were doing unlimited notice to the dinner the pretty girls were showing the boys all the pretty quilts for they were all spread out so you could see them and the girls were not ashamed of their work for there was the Log Cabin quilt, the Star quilt, the Crazy quilt and all sorts of quilts, some made out of all wool with wool bats in between and the comforts and the spreads all made by the fair heads. When you got a girl those days, you got one that surely knew how to keep house and work and not only that but knew how to make a crop as well. Those girls and boys are the mothers and fathers of the present generation but how changed. When the old folks had finished eating and taken some more bitters the young folks came in and ate their dinner. Some of the boys and girls could not eat much for they were in love, sick or bashful, no one could find out which. While the young folks were eating and having their fun the old ladies were taking the old men around and showing them all the nice quilts and comforts and they found out which one of the girls made them, too, and you could hear the old folks comment on the work by saying: "Well Sue or Rose she is a smart girl and will make any man a smart wife." You could see the girls blush with self pride as these remarks were made. The boys and girls had had their fun and work time was announced and commenced with a hearty yell from the boys as they made a rush for the new ground followed by the waving of many hands from the girls. After the young folks had gone to work the old women would get together and tell of how they used to do just as the old women do these days and will until the end of time. The old men would go over to see the boys try their strength with each other and the boys would do their best to show their Sires and Grand Sires what mighty men they were and what might be expected of them some day. After all the logs were rolled, the trash picked up and heaped in the log heaps all was left for the farmer to do when the proper time came by, putting fire in each heap. Then all returned to the house and the young fellows would amuse themselves with such sports as wrestling, jumping and running foot races. There was always plenty of good corn whiskey on hand, but never any drunkenness or improper conduct. "Get ready for supper" was announced then down to the barn all went who had stock they were all watered and fed. All washed and combed their hair and supper was announced and oh what a supper! Well the only way to describe it is to say we had every thing we wanted. The old folks stayed in the kitchen and the young people went into the big room. The fiddler would tune up his fiddle and the caller would call out "Choose your parteners" the next call was "Take your places" then the fiddle and the fun would begin. Some of the girls and boys would not dance but they would play to the music and keep step to it. After shaking hands with all they were off with the usual invitation: "Youn's must be sure to come. We'uns will look for youn's. Come now, you'ns must be sure to come." Such as one of our old time quiltings and log rollings. I will tell you of a new quilting with no logs to roll and only cider to drink.

Your Uncle Billy

§   Christmas Times.

By a Minister.

The boys had a good time rabbit hunting Christmas eve day and serenading at night. Christmas day preaching services were held at Bethel in the fore noon and at Ivy Hill in the afternoon which met with a good congregation at each place and we think it the best way to celebrate Christmas as it is supposed to be the birth day of Jesus, the saviour of all men who will have him.

We are glad that Mr. Ab Kirby's hog is a friend to prohibition and it done a good trick when it turned the keg.

Ask J. W. Ramey how he fell in the creek Christmas eve night.

Ask Mr. L. N. Shirley when he is going to Pine Mountain to see his best girl.

§   North Chechero.

Holidays are past and we hope every body had a nice time and imbraced Christ's Birth with thanks.

Mr. Logan White, a young man of Warwoman, and Miss Nannie Bell, a nice young lady of Clayton, were married Sunday, at the residence of J. M. Bell. Augustus Turpen, Esq., performed the ceremony.

B. E. Ramey arrived home Saturday night, Christmas Eve, from town at eleven o'clock.

I am sorry that Mr. J. M. Bell happened to the bad misfortune of losing his pet coon and opossum the other night.

§   The Clayton Tribune. Issued Every Friday. Official Organ of Rabun County. Entered at the Postoffice at Clayton Ga, as second-class matter. J. A. Reynolds, Editor and Business Manager. Terms One Year $1.00, Six months $.50 In Advance.

§   Blue Hights

Christmas is over and every thing passed off quietly, no one got hurt about here.

The sick of our community are all better.

Paul Dotson is preparing to build a new house.

Bill Huska is gone to Hartwell.

We were glad to have Hon. F. A. Bleckley, of Chechero, and H. B. Dotson and wife take dinner with us Xmas.

Questions for the readers of the Tribune.

1. We celebrate Dec. 25th for Christ's birthday. Can we prove by the Bible that it is the right day?

2. Have we any way to prove that He was born in winter?

3. Is Christmas any more than any other holiday?

4. Is it right to teach the little ones to hang their stockings or hats on the night of Dec. 24th, and a saint called Santa Claus will come down the chimney or through the key hole and fill them with presents?

Some one answer these questions through the Tribune and oblige.

§   Tiger

We are having some very cold weather.

Several of the young people of Tiger had the pleasure of attending a candy drawing at Mr. G. M. Oliver's a few nights ago.

Mr. Tom Elliot's family are very sick at this writing.

People have had a very nice Xmas considering the hard times and most everybody seems to be busy at work.

Mr. Marvin Ramey has moved from near Timson to Tiger Creek.

Prof. Irvin Price and Will Duncan paid Tiger a short visit last week.

Fletcher Johnson is placed under auspices of Gov. A. D. Chandler. He holds now a better paying position than Solicitor General.

§   Rev. Mr. Forester, of Macon Co., N. C., will preach at the Baptist Church 3rd Saturday and Sunday in Jan. 1899. All cordially invited.

§   Rev. Geo. Seay gave us a pleasant call Friday.

§   Thad Bynum smiles behind the counters of J. L. Hamby.

§   Mr. J. F. Earl visited Walhalla the latter part of last week.

§   Mr. M. V. McCrackin will attend school at Oakway, S. C., th yaer.

§   Mrs. J. I. Langston has returned after a visit to Walhalla of two weeks.

§   Mr. and Mrs. H. K. Cannon made a week's pleasant visit to Betor, N. C.

§   Mr. J. S. Ramey took charge of the Clerk of Superior Court's office last Monday.

§   W. F. Roane visited his sons Marvin and T. E. Roane, of Atlanta, last week.

§   Postmaster Arrendale reports that he fails to get the Tribune at his office, Grove.

§   John V. Arrondale is home from Dalohnegah, Ga., where he has been attending college.

§   The year 1898 is gone and its events will go down as an important part of our history.

§   Mr. Dock Isabell and Mr. Lory Merritt, of Fairplay, S. C., visited in town this past week.

§ Miss Blanch Wall, after a pleasant visit of several weeks to Anderson, S. C., has returned home.

§ Mrs. W. S. Long has been very sick for the past week. Dr. Green reports her condition improved now.

§ Mr. and Mrs. W. C. Norton visited the family of J. M. Crisp for several days the latter part of last week.

§ Col. W. S. Paris has moved from the Robbins residence to the newly finished house of W. H. Duncan, on main street.

§ Mr. A. L. Dillard had a delightful visit to relatives at Vissage and attended the marriage of Miss Bell Berong and Lon Wood.

§ Rev. C. W. Curry arrived last Saturday and has charge of the Clayton circuit, instead of Rev. Stilwell, who, it was announced, would supply this circuit.

§ See ad of J. E. Free. Some of the varieties of fruit we know to be something new and the very best. He is honest and you may be assured you get the variety you buy.

§ Mr. Augusta Wall informed us that a crowd of Egyptian horse swappers passed through Warwoman district a few days ago on their way to the horse swapper's convention at Hartwell, Ga., which convened there the 3rd inst.

§ Mr. John Scruggs aged 87 years died at his home in the Valley last Friday at 2 o'clock. Mr. Scruggs has lived in the county over half a century, being among the pioneers of the county. He was highly respeated and had gained much property by industry and careful economy.

§ Georgia, Rabun County. All persons interested are hereby notified that, if no cause be shown to the contrary, an order will be granted by the undersigned, on the 1st day of February, 1899, establishing a change on the Rogue's ford road, as marked out by the road commissioners appointed for that purpose, commencing near the Iron bridge on Chattooga river in said county, and running in a westerly direction, through the lands of H. R. Cannon and J. M. Swafford, and intersecting the old road near the residence of James Moore. Dec. 30th 1898. W. S. Long, Ordinary.

§ Mr. Finas Marsingale is home on a furlough of 30 days. He is just getting out of a very severe case of Typhoid fever.

§ Mr. Layfatte Wall and Mr. D. T. Duncan contemplate making improvements on the Fincannon block at an early date.

§ Georgia, Rabun County. J. F. Thompson, W. B. Watts, W. C. Kerby and others having applied for the discontinuance of a certain road, known as the Holcomb road, commencing at the foot of the mountain near the residence of J. T. McConnell, in the

597th militia district of said county, and running thence a Northwest direction to the district line.

Notice is hereby given that said application will be finally granted on the 18th day of January, 1899, next, if no sufficient cause is shown to the contrary. This Dec. 15th 1898. W. S. Long, Ordinary.

§   Georgia, Rabun County. All persons interested are hereby notified that, if no good cause be shown to the contrary, an order will be granted by the undersigned, on the 17th day of January, 1899, establishing a new road, as marked out by the road commissioners appointed for that purpose, commencing at the head of the lane between John B. York and Mary Crawford on the Scott's Creek road in said county, and running a south direction, through the lands of John B. York, John Crane and Jno. L. Watts and intersection the Tallulah Falls road at Jno. L. Watts' shop. Dec. 13th 1898. W. S. Long, Ordinary.

§   Georgia, Rabun county. All persons interested are hereby notified that, if no good cause be shown to the contrary, an order will be granted by the undersigned, on the 17th day of January 1899, establishing a change on the Ashley road as marked out by the road commissioners appointed for that purpose, commencing near the Pine School-house and running in a northerly direction through the lands of L. S. York. Starting on the west side of the old road, crossing the old road and running on the East side of the old road to the top of the first hill, thence, north up the top of the ridge, crossing the old road to the west side, thence up the side of the ridge to the gap, intersecting the new survey. This Dec. 13th 1899. W. S. Long, Ordinary.

§   Wolf Creek.
Nathan Jones, of Cornelia, Ga., is visiting his father and mother this week.
Miss Zenia Barker, of Whetstone, S. C., is among friends here this week.
Drew Smith and Elbert Jones started to the Horse-Swappers-Reunion yesterday.
Miss Rosa Jones is very sick at this writing.
Mrs. Sallie Dorsey is very sick. Hope she will soon recover.
John M. Cannon is preparing to go to Cornelia next week.

§   Warwoman.
Another year has passed and many will pause to say: "the time has passed so rapidly I have not finished my work." It is a fact time and tide wait for no man.
Oh! what a beautiful day has ushered the New Year, may we all be prepared to meet the seasons of the coming year.
Xmas holidays are about over, which has been very quiet and pleasant. People should go to work and try to make up the losses of last years freshets.
According to the ruling days the weather will be very favorable for out door labor up to June.
Mr. and Mrs. Tom Bleckley spent Xmas holidays with her father at Ellijay, N. C.
J. M. Bleckley Jr. closed his school at Wolffork last week. We are glad to have him home again.

§   Dillard.

Mr. Henry Mozely, of Toccoa, Ga., is in the valley this week.

Married, at the residence of the bride, Dec. 28, Mr. Robert Ritchie and Miss Minnie Tanner, Rev. J. S. Dickson officiated.

Mr. Thomas Price and two daughters visited friends in N. C., last week.

Mr. A. L. Dillard and Miss Addie Fuller went to Towns Co., last week to attend the wedding of Miss Belle Berrong.

Mr. Powell's daughter, Myrtle, has been very sick, but is improving.

Mr. Irwin Patton, of N. C., is in the valley this week.

Rabun Gap School will begin Monday Jan. 9. We are expecting a good school and several boarding students.

§   Any one wanting to buy a fine milch cow call on A. L. Dillard, Dillard, Ga.

§   County Directory. Senator, W. J. Green. R. E. A. Hamby, Representative. Ordinary, W. S. Long. Sheriff, J. B. Dockins. Clerk of Superior [Court], L. C. Hollifield. Tax Receiver, Monterville Kell. Tax Cllectr., James F. Smith. Treasurer, W. E. Thompson. County Surveyor, Presley Jones. [Coroner], William Wheeler. County School Commissioner, W. J. Neville. Members of Board of Education: M. J. Swofford, President; W. J. Green; Cisero Blalock; Z. B. Dillald; F. G. Holden.

§   Georgia, Rabun County.

Sealed bids will be received at my office in Clayton, Georgia, up to 10 o'clock A. M., Tuesday the 24th day of January, 1899, for the construction of a Steel Bridge over Tallulah river at Burton in said county, said bridge to be 90 feet in length besides approaches, with 12 foot roadway and must be built of first-class material according to plans and specifications now on file in my office.

I hereby reserve the right to reject any and all bids should it be to the best interest of Rabun county to do so. Term cash.

W. S. Long, Ord'y Rabun Co., Ga.

§   Tallulah Falls R. R. Co. Time Table No. 4. In Effect Saturday, Sept. 10, '98, 10 A. M.... Stations... Tallulah Falls... Turnerville... Anandale... Clarkesville... Demorest... Cornelia... W. V. Lauraine, A. G. M. & Supt.

The Clayton Tribune, Volume 1, Number 51, Friday, January 13, 1899

§   Sheriff Ritchie has four prisoners in jail.

During the holidays we heard of no trouble in our county, but last Saturday a number of crimes were committed. It was election day for constables and it seems the "dew" flowed freely in some portions of the county. The most serious difficulty occured in _____ dist. when Elec Coffee and William Madcap engaged in a fight. Madcap was seriously stabbed by Coffee and it is thought the wounds will prove fatal. Madcap has three ugly wounds in his left side, on of which is about four inches long and through to inside. Coffee has a very black eye. He is held by the authorities waiting results.

At Burton William Ritchie disfigured James Cordon by kniving him in the neck, forehead and nose. No arrests have been made.

Woot Worley a small boy of 17 is lodged in jail charged with an assault on the person of Mr. Lacounte, also there is a warrant against him for petty larceny.

Geo. Hurst and Alford Amonds are in jail charged with stealing a lot of baskets from a peddler near Pine Mountain. Hurst was tried here before Esq. Duncan Wednesday and bound over to the higher courts. Col. Hamby represented the state and Col. Paris represented Hurst.

§   The new Quilting.

I am now an old man and am not satisfied with the way this world is run, it seems as if the whole thing is wrong end backwards, it seems as if the whole thing is wrong end backwards. No stimulants that one can get and the rheumatism and diarrhoea and I don't know what else. I got an invitation to a quilting and like a fool went. I thought it would be like it used to be and I got there soon after sun rise and bless the good Lord the people were not up. I asked if the boys had not come to help roll logs, but they told me there was no logs to roll that they were only going to have a musical, I think they called it, with a tea late in the day after the dining, which would come off about two o'clock p. m. Well I did not understand all this, I wondered what a musical meant and what was meant by a dinning and a tea, but I thought I would wait and see. They treated me alright and asked me in to eat breakfast with them, but I told them I ate before daylight. About eleven o'clock some old folks and some young ones came. The young people all wore sharp toed shoes and white gloves. The girls all had on their spike toes shoes and gloves and what looked like a man's shirt. As they came in they were made known to each other as Mr. Jones, Miss Larkin, etc. Some of them went to the organ and played and some of them sung. They had a quilt in some frames that rolled up and they said it was a [?] quilt and was to put on a bed to show and not to use. It is like most every thing else these days—all for show. Dinner was served at 2 o'clock and I suppose that was what they called dining, it was alright, but scarce. When dinner was over I was invited with several other old men into another room and given a glass of cider they saying we needed some stimulants and that we could smoke our pipes and be to ourselves that we did not want to be bothered with the young people. About four o'clock we were invited in to tea so I was determined to see what it was and it was nothing but some tea, sugar and milk, and a little bit of sweet cake. It[?] wasn't fit for well folks, let alone sick people. So that was all of the new quilting. When I left they said "Uncle Billy you must be sure to call again, you will always be welcome." I told them just for manners same that they must come. I thought I saw a smile on the faces of all, but Mr. Editor I just be dad snatched if I ever go to another new fangled quilting. We have got too many new ways anyway. Well I must close for this time. Good bye,

Your Uncle Billy.

§   Warwoman.

Hurray! for the Black Diamond R. R. May God speed the time when we can hear the noise of the mighty engine puffing through Rabun county. A railroad is what she needs.

The bridge near Pine Mountain is finished, it is a real good one. Rabun people, don't stop until you get back all the bridges washed away in the recent freshet.

We are experiencing a cold snap at present, hope the weather will moderate soon and we may have a pleasant January.

Glad to see our old friend, Bill Williams, back on Warwoman again, his best girl seems perfectly delighted.

We are glad to introduce a new character in our communication, one, Mr. Samuel Bowers, a young gentleman who has just grown up, he seems to be a very conspicious character, especially among the young ladies. He glants[?] them all from the head of Warwoman to the far side of Mockasin.

Glad to welcome our old friend, William McCall, back to his old home near Mt. Carmel Church again.

Mr. Logan Bleckley is wearing bright smiles on his face.

§   Within the next 60 days $2415 will have been paid out to pensioned confederate soldiers and widows in this county.

§   Bridge Creek.
The weather is very cold and unsettled now.

Mr. John Derrick and wife and H. N. Burrell and wife, of Burton, visited relatives on Bridge Creek Sunday.

Mr. John V. Arrendale has returned to Dulohnegah to attend college until June. Mr. Eddie Marsongale accompanied him.

Mr. Thomas Gable thinks some of the young boys on Bridge Creek ought to be belled as they get scattered.

Sheriff Foster, of Towns Co., was on Bridge Creek attending to business.

Mrs. T. F. Arrondale is improving some at this writing.

Mr. J. C. Roberson's mill is moving up very lively now as Mr. Thomas Edwards and William Watts are pulling the belt.

The boys of Bridge Creek were very proud of having the pleasure to read the Tribune in four weeks. They say they had rather read it...than any other paper that comes to them as it is Rabun news.

§   Bethel.
Mr. Editor: If you will give me space in your colums I will say something to the questions asked by the Blue Hights.

As the first shall be last and the last first, I will give my time to the last one and leave the rest to some one else. I do not think it right to teach the little ones that Santa Claus will creep in and fill their stockings with gifts on that night, for we teach them false and we make them believe it and you know that it is wrong to teach and deceive the children, for Christ seeketh such to worship Him, as worship in spirit and in truth, and if Dec. 25th is the birthday of Christ we ought to teach the little ones that the presents gave to them on that day, only represent the gift that God gave into the world on that day to be the saviour of the world.

So I must not be too long on this subject as I hope to hear from some one else.
R. L. W.

§   Miss Ida Duncan is gone to Cornelia and Atlanta.

§   There will be no examination of state school teachers until next June.

§   Dept. John Godfrey is suffering greatly from inflamation of the face[?] and eyes.

§   The present month is keeping her record so far for rainy and cloudy days.

§   Mr. T. M. C. Hunnicutt, of Dillsborro, N. C., was in town Wednesday.

§   Benj. Marks and John Baker[?] have been the lively guests of the Blue Ridge Hotel the past week.

§   M-u-d, mud. Red mud, black mud, blue mud, gray mud, sticky mud and about half you hear is 'ain't it muddy?'

§   The friends of Mr. S. S. Hall will regret to know of his feeble condition. We sincerely hope he may soon recover.

§   The election of constables held here last Saturday resulted in the election of Mart Wall and Mart Holcomb.

§   Judge Long was very busy last Monday making reports for the old confederate soldiers and widows pension papers.

§   [?]. H. Coffee has been in Atlanta for[?] three weeks at the bedside of his sick son, Jesse. He is now much improved.

§   Dept. Collector Birdstrom and D. G. Doyer raided in the county and captured four coppers and destroyed six distilleries on Tallulah and Nantahala rivers.

§   We heard of no contests in the Bailiffs election last Saturday. We understand in some of the districts the election was very close. Mr. B. E. Ramey was elected by one majority in Chechero dist.

§   Mr. W. C. Speed and J. T. Smith, of Pine Mountain, Ga., accompanied by Miss Jane White paid our sanctum a pleasant visit to-day, both paid us the case for our paper. Thanks gentlemen.

§   It is now Sheriff J. R. Ritchie, Clerk Superior Court J. S. Ramey, Tax Receiver J. C. York and Tax Collector J. L. Dickerson and all begin with January and [illegible]. And again here is our merchants: J. L. Hamby, J. M. York and J. D[?]. Long and our retired merchants[?] [missing].

§   Dillard.
   Mr. Frank Singleton, of Chechero was in the valley the first of the week.
   Mr. Cart and Miss Carrie Berrong, of Towns Co., visited Mr. Grist last week.

Miss Stella Langston and Miss Willie Henson, of Clayton, attended the party at Mr. York's Friday night.

Mr. Bud York and Jeff Dixon were in the valley this week on business.

Rabun Gap school will not begin until the 16th as it is to be a subscription school.

Mr. John Tanner is sick at this writing.

Mr. Moore started to his house at White Plains Monday where he will stay until July when he will return to Rabun.

Mr. Judson Grist has been very feeble for some time.

I heard a young lady say she thought the paper would come out in mourning this week. In surprise I asked her why and she said, "Because Mr. M---- is going home."

B. H. Greenwood will start to Atlanta Wednesday to attend college.

§   The Blue Ridge Hotel, A Lovely Home for the Commercial Traveler. Table Furnished with the Best the market affords. Patronage Solicited.

§   Just Arrived. A Nice Line of Coffins, which make a neat addition to my old stock. My friends and old patrons will find me prepared to furnish them anything in this line, S. W. Dover, [Clayton], Ga.

The Clayton Tribune, Volume 1, Number 52, Friday, January 20, 1899

[Note: Please see page 53 for a full explanation of the symbol ‡.]

§   Intended for several weeks ago.

Burton, Ga.

Dear Editor:

This leaves us old folks in a sight of trouble. I promised to tell you of the two quiltings, but I must first give you a list of our troubles. Well, corn is selling at seventy-five cents a bushel and scarce at that, and what seems strange to the old folks, the boys and girls are marrying off and nothing to go on. How in the world are they to get on I don't see but as brother Kimsey says, the Lord will provide. Surely he will if you have anything to go upon. In the last month there have been six marriages and more in tow, but who they are the Lord only knows, for you never know until the thing is over. Miss Lily Stonecipher and Mr. Bryant Hill, they got married and are gone off to live for better or worse. We hope for the better on Lily's account. Miss Theodosia Wilson, she married a Mr. Mack Galbreath, an old widower, and he took her to Alabama. Now I don't think it fair, for the old widowers to take away our mountain girls. Then Miss Orphy Woodall married Mr. Mart Wilson, Miss Arty [illegible] married Mr. John [illegible]. Then Miss Ruth[?] Kimsey married Mr. Ben Holland, a prominent young mountaineer. Then Miss Lula Woods married Mr. Garnell, of White county, a very prominent minister of the Gospel. No, Mr. Editor, isn't that a sight with nothing to go upon? How in the Lord are they to get along? But the Lord will provide, or the old folks will have to take their girls back, it will be one or the other. Mr. John LaPrade and Rol Stonecipher have been consulting about marrying and have concluded that times are too hard—corn, scarce, possums scarce, taxes high, in fact every thing too uncertain—so they have acted with common sense and will wait till they make another crop and then if the girls are willing, taxes low, possums plenty, they will hitch up in a double harness forever, and if they can't get the girls to join in they say they will marry one another, and seem to think that the best plan anyway. Now, to cap it all off Mr. Mount Burrell, a widower with seven children married a widow with 2 children, now there will be weeping and knashing of teeth, scratching with toe nails. Lord deliver us from all such blessings. Well, I believe this closes all the matrimonial news up to date—but the worse of it all is, the revenues came in last Sunday morning and stopped between Uncle Billy's and Uncle Rocky's, they left their teams and were gone about two hours, when they returned they had cut up three stills, two in one house, and destroyed a large amount of slop which they called beer. When they returned they found that their harness had been cut by some one, but no one knew who, so they arrested Mart Beck, carried him to Blairsville and bound him over without any proof, so I heard. They found no one with the stills and they were over in Hamersham county except one and it was near the line. The revenues were a hungry looking set of men. They could get nothing to eat and had had nothing to eat in two days, so they said. Now, we old folks are in a bad fix, with no stimulants, rainy, wet, rheumaticks and pains, but the Lord will provide for the stomach's sake, so let it be, Amen.

Your Uncle Billy.

§   Ritchie-Pendleton.

Married, at the residence of Mrs. Pendleton at Smith Bridge, N. C., Mr. T. J. Ritchie to Miss Esther Pendleton. We wish the couple a happy future.

§   Rabun Friends, Please Note.

1. J. S. Jennings and J. M. McGuire are still at Oakway, S. C., and Oakway School is booming.

2. Oakway is 6 miles east of Westminster, S. C.

3. Westminster is 27 miles from Clayton.

4. Oakway is the nearest and best school for Rabun County patrons.

5. Board with the principal is $6.00 per month.

6. Send for circular!

§   The Harmony Grove Citizen came to us last week serenely with the announcement that it had tired echoing and wishes to pose hereafter as plain citizen.

§   Wm. Madcap is still improving. ‡

§   The weather is fine to-day. ‡

§   Miss Eliza Duncan is at Cornelia. ‡

§   See notice of sale of S. S. Whitmire in another column.‡

§   Come to Rabun county where you can get more money from an apple tree than you can for a bale of cotton. ‡

§ A drove of mules passed through town Wednesday. ‡

§ We see Dr. Long on our streets occasionally. Mr. Long is an old and honored citizen of the county. We wish the Dr. could be relieved from a cancer on his hand from which he has long suffered. ‡

§ We club with the Weekly Constitution. Send us $1.50 for it and the Tribune for the year 1899. ‡

§ Miss Manda Earl will assist Prof. O'Kelley in the Rabun Gap school. ‡

§ Heman Earl is attending school at Rabun Gap. ‡

§ Mr. J. C. Dickson had the misfortune to get his finger badly mashed in trying to manage his horse while in town yesterday. ‡

§ Milo Smith, of Westminster was in town Tuesday. ‡

§ Col. Paris has been confined to his room with an attack of grip the past week. ‡

§ Miss Ada, Virgil and James Green are attending school at Rabun Gap. ‡

§ Mr. John W. Green, of Warwoman visited the Valley yesterday. ‡

§ Henry Cannon is gone down to Toccoa after a first class shingle machine for W. E. Thompson and will attach it to his power and grind out shingles at the rate of ten thousand daily. ‡

§ Mr. N. L. Barnard, of Franklin, N. C. spent last night in Clayton on his way down the country with a drove of horses and mules. ‡

§ We have changed the date of publication of Tribune from Friday to Thursday. We [missing] this so the people can get their mail [missing] county, at least, on the Saturday following. ‡

§ Esq. Duncan says he had one hundred calls yesterday [and?] among these some warrants for same[?] offenders. ‡

§ Mrs. J. L. Hamby[?] visited her sister at Hale ridge [illegible] week. ‡

§ We are sorry to [hear?] of the illness of Captain Beavert[?] of the Valley. ‡

§ Old Tiger. ‡
   Rev. George Carrel, of Franklin county, Ga., will preach at Tiger the fifth Sunday of this month.
   Rev. Logan Whitmire was unamiously elected pastor at Tiger for the present year.

Mr. Andy Smith has moved to this section from Swain, N. C.

Mr. John Cannon and Miss Laura McCrackin visited relatives in Cornelia last week.

Mrs. Jess Green has returned from a visit to Chechero.

H. R. Cannon and his little son, Pearcey, were the guests of his sister, Savannah Bleckley, last Sunday.

Reuben Cheek has given up the post-office at Vandiver and moved to Moses Shirley's place near Clayton and John Rochester has taken charge of the office.

We were proud to see our old friend and neighbor Dud Vandiver among us last week.

Mr. Clifton McCrackin has taken up a school near Clemson College, S. C. He taught in this section last year and we wish him much success as he is one of Rabun's confidential young men.

U. S. Deputy Marshall John W. Godfrey and Deputy Marshall Loudermilk captured an illicit distillery in this section a few weeks ago.

Rabun county was ably represented in Hartwell last week at the Horse Swapping convention.

Mrs. Susie Green visited her son Jesse last week.

Mrs. John Jenkins is very sick at this writing.

Reed Bleckley visited her Uncle H. R. Cannon at Tallulah Falls last week.

Miss Ella Davis is expected to open a school at Tallulah Falls last week.

James M. Ramey is visiting in this section. He reports a good school at Cornelia.

Col. Crain passed up to Clayton last Saturday to look after some court case.

Rev. J. S. Dickson preached at Eden last Saturday and Sunday.

§   Upper Tiger. ‡

We are having some more disagreeable weather and the roads are muddy. The overseers are trying to have them worked so that Judge Estes will not grumble when he attends court next month.

Mr. T. A. Robinson of Tallulah Falls, visited R. E. Cannon Tuesday night.

Will Hunter, our barber, moved twice last week and is talking of moving again.

Mr. A. P. Smith is preparing to move to Wolf Creek.

We are informed Jackson Scott is drinking coffee three times a day since he received his Indigent Soldier check.

Dick Hunter purchased a good mare from Charley Cannon Tuesday last.

The people of Tiger heard a good sermon preached last Sunday at Ivy Hill by the new preacher, Mr. Hughes.

Mr. Milo M. Smith, of Westminster, S. C., visited relatives and friends Monday.

Messers Jesse W. Green and his son Porter passed by last week.

The Quarterly Conference of the M. E. church will convene at Ivy Hill on Feb. 6th 1899. Mr. Cooke, the presiding elder, will be here on Sunday, 5th Feb. and will preach at Ivy Hill on Sunday night previous. Hope every body that can will attend.

Mr. H. D. Dockins caught a fine wild rooster near the old saw mill place on Tiger Creek Tuesday. I guess it was one some wagoner had lost some time ago.

Mr. Marlor Whitmire returned from down the country a few days ago.

Candy drawings and singings seem to be the most numerous and pleasant things here now.

As Tiger has shown a scanty appearance of late, thought we would give you a few items.

Mr. Joseph Pitts is off on a tour to South Carolina.

Mr. Ramsey from South Carolina passed by Monday en route to White county on hunt of a stolen mule which had been taken from him last week. The man that stole the mule passed through here Friday. They were persueing him pretty closely.

The young folks had the pleasure of attending a candy drawing at R. E. Cannon's last Saturday night and all seemed to enjoy it. Uncle Bill Price was also there. He seemed to enjoy himself with the greatest sensation for a man of the fifties.

We are just in receipt of an interesting letter from our friend Clifton McCrackin. He is now teaching school at Fort Hill, S. C., and we wish him much success in his present and future enterprise.

Mrs. Hiram McCrackin paid Tiger a short visit Tuesday.

Mr. Rube Cheek is off to market.

§   Upper Warwoman. ‡
Mrs. Fannie Beck has her foot seriously burned.

Miss Lillie Beck is real sick at this writing.

Mr. William Ramey, of Chechero was on Warwoman last week.

Mr. Jeff Beck had the misfortune to get his hand badly cut while butchering a hog last week.

Miss Mary Beck returned home last week.

§   North Chechero. ‡
It is the muddiest time now we have had in quite a time. W. L. Carver arrived home last Friday and reports more mud and it in larger pieces.

Mr. J. W. Smith butchered a fine beef last week.

Mr. E. L. McConnell and wife and Miss Liza Williams spent a short visit with B. E. Ramey Friday.

A. J. Ramey, of Hart Co., has moved to Chechero.

J. B. Thompson, of Warwoman, has moved to Wolffork.

Mrs. A. M. Williams visited her two daughters in this community last week.

The mad dogs are raging on Long Creek and Chechero. Henry Cannon, of Long Creek, had three hogs and a yearlin to go mad.

J. W. Smith and W. J. Ramey have dissolved partnership.

W. S. Dickson has moved from Chechero to Warwoman.

The Clayton Tribune, Volume 2, Number 1, Thursday, January 26, 1899

§   This was our Local Column in No. 1, One Year Ago.
Mud.

More mud.

Mountains.

More mountains.

Mountains all around us.

See list of Grand Jurors.

All aboard for Port Royal.

See advertisements in this issue.

The High School Building is being enlarged.

We are just "stuck up" here in the mountains.

We will publish list of Special Jurors in our next issue.

Rabun County is a solid pillar of democracy in Georgia.

D. T. Duncan is building a nice residence on Broad Street.

Mr. S. S. Whitmire will soon have his factory completed.

After 30 days the Tribune will be the official organ of Rabun Co.

This has been drummer's week in Clayton, also revenue officer's.

We dare down country sand lapper to say anything against Rabun Co.

Little Fay Long, the three year old child of Judge Long, is quite ill.

Rabun County, is in many respects, the most interesting county in the state of Ga.

Diamonds are precious, but the Black Diamond is more precious to the people of Rabun County.

§   We call the attention of the voters of Habersham County to the announcement of J. L. Brown for Sheriff. "Jim" is a kind hearted and jolly fellow.

§   Capt. S. M. Beck killed a Ball eagle on Warwoman Creek Thursday that measured 7 ft. and four inches. The Capt. showed one foot which measured 7 inches.

§   Henry Blalock and Edley Derrick had a difficulty last Saturday near Burton in which the latter was struck by a weeding hoe. The result is quite an ugly wound.

§   Our friends W. D. Burch and L. D. Ewing, after leaving sunshine in the hearts of many people here, have returned—do not know where. Good boys they are.

§   County School Commissioner W. J. Neville is paying off the public school teachers of the county.

§   Mr. J. I. Langston is building a nice addition to his residence at corner Broad and Church St.

§   Mrs. J. L. Henson and Miss Stella Langston, after a pleasant visit to Fair Play, S. C., have returned home.

§   Rev. R. R. Sibley and his better half, after visiting in Clayton have returned to their home in the Valley.

§   Poets have been for a century trying to describe the beauty of Tallulah Falls, but have failed to do so to date.

§   J. M. Fletcher, of Nushua, New Hampshire and about a dozen of his Northern friends visited Tallulah Falls Monday.

§   Robert Burnett, traveling salesman for the McConnell M'f'g. Co., of Cornelia, Ga., was a pleasant caller at our office Thursday.

§   Deputy U. S. Marshall John Godfrey and Dept. Collector Carter captured a still and a rubber tube near Burton today.

§   Mr. C. F. Garret, of Leesburgh, Fla., is stopping at the Blue Ridge Hotel. He is much improved in health since a stay here of a few weeks.

§   The Post Mistress, Mrs. Henson, has made a considerable improvement in her office by adding a handsome cabinet of lock and call boxes.

§   Mr. Wesley Curtis, of Dillard, died suddenly to-day of heart disease. He attended church during the day and was apparently in good health.

§   If you have never heard the roaring[?] of the baech come to Clayton[?] and hear the atmosphere sing [missing] around Black Rock and [missing] mountains.

§   Black Diamond Contracts.
    A special to the Commercial Tribune from Vicennes, Ind., says:--The Vicennis, Vevay and South Atlantic branch of the Black Diamond Railway met here today. The contract for constructing the doubletrack railroad, 20 ½ miles in length, was let to Col. Albert E. Boone, of Zanesville, O., for $10,000,000. This includes a branch from Fredericksburg to Jeffersonville. Work will begin May 1, 1899, and will be pushed in both directions. Col. Boone also has the contracts for constructing the road in the states of Kentucky, Tennesee and Ohio at an aggregate cost of $50,750,000. J. M. Scott, President of the Vevay bank, was elected Third Vice President of the road.— Dover (Ky.) News.

§   The Clayton High School, under the able management of A. A. O'Kelley, Principal, and Miss Leila Moore assistant, is on a boom. The school is now 120 and rapidly increasing.

§   Wanted: Poets to come to Clayton and describe the top of Screamer, Black rock, Oakey, Rattlesnake, Pinnacle and Potata Hill at sunrise when they are robed in ice, as we haven't the language to describe them.

§   The extra term of the Superior Court ordered by Hon. Judge J. J. Kimsey is revoked, because [it is?] now apparent from what has transpired that business of importance cannot be done.

§   Wolf Creek.
    Mrs. Sallie Dorsey is very much improved.
    Dr. Cicero Kerby performed a surgical operation on Mr. Allen Williams' horse last week.
    Last Wednesday, Jan. 11, Miss Rose Jones died at her home of a lingering disease. Funeral services were conducted by Rev. J. M. Wall, and attended by a host of

friends and relatives.

Mr. Nathan Jones returned to his house in Cornelia last Saturday.

Mr. Will Cox visited his uncle, John Smith, Sunday.

§   Election of Masonic Officers.

At the last December meeting of the Rabun Gap Lodge No. 265 F. A. and M. the following officers were elected: R. E. A. Hamby, W. M.; F. A. Bleckley, S. W.; W. S. Price, J. W.; R. S. Sanders, Sec't'y.; J. L. Hamby, S. D.; W. T. York, J. D.; E. D. Swafford and J. A. Turpen, stewarts, and A. M. Wall, Tyler.

§   Judge Kimsey.

Judge J. J. Kimsey, of Cleveland is attending Superior court here this week. He is now back into practice and will most likely do a large legal business through the judicial circuit over which he has so recently presided.—Gainesville Eagle.

§   Burton Bridge Let.

Ordinary W. S. Long received the following sealed bids in response to an advertisement of the building of a steel bridge at Burton: Geo. H. Crafts, Atlanta, Ga., $1,925.25. J. R. D. Long, Chattanooga, Tenn., representing the Converse Bridge Co., $2,064. Chas. C. Marrison, of Cleveland, Ohio, representing the King Bridge Co., $1,983.74. Geo. A. Brocket of the Brocket Bridge Co., Cincinnati, Ohio, $2096. Gus Brown of Birmingham, Ala., representing the Southern Bridge Co., $2,000. J. G. Lancaster, of Roanoke, Va., representing the Virginia Bridge Co., $2,024. Geo. L. Austin, of Atlanta, Ga., representing the Geo. E. King Co., Desmoines, Iowa, $1,986. S. D. Brady, of Chattanooga, Tenn., representing the Canton Bridge Co.,, $1950. The contract was awarded to Geo. H. Croft, of Atlanta, Ga., he being the lowest bidder. Mr. Craft will have the bridge completed by May 25th next. That section is a heavy tax paying side of the county and they desire this recognition and we are glad they are to have a steel bridge. We congratulate the people of Burton.

§   Mr. and Mrs. W. T. York, of the valley, are receiving many inquiries for board in the valley the coming summer. You know with the proper effort this section would shine as gay as the butterfly in the summer season with the very best and wealthiest class in the south. We know they want to come to the mountains. If you fail to have thousands of these people it is your fault.

§   J. L. Henson is off the Clarkesville for two weeks.

§   Claude Green will attend school at Demorest this session.

§   Porter Green was up from Turnerville a few days the past week.

§   Count surveyor W. E. Jones was in town Wednesday.

§   Ordinary Long has received Indigent Soldiers checks.

§   Walter Hunnicutt has been in town this week taking pictures.

§ Mrs. W. S. Long is still quite sick, but much better than last week.

§ J. L. Robins is up from South Carolina doing some prepatory work before moving his family here.

§ Mr. Madcap, who was so badly stabbed by Ed Coffee, is doing well and it is thought his chances for recovery are good.

§ Dept. John Godfrey and D. G. Dover[?] came in from Persimmon with a sixty gallon still cap and worm. The worm was a new thing to us. Instead of calling it worm they called it a condenser.

§ Representative R. E. A. Hamby left last Monday for Atlanta to meet the special joint committe, consisting of two from the Senate and three from the House to investigate the Geoglogial department of the state of which he is a member and chairman of [the?] House section of said committe. Representative Hamby will be away from home about two weeks.

§ Dillard.
  School began Jan. 17 with 35[?] students.
  Mr. Jesse and Claude Green, of Turnerville, Ga., visited B. R. Dillard this week.
  Mr. Sidney Bradley found a hog in a hollow log Jan. 13th which had been in there ten weeks without food or water and still alive. Its hair had grown very long and for awhile it could hardly [stand?].
  [Illegible] Ramey, son of Tillman Ramey, died Sunday morning and was buried Monday. He was seventeen years of age and was until three or four days before his death a red faced healthy boy. He was a good boy and loved by both old and young. Mr. and Mrs. Ramey have our sympathy.
  The young people enjoyed themselves very much at a sociable at Mr. Drew Turpin's Saturday night.

§ Warwoman.
  The farmers are preparing their lands for another crop.
  Mr. Wm. King has moved to South Carolina.
  Miss Leila Long, who has been visiting her sister Mrs. Joe Bleckley, has returned to her home in South Carolina.
  Mr. Jay Freeman is visiting Mr. Andy Holden's quite often.
  Mr. Simmons of Persimmon is at J. M. Bleckley's on business.
  S. L. Bleckley is going to move to Young Harris for the purpose of schooling his children.

§ Bridge Creek.
  Mud and rainy weather seems to be plentiful.
  Meaks Arrendale is able to walk about again.
  Mrs. Polly Bramlet, one of Rabun's oldest citizens, died Friday morning.
  Some mischievous boys captured Marler Watts on Tallulah river near Cannon ford, claiming to be revenues, and gave him a chance to escape, which he did. He

split the water, crossed the river, and ran up to L. M. Chastain's and inquired the way to Glassy mountain. The next morning he was seen near Glassy telling every one he saw the country was full of revenues.

§   North Chechero.

I am glad to see nice weather again. The roads are drying out some.

J. M. Marsongale has moved to Chechero.

James Ramey, of the Ball Mt. had a fine mule to die at Mr. A. M. Williams last week.

Miss Mary Philips, of Long Creek, S. C., died last week.

J. M. Bell butchered a nice beef last week.

Mr. F. A. Bleckley had a stable raising last week.

Look out boys or you will miss a crop, it is time that all farmers were making preparations for a crop.

Miss Ada and Virgil Green and Tom Singleton entered Prof. O'Kelley's school this week.

Rev. John Fry will preach at Chechero the first Sunday in Feb. next. All persons are cordially invited that will come sober.

John Williams, of Arkansas is visiting relatives here now.

The way to enjoy life is to pay all your debts and doctor bills, have plenty of corn in the crib and fodder in the barn and have your stock nice and smooth.

Joe Ramey, of Damascus, S. C., is visiting relatives in this community.

The dogs are taking the day of killing sheep. They came in John W. Green's field and killed two sheep Sunday.

J. W. Smith has subscribed for the Clayton Tribune, that is alright. He is a man for my heart.

§   Vandiver. No. 1.

Rain and mud, no end to the mud.

Mr. J. E. Bleckley and wife started to Cornelia to-day. Hon. R. E. A. Hamby accompanied them to Turnerville.

Mrs. Emiline Jenkins has been very sick for the past week but is improving.

§   Vandiver. No. 2.

We are very proud of the beautiful weather and if it remains fair I think we will have less mud.

Mr. Will Shaw had a working the other day, all were lively. Among the boys were Joe McKay, of Tiger. All seemed to enjoy the day, though disagreeable.

Mr. Jeff McCrackin and family spent Saturday night with his mother, Mrs. Hannah McCrackin.

Miss Peril Alley spent Wednesday with Miss Martha Jenkins. Peril is a fine girl.

We are sorry to hear of the death of Miss Rosa Jones.

Mr. Jesse Dockins and wife spent Sunday night with Mrs. Hannah McCrackin.

Mr. Johny Cannon will soon start to Cornelia where he will remain for awhile.

There is a girl in this vicinity that mounted a Cannon on wheels with a cap on and started to the war. She got to Habersham before she learned the war had ended.

The Clayton Tribune, Volume 2, Number 3, Thursday, February 9, 1899

§   Grand Jury List.

William A. Swofford, James B. Powell, Isaac P. Coalman, Alpheus Benfield, Andrew J. Justus, Andrew J. Duncan, Monterville M. Kell, William T. York, Jeptha H. Taylor, James E. Bleckley, Adraham Jones, Hiram Dillard, Edmond C. Price, Boy F. Phillips, Robt. L. Ritchie, Turner F. Page, James H. Ramey, Horrace B. Stonecypher, Wm. H. York, Kinnie Cragg, James C. Roberts, James I. Langston, John M. Marsongale, Joshua F. Earls, W. B. Watts, Henry J. Taylor, Jesse F. Philyaw, Andrew J. Kell, J. S. Denney, James C. York.

§   Traverse Jurors.

John B. Smith, John B. Dockins, Martin C. Carver, John Hamby, Galveston F. York, Miles C. Canup, James Page, Henry K. Cannon, Russel H. Cannon, George W. Reed, Henry R. Lunchford, Walter Smith, Martin V. McCrakin, William T. Cragg, John T. Long, Joseph L. Dickerson, Damascus M. Forester, Marcus S. York, William S. Price, Jesse M. Wall, John T. McConnell, W. C. Norton, Berryman H. Atkins, H. M. Beck, Marcus L. Hopper, James I. FinCannon, John Martin, Jr., William J. Watts, Alford B. Parker, James T. Shed, George R. Stancil, John M. Philyaw, Emanual Smith, James M. Ramey, Lewis M. Crone, Edhriam H. Moore.

§   Old Tiger.

Court day at Stonepile last Saturday and a lively day too. Col. W. S. Paris attended court and several cases were disposed of. The most important case was between Bud Lovel and Joseph Godfrey. Col. Paris for Mr. Lovel and Mr. Godfrey plead his own case. Verdict for Godfrey.

Rev. Logan Whitmire preached at Tiger Sunday.

Dr. Green made a professional call on Stonepile last Sunday to the sick child of Ben Ellard.

Rev. D. D. Taylor has a daughter who is very sick with consumption. Very little hope of her recovery.

Messers H. B. Cannon, M. M. Hunnicutt and Clint Taylor attended Ordinary's court at Clarkesville Monday.

Road question seems to be agitated in this section. Boys, Judge Estes is just a man.

Miss Ella Davis is expected to open a school at the Falls soon.

Miss Fannie Dockins has been with her sister Lizzie Ramey for some time.

Reuben Cheek has returned from Elberton, Ga.

J. P. Harper has gone to Graham county, N. C.

§   Dept. Collector Bergstrom, E. L. Vigal and D. G. Dover and Dick Martin raided in the county the latter part of last week and destroyed 3 distilleries, one in the vicinity of Timpson Creek, two in the vicinity of Bridge Creek. At one of the latter distilleries about 75 bushels of grain was destroyed, and two large distilleries, the outfit was estimated to be worth about two hundred dollars.

§   Dillard.

John and Miss Matti Holden went to Clayton Saturday to the Quarterly Meeting.

Mr. Sam Holden and brother, of Pine Mountain, entered the Rabun Gap School Monday.

Mrs. John Godfrey is very sick at this writing.

The mail could not go to Franklin Saturday on account of high waters.

Martin Ramey is very sick.

Our school is progressing nicely. Prof. O'Kelly is a splendid teacher.

Lassie Rickman, who broke her leg several days ago, is improving.

Mr. Bill Scruggs was very seriously injured, Thursday, by his horse falling through the bridge with him.

Mr. Zac Dillard, who has been very sick, is improving.

§   Editor Clayton Tribune: Dear Sir:

I notice an extract in your paper headed "Mad Moonshiners" copied from the Georgia Cracker. It puts our people in an unenviable position. There has been but one side told and that was partly false. I will try and tell both sides as correctly as I can get up the facts. Just before Christmas a hack and pair of horses, a buggy and one horse came down the road and rove down in the field and stopped on Mockasin creek between Uncle Rocky Bottom Smith and Uncle Billy Stonecipher's. Birdstrom, Trammell and Johnson were the officers, Martin was driving the hack. He, I suppose, was a driver for them, and then there were two others in the crowd, one of them a boy by the name of Earnest Mushe, the other was Johnson's bodyguard, a fellow by the name of Canter, this boy Mushe was a reporter in this case. After taking out their horses two of them went up the creek, the rest went south and just across Wild Cat got one still but found no one at it, then they went over the mountain into Habersham county and there got two stills in one house, then returned to their teams to find that three pair of hurness[?] had been cut by some unknown person— so they started back to get some one—it made no difference who. They first put handcuffs on Jeff Day, then on Bud Day and then on Mart Beck. After a short time they took the hand cuffs off of the Day brothers and kept them on Mart Beck. After getting some strings and tieing up the harness they made a start when one of the strings broke and a halt had to be made for repairs. Then this fellow Martin, the driver, got out and commenced to curse Mart Beck, the prisoner. Mart only had the hand cuffs on one hand[. He] got out of the hack and picked up a rock and said, "You shan't curse me for what I know nothing about." When Martin got out a pistol and threatened to shoot Mart. All of the officers were there and not one opened their mouth to stop it or to interfere in any way. They carried Beck to Blairsville and put him under a bond of $500, on suspicion only. On their way down they stopped at a church on Dick's Creek and camped out, they burnt some of the seats, tied their horses to the church and done other damage. Now, Mr. Editor, that was the beginning and ending of the first raid. Now for the second one and how it ended with comments on both sides. The second time they came in, the first any one knew of their being around was the hearing of pistol shots at a neighbor's house. In this crowd was Johnson, Carter and Leanard, a hack driver. Martin, another hack driver, and Canter, Johnsons body guard or the foot artillery, as he had a very large army musket on his back and was afoot, the boys called him the artillery. The others were mounted on horseback. There were two others along, I think they were officers. They hunted around in his man's house, fired off their pistols in his yard and found nothing, then they found a still place with some beer on a branch above his house and found a still in a field above...his house. They arrested him, then came over to Jeff Day's and arrested him and then all hands started for Dick's Creek and stopped over night at Ransom Smith's. The next heard of them they had arrested a negro by the name of Bob Gomer... [*Note: The letter continues, but a portion of the right-hand side is missing, making it very difficult to transcribe.*]

The Clayton Tribune, Volume 2, Thursday, February 16, 1899 *

§   Upper Tiger.
  Dear Editor:
With the greatest of pleasure I will send you some local news to print and I would be glad to have a column in your paper every week as your paper has been a visitor at our home quite a while and it is a good paper. I would not give our county for any other paper. I do appreciate reading your paper.

Ask Mr. Walter Cannon who went to see his best girl the other night, missed the trail and got lost. I hope Mr. Marlor Whitmire don't feel bad since Walter beat him out.

I know of a young man that goes to see two girls and they are both named Nannie, wonder which one of them he likes best. Guess what kind of a business he says he is into.

Ask Mr. Jackson Watts when he is going to carry his girl back to the Ridge.

Mr. Charles Cannon, Mr. Virgil Thompson, Mr. Claude Keener, Mr. Jackson Watts and Miss Teril Turpin had the pleasure of going to the Blue Ridge Saturday to visit relatives and friends. They returned to their homes Sunday and report a fine time.

Mr. George Moore spent Monday night with Mr. Jackson Keener.

Mrs. Martha Keener says writing paper will take a rise if Teril don't quit getting such long letters, ten pages are nowhere with her.

Mr. Nathanuel Watts spent Sunday night with Claud Keener.

Mr. Jim Holcomb has a very sick child, hope it will soon improve.

Miss Lula and Warner Turpin returned home Saturday from Camp Creek where they have been visiting relatives.

Mrs. Emily Brewe and son went to the Blue Ridge Sunday to see her daughter, who is sick.

So I will close lest I make my letter too long. If I see this is printed I will try to send as often as I can.

§   Dark Murder in the Mountains.
  Bones of Man and Mule Found in Pile of Ashes in Rabun.
Clarkesville, Feb. 3.—Evidence of a mysterious murder for robbery have been discovered on the Rabun county side of Oaky mountain. The bones of a man and those of a mule have been found at a lonely place near a mountain path, and there is every indication that the bones and things found at the place are those of a man and a mule, both of whom are supposed to have been burned after being killed by

highwaymen. The bones were found in a pile of ashes and every evidence and sign point to the conclusion that the man who was riding the mule was killed and robbed and then his body and that of the mule were burned to destroy evidence of the mountain crime.

Two citizens discovered the pile of ashes and the bones one of whom was Mr. Joe Franklin, collected and has in his posession two kinds of hair, one specimen resembling that of the mane of a mule, the other that of the beard of a man. The bones of a mule's leg and foot were found and bones of a man were picked up in the ashes. There is a quantity of blood at the place and evidence of a struggle.

The fact that a horse trader who was reported as having started over the mountains two weeks ago is said to be missing lends support to the supposition that a man has been killed and robbed for his money. Every effort is being made to run down the mystery, and if possible to bring the murderers to justice.

At the place a large black gum tree had been burned in the effort to consume the mule and man. A bush some two or thee inches in diameter had been cut with a pocketknife with which to stir the fire. A saddle blanket was found not far away.

§   We publish an account of a supposed murder in this issue. We have tried to find out more about the matter, but cannot arrive at anything definite. The fact that a mule was burned naturally suggest a murder also. The place of the supposed murder is in the extreme south west corner of the county in a section called "Little Rabun," and in a lonely spot on the Oakey mountain near the Habersham county line. The place was found by a man turkey hunting. His dog scented the odor of the burnt mule, and in this way the owner of the dog was attracted to the place. We hope to be able to give our readers something more definite[?] soon.

§   News From Cuba By Clayton.
Nuevitas, Cuba, January 26, 1899.
To the Clayton Tribune.
Dear Editor:
Hoping you will appreciate a topic from the 3rd Ga., I will try to give your readers a brief outline of our trip to the West Indies. On the 13 inst. we went aboard the transport Roumanian, on the 14, she set sail, but at the mouth of the river she had to wait till morning of the 15, then off she went and by noon was at high sea and by the evening there was not any land to be seen. On the 16 she passed the Florida Keys. On the 18 we were in sight of land and on the morning of the 19, she case anchor six miles out in the Porto de Nuevitas channel...

The only thing that we Georgia boys miss is the good pure water. Here, the water we drink is rain water, it is caught in barrells and then boiled before it is used. This is all the fault I find with Cuba, but of course we will soon get accustomed to this. We are encamped on a beautiful hill just to the right of Nuevitas where a Spanish army once encamped...

Well, Editor, I think I have said enough on Cuba for the first time.
Clayton M. Dockins

§   From the Southern Record. Rabun's Quota.
In the past few months Toccoa has drawn extensively upon Rabun county for new

citizens. The latest arrivals are Rev. Mr. Turner and family. Mr. Turner will open a general merchandise store in the new Cooper building, which is about completed. Mr. H. T. Mozley and Mr. York came to Toccoa in the fall and are doing a nice business merchandising. Mr. Carter is another Rabun man who has taken an interest with Mr. Bright in the general Merchandise line[?]. Mr. Steve Whitmire is running a harness and leather shop, and also sells buggies and wagons. Hogsed & Garland, the livery men, have been in Toccoa for several years and they are good citizens and progressive business men who are making a success of the livery, sale and feed business. They also handle live stock, buggies, wagons, etc. There is plenty of room for more good men from Rabun, let them come on.

§   Warwoman.
Road working is the order of the day. They have built a foot bridge over the Warwoman creek on the road leading from Clayton to Highlands, N. C.
Marcus and Tom Bleckley have entered school at Rabun Gap.
The rivers have been pased[?] fording for the past few days.
All eyes are set on court as it is near.

§   Locals Intended for Last Week.
Mr. Sam Mitchell wishes us to say that he has been a citizen of this county for twelve years, that he has tried to treat every body right, and recently he has been blessed with the advent of twins at his house, one a democrat and he hopes that the other will marry a democrat. And that he has swapped 'hosses' 1899 times and is still in the business.
J. R. Stonecypher, of Burton, was in town this week and remembered ye editor— thanks J. R.
The citizens of Clayton join us in welcoming Mr. Robins and family as permanent citizens of our town. Mr. Robins owns one of the best farms in this section of the county.

§   ...Chamberlain Cough Remedy... For sale by J. L. Hamby.

§   North Chechero.
Intended for last week.
We have had more rain in the last six months than we have had in that length of time for seven years.
Canidy Philips, of Long Creek, S. C., killed four fine turkeys at one shot a few days ago.
Rev. John Fry preached an interesting sermon at Chechero Sunday.
Mr. C. R. Singleton and Miss Lizzie Williams were married last Sunday.

§   Revenue Stamp. You are required to put revenue stamps on the following...

§   When you are at Clarkesville don't fail to call on W. V. Lauraine at T. B. West old stand. You will find a well selected stock of goods and he will appreciate your trade.

§   Mrs. D. T. Duncan is convalescent after several days sickness.

§ Mr. Allen Watts' baby has been very sick, is now slightly improved.

§ We are delayed one day getting out our paper on account of the extreme cold weather.

§ Uncle Billy, of Burton, has a kinsman who styles himself as "Cousin" and has replied to his letter of last week.

§ It began snowing last Saturday evening and snowed until Monday morning. It covered the ground to the depth of about four inches.

§ Benjamin Ramey delivered to Sheriff Ritchie a load of pine which the sheriff turned over to the inmates of Rabun county jail and after an effort of about 48 hours to burn it, gave up in disgust and decided that Bennie had put off on them a load of Uncle Billie's spruce pine knots.

§ Mrs. W. T. Mosley, aged 86 years, died in Macon county N. C. last Thursday and was buried in the cemetery here last Saturday. She and her husband, H. T. Mosley, were among the first settlers of this town. After the death of her husband, about fourteen years ago, she removed over to Macon county where she lived at to the time of her death. Her request was to be buried here by the side of her husband. Mrs. Mosley's maiden name was Sloan and of prominent family of Pendleton, S. C., also a near relative of the Sloans of South Carolina, Georgia and Alabama.

§ See interesting letter from Clayton M. Dockins, of Nuevitus, Cuba in this issue. He is a Rabun boy.

§ Come to Whitmire's sale on the 18th.

§ Miss Martha Hawk, of Whetstone, S. C., visited in Clayton the latter part of last week and subscribed for the Tribune. Thanks.

§ J. M. Wilkerson will repair your watches, clocks and sewing machines. Address him at Clayton, Ga.

§ J. L. Hamby has returned from a business trip to Atlanta.

§ Mr. and Mrs. J. L. Hamby and Mr. and Mrs. William Bruce attended the funeral yesterday of Mrs. Jane Rogers, who died at her home near Pine Mountain Monday. Mr. Hamby is a brother and Mrs. Bruce is a sister of the deceased.

§ Mrs. Harrison Darnell, of the Valley died Sunday.

§ Dr. Henson is at home for the week.

§ The thermometer hid itself below zero here last Monday. Our thermometer is only marked 6 degrees below zero, but the mercury slid down below this mark and hid, so we do not know how cold it did get. But we know that we were out of wood and came near freezing to death.

§   Little Lady Clare, youngest daughter of Mr. and Mrs. R. E. A. Hamby, has been quite sick but is improved.

§   Superior court one week from Monday.

§   Mr. W. F. Holden, of Pine Mountain, is attending school at Rabun Gap. That's right, W. F., no young man can persue a better course.

§   "Sue and be sued" is experienced by many just now.

§   February is usually the toughest month for the merchants.

§   W. J. Green has had fortyfive men engaged, minus forty, to keep him in wood, but is now out. Not by yourself Doc.

§   Read the notice of administrator's sale in this issue. Mr. Ritchie has corn, fodder, tops and rye for sale.

The Clayton Tribune, Volume 2, Thursday, February 23, 1899 *

§   Old Tiger.
   Lawday at Tiger Saturday. On account of the cold weather most of the cases were continued.
   W. E. Jones and Allen Williams were at court Saturday.
   Rev. D. D. Taylor's daughter died of Consumption last Tuesday and was buried Thursday. A host of friends and relatives attended the funeral. They have the sympathy of this community.
   Jess Dockins has moved from Stonepile district to Mrs. Hiram McCrackin's.
   Sheriff Ritchie was here last week on official business.
   Mr. Ben Ellard's child is improving at this writing.
   Ed. Worley is the champion hunter in this section. He killed eight partridges at one shot. Who can beat this?
   Several of our boys attended the sale at Clayton Saturday and was a little late getting home.
   Mr. Tom Hunnicutt from North Carolina, is swapping horses and trading generally in this section. Tom, we don't think you ought to take Mr. Mitchell's trade from him.
   Mr. Andy Smith and wife were the guests of Mrs. Savannah Bleckley last Sunday.
   Our old friend, Hiram Moore from Stonepile, was among us last Sunday. Come again.
   Carrie, Ada and Ray Cannon visited here this week.
   Tom Bleckley visited his uncle, H. K. Cannon, last week.
   Road working is the chief occupation now.

§   R. E. A. Hamby, Attorney at Law, Clayton, Ga. Will practice in the Northeastern circuit, also in other circuits by special contract. Special attention will be given both criminal and civil cases in the U. S. Courts for the Northern District of Ga.

§   We notice a good deal being said in some of our exchange about good roads. Such things are unknown in this section now and we are afraid to publish anything lest our citizens think us visionary or crazy.—Franklin Press.

§   Hymenial.
   Mr. Charlie Rogers and Miss Eva Mosley were married at the residence of Mrs. Mosley Sunday evening last. Judge Long officiating.
   At Blue Hights, Mr. John Pelfrey to Miss Mary Love. Rev. R. S. Saunders performing the cermony.

§   Free Pills. Send your address to H. E. Bucklen & Co., Chicago and get a free sample box of Dr. King's New Life Pills... For malaria and liver complaint they have been proved invaluable...

§   Next week is court week and it is understood by a great many of our subscribers as pay week. We intend to publish the name of every person paying subscriptions to the Tribune, both old and new subscribers, if not otherwise ordered. We do this as we think it will be read with as much interest by our readers as anything we can publish, and that the people all over the county may know who reads the Tribune... A few days ago we saw clerk of the Superior Court, J. S. Ramey, deeply interested in reading the testimony of Horrace W. Cannon in a felony case. Why was it interesting? Simply because of it happened many years ago, and because of Mr. Cannon's prominence. Preserve your county paper...

§   Upper Tiger.
   Mr. J. R[?]. Stonecypher visited relatives and friends here last week.
   Messrs. Walter Cannon and Wm. Price visited relatives and friends at Long Creek, S. C., last week.
   Mr. James Kerby and William Roane went to see their best girls on Chechero last week.
   Miss Carrie Cannon passed through on her way home Sunday. She has been visiting her sister.
   Virge Philyaw and Jim Lovell, of Burton, Ga., visited relatives and friends here Saturday and Sunday.
   Mrs. Vickers is moving from Tiger to Cicero York's.
   Preaching at Ivy hill next Sunday evening at 3 o'clock.

§   Prisoners Escape.
   A. S. Hammond and Alex Coffe escaped jail last Sunday night by boring through the north wall of the jail. Hammons says they were about four hours boring through. The instrument used was a brace bit. They constructed a handle for the bit of a piece of chip. The following letters were left in the Jail addressed to Sheriff Ritchie, we publish them verbatim:

Clayton, Ga., Feb. 18, 1899
Mr. J. R. Richie
Dear sir I now take the pleasure this aftoo noon to drop yo a few lines to let yo Know that I am Gone and that I Thank yo verry much For the way yo hav Treated me and Wood of stade with yo But I had no money to stand my Trile and I thout it Best to Leave yo I am no Leaving this Country for the Dets I oo I am Leving this Country From the Truble yo know and as I am a Stranger and a Long ways from home it wood a bin the Jewery wood a found me Giltie and the Clerk wood of rote it Down the Judge he wood Past the sentens on me one yar in Jorgia Town
so Good By I must Go to see my Girl
yourse Trulie
Alfred Ammoin to J. R. Ritchie

Feb. 18, 1899, Clayton Ga.
Mr. J. R. Richie
Dear sir
I Think it is the Best for me to leev and stay out ountil after Cort And then I will Come and Give Bond For I think it is Best and I think yo for the way yo Treated me
T. A. Coffee

§   The following letter from a party in Grand Rapids, Mich., will be read with interest. It was handed us by our P. M., Mrs. Henson.
Grand Rapids, Mich., Feb. 15, 1899, P. M. Clayton, Ga.
Dear Sir:--
Will you kindly give me some information as to your country, climate, water, soil and timber? Are you on or near a stream of water? What fish and game in your locality, and how plentiful? What is lumber worth per thousand? Quote prices on provisions and etc. Do you have a newspaper? If so, kindly send a copy. We anticipate spending next winter in your state and some information as above will be thankfully rec'd.
Your truly, _____

§   W. P. McCrackin made our office a pleasant call last Friday and paid us for the Tribune. Thanks.

§   Mr. T. N. McConnell tells us he emptied the drugs of a wine barrell into his hog trough, and to the surprise of the family the hog became roving. Its actions frightened some of them, but when it was known that it was on a dead drunk the affair became laughable.

§   Mr. Irvin Price has been quite sick with fever in Atlanta, but is now able to be up.

§   Eddie and Lillie Norton are visiting in Highlands N. C.

§   Caney Thompson has been very sick, but is now able to sit up in his room.

§   Hill Williams, of Chechero says the timber is badly burst from the effects of the severe cold weather of last week.

§   Capt. Beck, Cannon Woodall and J. J. Ramey lost a lot of their hogs during the cold snap.

§   D. J. Hunter, of Pine Mountain, was in the villa Saturday.

§   The revenue officers made a raid again last Friday night in the neighborhood of Burton and destroyed three distilleries and arrested John Jones and Boyd Lovell.

§   W. F. Marsongale, son of J. M. Marsongale, received his discharge from the U. S. Army last Saturday. He was discharged on [account] of illness.

§   Mr. L. M. Chastain, of Burton, was among the crowd here Saturday. He expects to attend the Normal in Athens this year.

§   During court week you can get board and lodging at Mrs. J. L. Henson's at 50 cts. per day or 15 cents single meal.

§   Mr. E. C. Price lost a lot of his chickens during the cold snap.

§   J. T. Long is on the sick list but still able to attend his mercantile business.

§   We see many fine looking, bright young men and boys on the streets that ought to be in school Now, let us advice you young men and boys to get into the school room at once.

§   Harry and Willie Duncan are in school at Rabun Gap. Right you are boys, stick to the school room, that is the place to prepare yourself for life.

§   Mr. W. F. Roane is making some improvements on his farm south west of town.

§   Mrs. W. C. Norton is at Pine Mountain for a few days.

§   Persimmon.
   I have been noticing the columns of the Tribune and have not seen anything from Persimmon. I will try to give you a few sketches.
   We have had snow and now we have mud.
   The farmers are not doing much in the line of farming.
   We extend our sympathy to the bereaved family of Mart Wellborn. Their little boy departed this life last night, to await that grand gathering in the sweet bye and bye.
   T. E. King started his wagon to the Railroad this morning.
   G. H. Thompson had a store raising to-day.
   Tom Ritchie passed down the creek yesterday with the mail boy. I suppose he was wanting to see if the mail boy got any more liquor. I would like to know if the mail

carrier has any right to carry whiskey. If not, has the Postmaster any right to let them have the pouches when they are intoxicated?

<u>The Clayton Tribune, Volume 2, Thursday, March 9, 1899</u> *

§   Grand Jury Presentments.

Georgia—Rabun County. To the Superior Court of said county:

We, the Grand Jurors selected, chosen and sworn to serve at the February term, 1899, of said Superior Court, respectfully submit the following general presentments:

County Officers.

Through appropriate committees we have examined the various offices of the county, and found books of the Ordinary, Sheriff, Tax Receiver, Treasurer and County School Commissioner to be neatly and correctly kept with proper entries...

We have also examined the office and books of the Clerk of Superior Court and find some correctly kept, except as to the book in which is entered the Insolvent costs. This book appears to have many erroneous entries, and is otherwise confused and not kept in proper shape...

We therefore recommend that A. J. Duncan and W. H. York, acting as a committee in conjunction with the Ordinary of the county, do employ a competent attorney to represent the county in recovering to the County Treasury any sum that may be due to the county on account of said Insolvent cases...

Public.

We have examined the dockets of the various Justices of the Peace and Notaries Public and find them all properly kept except that in one case, the Notary Public of the 636th District, G. M., has failed to state the style of the case.

We find vacancies to [missing] in the office of Notary Public in the 495, 509 and 597th Districts, G., M., by reason of the expiration of the terms of office of the incumbents. We recommend the appointment of John S. Denny as Notary Public [missing] ex-off. Justice of the Peace for [missing] District, G. M., Jesse F. [Phil---] said office for 509th [District G.] M., and H. B. Cannon for [missing] for 597th District G. M.

Paupers.

[Missing] have examined the Pauper [missing] the county and find those [missing] entitled to aid from the [missing] We recommend that the [missing] persons be added to said [missing] paid the amounts as [missing] Cloy Metcalf $25 per annum. Liceny Teague $15 " ". Liddie Ann Gaines $25 " ". Mary Fowler $12 " ". Russel Woodal $20 " ".

Public Roads.

We recommend that all Commissioners of roads in the county take active and diligent measures to have the roads put in good condition. We condemn the practice of working the roads only twice a year and then just before court...

We recommend the following changes on the public road: That the ordinary change the road in Tiger District, commencing at the five mile ford, running on the east side of the creek to near the ford south of James E. Bleckley's...

[Illegible] Hiwasse road, where the same runs over the Pickett, Mosely, York and

Long hills, the [illegible] be changed as to secure a better and easier grade.

That in the Valley road where it crosses the Whitmire hill, the same be made sufficiently wide to enable wagons to pass each other.

Pensions.

We have examined the Pension rolls and we find that all persons whose names appear thereon are justly entitled to the pensions they draw.

We recommend that Dr. W. J. Green be paid twenty dollars out of the County Treasury for services rendered in the lunacy trials of Mrs. John Norton and Mrs. M. Blalock.

We recommend that A. J. Duncan be paid one dollar extra of his pay as Grand Juryman for his services as Clerk of this body.

Public Buildings.

We recommend that the blinds on the upper story of the court house be removed and that good, substantial shades be placed on the inside of the windows.

We find the jail to be not entirely secure... We recommend that the Ordinary take immediate measures looking to the putting said jail in a safe and secure condition, so as to prevent any prisoner from effecting an escape therefrom... That part of the jail occupied by the Sheriff's family should be supplied with locks and other protection...

Having recommended that Liddie Ann Gaines be placed on the pauper list, and so far as the county is concerned believing that Jesse W. Green has fully performed his duties as her guardian, we recommend that Jess W. Green be relived from such guardianship...

We extend to his honor, Judge J. B. Estes, and to Solicitor General W. A. Charters our thanks for courtesies extended us, and for the despatch and ability with which they have administered the business of the court.

We also thank our Bailiff, B. E. Ramey, for his very efficient services.

James I. Langston, Foreman, William A. Swofford, James B. Powell, Isacc P. Coleman, Edmond C. Price, James E. Bleckley, Boy F. Phillips, Kinney Cragg, John M. Marsongale, Wm. T. York, Monterville Kell, Turner Page, Andrew J. Justice, Abraham Jones, Horace B. Stonecypher, Jeptha H. Taylor, Alford Benfield, James C. Roberts, James H. Dillard, James H. Ramey, William H. York, Andrew J. Duncan, Rob't. L. Ritchie.

§   R. R. York murdered on Persimmon.

Was Found Dead Last Friday.

Dan Dover Charged with Murder.

Found Guilty at the Coroners Inquest But was Released After being tried Before a Court of Four Justices of the Peace.

On last Friday there was a great excitement on Persimmon creek and surrounding country over the finding of the dead body of R. R. York. As the following evidence will show, Dept. Collector Vigal, D. G. Dover and James Eller were raiding in that locality last Thursday, and was at a distillery destroying some beer, when three men were seen by Mr. Vigal and he ordered Dover to catch them. The three men started to run, and Dover after them. It developes from there that the men were Roe Welborne, John English and R. R. York. The testimony shows that here York was seen last and the mystery of the murder may lie hidden till the day when all things will be known... Dover was tried here last Monday and was found not guilty. Some theories are floating and it may be that "murder will out". Below is the statement of Dover before and after conviction, and the testimony of all witnesses before Justices of the Peace W. S. Price, D. T. Duncan, V. C. Kerby and Julias Parker.

Dr. Green's testimony in the trial was as follows:

"Well, I don't know R. R. York. I saw a dead man last Saturday who they said was R. R. York. His neck was broken and was the main cause of his death. About two or three o'clock I received a notice summons to attend the Coroner's Jury trial and to come to a ridge near J. N. Crunkleton residence—that R. R. York had been found dead and the summons was issued by request of the Coronor's Jury..."

Roe Welburn swears:

"Well, about all I know it is: Me and John English and R. R. York had met at J. N. Crunkleton's on last Thursday last, and we consented to go to a place where we could get us a drink of beer... Just as they said that I looked down the hill below a few steps and I seen Mr. Dover coming up the hill first below us (Dan Dover) and we all turned to run to get away...and this fellow York says: "I will be d-----d if I can go any further". He was near the top of the ridge and that was the last time I saw him...Dan Dover was about 20 or 30 steps behind him the last time I saw him."

Alph Teams swears:

"I don't know much. I was down in the field at work, heard some one say, "Shoot him, G-d d----m him." I saw Mr. Dover coming back. It was about one hundred yards from Dover to where the boy was dead. About twenty minutes after I saw him coming back. I could see nearly to the distillery."

Miles Head swears:

"I saw some men running. I saw some men running. I saw one after the other and heard some one say. "Shoot him, G-d d----n him, looked like he was about 20 or 30 steps behind him. I saw the man lying there dead and these fellows running was about 150 yards from where I saw them running."

John English swears:

"Well, me and Mr. Welborn after we crossed down about half the ridge and saw some men and some of the boys said it was the Revenue. I saw Mr. Dover and he was after us. We ran and the last I saw of him Mr. Dover was after him... I never saw Mr. York any more until I saw him dead..."

John Frady swears:

["] I was not the first to find him... One of Mr. English's boys first saw him..."

W. H. York swears...

Mr. Vigel swears:

"On March and me in company with Mr. Dover and Ellar were near Blalock, Ga. We had information that Mr. Welborn and English had a still... Dover was not out of sight of me at any time and I could see him plainly and he was at no time nearer than 100 yards of those fellows he was after..."

James Eller swears:

["] We went to the distillery and the still was out and gone and Mr. Vigel told Dan to go up and look for the still and Mr. Vigel cut the stands down and looked upon the ridge and says: "There they are, Dan, catch them."... We got on our horses and left...and we went and destroyed another distillery and then came to Clayton. I heard of the death of York when Mr. Langston arrested me Saturday morning..."

Defendant's Statement:

"On this same road after going to this distillery I left Mr. Vigel and I looked for the still... We went to another distillery and staid, I guess, an hour. There we saw a lot of men over the left of Mr. Louin..."

Dover's Statement Before the Trial.

We called on Dover for a statement Saturday evening last and he readily gave it as follows: While on a raid, in company with Deputy Collector Vigal and James Ellar last Wednesday near Persimmon Baptist church. We had cut a distillery just below there and came up near the church to cut another one. In looking around for the still, it having been moved, Mr. Vigal saw three men running up the hill and said, "Catch them! Catch them!" I started after the men and only run fifteen or twenty steps and returned to where Mr. Vigal was, at the still place. Not at any time were we out of sight of each other. From there we came down to the public road and followed the public road up to Frady's saw and grist mill. Near this mill we took a right hand road up to another distillery and destroyed some beer but failed to get the still. From there we returned to Clayton.

Dover bitterly denies any knowledge of the murder and expressed himself as being greatly surprised at his arrest.

§   Traverse Jury Drawn for August, 1899.

1 Rolin L. Whitmire, 2 Julius M. Carver, 3 Alexander Roane, 4 Thomas J. Ritchie, 5 Joseph M. Watts, 6 James W. Derrick, 7 Wm. T. Smith, 8 David Garland, 9 John B. Kell, 10 John B. Jones, 11 Joseph E. Beard, 12 Geo. J. Hix, 13 Wm. B. Watts, 14 Ethel D. Swafford, 15 John A. Reynolds, 16 Wm. B. Parker, 17 John Speed, 18 Robert N. Dover, 19 John Darnell, 20, Geo. W. Elliot, 21 Ephraim H. Williams, 22 James Z. Hopper, 23 John Nix, 24 Monroe Turpin, 25 John F. Ritchie, 26 John W. Watts, 27 Abel R. Williams, 28 Jesse R. Jones, 29 Tillman Ramey, 30 Jonathon C. Ford, 31 Major L. Scruggs, 32 Jesse E. Singleton, 33 John H. Collins, 34 John C. Howard, 35 James E. Bleckley, 36 Drew Turpin.

§   The presentments of the grand jury, which appear in this issue, is an interesting document. They condemn the practice of working the public roads twice a year, and that just before court. Their presentments speak well for that honorable body and show good business judgement. Especially is this true of that part of the presentments reccommending the public road surveyed by a competent surveyor.

§   We are in receipt of a copy of The Dahlonega Signal—aged 59 years and six months. But it still has a youthful appearance, and of course the good people will continue to give it a generous support in its old age.

§   March is here with her usual wind.

§   Irvin Price is at home from Atlanta.

§   Mr. F. A. Bleckley is somewhat improved in health.

§   School began here last Monday with a fair attendance.

§   Mr. Gus Turpen is fearfully sick at his home on Warwoman.

§   S. S. Whitmire is being confined to his room on account of Grip.

§   Mrs. Emily Wall has been quite sick, but is now improved.

§   The two very cold days this week delays us in getting our paper.

§   We thank the members of the grand jury for their rememberance[?] of us in their presentments.

§   J. F. Earl, James M. Bell and others are building a bridge across the creek east of town, which is much needed.

§   Giving an account of the murder has crowed out some communications. They will appear next week.

§   Some friends have asked us to make inquiry about the minutes of the last singing convention. They say they have never received them.

§   Only two subscribers discontinued the Tribune last week, and [their] reason for doing so was that [missing] failed to get it promptly.

§   [Missing] announced in our last issue [missing] would publish the names [missing] subscribers who paid on subscription during court. We also [missing] a list of new subscribers.

§   There is a premium of five [dollars?] offered to the party raising the [missing] watermelon in this county. [Missing] melon must be pulled in the [missing] of witnesses and weighed [missing] the Ordinary.

§   We are in receipt of a letter from [?]mmons and Hurst, who were convicted for offense of larceny last court severely abusing the citizens of Rabun county, and especially the people of Pine Mountain.

§   The many friends of Dr. Jesse C. Dover will be pleased to know that he will return to Clayton after completing[?] his course in college.

§   The friends of Mr. Gaston King, of Burton, will greatly sympathize with him in the loss of his wife which occurred this week. No better men live in the county than Mr. King and the loss of his good wife is a great calamity to him.

§   Hon. R. E. A. Hamby left for Atlanta Monday. The committee of the State Geological Bureau has been called together this week, and when this duty is performed, Col. Hamby will go to South Georgia on legal business and on his returned will be detained there several days on account of business before the Supreme court. The date of his return is somewhat indefinite.

§   Sheriff Ritchie has five men in jail, some of whom made an attempt to escape by tearing up the sheet iron floor. They were mildly punished by the sheriff for this act.

§   Warwoman.
Ms. Fred Bowers and Miss Lena Bleckley have just returned from Whetstone, S. C., where they have been visiting relatives and friends.
Married at the residence of Mr. Jim Teague, his daughter Minnie, to Mr. Logan Hamby.
A thief broke in A. D. Hunter's store at Pine Mountain and stole about fifty dollars worth of goods.
Rev. A. B. Thomas is holding a series of meeting at the Flatt N. C. Hope he will be the means of bringing many souls to Christ.
Mrs. Dan Garland is visiting her sister, Mrs. H. L. Garland, in the Flatts.

§   Bridge Creek.
Great excitement on Bridge creek over the report of Dan Dover killing Bob York. We don't think it is to kill a man that is running from you.
James Crawford is the boss rabbit hunter, as he killed four in a few minutes the other day.
Mr. W. P. Nix has gone to Clarksville to see his father who is very sick.
Mr. J. M. Arrendale, W. J. Watts and others are very sick with grip.

§   Paid Subscriptions.
Clayton. A. J. Duncan, D. W. Tow, M. W. Swofford, L. D. Echols, S. W. Dover, A. B. Wall, H. K. Cannon, J. C. Singleton, F. A. Bleckley, J. A. Arrendale, James M. Bell, W. E. Thompson, M. L. Shirly, W. C. Donaldson, J. F. Earl, W. C. Norton, W. J. Green.
Tiger. Albert Smith, Jacob Hunter, W. B. Watts, L. N. Shirley, J. C. Green, E. L. Roane, S. H. Robinson, J. R. Godfrey, A. J. Keener, B. M. Kerby, J. C. Bramblet, J. F. Thompson.
Rabun Gap. H. A. Keener, John F. Ritchie.
Wolffork. W. M. Parker, Alford E. Dickerson, Turner Page, M. L. Keener, J. B. Powell.
Chechero. E. L. McConnell, J. F. Godfrey, W. A. Swafford.
Grove. J. M. Arrendale, I. J. Hunnicutt, J. B. Smith.
Vandiver. W. E. Jones.
Dillard. L. L. Long, A. J. Grist, J. A. Collins, B. R. Dillard.
Persimmon. J. N. Crunkleton, E. P. Parker, H. M. James, L. T. Teems, T. M. Justus, H. V. Moore.
Burton. H. M. Beck, G. H. King, Kennie Cragg, J. H. Laprade, James F. Smith, T. A. Powell, Cicero Blalock, J. H. Derrick.
Blalock. P. E. Thompson, J. T. Bradshaw, G. H. Thomson, H. R. Lunchford.
Turnerville. J. F. McCrackin, Y. C. Dickson.
Tallulah Falls. B. H. Atkins, W. M. Lee, W. M. Kendrick, Lonie Gibson.
M. V. McCrackin, Oakway, S. C.; E. N. York, Mountain Rest, S. C.; Claude Green, Demorest, Ga.; L. V. Littleton, Cullasajah, N. C.; John A. Earl, Atlanta Ga.; J[?]. N[?]. Keener, Boise[?] City, Idaho; A. J. Kell, Scaly, N. C.; H. T. Mosely, Toccoa, Ga.; J. B.

McCrackin, Clemson College, S. C.; Rev. W. A. Simmons, Acworth, Ga.; J. C. Langston, Walhalla, S. C.; M. S. Arrendale, Savannah, Ga.

§   List of New Subscribers.
    Clayton. M. M. Marsongale, J. C. York, Jeff Bradley, L. N. Philyaw.
    Rabun Gap. C. F. Bleckley, H. A. Keere, I. A. McCurry, A. E. Burrell, M. M. Moore, H. L. Dickerson, Henry Dailey.
    Dillard. J. J. Smith, G. W. Greenwood, W. T. Angell, J. H. Ramey, M. B. Darnell, J. B. Gillespie, T. B. Carter.
    Vandiver. W. H. L. Ramey, J. B. Smith, Jeptha Taylor.
    Wolffork. John B. Carnes, J. G. Wellborn, Jesse Taylor, E. C. Dillingham, Sam Wellborn, Samuel Taylor, H. M. Hopper, John Martin.
    Pine Mountain. J. C. Powell, W. E. Owen.
    Chechero. W. A. Swofford, Bry F. Phillips, Leander M. Ramey.
    Tiger. E. L. Roane, R. H. Cannon, Rev. J. S. Dickson, G. R. Dickson, J. F. Thompson.
    Tallulah Falls. A. J. Jones, W. M. Lee.
    Burton. H. M. Beck, B. M. Kerby, F. Philyaw, John M. Philyaw.
    Blalock. J. T. Bradshaw, John English, E. M. Welburn.
    Persimmon. John A. Burrell, I. P. Coalman.
    E. H. Baker, Grove; John A. Green, Dixon, Ga., by D. M. Green; Mrs[?]. M. E. Farmer, Betor, N. C., P'd by J. N. Fisher; H. C. Farmer, Bleakfoot, Idaho, P'd by J. N. Fisher; M. W. Lyon, Climax, Tex.; John V. Arrondale, Dahlonegah, Ga.

§   Dillard.
    No school Tuesday on account of cold weather.
    Miss Essie Wall, of Warwoman, entered school at Rabun Gap last week.
    Miss Genelia Bynum has had the Grip, but is better.
    Fannie Scruggs is spending the week with Ethel Powell.
    Charlie Langston, Harry Duncan and Heman Earl have stopped school and gone home.
    Mr. O'Kelly went to Clayton Saturday.
    Mr. Hiram Dillard went to Sapphire, N. C. last Saturday.
    Mr. Porter and Tom Ritchie are buying cattle this week.
    Sam Mitchell and George Oliver went to North Carolina.
    Mrs. Rachel Dillard is going to stay with her son, John Dillard a while.
    We all enjoy reading Uncle Billy's letters very much.

§   Upper Tiger.
    We have had almost as cold snap recently as the one some time ago.
    Messers Andrew Smith, William Brindles and others from North Carolina, are visiting friends in this section.
    Mr. Tom Ritchie bought twelve head of nice small cattle from J. E. Bleckley last Tuesday.
    Mr. Banjo Dave Ramey, from Chechero was in town Wednesday.
    Nearly everybody has had the Grip in this vicinity.
    Miss Lola Stonecypher and her little nephew visited relatives here last week.

The quarterly Conference will convene at Ivy Hill on Saturday and Sunday the 18th and 19th inst. We are expecting presiding elder Cooke with us this time, as he was not able to come before on account of the Grip. Hope every one that can will attend.

The Clayton Tribune, Volume 2, Thursday, March 16, 1899 *

[*Note: Please see page 53 for a full explanation of the symbol ‡.*]

§   Man Found Dead.
   Is it Murder Again?
   News reaches us that a man was found dead on the S. C. side of the Chattooga river, one mile below the residence of B. H. Atkins, the first of this week. It was first thought that the body of John Hays, colored, had been found, as he has not been heard of since last fall. Some time during the latter part of last year, Hays was near Whetstone, S. C., late one afternoon, coming toward Clayton, and stopped at the residence of Thos. Page and as it was dark, and the river swollen, and no way to cross except by batteau, he was asked to remain the night, which he refused and that was the last of John Hays. His hat was found, as was the batteau, some distance down the river. When the news of the finding of the dead body, at the above named place, the circumstances naturally suggested that it was the body of Hays. Such is not the case however. The body found is that of a white boy, about 17 years old, and is thought to be Cliff Gaines. We are told that Gaines has not been seen in about four weeks, and he has been accused of reporting stills and it may be that he has been foully dealt with. Others say Gaines is alive and is now at Anderson S. C. We are in receipt of a letter from Mr. B. H. Atkins which we give our readers.
   Chattooga River, March 12, 1899. Mr. Editor Tribune: Another horrible discovery. Found the body of an unknown man to-day, was found about one mile below my house in Chattooga river. The body is suspended by the arms to some bushes. The flesh has left the skull and the under jaw misplaced. No identity has yet been made. No clothing on the body except the bosom of a shirt. Yours truly, B. H. Atkins.
   Since writing the above we are in receipt of a letter from Wyly Pitts, Esq., Tallulah Falls, and from it we gather the following:
   On the 12th instant, there was in the Chattooga and Tallulah rivers on the South Carolina side the dead body of an unknown boy about sixteen years old. After due process performed, according to the South Carolina law, the body was buried on the bank of the river by M. H. Lee, Esq., F. D. Rathell, D. F. Carter, J. T. Rohletter and others of South Carolina and John V. Stone, J. W. Woodall, Wyly Pitts and others of Georgia.
   The verdict of the jury was, That the dead body was unknown to any of them and that he had come to his death by some unknown cause, and was supposed to have been between the age of twelve and sixteen years. No clothing on him except a part of a shirt—dark striped goods with metal buttons. Respectfully, Wily Pitts.

§   Upper Tiger.
   Mr. Jno. Green from Warwoman, is visiting his son on Tiger.

Mr. W. P. Ramey purchased a good mule from C. E. and W. R. Cannon last week.

We have had so much bad weather that the farmers are badly behind in this section.

We had a nice singing at Bethel last Sunday.

The people organized a Sunday school and put in their nickles and dimes for literature. There will be Sunday school there next Sunday afternoon at 8 o'clock.

Mr. M. L. Shirley is off to Clarksville this week.

J. M. Ramey, of Cornelia, was up last week.

The young people from Tiger and other places had the pleasure of attending a nice candy drawing at Henry Cannon's last Saturday night. All seemed to enjoy themselves.

Guess who started to candy drawing and stopped on the way at his girl's house and would not go any farther or let her go. We do not know for what reason unless he was afraid the clerk of court would defeat him.

§   Black Diamond R. R.

Charlston Is Given an Opportunity to Show her Hand.

Charleston Post. The Black Diamond road, a railroad which is proposed to be built from the Ohio river to the tide water region, is receiving the liveliest attention of the public, both in the West and in the South. The contract, it is understood, has been let for the construction of a portion of the road, and this will be under the supervision of Col. E. A. Boone, the promoter of the project. The road will be built from the Ohio river to Port Royol, but there is a probability of its running to Charleston, as will be seen from a letter written by Col. Boone, published in this article.

Colonel Boone has always held that the construction of the Black Diamond to Charleston will mean much for Charleston...

The following letter has been received from Col. Boone.

Zanesville, O., Feb. 21, 1899. Editor Evening Post:

Sir—I notice a late article in your paper saying the Black Diamond was going to Port Royal S. C. and Savannah, Ga., but not making any effort to reach Charleston. I want to state the exact situation... I am laying my plans to build both Charleston, S. C., under the charter Ohio River, Anderson & Tidewater railway, whose charter was amended by your legislature February 11, 1898. We propose building a double track road or none...

Knoxville, Tenn., will invest $1,000,000 in the Black Diamond system...

I send you under separate cover other data for you to digest and reserve for reference.

Truly, etc., Albert E. Boone.

§   Wolf Creek.

We had a nice little snow Monday and some cold weather.

A. S. Williams caught a large polecat in a box Sunday night.

The people are sorry to hear of Mr. York being killed, also sorry to learn he was in a business contrary to law. The Bible says: "There is a way that seemeth right unto men, but he end thereof is death." If the moonshiners are not in this way we are not able to tell. If the citizens of the county would stand up for the right and help to surpress crime we would see a great change in the priest hood, but there are so many of us guilty we can't take hold. The professing people are violating the laws of church government by the sin defiled stuff that is called mountain due. Let us stop and think before we are lost in eternity.

§   New Hotel for Tallulah Falls.
    (Atlanta Constitution)
The contract for a large modern hotel to be built at Tallulah Falls was let Saturday, and work on the building will begin this morning. The building is to cost about $35,000, and will be run by a syndicate of Atlanta men.

Mr. Fred Wagener, of this city, is the contractor, and one of the terms stipulated is that the hotel shall be completed for occupancy not later than the middle of June. Mr. Wagener will send a full force of men to Tallulah Falls this morning to begin the preliminary work on the building.

The hotel is to consist of three stories...and will have 100 rooms. It is to be build of wood, but will be constructed with a view to being operated both as a summer and winter hotel. The entire building will be heated with steam, and be supplied with electric lights from its own plant.

Each room will be provided with a fireplace and with a private bath, and the hotel will fitted up with all the modern conveniences. The plans for the building were made by Messrs. Bledkley & Tyler, and the work on the hotel will be pushed as rapidly...as possible in order to have the opening this summer.

As soon as completed, the hotel will be handsomely furnished throughout, and it is said that when finished it will be one of the best appointed resort hotels in this section of the country. It will be built a short distance from below the grand chasm and immediately on the line of the Tallulah Fall railroad.

§   Spring. Oh, when will spring come? ‡

§   A heavy rain fell here last night. ‡

§   Mrs. Emily Wall is still improving in health. ‡

§   Superior court at Hiwassee next week. ‡

§   The time for shooting game has expired. ‡

§   Thanks to Mr. D. T. Duncan for some fine beets. ‡

§   Easter comes on the second day of April this year. ‡

§   We will pay the cash for green or dried apples. ‡

§   Mr. J. L. Hamby returned from Atlanta Saturday. ‡

§   It now seems that the Black Diamond is going to be built. ‡

§   J. C. Pickett and Willie Bradley are off to Walhalla, S. C., to-day. ‡

§   Rev. C. W. Curry returned from Griffin yesterday after a visit of two weeks. ‡

§   The press all over the country is talking the Black Diamond Railroad. ‡

§   Mr. F. A. Bleckley was in town Tuesday for the first time since his illness. ‡

§   Treasurer W. E. Thompson is suffering from the effects of a sprained arm. ‡

§   Mr. and Mrs. W. C. Norton are quite sick. Mr. Norton is confined to his room. ‡

§   Marion Long scored a victory over some of the crack shots of the town last evening. ‡

§   From all accounts there will not be peaches enough in Rabun County this year to make a pie. ‡

§   Parties wanting cane seed can get them by calling J. J. Greenwood. Dillard, Ga. ‡

§   Mr. Mart Wall has added to the appearance of his residence by putting on a good shingle roof. ‡

§   Dr. Green had several acres of his land terraced this week. Who will follow in this needed improvement? ‡

§   Geo. Dallrimple, of Franklin, N. C., is in Clayton to-day, but his friends say his affections are in the Valley. ‡

§   W. C. Donaldson and his brother are putting the finishing touch on Turner Page's grist mill at Wolffork. ‡

§   J. I. Langston returned from Turnerville Tuesday. ‡

§   Mrs. T. N. McConnell is quite sick at her home. ‡

§   We notice Mr. Warren Dunlap on our streets after an absence of several months. ‡

§   The South end of the Tallulah Falls Iron bridge fell to the distance of ten feet last night. The iron is terribly twisted and it is feared the worst is to come. Judge Long wired Geo. H. Craft, of Atlanta, to meet him there Monday and steps will be taken to adjust it at once. The traveling point is now cut off in that direction. ‡

§   Dillard. ‡
    Mr. Irvin Price visited friends in the valley the first of the week, and some of them were all smiles, so come again Irvin.

Charlie and Jesse Langston, Harry Duncan and Heman Earl were in the valley Sunday.

Miss Mary Ramey, of Pine Mountain, entered school Monday.

Willie Duncan has stopped school and gone home.

Mr. A. L. Dillard went to Atlanta this week.

No school on Tuesday on account of rain.

Mr. James Fuller went to Tallulah Saturday.

Marvin Powell has quit school and gone home.

§   Notice. Jan. 16th, 1899. ‡

Don't go to the public works to make a living, stay at home and set out an apple and peach orchard and grape vineyard. When you want anything in the line of fine varieties of apple trees address B. E. Ramey at Chechero Ga. He will sell you trees from ten to fifty [?] trees.

§   Church Directory. ‡

Below are the appointments for the Clayton Circuit:

Clayton, First Sunday in each month, 11 a. m., 7:30 p. m.

Pine Mt. Fourth Sat. and Sun. in each month, 11 a. m.

Antioch, First Sun. in each month, 3:30 p.m. and Fifth Sat. and Sun. 11 a. m.

All are cordially invited.

Chas. W. Curry, P. C.

§   Blue Hights. ‡

News scarce.

Rain and wind.

The farmers are all late, but I guess we will get to work after while.

The people are building a new church at Pleasant Grove.

Paul Dotson goes to Westminster, S. C., to-morrow to buy acids.

§   Old Tiger. ‡

Mrs. Eliza Williams died at her...home near Vandiver last Saturday and buried Sunday at the grave yard. She was one of Tiger's oldest and best women.

Mrs. Martha Swafford is very low with Consumption at this writing.

Leander Smith has moved from this section to the ford of the river in Stonepile district.

Reed Bleckley attended the candy drawing at her Uncle H. K. Cannon's.

Ruben Cheek returned from Elberton, Ga., last week. He says they are clever people there.

Aunt Emily Smith made a business trip to Turnerville last week.

James Ramey is up from Cornelia on business.

H. B. Cannon attended court at Clarkesville this week.

Law day at Tiger last Saturday.

Messrs W. E. Jones, Clint Jones, H. B. Cannon and Uncle Ned Shirley attended court at Clarkesville this week.

Mr. Tom Edwards moved to this section last week.

Rev. Taylor preached at Tallulah Falls last Sunday.

§   Robins—Quarles. ‡

Married, on Sunday, Marth 5th, 1899, at the residece of the bride, by Rev. Robert Cobb, of Walhalla, and Miss Fannie Quarles, of Double Springs [sic]. Our warmest congratulations are extended to Mr. and Mrs. Robins in their new relations. May happiness and joy be their through life's pilgrimage. The groom is well known to the Oconee people, having filled the office of sheriff for several terms with great acceptability and satisfaction.—Keowee Courier.

The Clayton Tribune, Volume 2, Thursday, March 24 23, 1899 *

§   Persimmon.

Rain and mud.

The farmers have their fences to mend.

Last Saturday night we had the worst rain we have had during the winter.

I. P. Coleman and his brother have returned from the railroad.

If you never saw a baby that just weighed one pound and a half with it's clothes on, go to P. E. Thompson and you can see it.

J. C. York's wife is on the sick list.

Sheriff Ritchie and Albert Dillard, accompanied by two other fellows, passed through our settlement last week.

J. C. York don't know whether he will get to meet the people on his first advertisement yet or not. The comptroller has never sent his blanks and instructions yet but he will get them in time to save disappointment.

The roads are impassable in some places and the foot logs are gone on the side towards the Gulf.

A North Carolina wagon and a load of corn, with some other things got washed away Saturday night. Some pieces of the wagon were found.

T. E. King's spring house, wash pot and some jars of fruit were washed away by the water.

§   Mr. J. C. Pickett sold about four hundred dollar's worth of stock cattle yesterday to a Mr. Bryson, of North Carolina. Mr. Picket got good prices and the sale brings the money among us. Georgia needs thousands of such men as producers, and if we had them, instead of the per capita being about eighteen dollars in Georgia, it would soon be from one to three hundred dollars, like a number of the New England States. The reason the New England states have money is, because they produce something at home.

§   Bridge Creek.

Cold rains and Grip.

Toma[?] Allen is suffering very much from what is called Inflamationary rheumatism.

Rev. A. Shook and E. H. Baker visited[?] M. L. Arrendale last week.

Mr. M. L. Arrendale and Rosa [?]ans, of Flat creek, were married last[?] week. E. H. Baker officiated.

Thomas Woods happened to [missing] accident of getting his smoke house[?] and some 70 or 80 syrup[?], a syrup boiler, sack or two [missing] burned up. He was very badly[?] burned himself.

At the last Singing Convention which was held at Ivey Hill [missing], there was money made up [missing] of the convention and [missing] was given to some person[?] have them printed and sent out which[?], so far as I can learn, has never[?] been done. Any one who can[?] give information through the[?] Tribune would be highly appreciated[?].

§   Early this morning Mr. T. B. Carter, of Rabun Gap, was brought down by friends and was carried before Dr. Green and he was pronounced by the Doctor as mentally deranged. At 2 o'clock he was tried before a Jury of 12 men and they sustained Dr. Green. The following composed the Jury: W. J. Green, H. B. Dotson, M. L. Shirley, J. M. Wilkerson, J. T. Long, J. M. York, David Garland, Eugene Mozely, H. L. Ramey, M. B. Darnell, W. E. Thompson, A. M. Wall.

§   Persimmon.
Rev. Hughes preached here Saturday.
Jim James is improving.
Little Dick York is not expected to live.
A. M. Keener is preparing to build him a house.
A. E. Dickerson and wife were over Sunday.
Rev. Hughes changed his appointment from the second to the third Sunday and Saturday before.
Let's not estimate our property so low this year. Mr. Editor, make them recollect what I say and Pass me not.

§   Rainy Mountain News.
Rev. J. S. Dickson preached an interesting sermon at Chechero Sunday.
Mad dogs are raging in this community again. Many hogs and dogs are supposed to have been bitten.
D. S. Williams, F. A. Bleckley, Marinda Ramey and little J. M. Ramey are quite sick at this writing.
Mr. A. C. Godfrey died Monday morning at 3 o'clock—aged ninety-five. He leaves many friends and relatives to mourn his death.
B. E. Ramey visited A. C. Godfrey Sunday.
R. A. Whitmire has been in this section buying mules. He says he going is gamble on them. R. A. is a hustler.
The widow of Will Cox needs the[?] sympathy of her friends.

§   Upper Warwoman.
Sunday was a windy day.
Little Fred Beck had the misfortune to get his hand badly burned last week.
Mrs. Mary Knox, of Westminster, S. C., is among friends on Warwoman.
Mrs. S. M. Beck, who has been very sick, is improving.
Mr. Andy Speed visited relatives here this week.
A lively crowd of young people visited Jeff Swafford's family Sunday.

Mr. Gus Turpen is improving.

Mr. J. L. Hamdy was on Warwoman last week. He pulled twelve teeth in five minutes. We think Mr. J. L. will make a good doctor yet.

§   L. C. Hollifield is in feeble health.

§   Mrs. Emily Wall is improving.

§   Dr. Henson is gone to Clarkesville.

§   Twelve inch pie pan for a dime at Long's.

§   We have some fine spring weather to-day.

§   Mr. M. L. Shirley has returned from Clarkesville.

§   A 14 inch dish pan at Long & Son's for ten cents.

§   Mrs. W. C. Donaldson has an attack of the grip.

§   The Tribune is continually increasing in subscription.

§   S. S. Whitmire is still confined to his room from an attack of Grip.

§   It will be some time before the people can cross the river at the Falls.

§   J. E. Derrick has been on the sick list since court but is now improving.

§   Judge F. A. Bleckley is still improving in health but his wife is very sick.

§   J. T. Long & Son have paid the cash for a portion of our columns this week.

§   If you want to see the biggest bargains ever sold in Clayton go to Long's store.

§   Col. Paris attended Clarkesville Superior court last week. Col. Paris is among the foremost lawyers of the state.

§   One gallon oil can at Long & Son's for ten cents.

§   With the help of our correspondents we shall endeavor to put lots of spice in the columns of the Tribune this year.

§   Long, come along, come a long way to get Long's prices. They are low, thats the long and short of it.

§   Dr. Geo. W. Long and family were greatly alarmed Tuesday. It was thought their residence was on fire, but soon found that the soot in the chimney was burning out.

§   Are you hunting bargains? Call on J. T. Long & Son.

§   M. M. Moore, of Rabun Gap, went to Atlanta yesterday to stand his trial in the United States court. The charge against Mr. Moore is working in a distillery.

§   Fourteen inch stove pan at Long's for two nickles or a dime.

§   It is rumored in town to-day that a new discovery has been made in the murder case of R. R. York. Rumor says that some distance from this place blood has been found and signs of a struggle on the ground.

§   Judge Long is improving his residence by doing some ceiling.

§   We are glad to see the Misses Maud and Ina Coffee in school here.

§   L. C. Hollifield is off repairing his mill property which was damaged by the heavy rains a few days ago.

§   J. I. Langston has added much to the appearance of his premises by putting a neat picket fence in front of his lot.

§   Work has begun on the one hundred room hotel room at Tallulah Falls. It is to be finished within 90 days. Hurrah for the falls!

§   Geo. H. Craft, of Atlanta, has the contract to repair the Tallulah Falls bridge and will do so just as soon as it is possible.

§   Receiver of tax returns J. C. York will be here on the third day of April for the purpose of receiving tax returns.

§   The Southern Record has changed its form to an eight page, and has E. P. Simpson assistant editor. The Record changes often, but for the better however.

§   We are in receipt of a letter from an ex Cuban soldier, but he failed to sign his name, and it goes with all other such communications—to the waste basket.

§   The railroads have reduced the fare to one cent a mile each way to the Confederate Veteran's Reunion which will be held in Charleston on the 10, 11, 12 and 13th of May next.

§   Upper Tiger.
    We had a very nice Quarterly conference at Ivy Hill Saturday and Sunday and a very good attendance considering the weather.
    The weather has moderated some and the farmers are putting in good time.
    V. C. Kerby had a stable moving last week. He moved them forty yards further away from his house.
    Porter Green passed by Monday on his return to Turnerville.

Mr. Albert Lovell and Hamp Nimons made a flying trip to South Carolina last week.

We are requested to announce that there will be no more preaching on the first Saturday and Sunday as heretofore, as it is changed from the first to the fourth Saturday and Sunday in each month.

Charley McKay is off to South Carolina this week.

Mr. John Marsongale, of Chechero, visited Mr. Tom Dotson on Tiger Saturday.

Mr. Devero Duncan and Miss Lela Bleckley attended the quarterly Saturday.

Elder Cooke was not with us as he was sick, but Mr. Landrom, from Dalonega, filled his place and preached some good and able sermons.

Messrs C. E. and W. R. Cannon have purchased a good lot of acid and if you need anything of this kind now is the time to buy. It will sell fast as there is no way to haul from the railroad.

How about new road on Tiger that the grand jury recommended to be built? We think the best and cheapest plan would be to make new changes to the old one and build two good bridges across Tiger creek.

Russell E. Cannon is preparing to go to Atlanta in a few days.

Uncle Billy's cousin says that a drunkard's breath is as bad as the smell of a pole cat. He also says that the reporter sees his country is going to ruin. Now, if the reporter was working for the good of his country we could sustain his argument, but ninety-nine reporters out of one hundred have been and are blockaders or are reporting for the almighty dollar.

§   Time Only Is Now Between Us and the Black Diamond.

We are indeed very much encouraged at the result of the Black Diamond Railroad meeting in Cincinnati Tuesday.

Private advices are to the effect that success is certain and beyond all doubt. We give below an article taken from Wednesday's Enquirer:

"The much talked of and long-projected Black Diamond Railroad appears to have reached a culminating point in the important meeting held at the Grand Hotel yesterday of the Directors of the different corporations in the several states through which the system is contemplated... Hon. T. C. Dickinson, the financial agent of the company, who has been in England for two years in its interest said to The Enquirer man:

"The funds necessary to commence the construction of 550 miles of the road from Clay City, Ky., through the rich coal, iron and timber regions en route to the magnificent harbor of Port Royal, S. C., will be available immediately, and we expect to commence the actual construction of the road within three or four months or earlier.

Mr. Thomas Tancred, the eminent civil engineer, who [?] thorough inspection of the projected lines last fall, has made a preliminary report to his associates in London...

"This road will be one of the grandest ever built on this continent. Its seaboard terminus, Port Royal, S. C., is on a straight line north from the Nicarauguan Canal, and when both these commercial highways are completed they will shorten the communication from China to Chicago and the Northwest 12,000 miles, as against the San Francisco route."

Col. Albert E. Boone, of Zanesville, Ohio, the original projector and promoter of the Black Diamond system, said:

"The whole scheme now passes into the hands of the British syndicate... Not a dollar of stock will be owned in the United States..."

There were over 30 men in the meeting yesterday from five states, and a representative body of Americans they were. One of the chief officials present was Col. Ross, President of the Knoxville Chamber of Commerce and President of railway lines of that city.

The Dover, Kentucky and South Atlantic Division was represented by James N. Boyd, President, Dover, Ky.; Samuel W. Stairs, Vice President, Dover, Ky.; E. S. Montgomery, Mt. Olivet, Ky.; W. H. Thomas, Treasurer, Dover, Ky.; Wm. McNutt, Assistant Treasurer, Dover, Ky.

§   Steve Lawen has attracted more attention in town this week than a one horse circus show. To one not accustomed to the street exhibitions, it would be hard to tell who in the crowd was the Idiot.

§   J. T. Long and J. M. York went to Turnerville Tuesday and returned last night with their feet badly [?]. They walked down there and back, but a V will not induce them to do so again.

§   Mr. S. S. Burnett is in town today on his usual round selling shoes for Grambling and Spalding. Mr. Burnett has traveled this mountainous section for nearly nine years and the number of his friends are all who know him.

§   Judge Long informs us that he has appointed James Turpen, Walter Smith and H. B. Stonecypher to make a survey of a new road from Clayton to James E. Bleckley's, and next Monday is the day set apart for the work to begin.

§   A new post office has been established in this county by the name of Quartz. It is located near the Moore gold mines in the northwest portion of the county with Lee T. Teems as post master.

§   Joseph E. Nevill, David Garland, L. L. Long, J. P. Norton, John F. Ritchie and A. A. Darnell, of the valley, passed through town Tuesday on their way to Walhalla after acid. These gentlemen do not want it for cotton but to make compost.

§   Last Saturday night, during the thunder storm, lightning struck a tree about eight feet from the residence of Monroe Turpin, almost instantly it struck another tree at the other side of the house about the same distance from the house and shocked some of his children, but not at all seriously.

§   Dr. D. L. Garland arrived home last Sunday night from the University, medical department, of Nashville, Tenn., where he graduated last Friday. The Dr. is somewhat undecided as to where he will locate at present. Dr. Garland has many friends and we predict for him success in his chosen profession.

§   Dear Editor:

I herewith hand you a beautiful poem entitled, "I am Dying," which I hope you will publish. The lines therein will explain the condition of Mr. Page when they written. I am proud to say that he had the fortune to recover from what he thought, at the time of writing, to be a fatal disease, and, beyond his expectation at that time, got to see and caress his dear old mother again in life. I am sure it will be of some interest to your readers when they know that Mr. Page was born and reared in Rabun county, and his parents lived here when the poem was written. He is the author of a number of other beautiful poems and songs and has made quite a local reputation as comic composer and singer.

Yours Truly, R. E. A. Hamby.

I am Dying... J. J. Page, Piedmont, S. C.

The Clayton Tribune, Volume 2, Number 10, Thursday, March 30, 1899

§   Quartz.

The people are well pleased at getting a new post office at the Moore mine.

Dock York, brother of the murdered R. R. York, is still in a very critical condition.

The infant child of P. E. Thompson, aged about three weeks and weighing one and half pounds, died last Sunday. Our sympathies to the bereaved.

Mr. James Wheeler and Miss Nancy Harvey were married last Thursday.

The Sunday school is quite promising under the management of Mr. Sam Gates as superintendent. He gave a very instructive lecture last Sunday.

Our most genial friend, M. C. York, of Clarkesville, paid us a pleasant visit Sunday. Mr. York is a very popular young man. He has made a success in business by his own energy and honest, upright dealings. His example should encourage other young men to strive to elevate themselves in the right direction.

Mr. Chas. F. Renner, of the Eureka Mining Co., Canton, Ohio, has returned to the More mine accompanied by two other gentlemen of the same place. Mr. Renner will have the tunnel cut further in the hill, as the hands have struck rook and it is thought the real vein will be reached soon. They are inspecting mining property and anticipate puting an expensive plant somewhere near here, if they find indications that will justify and[?] other satisfactory arrangements.

§   Rabun Gap.

Too late for last week.

It has rained and rained and is still raining. The river has washed the bottom land in the Valley very badly.

Mrs. John Tanner has been very sick but is some better now.

Joseph Neville, David Garland and Emery Keener have gone to market this week.

Mrs. Rosana Garland spent a week with relatives and friends and returned home Friday.

§   Old Tiger.

Too late for last week.

Mrs. Martha Swafford, who was sick at the last writing, died last week and was buried at the grave yard near Vandiver. She leaves a husband and many friends and relatives to mourn her loss.

Ordinary Long and Col. Paris passed through this section last Monday looking after the iron bridge at Tallulah.

Mr. and Mrs. Frank Morton, of Looky, N. C., are in this section.

Rev. Will Ellar from Towns county preached at Camp creek last Sunday.

The prospects bid fair for a lively at Tallulah Falls this summer. Miss Ella Davis has opened a school there. She is one of Franklin county's best teachers.

Messrs Dav Nation and Ed Worey are helping run U. S. court now.

§   County Directory. Judge Superior Court, John B. Estes. Solicitor General, W. A. Charters. Senator 40th Senatorial District, W. J. Green. Member of Legislature, R. E. A. Hamby. Ordinary, W. S. Long. Sheriff, J. R. Ritchie. Clerk Superior Court, J. S. Ramey. Tax Receiver, James C. York. Tax [Collector], Joseph L. Dickerson. County Treasurer, W. E. Thompson. County Surveyor, W. E. Jones. Coroner, William Wheeler. Justice of the Peace, V. C. Kerby. Notary Public and Ex Justice, D. T. Duncan. County School Commissioner, W. J. Neville. Members, Board of Education: M. W. Swofford, President; W. J. Green, Cicero Blalock, Z. B. Dillard and F. G. Holden.

§   Black Diamond.

Complete Transfer of Property to British Financier.

Cincinnati, March 22.—A meeting of the American stockholders of the proposed Black Diamond route, a railroad to run from Ohio to Port Royal, S. C., was held here today for the purpose of completing the sale to English capitalists. Mr. W. P. Dickinson of Washington, was authorized to transfer the franchises and rights to the British financiers. Mr. Dickinson will leave for England in a few days. It is expected that the construction will begin in a few months. The first portion to be built is that running from Clay, Ky., to Port Royal, 550 miles.—Augusta Chronicle.

§   Ordinary's Citations.

Road Notice. Georgia, Rabun County.

All persons interested are hereby notified, that if no good cause be shown to the contrary, an order will be granted by the undersigned, on the 24th day of April, 1899, establishing two changes on the Persimmon road in the Valley district as marked out by the road commissioners appointed for that purpose, 1st commencing near W. R. Coffee's and intersecting the Betty's creek road near David Garland's, thence the Betty's creek road.

Second change. Leaving the Persimmon road near James W. Carter's gate and intersecting the old road near Rabun Gap Institute, through the lands of W. R. Coffee, David Garland[?], J. S. Tanner and school property.

This March 21st 1899. W. S. Long, Ordinary.

§   Georgia—Rabun County. All persons interested are hereby notified that, if no good cause be shown to the contrary, an order will be granted by the undersigned, on the 28th day of April, 1899, establishing three changes on the road leading from Clayton to Tallulah Falls, as marked out by the road commissioners appointed for that purpose.

1st change leaving the old road on top of the hill east of Allen Turpen's and intersecting the old road west of Allen Turpen's.

2nd change leaving the old road near the west end of said new turn and intersecting the old road at the foot of the hill.

3rd change leaving the old road near the foot of the hill at L. D. Smith's and intersecting the old road at the foot of the hill near J. M. Ramey's road. Through the lands of I. J. H. Hunnicutt, J. A. Cannon, Z. N. Turpen and J. E. Bleckley.

March 27th 1899. W. S. Long, Ordinary.

§ Upper Warwoman.

Mr. A. L. Dillard and Charley Langston passed through on their way home from Hartwell Ga.

Miss Maud Holden, who has been real sick, is up again.

Mr. Clint Jones is very sick at this writing.

Mr. and Mrs. Logan White were the guests of Mart Beck Sunday.

Mr. and Mrs. Bowers spent a few days with Jeff Swafford's family last week.

Mr. John Carves, of Scaley N. C., moved to W. P. McCrackin's last week.

W. S. Dickson is off to market this week.

§ Ordinary Long Shot.

While standing in front of the Blue Ridge hotel last Monday night about 8 o'clock, in company with J. I. Langston and M. L. Shirley, who were standing within two or three feet of him, two men drove up hurriedly and without a moment's warning Judge Long was shot through the right arm by one of the men in the buggy. The ball, 38[?] caliber, passed through the muscle of his arm about half way between the shoulder and elbow and lodged just under the skin on the back of the arm. In a short time the ball was taken out by Dr. Green, his wounds dressed, and we are proud to tell our readers that Mr. Long is resting quietly. We do not believe the party knew at whom he was shooting, as Judge Long is an exceedingly quiet and inoffensive gentleman and a more deservedly popular man, where he known, is not to be found. It was a narrow escape and created quite an excitement in town.

§ Dillard.

Mrs. Martin died Monday and was buried Tuesday at the Baptist cemetery at 2 o'clock. She leaves many relatives to mourn her loss.

Misses Lula Howard and Ethel Powell visited Miss Nora Earl at Clayton Saturday and Sunday.

Misses Carrie Whitmire and Ella Ramey went home Friday and returned Monday.

Mr. Irvin Price was in the Valley Sunday. He was all smiles.

Mrs. Lafayette Hamby was in the Valley Sunday.

Major York is at home again after an abscence of three or [four?] weeks.

§ Henry Algary is out after being confined to home for some time—grip.

§ Mrs. D. A. Henson has a new pattern of quilt top entitled the "Smoky Mountain" and she will take great pleasure in exhibiting the pattern to her lady friends in town.

§   We venture the assertion that there are more young in Rabun county attending the different colleges in the state and United States than any county in the state, population considered.

§   Mr. W. H. Price has not been in town since before the holidays till last week. He has been ill at his home, but is now out again to the delight of his many friends.

§   Mr. W. C. Scruggs will have prepared a minature mill stone to put on exhibition at the state fair this fall. Next, what do you say Capt. Beavert? We are told you have some fine asbestus.

§   It is said that Turner Page has the best grist mill in the county. The mill is just completed and was built by our townsman, W. C. Donaldson. Some of the boys up there say that it takes two men to dip up the meal it grinds so fast.

§   Judge J. B. Estes was in a humorous mood during the session of court at Hiawassee this week, and the Judge's friends attribute the marked change because he was forced to hold court in a church house, as the court house is considered unsafe.

§   Mr. D. M. Green, of the Valley, was in town yesterday and stated to us that the damage of his neighborhood by the recent rains is estimated at ten thousand dollars. He stated the character of the damage is lands[?] washed, immense drifts settled in the creeks and on the land and filling up of the ditches.

§   Killed by Lightning.
Freeman Martin aged 26, and his nephew Willie Martin aged 15 were killed by a stroke of lightning at the home of the former in Washington district on last Saturday evening about 5 o'clock.
The wife of Freeman was sitting near him, and was terrible shocked.
A boy in an adjoining room was also terribly shocked. No other persons in the house.
Freeman was a son of William A. Martin, a prominent citizen of Washington district, and Willie was a grandson of William A. and a son of Jonas A. Martin.
The burial took place at Prospect church on Monday.—Banks County Journal.

§   Mrs. W. C. Donalson is still in poor health.

§   The Tribune is increasing daily in subscriptions.

§   Read in this issue what work will do for you.

§   "Howdy do you do?" "Oh, I've got the grip."

§   Mrs. James M. Bell has a severe attack of the grip.

§   D. T. Duncan, Esq., is quite feeble at this writing.

§   S. S. Whitmire is out in town much improved in health.

§   Mr. N. L. Robins is at Whetstone, S. C., for a few days.

§   Pickins' Nose mountain was covered with snow yesterday.

§   W. J. Robins has been quite sick at his home for the past week.

§   Albert Dillard, of Dillard, has returned from a trip down in Georgia.

§   It is thought the Tallulah Falls bridge will be repaired by Wednesday of next week.

§   Mr. T. L. Wilkerson has been seriously sick at his home but is slightly improved.

§   Mr. Warren Dunlap, who has been in the West for several months has returned home.

§   Col. Paris and Sheriff Ritchie [attended?] Hiawasse Superior Court [Monday?] and Tuesday.

§   See an interesting letter from Quartz in this issue. Such letters make interesting news.

§   Jesse Langston, of Whetstone, was in Clayton Saturday mixing among his many friends.

§   Mr. and Mrs. W. C. Norton are much improved in health. Mr. Norton was on the streets yesterday.

§   Miss Stella Langston, of Clayton, Ga., is on a visit to her brother, Mr. J. C. Langston, and family.—Keowee (S. C.) Courier.

§   Ex-tax collector James F. Smith, [?] Burton, was in town Saturday. Mr. Smith has made final settlement with the state and county.

§   I want to buy old copper of every [description?]. Will pay 3 cents per [pound?]. J. L. Hamby.

§   Mr. Editor—
This is Sunday and I do feel very poorly. The rheumaticks is powerful bad. It is warm and cloudy and is raining some. Mr. Cannon and Miss Len Hooper got married this a. m. and he took her home. The Lord will provide, but I do know that Cannon will never get himself another new suit of store bought clothes—none of them do. I know by myself, for I have been married now goin on forty years and hain't got but one gallus and only one button on my breeches and none on the shirts. I can't afford to wear only a hat, a pair of socks, a shirt and one pair of breeches—that's all, and have to stay in doors and wrap up in a quilt when the old ooman washes but the Lord

provides. Folks is away behind up heare about plowing. All the small grain killed and it still rains. Mr. Jim Smith has put up two bridges on his place. He had to do it to get out. Nelson Tilly has a full stock of goods on hand and is getting all of everything else he can. He has got the contract to furnish the bridge timber for the new bridge and has got the contract to haul out the new bridge and is fixing to get the mumps and the smallpox and all the money that he can get hold of and what he can't get will take notes for. Uncle Rocky is getting up some shot to kill spring squirrels with. Uncle Billy Stonecypher has sown his tobacco bed and spend his time looking after his sitting hens. Roll and John Leprade has not married yet. I think they have fallen out and this is a good sign. Virge Stonecypher will soon have his mill going. It will be a great convenience to our people. The old ooman and Grandma Tilly both say that Cousin Billy ain't no kin to she or me neither[?], so I reckon he hain't, but is a sort of a one gallus feller that claims kin with all on Adam's account. I intend to discuss this licker business. I [missing] the way the distillers [missing] look at it, then I will [missing] the law abiding [missing], then I will write [missing] side, then I will [missing].

§   The average attendance of pupils in school this week is twenty. Several being out on account of sickness.

Honor Roll. Heman Earl, Bert Paris, Ed Norton, Marlor Swofford, Sam Hopkins, Alex Hopkins, Lillie Norton, Maud Coffee, Ina Coffee, Nettie Rhodes, Delphia Hopkins.

The Clayton Tribune, Volume 2, Number 11, Thursday, April 6, 1899

§   Rainy Mountain.

Martin Wall is building a nice cabin and will move soon.

D. S. Williams shot a fine turkey gobler last week, broke its wing, run it one fourth mile and lost it.

Sephes Johnson killed a turkey last week.

Miss Martha and David Williams and Miss Serine Stubblefield visited Jeptha Taylor Sunday.

The youngsters of Chechero swarmed and settled at Mrs. Eliza Ramey's Sunday.

The farmers are getting scared, afraid they be too late about planting corn.

T. M. Williams and his sister, Martha, made a business trip to Westminister this week.

J. D. Smith went to see his best girl Sunday for the second time in a week.

The Justice court of the 436th District, G. M., dismissed a suit between Marshal Bleckley, col., and Harve Penland, col., on account of the plaintiff and W. S. Paris not appearing.

A young man went to see a young lady Saturday night and as he entered the door of the sitting room she occupied the bed room and remained there during the night. So come sooner young man. Do not be so slow.

B. E. Ramey purchased a fine load of shucks of J. D. Price Sunday.

W. H. Denny and the widow of the late A. C. Godfrey made a business trip to R. E. A. Hamby's office Monday.

As Mr. L. P. Wall was enroute on a business trip to Tallulah Falls he lost his artificial teeth and some money. The whole sum was twenty dollars or more and we all can guess what was the trouble with him.

§   The North Carolina legislature has agreed that the Black Diamond railroad shall write "gold" in its bonds, because a large part of them are to be floated in England, and England does not want any except gold bonds. Thus it seems that the North Carolinians have recognized, after all, that we cannot do precisely as we please in money matters, without consulting any other country.—Gainesville Eagle.

§   Upper Tiger.[1]
We are having some more severe cold weather but are proud to see it fair as the farmers can plow a little which is badly needed as they are mightily behind. It doesn't seem now that there will be any peaches and plumbs and not very many apples.

Mr. John McCay and two sons, Will and Joe, have gone to Tallulah to work on the new hotel which is being erected.

We are glad to learn that the new trestle below Tallulah is being rebuilt and that the bridge over Tallulah River will be completed again next week.

Mess[rs.] Dick Hunter and Charley Cannon attended Chechero court Saturdy.

Mr. A. L. Roane has moved from here to the Ridge.

We are proud to see our barber, Will Hunter, up again. He has been confined with Grip.

Walter and Jim Kerby are off to Westminster, S. C., this week.

H. B. Stonecipher and wife are up again.

§   Wolffork.
As I have not seen anything from Wolffork lately I will try to give you a few dots.

Married, at the residence of the bride's father, Miss Nancy Harvey and Mr. James Wheeler.

Wolffork will soon afford two new mills. A grist and a saw mill will be completed this week, the grist belonging to Mr. Turner Page and the saw to Mr. Mart Dickerson.

Lizzie Page and Lillie Moore spent Saturday night at Rev. Samuel Taylor's and enjoyed it very much.

The people of Wolffork were very much alarmed on Wednesday last as they thought they heard the Black Diamond and looking out they found it to be a young man with a large bar on a wagon.

Mr. M. L. Keener has planted out his garden. Lookout girls.

We suppose the Marsongale crowd enjoyed themselves very much on Sunday last.

Miss Mary Pills and Miss Dora Dickerson, of Germany, spent last Saturday night at Mr. John Moore's.

Mrs. Lizzie Moore is very ill at this writing.

Sunday School opened here last Sunday and elected Mr. D. W. Rickman superintendant.

Mr. E. F. Page, don't be so shy the next time the girls visit you.

---

[1] By a different author than the succeeding report of the same community on page 109.

§   Hartman—Ramey.

There was a very quiet wedding at the Blue Ridge Hotel Monday morning last. The contracting parties were N. M. Hartman and Miss R. M. Ramey. D. T. Duncan performed the ceremony in [illegible].

§ Blalock.

The last freshet on Tallulah was the biggest one yet and did more damage to lands than any in years. The river was a foot and half higher than it was last fall.

Mr. Geo. H. King will soon have his new store house completed. He says he is in the business to stay.

The community is terribly aroused and uneasy about the queer acts of Thomas Youngblood. It seems that he has lost his mind entirely. For several days he has repeatedly attempted to commit suicide by trying to shoot himself with an unloaded hoe handle.

We are sorry to hear of the death of old man Benfield, who departed this life March 28th, at the age of eighty-three years.

There are some postmasters at fault somewhere. We can't get our mail regular, even our Clayton Tribune over half the time does not come to Blalock in a week after it is printed. Can nothing be done?

§   Upper Tiger.[2]

It seems now that there will not be much farming done as the weather is so bad.

Charley Oliver and Willie Roane Jr. returned from a trip down the coutry Tuesday.

Mr. Claude Keener and Miss Texie Turpen attended church at Tiger Sunday.

Mr. A. M. Wall, of Warwoman spent Friday night with R. E. Cannon.

Ask Mr. Joe Godfrey what the fine is for throwing the side walk at a person in Tiger.

Jackson Watts has gone to farming.

Will Erwin (col.) has returned from down the country.

Mrs. Pitts, wife of Kimsey Pitts, is very sick at this writing.

§   Snow is on the ground in Rabun.

§   J. W. Robins is improving slowly.

§   Dr. J. C. Dover is expected home to-night.

§   Miss Maude Coffee visited home folks Sunday.

§   Dr. Henson has returned home from Clarkesville.

§   The sick of the community are generally improved.

§   Sheriff Ritchie made an official trip to the Flats yesterday.

---

[2] By a different author than the previous report of the same community on page 108.

§   Mr. Charles Hurbert, of Athens was in town yesterday.

§   Mr. and Mrs. S. S. Whitmire returned from Toccoa yesterday.

§   There are five inches of snow in some parts of North Carolina.

§   Mrs. M. M. Marsongale is much improved after a severe sickness.

§   Mr. and Mrs. Charlie Grant, of Walhallah are in town to-day.

§   Mrs. Wall and Mr. F. A. Bleckley are much improved in health.

§   Judge Long is fastly recovering from his recent pistol shot wound.

§   H. K. Cannon had some terracing done on his farm last Saturday.

§   J. I. Langston returned from a business trip to Walhallah yesterday.

§   Mr. D. T. Duncan is numbered among the grip patients the past week.

§   Mr. Fred Hunt, of Demorest, Ga., visited relatives in Clayton Sunday.

§   Mr. and Mrs. W. C. Norton are decidedly better now, but Miss Lillie is not so well.

§   Miss Stella Langston has returned from Walhallah, S. C., after several weeks visit.

§   We had considerable frost yesterday morning and it is feared the apple crop suffered.

§   We publish in this issue by request of Mr. R. J. S. Dickson, the first prayer in Congress.

§   Mr. W. A. Martin wishes to say that the accounts of his father are with R. B. Ritchie, at his residence.

§   Mr. F. G. Holden, of Russel, S. C., was here at the meeting of the board of education Tuesday. We thank you for the $.

§   Mr. and Mrs. S. W. Dover have been in Atlanta for the past week. They went down to visit friends and to witness the graduation of their son, J. C. Dover.

§   Z. M. Turpen, James E. Bleckley, representing Dr. J. A. Cannon, of Jeptha, N. C., as well as his own interest, had some land lines established on Tiger creek yesterday.

§   The people of Clayton were pleased to have Judge Logan E. Bleckley and Mrs. Bleckley, of Clarkesville, with them since last week. They returned to their home yesterday.

§ Thomas Coffee, of Germany, was in town Friday limping on account of having lost part of his foot. He accidentally severed two of his toes off while chopping with an ax.

§ Jess Langston and Will Angel caught a large[?] fox yesterday morning. They caught it east of town near the residence of P. N. McConnell. This is the second one they has caught within a week.

§ The farmers are much discouraged on account of the continued cold and rains. Be cheerful, you have never failed to be liberally rewarded for labor wisely performed and there is ample time to make crops yet.

§ Mr. H. Long and Mr. L. N. Robins drove in town to-day with 32 copper stills cut into smithereens. The stills were well perforated, as was the caps and worms. This is in response to a small ad in the last issue of the Tribune.

§ At a meeting of the county Board of Education to-day Prof. A. A. O'Kelley was elected to conduct the County Teachers Institute, to be held in Clayton on the week before the general examination. Prof. O'Kelley has been in our county for more than two years and has the confidence of all school officers and patrons.

§ Chechero.
We are glad to see Sutton Price on foot again after an attack of rheumatism.
The farmers would be glad to see nice weather.
Nathan Hartman, of Pennsylvania, came in this community Saturday, remained till Monday. It is said that he and Rebecca Ramey were married Monday.
Many friends visited Mrs. R. E. Williams Sunday.
The fox hunters, J. R. Ritchie, Jess Langston and Marler Swafford caught a fox near here Saturday morning.
We have a good Sunday school at Chechero every Sunday.
William Thrift, of Longcreek, was in this community Sunday.
They organized a Sunday School at New Hope Sunday afternoon.
Grip is still raging in this section.

§ Upper Warwoman.
Rev. Curry preached an interesting sermon at Antioch Sunday.
Mr. Gus Turpen is still on the sick list.
Mr. and Mrs. Julius Carver, of Chechero, was on Warwoman Sunday.
Misses Ella and Mary Hamby, of Pine Mountain, were at church Sunday.
W. M. McWharter, of Chechero, was here last week.
Mrs. Savannah Dickson is real sick.
Miss Lula Holden has neuralgia.

§ Old Tiger.
Wedding bells are ringing in Stonepile district.
Miss Fannie Dockins and Mr. Andrew Watts were married at the residence of Mrs. Nancy Dockins today.

Mr. Will Shaw has been very sick, but is some better at this writing.

It is reported that the bridge at Tallulah is ready for travel.

§   Bridge Creek.

We are having some [illegible] weather after so much stormy, rainy, haily, snowy weather.

The farmers are very busy preparing to plant corn.

Rev. E. H. Baker preached a very interesting sermon at Rocky Grove Sunday.

Mr. Thomas Edward and J. C. Robertson are moving their saw mill from this place to Tiger.

We are glad to hear that Thomas Allen is improving.

§   Wolfcreek.

The people seem to be very anxious to get to work.

Dr. Green came down to see E. H. Williams, who has grip, this week.

Virgal Ramey killed a large wild cat the other day.

There has been a good many cases of Grip in our community this spring.

We are informed of another murder case over in the edge of Habersham county. Cife Smith killed a drummer named Bell. You can guess the cause. We only have one cause and that is well known, yet, some people will justify the stuff. Let us all see who can do the least harm and the most good and see if times wont change for the better.

§   A Month Earlier.

Below is the act of the last Legislature, changing the time of giving in taxes. Mr. York, our tax receiver, desires its publication as some of the tax payers are confused when informed of the change.

It is therefore ordered, That the first day of February, 1899, be and the same is, hereby fixed and designated as the day for making returns of taxes for the year 1899, hereby requiring the values of all property owned and possessed on that day to be the basis of said tax returns.

§   Betty's Creek.

Mr. Sam Corn and Miss Lena Norton were married last Thursday.

Mr. L. L. Long and Mr. J. P. Norton went to market last Thursday.

We are having a very nice Sunday School here. Mr. T. A. Williams is superintendant.

Mrs. Louisa Hopper is very feeble at this writing.

Mrs. A. A. Darnell has been on Persimmon visiting relatives this week.

The farmers had better get to work if they mean to live this year.

There was quite a crowd at Bud Darnell's Easter.

There will be singing here Sunday.

George Dillard has some nice lumber at his saw mill now.

Miss Nannie Williams and Effie Darnell went to the valley Saturday.

Mrs. Francis Garland is staying with her daughter.

§   Ordinary W. S. Long is putting a nice picket fence in front of his vacant lot adjoining his residence property.

§   S. James and F. B. Blackwell, of Scaly, N. C., made our office a pleasant call Tuesday, and enrolled as readers.

§   The prospects for the Black Diamond is still encouraging.

§   Jumius Henson, Gordon and Jesse Langston were out chasing rabbits Tuesday and caught a large raccoon.

The Clayton Tribune, Volume 2, Thursday, April 13, 1899 *

§   It gives us pleasure to inform our readers that Dr. J. C. Dover is placed among the honor roll of graduates at the annual graduating exercises of Atlanta College of Physicians and Surgeons which was held in Atlanta April 3d. Dr. Dover merits the distinction and we predict for him a distinguised career in his chosen profession. Honor has been placed where honor is due. We publish the following letter from the secretary of the Georgia Board of Medical Examiners:

Griffin, Ga., Apr. 19, 1899. Dr. J. C. Dover. Dear Doctor: It gives me pleasure to inform you that your recent examination before the Georgia Board of Medical Examiners—Regular—was satisfactory. Your license will follow in a few days. Yours truly, E. R. Anthony, Secretary of Board.

The Georgia Board of Medical Examiners has no connection with the Medical college; but is in independent body created by the legislature of Georgia to suppress quackery. Dr. Dover, as did all others [illegible] graduating class, successfully passed this Board.

§   As a rule the people of Rabun certainly know a thing when they see it, but a few days ago a certain young man, at whom fortune has not smiled, wanted to get married but had no funds. A confederate bill was handed him and to Clayton he proceeded, but Judge Long quietly informed him of the character of his money to the astonishment and embarassment of the young man. But we understand the young man got married just the same.

§   Communication From Blue Ridge.

The people met at the Ridge and organized a Sunday School. Hope they will have a good school. The prospects points to success. It is absolutely the duty of parents to attend Sunday School with their children and help instruct them in the way of life. Then instead of the children going to church to jump and have a gay old time they should be under the eye of their parents. Questions. If it is not their duty to do this, upon whose shoulders rest the responsibility? If we don't teach and instruct them what will be the result in the last and great day? But many people, parents, too, would prefer to go visiting on the Lord's day, in order to gossip. Bro. and Sister A will go to your house to parrade my faults before you and your family and then come to my house and do the same thing for you and very soon the whole community is in an uproar. Brother, what kind of Christianity is this? What kind of wisdom? We are required by God's law to bring up our children in the nature and admonition of the Lord. And when this is done, you will not find the child when it is grown up visiting grogg shops and houses of ill repute and bringing down upon the gray hairs of their parents[?] an everlasting shame.

Yours, Mrs. Jonella.

§ At a meeting of Black Diamond people at Cincinati Tuesday all the necessary preliminaries were arranged to close the contract for the funds to build the road. As soon as the financier, Mr. Dickinson can reach London the deal will be closed and arrangements made to begin the work at once. The road is now an assured fact. We who have made such an up hill fight for the enterprise feel much elated over the final success.

"We told you so."—Dover (Ky.) News.

§ Persimmon.

Sunday School was quite small Sunday.

Some of those men that think they have the power in this and the world to come were on this side last week. I look for them before they die to meet with some of the same things that they send whizzing through the air without cause.

Miss Gooley Justus has gone to Toccoa.

Mrs. M. V. York has not returned from Cornelia.

Jas. C. York has the measles.

Esco Nichols has gone to the railroad.

§ Wolffork Dots.

Mr. Ed and Charley Page made a business trip to Westminster last week.

John Justus and wife and Miss Nora Powell, of Germany, were at Sunday school Sunday.

Mrs. Polly York, of Persimmon, is visiting relatives on Wolffork this week.

We sympathize with W. R. Keener for the loss of his sheep that got killed last week.

Mrs. I. M. Keener and also Mrs. Emma Page have gone to Atlanta to be treated by physicians there.

Mrs. Rufus Keener is very feeble at this writing.

We would like know what has become of the young man that was so handy about carrying lanterns last fall[?].

§ Gardening. Every one is gardening.

§ Little Mary Coffee is very sick.

§ Mrs. C. C. Wall is on the sick list.

§ John H. Donalson is off to Turnerville.

§ L. N. Robins is at Whetstone for a few days.

§ A. M. Wall is suffering from throat affection.

§ Little Bessie Bruce is quite sick at this writing.

§ Mrs. Emily Wall is improving rapidly in health.

§ The bridge at Tallulah Falls was repaired last week.

§ We have a good prospect now for a good apple crop.

§ James Robins, of Whetstone, S. C., was in town Monday.

§ Drummers Jackson and Beacham, of Athens, are in town to-day.

§ John M. Moore passed through Tuesday enroute to Toccoa.

§ One of the busiest men in this community is Mr. S. S. Hall.

§ The family of W. C. Norton is decidedly improved in health.

§ Miss Dovie Williams, of Chechero, entered school here this week.

§ We presume there is no fault found to the weather the past week.

§ Miss Susie Ramey has been a pleasant visitor in town this week.

§ Mr. J. F. Earl's premises had the appearance of[?] a bonfire last evening.

§ Reports are that work will begin on the Black Diamond R. R. in a few days.

§ Mr. J. L. Hamby is feeling badly. He is not able to attend to business.

§ H. C. Erwin, of Clarkesville, was in town on business for several days this week.

§ Mr. W. E. Thompson is very sick. He has been confined to his room for several days.

§ Mr. J. S. Ramey has returned from a pleasant visit to the "old folks at home" in Cornelia.

§ Mr. S. L. McKinney, of Blue Ridge, Ga., representing Stovall Callaway & Co., of Atlanta, was among the...merchants here yesterday.

§ Mr. S. S. Whitmire is off to North Carolina this week looking after machinery to place at his mine. He may visit Ashville before he returns.

§ Mr. R. P. Burch, of Hiawasse, was mingling with friends in town Monday, and we had the pleasure of his acquaintance and enrolling his name on our mailing list.

§   Dept. Collector Vigal and others have been in the county a few days with poor success. John Godfrey says they are trying to get a person from the county jail and that this class is the only kind they can catch now.

§   Dr. G. W. Long, accompanied by his son, W. S. Long, Dr. Green and Representative Hamby, left for Atlanta Monday where he will go before a board of physicians and will be advised as to whether his hand should be amputated. Dr. Long has suffered about seven years from a cancer on the hand. It may be that the physicians will recommend amputation. The friends of the Dr. will anxiously await results in the matter.

From a letter from Judge Long to J. T. Long, we learn that Dr. Long was considered able to stand the operation of having his arm amputated and that the operation was to have been performed yesterday at 2 p. m. The friends of Dr. Long will anxiously wait the result of the operation.

§   Mr. S. S. Whitmire has purchased the noted Kell mica mine ten miles northeast of Clayton, and will begin operation about the first of May. This mine is one the best of its kind in the South. A solid piece of mica weighing about five hundred pounds in the rough and would square twelve inches, was taken out of this mine some time ago. The party was offered five hundred dollars for the piece before it was taken out of the cut[?].

It gives us much pleasure to publish the above facts. Mr. Whitmire will pay the cash for labor and we wish him much success in the enterprise.

§   If some of the citizens in town are not lazy it is not because they are indexed.

§   Col. Paris is acting farmer to-day, he has his coat off and talking, gee wo, haw here, to his horse.

§   Bro. Curtis, of the Franklin Press, is pouring hot shot into the ranks of the abvocates of the dispensary law.

§   There was a mortgage recorded in the clerk's office here this week containing about twelve thousand words.

§   Whipporwills, bumble bees, blue birds and other migratories, we think, will be safe making their advent among us now.

§   Dock Keener, of the Valley, left Monday for Atlanta. He has an...affection of the eye and will go before Dr. Calhoun, eye specialist.

§   A crowd of Egyptians with horses, vehicles, dogs, cats, "niggers" and etc. passed through Clayton yesterday headed for North Carolina.

§   The continuous low temperature and amount of rain have greatly retarded all farm work so that comparatively little has been done preparatory for coming crops.

§   See ad of the Normal school at Mt. Airy. Mt. Airy is a delightful place to live and you will be much pleased with the management of the school.

§   Mrs. Turner Page, accompanied by Eddie Page, went to Atlanta the first of the week. Mrs. Page went to be treated for a disease of the throat.

§   Rabun Gap.

The people here are very anxious to get to work on the farms. Hope they will hold[?] out that way.

Miller Rush came through the Valley Sunday on his way home from Texas. He seems to be better in Macon county than in Texas. So boys, you had better not be so anxious to go West.

N. L. Garland, of Toccoa, was in the Valley this week. He carried Mrs. Angel and Miss Carrie Carpenter to their home in Macon county.

The Rabun Gap school is getting along nicely.

Rev. Curry preached in the Valley Saturday and Sunday.

Several of the boys are off to market this week.

§   Upper Tiger Dots.

Mr. H. K. Cannon, Billy Winters and others passed through this section Tuesday enroute to Toccoa.

Charley Oliver and family have moved to Tiger.

A nice party from near Tiger, consisting of Mr. Frank Martin, Miss Lillie Singleton, Mr. Austin Mitchell and Miss Lizzie Martin visited the top of Screamer mountain Sunday.

Mr. Willie Duncan and Miss Gussie Price were at Bethel Sunday.

The farmers are making good use of the time since the weather has moderated.

Guess what young man has rented land and says he thinks he can grow enough corn bread for two.

Mr. John Cannon, of Cornelia, was mingling with his friends around and near Tiger Sunday.

Dr. Green and Col. Hamby passed by enroute to Atlanta Monday.

The two year old child of Babe Lacount died the third day of this month and he has two more sick.

A. W. Kerby is sowing oats this week. Ab is a skillful farmer and a good blacksmith.

J. S. Ramey passed by Monday on his return from Cornelia, Ga.

Ask Claude Keener when the[?] wedding will occur.

§   Bridge Creek.

Rain and snow.

The time to plant corn is here.

Mr. Joseph Marcus is improving.

Mr. W. P. Nix is at Tallulah Falls working on the new hotel.

The patrons of Grove post office are well pleased with Harvey Keason carrying the mail. He is always on time.

Uncle William Watts is ninety two years old and can preach as good sermon as he ever could.

We regret very much the death of Mr. A. D. Watts' little child. Mr. Watts has the sympathy of the entire community.

§   Black Diamond News.

Dover (Ky.) News.

The "know-alls" admit that the Black Diamond will be built, but it will be built some other route...

Some bright mind at Maysville has started the report that the Black Diamond will be built from Port Royal to Clay City, but from that point it will not be built through Dover, as surveyed, but will be run to Columbus...

A private letter from Sir Thomas Tancred says: "We are quite ready to proceed at any moment. The delay is on the other side." The delay mentioned has been over come, and when Mr. Dickinson arrives in London we may expect the Black Diamond affairs to "proceed at any moment." Mr. Dickinson was delayed in getting papers certified on account of the absence of the Embassador, but sailed yesterday from New York on the steamer New York.

§   Chechero.

Mrs. J. W. Green is very sick at this writing.

E. L. McConnell visited Martin Wall Sunday.

Mrs. James Smith is quite sick.

The cool weather continues till April 10th. We are afraid the fruit is ruined in this section.

§   At the last meeting of the Board of Education, held last Tuesday, a committee of three of the Board, W. J. Neville, Cicero Blalock and Z. B. Dillard, was appointed to investigate the matter of complaint in reference to the location of schools in Pine Mountain district. The committee, after making investigations, decided to let the matter be as arranged by the district trustees in the year 1894.

§   The Black Diamond.

Anderson Advocate, March 13: J. L. Tribble and Capt. P. K. McCully left here yesterday afternoon for Cincinati, Ohio, to attend a meeting of the promoters of the Black Diamond Railroad, at which[?] Col. T. C. Dickinson, the financial agent, who has been in London working up the financial arrangements, will make a report.

The Clayton Tribune, Volume 2, Thursday, April 20, 1899 *

[Note: Please see page 53 for a full explanation of the symbol ‡.]

§   Dr. Henson is off to Clarkesville. ‡

§   See town ordinances advertised in this issue. ‡

§   Mr. F. A. Bleckley is still in feeble health. ‡

§   Mr. W. C. Noron is not improved in health. ‡

§   Mr. Geo. Oliver is marshaling the town this week. ‡

§   J. L. Hamby is able to be out at his place of business. ‡

§   Tyre Queen's condition is quite precarious at this writing. ‡

§   Ransome Hunt visited the family of W. C. Norton this week. ‡

§   Mayor pro tem Donaldson has presided in municipal affairs this week. ‡

§   Mr. W. E. Thompson is able to be out after quite a continued sickness. ‡

§   Mrs. W. S. Long is much improved[?] after suffering intensely from[?] earache. ‡

§   Mr. W. C. Donalson put a nice [missing] on Judge Long's residence a [missing] days ago. ‡

§   Look for a huge advertisement [missing] E. P. West & Co., of Clarkesville[?], in our next issue. ‡

§   Dr. Green and Col. Hamby returned home Monday night. They visited Brunswick, Ga., during their absence. ‡

§   T. J. Coffee has sold his farm in town to Jesse McCurry, of Rabun Gap. Mr. McCurry will move his family down soon. ‡

§   Mr. B. H. Greenwood, of Dillard, has completed his course in the Atlanta Business College. He returned to his home Thursday. ‡

§   J. M. Collins, a well known resident of this county, was accidently killed by being shot, near Westminster, S. C., last Friday. ‡

§   Mr. M. L. Garland, of Toccoa, made our office a call Saturday. Mr. Garland was viewing the scences[?] of his native heath. ‡

§   Black Diamond News.
   Dover (Ky.) News.
   A letter from Mr. Kirby written while on the road states that he and Chief Engineer W. B. Crenshaw would arrive in Anderson, S. C. Tuesday morning, ready for work on that end of the line.
   We expected to have a cablegram from Hon. T. C. Dickinson, European financier of the Black Diamond, who was due to arrive in London Tuesday or Wednesday, and

are somewhat disappointed that he has not arrived in time to give information for publication this week.

An editorial from the Charleston, S. C., News and Courier reproduced in another part of this paper shows that that city is awakening to the fact that the Black Diamond is sure to be built and with out necessarily running to that city. Charleston, like some [missing] self-important towns, ridicules[?] the proposed road and refused to give Col. Boone and his associates a respectful hearing. They ignored his proposition, and the road was run to Port Royal... But, just the same, the main double-track line of the Black Diamond will go to Port Royal for two reasons—first, that Charleston has allowed the day of grace to pass by without action; and, second, because Port Royal harbor is a deeper and better harbor than either Charleston or Savannah—in fact it is the best natural harbor on the South Atlantic coast.

§   Upper Tiger Items.
Miss Lizzie York is visiting relatives and friends here.
Rev. Dickson preached an interesting sermon at Bethel Saturday.
Mrs. Kimsey Pitts is very sick at this writing.
Mr. Virgil Thompson seems to be a Sunday boarder at Mr. Cannon's.
The Bethel and Ivy Hill singing classes will have a singing at Pine next Sunday at 3[?] o'clock.
Misses Nannie Oliver and Gussie Price think that they are nearly ready to go to war as each of them has a Cannon.

§   Wolfcreek.
The people are looking ahead to corn planting during this fine weather.
M. L. Jones lost his baby Friday night. It was found dead in the bed Saturday morning.
We are looking for some better times when our trading place gets built up again, the big hotel done and the trestle built up, which is fastly being done.
We saw in our last issue that a portion of Uncle Billy's letter was left out. We like to read the Tribune, but would like it better with more of it left out unless it was based upon better things. The apostle says, "Fear God and keep His commandments is the whole duty of man." If we would do this, we would be a happy people and would not be brought down to degration[?] by supporting the evil of our country.

§   Tallulah Falls.
The learned Robert B. Barnwell died at Tallulah Falls, supported by his warm personal friend, Dr. Percy Nide Daboeay, and was laid to rest in accordance with the services of the Episcopal church on the Sabbath day. Through four score years his career has been a picturesque and romantic one.—Mt. Airy Protectionist.

§   To Whom It May Concern: My son Charles C. Swofford has left home without my consent and all persons are hereby notified not to board, clothe, shelter or in any way harbor the said Charles whose age is thirteen years. W. A. Swofford.

§   We are requested to state that the Rabun County Singing Convention convenes at the Tallulah Academy[?] on Friday before the [illegible] Sunday in August next.

§   The students at Rabun Gap High School will give a public debate on the evening of May 12th. The subject for discussion is, "Resolved: That the United States should not annex the Philippian Islands." All cordially invited to attend.

§   Last Sunday, at the residence of Mr. Oliver about two miles south of town, Tyre Queen was shot by M. H. Wall. The ball, 38 calibre, entering the left shoulder and winging[?] downward. All the reports say that the act was done in self defense and Wall tried to avoid any difficulty and that Queen was striking at him with a knife. No warrant has been issued, but Wall has surrendered to the Sheriff.

§   That great big 200 pound Tom Haralson representing Hynds & Co., of Gainesville was persuading our merchants this week.

§   Many thanks are due to Mr. N. L. Robins by the citizens east of town for permitting them to cross the creek on his water gap for the past nine months.

§   Our Sheriff says he has been persuing Tallulah and Burton sections for two weeks and he says that he is satisfied the "Si" Smith is not in that section of the county.

§   Rev. Charles W. Curry passed through town yesterday on his way to the international Sunday School Convention which will be held in Atlanta embracing the 28th. Mr. Curry will visit home folks at Griffin before his return.

§   Henry Blalock, of Burton, who is accused of assault and attempt to murder a Mr. Taylor of Habersham county, has surrendered to Sheriff Ritchie and has made bond for his appearance at the August term of the Superior court.

§   Sheriff Ritchie had a very unpleasant duty to perform Tuesday. He dispossessed A. J. Trusty on Persimmon. The Sheriff says he was treated kindly by the unfortunate parties.

§   Now is the time to clean your premises. We would advise all to burn the chip piles and all vegetable matter, and above all clean and disinfect your cellars. The council will take action in the matter. Do what you ought to do without being made.

§   Rabun Gap.
   It has cleared off at last and the farmers were very glad of it. They want to have something to feed the Black Diamond hands on.
   Mr. Fate Garland died in Toccoa last week and was buried in the Valley last Saturday. Many friends and relatives attended the funeral.
   Mrs. R. Garland, who has been sick, is better.
   Mr. Amos Gillispie and family and Mrs. Sallie Garland were the guest of J. A. Hopper and wife Sunday.
   Rev. A. B. Thomas preached at the Baptist church Sunday and Rev. Curry at the Methodist.

§   Part of Ordinances of the Town and Council. Courts... Peace; Good Order and Morals... Liquors...

§   Judge Bleckley's Lecture.

Notwithstanding the very bad weather last Friday morning, Judge Logan E. Bleckley delivered his lecture on Value, as had been advertised. The audience was not what it would have been had the day been better, but all who were there counted themselves fortunate. Judge Bleckley's subject is a very deep on and he has given it much thought. His arguments were masterly, and his witicism keen. He has been requested to repeat the lecture at a later date, when the elements are in a more agreeable humor, for the benefit of those who could not get out before, especially the ladies. His lecture will doubtless arouse an interest in that great subject never felt before.—Clarkesville Advertiser.

§   Persimmon. ‡

Too late for last week.

Rev. Hughs was not able to preach long last Sunday.

Mrs. M. V. York has returned from Cornelia.

M. B. and Henry York, sons of J. C. York, came home on a visit last week.

We are glad to have Prof. John C. Howard back in this community.

H. M. Nichols has been planting corn.

H. V. Moore has the contract of carrying the mail from Persimmon to Quartz.

The people of this vicinity in general are well.

Sam Gates has turned his place as S. S. superintendant over to Prof. Howard.

Thomas King and wife spent the day with T. M. Justus last Sunday.

There was quite a crowd at Sunday School Sunday.

<u>The Clayton Tribune, Volume 2, Number 14, Thursday, April 27, 1899</u>

[*Note: Please see page 53 for a full explanation of the symbol* ‡.]

§   Persimmon. ‡

The people of this vicinity are driving their farming work to the best advantages.

Quite a number attended preaching Sunday. We will compete with any Sunday School or Singing class, as to interest taken in them.

Next Sunday we have a day of interrerest in Singing and Sunday School. Would be glad to have as many as possible to attend.

Mrs. Mart Justus is very sick at this writing.

Mr. Caney Thompson passed through with his family Sunday.

Mrs. Sarah Crunkleton, of Highlands, is still here among friends.

We are glad to see in the Tribune that our town has adopted some rules of government, which we hope they will carry out.

§   Notice.

I will be at the following places on the time mentioned below for the purpose of receiving the tax returns of Rabun county for the year 1899.

Wolffork, Monday, May 1st... Bettie's Creek, Monday, May 1st[3]... Valley, Tuesday, May 2nd... Hale Ridge, Wednesday, May 3rd... Moccasin, Thursday, May 4th... Warwoman, Friday, May 5th... Chechero, Saturday, May 6th... Tiger, Monday, May 8th... Tallulah Falls, Tuesday, May 9th... Stonepile, Wednesday, May 10th... Tiger Po., Thursday, May 11th... Clayton, Friday, May 12th... Persimmon, Saturday, May 13th... Tallulah, Monday, May 15th... Dicks Creek Church, Tuesday, May 16th... Cross Roads, Wednesday, May 17th... Jermany Church, Wednesday, May 31st... Clayton, Thursday, Friday and Saturday, June 1st, 2nd and 3rd...

The above are your last chances. J. C. York, T. R.

§   Betty's Creek Dots.

The farmers have been working very hard this week, they think it is about corn planting time.

Docia and little Bry Darnell have been visiting relatives in the Valley this week.

Mrs. Louisa Hopper, who has sick, is improving now.

Mr. Asbery Darnell, of the Valley was on Betty's Creek Sunday.

Mr. Lex and Misses Effie Darnell and Nanie Williams went to the debate Friday night.

The estate of Harrison Darnell was divided last week.

Mr. and Mrs. James Bradley were visiting relatives here Sunday.

Mr. Charles Hopper has been very sick, but is improved.

George Ledford was at Mr. William's [illegible].

§   Gen. Wm. Kirkby and Col. L. W. Crenshaw, of the Black Diamond Road, reached the city this morning, looking after the interests of the road. Mr. Crenshaw is the chief engineer of the road and will ride horseback over the entire line from here to Hampton, and the line will be permanently located. Gen. Kirkby says as far as money matters are concerned there is nothing to prevent the construction of the road from beginning in May or June.—Anderson Advocate, April 10th.

§   Wolffork.

Mr. Lester and Leona Hopper have gone to Toccoa.

Mr. James Keener and wife, of Persimmon, were on Wolffork Sunday.

Mr. George Dorsey passed through this section to day.

Ask Miss Rhoda Hopper why she goes to Rabun Gap Post Office when there is one nearer home.

Mr. Rufus Keener has purchased a farm bell. Wolffork is improving.

M. L. Keener visits Germany very often.

Mr. Mart Dickerson has got his mill to sawing and several boys want a bill[?] of lumber. Look out girls.

§   Warm. These are nice spring days. ‡

§   W. C. Norton's family are improved in health. ‡

---

[3] Day and date indicated by ditto marks in this entry, and month indicated by ditto marks in the remaining entries of this item.

§   Next Tuesday is regular meeting of the town council. ‡

§   Mrs. Jane Smith is seriously sick at her home in Chechero. ‡

§   Tyre Queen, who was shot by M. H. Wall, is improving. ‡

§   Mrs. Susan Sweatman moved into the Simmons cottage Tuesday. ‡

§   Mrs. S. S. Whitmire has returned from a pleasant visit to Toccoa. ‡

§   Miss Dovie Williams visited home folks Saturday and Sunday. ‡

§   Mrs. J. M. York and children visited relatives in Germany last week. ‡

§   Mr. Jesse W. Robins is not so well. He is confined to his room again. ‡

§   If you want the best chewing gum at 5 cent a package, go to Ruby Paris. ‡

§   About 15 citizens of the town are raising the bridge across town creek tomorrow. ‡

§   Marshall Oliver is making some nice improvements on the streets and side walks. ‡

§   Mr. J. L. Hamby is off to Franklin, N. C. after a load of home made flour. ‡

§   Marion Long took a vacation from his store and was on the farm a few days this week. ‡

§   Mrs. D. L. Parker, of Burton, is spending this week in town the guest of Mrs. J. I. Langston. ‡

§   Mayor pro tem Donalson is faithfully performing the duties of his office in the absence of Mayor J. L. Henson. ‡

§   Bud York says he is the laziest fellow you ever saw, and that it is no[?] lie, but he wishes it was. ‡

§   Mrs. Lizzie Coffee, of Atlanta, is expected to be up from Atlanta to-morrow, the guest of Mr. and Mrs. J. H. Coffee. ‡

§   Dr. Long has returned from Atlanta. The physicians before whom he went thought it best not to amputate his hand on account of the weakened condition of the Dr.

§   A stranger, a printer by trade, passed through Clayton Tuesday and said he was assaulted by two white men at Alto, Ga. while passing through that town last Sunday.

§   J. A. Swafford and family arrived from Atlanta last Friday and will remain here the summer. Gus is a good fellow and we hope he may fully recover his health which has been poor for some time.

§   A very sad funeral service occurred here Monday last. Mrs. Catharine Hunnicutt, an aged and highly respected lady and Miss Pearl Brock, a niece of Mrs. Hunnicutt, were buried in one grave. Rev. Chas. W. Curry conducted the funeral services in an impressive manner. The departed ones have many relatives in this county. The bereaved have many sympathizers.

§   Wolf Creek.
The people have been busy at work the last few days.
Spring seems to be coming at last.
Some are planting corn. Get your ground in good fix before you plant if you can.
E. H. Williams is improving in health.
Mrs. David Smith is very sick.
W. E. Jones has built some new bridges across the branch in his field.
D. M. Smith and family made a flying trip to the Falls last week.
John Smith is in Fulton county Jail.
The tax-receiver will be around the 7th of May to get the value of property from a seedtick to a bear. Be liberal and give in your property, they are going to have it anyway.
J. J. Ramey has a lot of new goods to sell. Come around and trade with him.

§   Rabun Gap. ‡
Every thing seems to be quite. We had a big rain Monday night, the forest is getting green rapidly and grass is coming.
We had a nice singing at the M. E. Church Sunday.
Miss Alley Henderson is much better at this writing.
Benny Grist is on the west side of the River. We are always glad to see him come.
Several youngsters went to the Negro meeting Sunday.
A Tennessee cow buyer drove 80 head of cattle out of this vicinity Saturday.
Mr. Jess McCurry and family have moved to Clayton.

§   Ramey—Wall. ‡
Last Sunday at the residence of Rev. R. S. Sanders, J. S. Ramey and Miss Essie Wall were united in holy wedlock. Rev. R. S. Saunders pronouncing the solemn words that united them for life. Mr. Ramey is the popular clerk of the superior court of this county, while Miss Essie is a young lady who merits the love and esteem of the man to whom she has intrusted her heart and hand.
We join their many friends in wishing them a long life of prosperity and happiness.

§   From Clarksville Advertiser. ‡
Judge Logan E. Bleckley went to Atlanta last week to attend the funeral of Col. Hammond.
Mrs. L. E. Bleckley expects Miss Blanch Wall of Clayton, to visit her next month.

The face of Prof. J. C. Howard is missed in Sunday School, for he is a great Sunday School worker wherever he is, so perhaps our loss is some others' gain.

§   Honor Roll. ‡
Delphia Hopkins, Maude Coffee, Ruby Paris, Ina Coffee, Lillie Norton, Dovie Williams, Ronnie Paris, Luther Swofford, Bert Paris.
Average attendance nineteen.

The Clayton Tribune, Volume 2, Number 15, Thursday, May 4, 1899

[Note: Please see page 53 for a full explanation of the symbol ‡.]

§   Three Forks.
Gentle spring is here again after so long a time. Many a poor old cow and sheep if they could would say, "Welcome spring, welcome."
Corn planting time is here and nobody done planting. I heard of one man who was done and the people were talking of whitecaping him, but I think it would be better to whitecap those who are not done. If this was done this settlment might well be called the Whitecap sestlement. Maybe that would give some of them courage.
Mr. Thomas Carver has been sick for some time and we are sorry to say he doesn't seem to get any better.
Tax receiver York met quite a crowd at one of his advertised places yesterday at a very late hour of the day. Some of us who had been waiting all day got pretty blank from doing without dinner.
Would be glad for some one to tell us how Mr. John Carver and family, who some time ago moved from this settlement to Chechero, are getting along.

§   Rabun Gap.
Rev. Brown has been in the valley for a few days in the interest of his church and community and preached Sunday.
J. M. Hopper passed through Sunday enroute to Toccoa on business.
Mrs. J. C. Carter has moved to Bryson City, N. C.
Mr. David Garland has taken his wife back home to live. We wish them much happiness in their future and hope they will live for God.
Mr. John Tanner is very feeble and Texie McCurry is very sick at this writing. She has a case of fever.
There will be children's day services at the M. E. Church the third Sunday in this month.
Mrs. J. A. Hopper is very poorly at this writing.
Mrs. Rosana Garland has a very severe attack of sick headache.

§   Upper Warwoman.
The revenues raided on Warwoman and Dick's Creek last week and captured one copper and a lot of beer.
Mr. Curry failed to meet the people at the M. E. Church Sunday but he will come next time.

We were glad to see our old friend Rance Hunt on Warwoman last week.

Fred Bowers visited friends here last week.

Miss Addie and Crese[?] Carver spent Saturday and Sunday with people on Warwoman.

Miss Marsongale is in feeble health.

Sam Holden is wearing long pants now. Look out girls.

§   To Teachers. The Normal Department of the Mt. Airy Institute opened April 3rd, 1899, and will continue until the county examination. This session will be conducted by Prof. J. E. H. Fry, who will use the Text Books on which the State School Commissioner will base the Examinaton. Do you wish to increase your pay by raising your grade from second or third to first? Do you desire to secure a license to teach? Come to the Mt. Airy Institute. Tuition costs $1.50 per month, board $6 to $8 per month. G. B. Gard, Sec. to the Faculty.

§   Wolffork Dots.

Mr. Joseph Dickerson and Mr. Isaac Justus have returned from market.

Mrs. Emma Page is improving from a severe spell of sickness.

Mrs. Carnes, of Germany, is visiting relatives on Wolffork this week.

Mr. George Martin was at Sunday school Sunday.

Mr. James Pendergrass is ready to plant corn.

§   This is beautiful farming weather.

§   J. L. Henson is home from Habersham.

§   Sheriff Ritchie is not very well this week.

§   Miss Beulah Green was in town Saturday.

§   Miss Effie Duncan is on the sick list this week.

§   Mr. Claude Green has returned form Demorest.

§   Mr. J. C. Langston of Walhalla, is in town today.

§   The health of the community is excellent at present.

§   Ordinary Long had his well cleaned out yesterday.

§   Nature is rapidly putting on her beautiful robe of green.

§   The Black Diamond seems to be [missing] thing now.

§   [Missing] farmers are putting in good [missing] planting their crops.

§   The bridge across Town creek was completed last Friday.

§   When the Black Diamond comes Clayton will blossom into a city.

§   This is the time of the year when people are afflicted with that "tired feeling."

§   Dr. Davis, of Haywood, N. C., was in town a few days this week.

§   Some of our merchants say they have a much better trade than usual now.

§   Drummer Church, representing John B. Daniel & Co., of Atlanta, was in town this week.

§   Mr. Clifton McCrackin, of Fort Hill, S. C., was in town Saturday and made us a pleasant call.

§   Mrs. D. L. Parker, who has been here the past week to receive medical attention, is much[?] improved.

§   Fine growing weather now.

§   Son Henson is regularly on the farm these days.

§   Mrs. J. S. Ramey has been quite sick with roseola this week.

§   Rev. Chas. W. Curry is on a visit to Walhalla for a few days.

§   There was a large attendance at the Justice's Court last Friday.

§   W. C. Donalson purchased a tract of land from J. F. Earl Monday.

§   Farmer's have their crops well in hand and we predict a good harvest.

§   Creditors should be as lenient as possible at this season of the year.

§   The atmosphere is laden with the sweet fragrance of the wild locust blooms.

§   Mr. W. C. Norton has recovered from his continued sickness and is now between the plow handles.

§   Mr. George Bowers, of Franklin, N. C., is visiting his sister, Mrs. Turner Page.

§   Misses Ina and Maude Coffee and Dovie Williams have stopped school and are at home.

§   Mr. J. C. Langston, who has been on a visit to home folks a few days, returned home to day.

§   Mr. J. L. Hamby sold a fine team of horses to R. Hunt, of Demorest, Ga., last Friday.

§   Mrs. Emily Wall left Tuesday for a visit of a few days to her sister, Mrs. Dr. Bell, at Walhalla.

§   Mr. and Mrs. A. Henry, of Highlands, were the guests of Mr. and Mrs. L. N. Robins several days this[?] week.

§   Miss Manda Earl, one of Clayton's most charming young ladies visited home folks Saturday and Sunday.

§   We say emphatically that Georgia has as good chief executive officers as Kansas or any other state in the union.

§   Dr. P. N. DuBoeay, Mrs. Hunnicutt and Cecil Cannon, of Tallulah Falls, were among friends in Clayton Monday.

§   The friends of Mr. and Mrs. D. C. Brown, of Chappel hill, Ga., were glad to have them among them the past week.

§   Mrs. Jane Smith died at her home on Chechero yesterday. She has been sick since January last. She was about six-five years and highly respected.

§   Jesse Robins is out on the streets after a few weeks of sickness. He says he doesn't care for any ordinances the council may pass except he does not want the ante-whittling law passed.

§   Mr. R. C. Wilhite, of Burton, is in town to-day and says the steel bridge across Tallulah will be completed to day. Mr. Wilhite says that Mr. Craft has done a good job and is one of the best bridges he ever saw.

§   Mr. A. J. Nix died at his home in Clarkesville last Monday after a protracted illness. Mr. Nix was a prominent man in that county, he was for many years sheriff of the county and held other offices of trust. With him goes an old landmark of that section.

§   Chechero.
   Mr. M. B. Ramey sheered five pounds of wool off of one sheep last week.
   W. A. Swofford has arrived home with his son Charles.
   It is reported that the Rogue's Ford Iron bridge gave way and sprung down the river two inches or more.
   Mrs. Smith is no better at this writing.
   J. R. Ramey, of Long Creek, visited in this community Sunday.
   Mr. John W. Green visited Marinda Ramey.

§   A Rare Old Letter on Georgia Scenery. (Atlanta Journal)

The following letter, describing a trip from Stone Mountain to Tallulah Falls in 1846 was written by a gentleman who afterward became distinguished in his native state, Pennsylvania. It is one of the finest descriptions ever written of Georgia scenery...

It will be seen that the author of the letter was a man of culture literary taste. He became eminent as a naturalist and occupied a chair in LaFayette college, Pennsylvania. He was a minister of the gospel and his first charge was at Montscello, Ga. From there he wrote this letter to his cousins, Miss Johnson and Miss Allen, of Philadelphia.

Monticello, Jasper Co., Dec. 8, 1846.

My Fair Cousins, Annie and Sue:

I have long had it in mind to write you, and now, as a good occasion offers, I hope that you will not take it amiss...

About the middle of August, while recovering from attack of fever I had the good fortune to receive an invitation to join a party of ladies and gentlemen in a tour through the eastern portion of upper Georgia. Having heard much of the magnificence of the scenery of that region, the paradise of the Cherokee Indians, from which they were driven but a few years since by the encroaching "paleface," and anxious to breathe once more my native element, pure mountain air, I accepted it gladly...

The first party was composed of choice spirits from Macon and Savannah... He to whom we looked up as our leader, because he had traveled over the same ground before. Dr. Joseph Le Conte is a finished scholar, a man of science, especially skilled in ornithology and music, and possessed of polished manners...

The first point of interest which we visited was the celebrated Rock Mountain in De Kalb county... Far as the eye could reach, from the distant western horizon, where stretched the Altonah Hills and[?] the Blue Mountains, dimly visible...

Our course now was[?] northward to Gainesville, crossing the Chattahoochee about four miles from that place... Yonah (or the Bear) mountain standing alone, proudly pre-eminent, its lofty head still rosy with light... The next moon saw us in a cool atmosphere, amid strange plants and weather beaten pines on the height of Yonah, seated on the verge of a tremendous precipice, around whose cliffs ravens and buzzards floated, the valley spread out like a map beneath, and watered by streams abounding in gold, and in the distance to the left thirty miles off, Dahlonega, where a branch of the United States mint is established...

...we arrived in Nacoochee[?] valley. And all that [missing].

This was deversedly the chosen residence of the Cherokee Indians, the remains of whose wigwams are yet to be seen. Nacoochee was taken from a celebrated beauty of that name, and signifies evening-star. The Chattahoochee and Soukee[?] rivers flow into the valley and are full of gold. Near their junction a conical hill is situated, which exhibits evident traces of having been once fortified. It is supposed to have been done by the Spaniards long time ago, when they came eagerly searching the most precious metal. This supposition is confirmed by the discovery of buttons, and sundry relics of Spanish manufacture.

From Nacoochee we went to Clarkesville, a pleasant village and a favorite place of resort, during the last few months, to the citizens of Charleston and Savannah... Not delaying long here we pushed on 15 miles further to Tallulah Falls.

They are the children of Avera Terrora, which is by interpretation "The Terrible." Taking its rise in the neighboring mountains, it runs into an awful chasm, rent in some premival convulsion 1,000 feet deep, and foaming and tumbling along its rocky bed for miles through the dark abyss, it pours at length over the brink of a steed[?] ledge, and dashed into white spray, falls into a pool below, hemmed in by lofty walls of rock. This is the first cascade and is Lodore. Pausing, as if to collect its whole might, it rushes on through a narrow gorge and repeats the same glorious wonder, by three graceful leaps from bench to bench, throwing out large masses of spray made up of globules, glittering like pearls in the sunlight, and filled with segments of sunbows, and seventy feet below breaks with a roar of thunder on the surface of an immense rock, and driven with terriffic violence against the adamantine ribs of the basin and hissing and boiling, sends up continual volumes of thin mist, keeping perpetually fresh and green the fragrant flowers and moss on trees, pines, hollies, and magnolias that stand or wave in clefts of[?] the crags, rank. This is called Tempesta.

Then further down comes the Oceana Cascade, like this and yet different, and if possible still more beautiful. Here one of the ladies threw her handkerchief to an undine, or Water Nymph, and we feared for herself, for the attraction is strong to move with the moving flood...

The house of our entertainment is in perfect keeping with the place, and its owner much like the fortress of Robinson Crusoe built by Captain Beall's own self, as he loves to tell...for the captain is a character. Of good family in Virginia he ran away when a boy, not liking books, and after various wonderings up and down, enlisted as a dragon in Florida, married a wife, came into the woods, and by his own ax and energy erected a house without nails, to which he added as he prospered...

The captain calls his three children, "Rolla, Tallulah, Magnolia," as he says, "Historical, Geographical, Botanical."

I had something to say about Toccoa Falls, whose height is 184 feet, but must now close. The little fern (Asslenium[?] Rutamurania) and moss (Lycododium apodum[?]) were gathered from rocks wet by the mists of Oceana Cascades. To hear from you would give me exceeding pleasure for I am much interested in all that concern you. In May next I expect to be in Piladelphia. My kind regards to Mr. and Mrs. Allen.

Yours with esteem, Thomas C. Porter.

§   Black Diamond.

We learn through exchanges that the money to build the Black Diamond Railroad has been secured and that contracts for grading the entire line will be let[?] out at an early day. This is news glorious to our readers. We hope soon to see the engines and cars whirl through the famous Rabun Gap and run gracefully around Pinacle mountain and through Saddle Gap, and vice versa.

§   Wolfreck.

Corn planting is in a rush. Some are about done, others but little done.

The people generally well in our part.

Green stuff has taken the place of dry at last with our stock.
Some of the young people had a candy drawing Saturday night.

§   Chub and Miss Lillie Wall and the Misses Oliver went to Chattooga river to-day on a fishing trip.

§   Miss Arah Coffee shot and killed a rattlesnake measuring four feet in length last week. Good for Miss Arah.

§   Mr. S. S. Whitmire is off this week to his mica mine. He is working several hands and we hope Sylvester will "strike it rich."

§   Mrs. Martin Justus, of Persimmon, has been quite sick for the past two weeks. Dr. Green reports her condition improved to-day.

§   The revenue officers have raided in the county this week, and, we are told, have had success in their line of business.

§   We notice the next Quarterly conference for the Clayton circuit will be held at Antioch June 11th and 12th.

§   We are still agent for the daily Constitution. If you desire to remit through us hand in the amount next Saturday or Monday.

§   The friends of Mr. P. D. Coffee, of Covington, Ga., will regret to know that his house was burned Tuesday of last week. His loss reaches into the thousands of dollars.

§   Miss Ida Duncan, after several months' absence, returned home last Monday to the delight of her friends, and she was delighted herself.

§   A pleasure party will picnic on Screamer's summit in the near future. A more delightful and picturesque place could not be selected.

§   Squire Derrick won the button yesterday killing squirrels. It is reported he killed five and his new dog treed twice that number.

§   Isaac McCurry, of the Valley, has moved to town and is occupying the house on the corner of Maine and Academy streets.

§   Mr. W. S. Whitmire, of Toccoa, accompanied by his father, W. R. Whitmire, returned to his home Monday after a pleasant stay of several days among relatives and friends in Clayton, his former home. Mr. W. S. has many friends here who always glad to see him.

§   Mr. Jeff Duncan has been off a week visiting, hunting and fishing on Warwoman. He killed six squirrels and among others caught about one hundred fish. Uncle Jeff was agreeably surprised on his return this morning when Judge Long handed him a sixty dollar pension check. This is his first as he is one of those who recently made applications and is one of the county's most worthy applicants.

§   Upper Warwoman.
   Rev. Curry preached at Antioch Sunday.
   The farmers are about done planting here.
   Mrs. Bowers and Mrs. Josie Swafford visited Johie[?] Worton last week.
   Eugene Swafford made a business trip to Walhalla last week.
   Chub Wall and Bert Robins were on Warwoman last Sunday.

The Clayton Tribune, Volume 2, Number 16, Thursday, May 11, 1899

[Note: Please see page 53 for a full explanation of the symbol ‡.]

§   Judge Long, in company with your humble servant, went over to Burton last Saturday. Judge Long went over to inspect, receive and pay for the iron bridge, all of which he did. From appearance the bridge is an excellent one and the people over there are real proud of it, and we are glad for them; they needed it badly. Burton is surrounded by good farm land and the people seem to be prospering financially.

While we have a pretty good sized subscription list at that place, we know after visiting there, that it is not what it ought to be. We expect to go there again soon and never leave till we enroll many more names of the substantial citizens, and they had just as well make up their minds to subscribe for the Tribune.

The bridge was constructed by Mr. Craft, of Atlanta, but the work was managed by a darkey and we saw Mr. Craft pay him one hundred and fifty in cold cash for his services. This negro conducted himself in such a way as to gain the respect of the people there.

§   Black Diamonds R. R. news remains flattering according to all reports. Rabun would be one of the banner counties of the state if fate should smile on her with this road. Her natural resources are unsurpassed, especially her timber and mineral. When it comes to climate and magnificent scenery we will compare favorably with any country.

§   Chechero. ‡
   The Chechero Sunday school is moving along nicely and has forty enrolled.
   Mrs. M. J. Smith died May 3nd and she leaves twelve children and fifty-five grandchildren to mourn her loss.
   George Smith, of Longcreek was on Chechero Sunday to see his best girl.
   L. M. Ramey had a log-roling Monday and had one hand to help him.

§   Matrimonial. ‡
   Tuesday evening just as old Sol was paying the Eastern foothills his last respects, there was something of a surprise party at Dr. Hensons.

Mr. Marion Long, accompanied by his Uncle Judge Long, in an unassuming and unpretentious manner, called at Henson's residence and in a short time informed those interested that a quiet home wedding would soon occur. There being no dissenting voices, Mr. Long and Miss Willie Henson were united.

We wish for them a long, happy and prosperous life.

The Clayton Tribune, Volume 2, Thursday, June 1, 1899 *

§   It is hot. A fine [illegible] yesterday.

§   Justices court to morrow.

§   Ordinary's court next Monday.

§   See farm for sale by M. L. Shirey.

§   See administrator's ads in this issue.

§   Harry Duncan is on the sick list today.

§   Mr. and Mrs. J. E. Derrick have the boss onion patch of the town.

§   The friends of Mrs. J. S. Ramey will regret to know that she is quite sick.

§   R. E. A. Hamby has returned after several days absence in Atlanta.

§   Prof. O'Kelley and Virgil Green are off to the commencement at Cornelia.

§   J. C. York will be here on the 1st, 2nd and 3rd, the last chance [to?] make your returns.

§   From exchanges we learn that something "interesting" will be given the public soon.

§   Porter Green, of Turnersville made Franklin a visit this week. He returned home to-day.

§   Claude Green, of Turnersville, was the guest of his brother, Dr. Green a few days this week.

§   Mr. L. C. Hollifield is off for a few days to Toccoa on a combination trip of business and pleasure.

§   The quarterly meeting of the Rabun Mission will be held at New Hope Church Saturday and Sunday next.

§   Go to W. B. Watts Two and one half miles West of Tiger For Lumber.

§   Husband Shoots His Wife.

Last Tuesday about noon, M. L. Shirley came to his house from the farm in an intoxicated condition and he and Mrs. Shirley engaged in a family unpleasantness. Shirley in a rage of passion shot his wife.

The ball pierced her head between the right eye and cheek hollo[?] and lodged near the ear. She is in a very critical condition, and very little hope of her recovery.

Shirley is held in jail waiting results. He is a man of much property and the affair is deeply regreted.

§   The second Quarterly Meeting of the Clayton circuit will be held at Antioch June 10th and 11th 1899.

Rev. E. R. Cook, P. E., will be present. A full attendance of all the official members will be necessary. Let every steward be there without fail. God has placed it upon you to act in this capacity and how can you neglect so great a duty?

Rev. Cook will preach at Clayton Sunday evening at 8 o'clock, June 4th. Let every body attend as Bro. Cook has not been with us before this year. It is important that we come out to these services.

May the God of all Grace direct you in paths of peace is the prayer of

Chas. W. Curry, P. C. Clayton circuit.

§   Mrs. Lucy Watts, of Tiger, who has been in lingering health for some time, is stopping with Mrs. L. C. Hollifield, and is being treated by Dr. Green.

§   Mr. Henry Mosely, after a very pleasant stay of several days among friends and relatives returned to his home last Monday. Mrs. Mosely returned with him after several weeks stay among her relatives and friends.

§   Mr. and Mrs. W. J. Grist, of the valley, were in town Saturday, the guest of Mr. and Mrs. W. J. Green. Mr. Grist's friends will be pleased to know he has regained his health after a continued sickness since December last.

§   Shocked by Lightning.

Yesterday about noon a small cloud made its appearance over town and a bolt of lightning struck a fence post, within a few feet of Representative R. E. A. Hamby's house, severely shocking Mrs. Hamby, Mrs. D. L. Parker, and Jeff Duncan. Mr. Duncan was burned by the lightning on the top of his head, and suffered from it during the afternoon.

§   We call attention to the advertisement of the "History and Conquest of the Phillipines and our other Island Possessions" in this issue. Mr. E. F. Blalock, of Burton, is agent for this county. He is a worthy young man and is making a successful agent. We subscribed for a copy and advise those who desire a thorough knowledge of the new posessions to obtain a copy of the book.

§   Upper Warwoman.

Mr. Tom Price, of the Valley, was on Warwoman last week.

Misses Lula Ramey and Amanda Carver, of Chechero, were on Warwoman Sunday.

In answer to Three Forks' letter of last week, I will say that Wilbanks is getting along nicely.

§   Dillard.

Marlor Whitmire and Miss Lillie Wall, of Clayton, were in the Valley Sunday.

Mr. Henry Mosley and wife, of Toccoa, who have been visiting friends here for a few days, returned home this week.

Mr. Billie Whitmire and granddaughter, Miss Carrie, were in the Valley Sunday.

Mr. Free and daughter Nerva, of Soque, Ga., visited friends at this place last week.

Rev. A. B. Thomas baptized Mrs. Belle Daily in Betty's Creek Sunday morning.

The farmers are getting along nicely with their week.

Mr. John Winters and family of North Carolina, were in the Valley the latter part of last week.

Mrs. Ida Brown, from below Gainesville, who has been visiting her father, W. C. Scruggs, started for home Tuesday accompanied by her little sister Fannie.

§   Notice to Teachers.

All applicants for teachers licenses are hereby notified to be at Clayton on Thursday the 22nd day of June next, as that is the date of the next general examination. By order of the State School Commissioner.

The Teachers Institute will be held on the week beginning on Monday the 12th day of June.

Prof. A. A. O'Kelley can be employed for the time between the close of the Institute and the examination. Teachers will do well to confer with him.

Respectfully, W. J. Neville, C. S. C.

§   Rabun Gap.

J. A. Hopper has corn waist high in his garden.

The two Dr. Garlands are gone to Nashville, Tenn., to attend the examination. We wish them much success.

Mrs. John Howard is worse again.

Mrs. R. Garland has gone down to see her sick brother.

We are needing rain very badly. The plants are dying in the beds.

Mrs. Lafayette Garland is visiting friends and relatives here for a few days.

Mr. John Tanner is not doing any good. He is in very feeble health.

Mrs. Henry Mosley was among us Saturday and Sunday. We were[?] glad to see it.

§   Some Things That Happened in Rabun Many years Ago.

About fifty years ago Mr. John B. York, who lives near town, shot a wild turkey on a mountain side, and it sailed, as they usually do after being shot, and when he reached home the turkey was lying dead at his door. Among the many deer he has killed one was as white as snow. He killed it on Slick Rock Mountain.

About a quarter of a century ago, Mr. Ira Holden of the Tennessee valley, then quite a youth, passed a school house off Warwoman, and hollowed[?] "school butter." He was riding a swift animal and felt safe in throwing the old "condesending phrase" at the school, but the larger boys chased him to his home, (about the distance of eight miles), and besides the embarrassment the students subjected him to, Mr. Holden tells us that the whipping he received from his father still holds a place in his memory and that he has been cautious since on what occasions he used the words "school butter."

If a couple of strangers are living that passed the academy in Clayton fifty years ago they remember hollowing "school butter" and a ducking they received at the hands of the Clayton school boys. As they were passing the old Academy they rang out oaths and "school butter" in the school and when they did this the teacher, a Mr. Brawnson, pointed to this one and that one of the students, saying, "You go and catch them." The boys went but not before they reached Burton, ten miles from here. The two strangers were left barely alive in Tallulah river.

Thomas Fountain is, according to the opinion of nearly all the citizens of this county, wrongfully serving a four years term in the Ohio Penitentiary. He was accused of whitecapping. One Hamet, whose character was unsavory, was severely whipped by a party in this county, and Fountain was convicted for the offense.

Mr. Bob Pelfry tells us that Fountain, however, will be given his liberty about the first of August next.

During a summer month about eight years ago, Mr. and Mrs. J. C. York were out hunting cattle in the mountains on the head waters of the Tuchaleech, seven miles from the public road, and the same distance from his home. When they reached a place called the milk sick cover Mr. York's dogs treed a squirrell and they were looking up a tree for the squirrell when Mrs. York was bitten by a large rattlesnake. Mr. York knowing the distance from home and remedy, hurriedly corded the bitten limb and picked his wife up in his arms and made double quick time the seven miles to home and remedy and the life of Mrs. York was saved. Mr. York asserts, as well as others who saw the snake, that it had long bristles on its back.

About ten years ago, there lived a family of six, by the name of Wood, in a typical mountain cabin, a little over a mile from Clayton, on the banks of a beautiful mountain stream... Fortune had never smiled on this home, but the fact that it had not does not prove that the occupants were not happy. It does not prove that those five small children did not dreem as sweetly as the children of the millionaire. They may have worn tattered garments and luxuries were not known to them, but their hearts were as pure as the air they breathed or the snow that mantles the forest in the rigor of winter on the Pinacle mountain. In this lonely cabin there was but one door. One dark night, in the absence of the husband who had gone away to work for bread for his wife and children in a distant neighborhood, the wife and children retired for the night... Sometime about midnight when sleep is sweetest, it is supposed that fire caught the building near the door and the inmates perished in the flames. Many people living in Clayton remember the sad scene of the charred bodies of the six unfortunates. The six bodies lie to-day in the old church yard at the Clayton Baptist Church.

§   Persimmon.

Quite a crowd attending commencement at Cornelia.

It is reported that James Thompson has received appointment as Deputy U. S. Marshall.

No one sick.

No rain yet, but are needing it.

John Howard escorted the beelle of Persimmon to Cornelia this week.

The Clayton Tribune, Volume 2, Thursday, June 8, 1899 *

§   Program of Children's Day Exercises at Rabun Gap, June 17.

...Invocation, by Rev. Chas. W. Curry...

Address, by Jno. Howard...

Recitation—"Hitherto and Henceforth" by six boys and girls...

Sermon, by Rev. J. W. Hughes...

"Important questions regarding our new fields," by Supt. and school...

Recitation—"Beautiful Things," by Miss Lizzie Dillard...

Recitation—"What is a farm fit for?" by Frank Dillard.

Recitation—"A Liberal Education," by Oscar Powell.

Recitation—"The Way to Heaven," by Miss Ethel Powell...

Recitation, by Leila Curry, Griffin, Ga.

Address, by W. A. Curtis, Franklin, N. C....

Address, by Prof. A. A. O'Kelley.

Solo.—"I'll go when you want me to go," by Rev. Chas. W. Curry.

Address, by Hon. R. E. A. Hamby, Clayton, Ga....

§   ...Chamberlain's Pain Balm... For sale by J. L. Hamby.

§   I want to buy old copper of every description. Will pay 3[?] cents per pound. J. L. Hamby.

§   [Missing] rain badly needed.

§   [Missing] B., Henry and Miss [missing] and C. J. Crunkleton returned[?] home from Cornelia [missing] they[?] have been spending a [missing] months preparing for a more [missing] life. We gladly received them[?] to Sunday-school Sunday.

§   We are sorry that Prof. Howard is going to be away for a while as he is such a good stake in the Sunday school.

§   The long looked for minutes of the singing convention have come at last. Some of those that were present are not very well satisfied with them because they don't show the report of the finance committee.

§   The U. S. D. M. was on the river Sunday. It is thought he came over to let the Marshal Thompson have some of his papers and help him to drink a run of liquor.

§ J. C. York had some corn borrowed while he and his family were away last week. The borrower is unknown at the present.

§ The general health of the community is very good at this writing.

§ The prospect for rain now is good for it is cloudy and sprinkling.

§ Some of the girls visited the tunnel Sunday, where they could go some two or three hundred feet under ground.

§ Betty's Creek.
The people are needing rain on Betty's creek.
Rev. Thomas preached a very interesting sermon Sunday evening.
Mr. Free and daughter were in this community last Sunday.
Mr. George Dillard has quit sawing on Patterson creek and has gone to the Flats.
Our Sunday school is progressing nicely.
Mrs. Nancy Wilbanks is very sick, but hope she will soon recover.
James Bradley, of Peesimmon, was among us Sunday.
We would like to hear from Asbury Darnell. The last we heard of him he was at Mr. Wall's.
Mr. Charles Hopper and Misses May and Carrie Garland have gone to Mulberry, N. C.
Mrs. Louisa Hopper departed this world Friday morning about six o'clock. She was a kind and tender mother and leaves seven children and many relatives and loved ones to mourn her loss.

§ Dillard.
Mrs. Will Greenwood, of Franklin, is visiting relatives here.
Mrs. Mary Enloe is very sick at this writing.
Dr. Garland moved into the Will Greenwood cottage last week. We are glad to have him with us again.
Little Lena Garland and Fred Burrell are both very sick.
Mrs. Louisa Hopper, a highly respected old lady, who lived on Betty's Creek, died Friday morning and was buried at the Baptist cemetery Saturday morning.
Mr. Tom Coffee and family of Clayton, visited relatives in the Valley last week.
Mr. Irvin Patton, of North Carolina, was in the Valley Tuesday.
Mr. Ben Greenwood went to Franklin last week.
Little Lizzie Ritchie, who has been visiting her Uncle John Carter[?], at Toccoa, for some time, came[?] home last week.

§ Old Tiger.
Rev. D. D. Taylor is very sick at this writing.
Prof. O'Kelly and Virgil Green passed this section from Cornelia commencement a few days ago.
Rev. R. L. Whitmire preached at Tiger last Sunday to a good congregation.
The train is expected to arrive at Tallulah Falls by 15th of June.

Mr. Tatum Taylor was at church Sunday and left for home near Mayesville Monday.

Camp Creek was well represented at church Sunday. A number of people from that section was with us.

The farmers are doing all they can in this vicinity to make bread for another year.

Mr. Frank Morton has been given a common guard's place in some convict camp of Georgia. He left Friday to go to work.

Mrs. Savannah Bleckley arrived home last Friday from Tallulah where she has been sending her children to school this spring.

Mr. John Jenkins is seeing a great deal of trouble. He is about to lose one of his best farm hands. Lookout boys, John has plenty of guns.

The fruit crop in this community is almost a failure.

§   Rabun Gap.

It is very warm and dry, and rain is much needed. The bug and cut worms are doing lots of damage to the corn crops and the bottoms have a bad stand so far.

Mrs. Louisa Hopper, of Betty's Creek, died last Friday morning and was buried Saturday.

Mr. William Neville, a young man from Walhalla, S. C., was in the Valley Saturday on his way to Franklin, N. C.

Mr. Keen Garland's little girl is right sick at present and also Dock Burrell's baby is very sick.

Dr. Garland has moved back to the Valley, and I guess he came in a good time for the children nearly all seem to be sick in the Valley.

§   See Sheriff's sales for July.

§   Honey for sale at this office.

§   Marshal Oliver is on the "puny" list.

§   Judge F. A. Bleckley is slowly improving.

§   See notice of change of public road in another column.

§   Mrs. W. S. Paris returned from Atlanta yesterday.

§   Rev. J. W. Hughs will preach at Ivy Hill next Sunday.

§   J. C. York has very much improved in health the past week.

§   Post Mistress D. A. Henson is gone to Walhalla, S. C., to-day.

§   Drs. Green and Dover report Mrs. Shirley's condition very critical.

§   Mrs. J. W. Hughes, of Cumming, Ga., will visit some time at Tiger.

§ Mr. and Mrs. S. S. Whitmire are off to their mine this week.

§ Mr. and Mrs. L. C. Hollifield are visiting on Timpson creek for a few days.

§ Harry Duncan and Charlie Langston have been feeling badly for the past week.

§ W. C. Calwell, who sells Rabun county nearly all its groceries, is in town to-day.

§ It is reported here that Si Smith has been captured near Bryson City, N. C. yesterday.

§ Mrs. J. S. Ramey has been very sick for past few days, but is better to-day.

§ Misses Stella Langston and Lillie Norton are visiting in Highlands, N. C., this week.

§ J. C. Dickson and Mrs. Dickson, of Turnerville, visited the father of the former on Chechero Tuesday.

§ Mr. J. W. Bigham, representing the Foote & Davies Co., of Atlanta, was in town first of the week.

§ You low landers come to the mountains and keep cool. We have plenty of cool water and dense shades.

§ Late yesterday evening, during a thunder storm in the Valley, two of Mr. John Neville's horses were killed by lightning.

§ We made an error in advertising the sale of 100 bushels of corn by John F. Ritchie. It will be sold on the 17th, instead of the 11th.

§ Mrs. D. L. Parker, who has been under treatment of the doctors here, returned home last week somewhat improved in health.

§ Mr. M. L. Shirley, who is confined in jail for shooting his wife, requests us to say that the shooting was an accident and he would not have purposely done the act for the world.

§ J. C. York, Tax Receiver, closed his last round Saturday. Mr. York informs us that parties who may have failed to make their returns can do so at his home, in person or by mailing him returns properly accompanied by an affidavid.

§ Miss Lizzie Duncan happened to a very painful accident last Monday night. As she started to the window to pull the shade down she stepped on a crochet needle and it stuck into her foot an inch deep or more. She is unable to walk.

§   Keowee Courier: We regret to learn of the serious illness of Capt. W. J. Neville. He has been quite feeble for the past week, but is reported slightly better this morning.

§   Warren Dunlap brought to our office last Saturday a rattle snake's hide stuffed measuring 4 feet and 11 inches in length, and the hide of its head not counted and the rattles gone. It measured over seven feet when first killed.

§   Mr. and Mrs. Geo. W. Greenwood, Mrs. James Greenwood and two children, of Rabun county, and Mrs. J. L. Garland, of Toccoa, Ga., were visiting Mr. W. H. Greenwood and family from Wednesday evening to Friday morning.—Franklin Press.

§   ...Chamberlain's Colic, Cholera and Diarrhoea Remedy... For sale by J. L. Hamby.

§   The political pot has begun to simmer as the summer approaches. According to the rotation system Towns County is entitled to the senator from the fortieth. We know very few people in the county, but we know J. Miles Berrong, of Hiwassee, and we hear his name frequently spoken of as a probable candidate. Mr. H. A. Keener says the republican element is for him.

§   Warwoman.
   Crops are looking quite[?] well, regardless of the drouth we are having.
   Mr. Marcus Bleckley and sister, (Miss Lena), have returned from the Valley where they have been going to school.
   A jolly party from Warwoman went fishing last night. They caught enough for one of the party to eat.
   Mr. and Mrs. Long, of South Carolina are visiting their daughter, Mrs. Joe Bleckley.
   Mr. and Mrs. L. H. Garland, of Macon, N. C. passed through this section last week going to Walhalla, S. C.
   The revenues of South Carolina raided in this section last week, but availed nothing.
   Rev. Curry delivered a very able sermon at Long Bottom church Sunday. There was quite an attentive crowd to hear him.
   Robt. Simmons has moved to Walhalla.
   Mr. Daniel Teems and family have mysteriously disappeared. Daniel come back and finish your crop.
   Mr. Eddie Norton, of Clayton, is visiting Lafayette Dockins.

§   There will be religious services held at the Black Rock on Black Rock mountain the fifth Sunday in July. Services will be conducted by Revs. J. A. Almond, Samuel Taylor and R. S. Saunders. Bring your lunch and let us have a glorious time. Services at 11 o'clock a. m. and 2 p. m.

<u>The Clayton Tribune, Volume 2, Number 22, Thursday, June 22, 1899</u>

§   County Directory: Judge Superior Court, John B. Estes. Solicitor General, W. A. Charters. Senator 47th Senatorial District, W. J. Green. Member of Legislature, R. E. A. Hamby. Ordinary, W. S. Long. Sheriff, J. R. Ritchie. Clerk Superior Court, J. S. Ramey. Tax Receiver, James C. York. Tax Collector, Joseph J. Dickerson. County Treasurer, W. E. Thompson. County Surveyor, W. E. Jones. Coroner, William Wheeler. Justice of the Peace, V. C. Kerby. Notary Public and Ex Justice, D. T. Duncan. County School Commissioner, W. J. Neville. Members Board of Education: M. W. Swofford, President, W. J. Green, Cicero Blalock, Z. B. Dillard and F. G. Holden.

§   Church Directory.
    Below are the appointments for the [illegible]:
    Clayton[?], first Sunday [illegible] 11 a. m., 2.30 p. m.
    Wesley Chapel, 2nd and 3rd Saturday and Sunday in each month, 11 a. m.
    Pine Mt., Fourth Sat. and Sun. in each month, 11 a. m.
    Antioch, First Sun. in each month 2.30 p. m., and Fifth Sat. and Sun., 11 a. m.
    All are cordially invited.
    Chas. W. Curry, P. C.

§   Clothes at close prices at Earl's. Be good and look good by getting a suit at Earl's.

§   The Tallulah Lodge opens for guests July 1st.

§   Mr. F. A. Bleckley is able to be up and visit the cuisine.

§   Miss Beulah Green spent yesterday afternoon in town.

§   Sheriff Ritchie made an official trip to the Falls Tuesday.

§   Applicants for teachers license are being examined today.

§   Mister Jimmie Reynolds has been quite sick for a few days.

§   Augustus Wall has been very sick but is now slightly improved.

§   Mr. Kirke Rhodes had the misfortune to lose one of his horses Tuesday.

§   A swarm of bees took leave of absence from Mr. Millard Marsongale Tuesday.

§   Miss May Ramey of Cornelia is visiting her brother, J. B. Ramey, this week.

§   Miss Liza Duncan has been very sick for some time but is improving a little.

§   If you want a saw mill located on your premises, write to F. H. Thomason, Alto, Ga.

§   Quite a number of our people attended Children's Day exercises at Rabun Gap last Saturday.

§   There will be Sunday school at the Methodist church at 9:30 o'clock next Sunday. All invited.

§   J. L. Sumpter, of Toccoa, Ga., in company with "Vig" Arrendale of Grove, was in Clayton last Saturday.

§   Nin Ramey said the boys told him wrong a year ago at the examination. Don't let them fool you to-day, Nin.

§   Misses Kate Bell and Bessie Strother and Mr. Jude Strother, of Walhalla, S. C., are visiting Miss Blanche Wall.

§   Burgstrom came up yesterday [illegible].

§   Thanks to Jessie Smith of Tiger, W. J. Neville of Rabun Gap, Mrs. M. E. Farmer of Betor, N. C. for their cash this week, to help hard times.

§   Mrs. M. L. Shirley is somewhat improved since our last issue, and her physicians state she will probably recover with care and prudence.

§   I am compelled to have what you owe me to pay what I owe by the first of July. Please don't come with a promies come with the cash; that is what I have to pay for goods. I can't live much longer on promises. Lizzie Duncan.

§   Mr. John A. Earl has sold his mercantile interest in Atlanta and is with home folks here. Mr. Earl has not decided just what he will do for a livelihood, but we hope he may see his way clear to remain in Clayton.

§   W. S. Whitmire has been up from Toccoa a few days visiting the noted Kell mica mine. It is being worked by S. S. Whitmire and he will be taking out the mica in a few days.

§   Mr. M. W. Swafford wants the public to understand that the North Chechero correspondent is mistaken in saying he has sheep-killing dogs. We will say for Mr. Swafford, that if his dogs kill sheep it is not because he has nothing to feed them.

§   Si Smith, the murderer of W. B. Bell was captured at the home of his father about noon last Monday, by a posse of men from Gainesville. Smith was carried to Clarkesville and is now in jail waiting trial at the September term of superior court. Since publishing the above we are reliably informed that Smith waived trial and was sent to Gainesville.

§   Uncle Pink Mosley, the boss cradler of this county is harvesting J. F. Earl's rye crop. Uncle Pink has lived about four score years and says he is going down the road of life, but some of the young men would be tired if they kept up with him with his cradle.

§   On last Thursday evening an interesting debate was held at the court house. The question discussed was: Resolved, that expansion is a wise political measure. The speakers were, Prof. A. A. O'Kelley, Hon. R. E. A. Hamby, Prof. L. M. Chastine, Garnett Williams, Luther York, F. D. Singleton, R. C. Ramey, J. M. Bleckley and Jackson Crunkleton.

§   Big Masonic Festival. Every Body Invited.
There will be a Masonic Festival under the auspices of Rabun Gap Lodge No. 265 F. & A. M., in the Masonic Hall at Clayton, Ga., on Saturday, June 24th 1899.
A number of eminent Masonic speakers, who will deliver addresses on that occasion, will be present.
We have already received the promise of Dr. Oslin and Ex-Senator J. E. Redwine, of Gainesville, Ga., to be present. Their addresses will be highly [illegible] entertaining.
[Program]... Prayer by A. P. Turpin; music by Choir led by G. H. King; Address by Ex-Senator J. E. Redwine, Gainesville, Ga.; Address [by] Dr. Oslin, Gainesville, Ga.; Prayer by Rev. Bro. R. L. Whitmire; Benediction by Rev. Bro. J[?]. M. Wall.
Every body is cordially invited and every Brother with his family belonging to Rabun Gap Lodge is especially requested to be present with a goodly supply of the necessities of life, such as [illegible], beans, potatoes and etc.
Fraternally Yours, R. E. A. Hamby, W. M. Rabun Gap Lodge No. 265 F. & A. M.

§   A goodly number of the teachers of the county are receiving instructions from Prof. O'Kelley this week. They are preparing for the examination. The following teachers are attending: Amanda Earl, Mary Bynum, Genela Bynum, Maybelle Coffee, Ina Coffee, Ada Green, Beulah Green, Dovie Williams, Ella Ramey, John Holden, J. M. Bleckley, W. F. Holden, Garnett Williams, Virgil Green, James Green, F. D. Singleton, J. M. Hopper, Oscar Powell, Claude Green, Thomas Hamby, Netherland Bynum, Jack Crunkleton.

§   W. J. McCurry's dog went mad at his home Tuesday and was shot by his brother I. A. McCurry. Fortunately no one was bitten except Mr. McCurry's little boy and the bite is so slight that no fears are entertained. About a month ago Marion Long killed a mad dog near town and it is supposed that his dog was bitten by it and it may be other dogs will go mad and receive the same fate.

§   Tallulah Falls
Tallulah is on a boom.
Some boarders are coming in this week.
They are getting rooms ready at the new hotel as fast as possible.
Henry F. Ramburn, a Methodist minister, preached a good sermon here Sunday.
We organized a new Sabbath School at the new hotel Sunday. All are invited.
There are a good many people camping around here now.

§   Upper Tiger

We are having good Sunday schools both at Bethel and Ivy Hill.

Messrs. Claude Green, Thad Bynum and Frank Singleton attended Sunday school. Mr. Singleton gave us a nice lecture which was appreciated by all who heard him.

Mr. R. E. Cannon and family visited the family of James E. Bleckley last Sunday.

James Kerby, who has been sick threatened with fever, is up circulating himself again.

Dr. W. J. Green passed by this place Tuesday enroute to Stonepile to see Mr. Andrew Watts who is threatened with fever.

V. C. Kerby will soon have the new addition of his house finished.

Mr. D. P. Lacount's four-year old child is very sick at present.

H. D. Dockins had a fine horse to get snake bitten last Sunday.

Willie Duncan visited the family of W. P. Price Sunday.

Mr. Charlie Oliver and William Holbrooks have sold out their stock of goods and moved to W. F. Roane's old place.

Uncle Charlie has been very sick for the past week but is convalescent.

Mrs. Rube Cheek has moved from M. L. Shirley's to her mothers on Tiger.

Claude Keener, what happened to you the last time you went fishing?

V. C. Kerby gave G. M. Oliver's boys a fine large horse a week or two ago.

§   Old Tiger

Mr. R. E. Cannon and wife spent the day with James E. Bleckley last Sunday.

Miss Ada and Ray Cannon visited relatives and friends on Tiger last week.

Miss Martha Jenkins spent the day with Miss Reed Bleckley last Sunday.

Mr. Andrew Watts is very sick this week.

Mrs. J. C. Green has been sick, but is improving now.

Mr. Harrison Roletter was with his best girl Sunday.

Miss Bessie Cannon, who has been spending some time with her grandparents, returned home yesterday.

Our Sunday School was [illegible] Mr. Nin Ramey and the other by Uncle Ned Shirley.

§   We learn from the Dover (Ky.) News that Hon. T. C. Dickinson, European Attorney and Financier of the Black Diamond Railway, sailed from London on the 10th inst. on the steamer New York, and will land in New York City Saturday or Sunday... He comes to perfect some necessary papers in the South which requires his personal attention, and to give what assistance he can in pushing the surveys now being mad[e] in South Carolina...

§   Ordinary's Citations.

Georgia—Rabun County. H. J. Ramey, having made applications to me in due form to be appointed permanent administrator upon the estate of James Dockins, late of said county, notice is hereby given that said application will be heard at the regular term of the court of ordinary for said county, to be held on the first Monday in July 1899. Witness my hand and official signature. This 30th day of May, 1899. W. S. Long, Ordinary.

§   Georgia—Rabun County. All persons interested are hereby notified that, if no good cause be shown to the contrary, an order will be granted by the undersigned on the 10th day of July, 1899, establishing a change on the road leading from Clayton to Tallulah Falls, as marked out by the road commissioners appointed for that purpose, said change commencing about 150 yards west of the upper ford of Tiger creek at the first branch, and running down the creek to the left of the old road, through the lands of Mrs. M. E. Farmer intersecting the old road near the residence of J. E. Bleckley. W. S. Long, Ordinary. This June 8th, 1899.

§   Rabun Sheriff Sales for July.
Will be sold at the court house in Clayton on the first Tuesday in July, within the legal hours of sale, the following property, to wit:
A tract of land in the second land district of Rabun County, it being part of lots 79 and 80, and bounded as follows: Commencing on a chestnut stump near Black's Creek; thence north with T. R. Fountain's line to top of knob; thence southeast with W. R. Pelfrey's line to the branch; thence up the branch to a line stump; thence northeast to the original line; thence north the original line to the corner; thence west the original to the top of the ridge; thence north the top of the ridge with T. R. Fountain' line to Black's creek, the beginning corner. The same being improved land. Levied on and to be sold as the property of W. I. Ledbetter by virtue of four fi fas each issued from the justice's court of 556th district of G. M. of Rabun county, one in favor of J. I. Langston, one in favor of J. C. Langston, one in favor of T. N. Carter & Co., and one in favor of J. F. Earl; all against said W. I. Ledbetter. Levies made and returned to me by J. H. Dillard, L. S[?].
Written notice given in terms of the law.
This June 5, 1899. J. R. Ritchie, Sheriff.

§   I want to buy old copper of every description. Will pay 3 cents per pound. J. L. Hamby.

§   Notice.
Beginning Monday June 26th for evening train, we will sell round trip tickets at one fare good returning any day until one week from date of sale, [illegible] July 9th account of the Gainesville Chataqua.
On morning of July 9th a train will be run to connect with the Bell train on the Southern Ry. Account of W. J. Bryan day.

§   Fletcher M. Johnson, Attorney at Law, Gainesville, Ga.

§   H. H. Dean, Attorney at Law, Gainesville, Ga.

§   W. S. Paris, Attorney at Law, Clayton, Ga. Will practice in all courts of Georgia. Office No. 4 Courthouse.

§   J. M. Wilkerson. Will repair your Watches, Clocks and Sewing Machines.

§   Go to W. B. Watts, two and one half miles West of [illegible] for lumber.

<u>The Clayton Tribune, Volume 2, Number 23, Thursday, June 29, 1899</u>

§   Sales day Tuesday.

§   Ordinary's court Monday.

§   Justices' court to-morrow.

§   Did you hear the lecture of Dr. Oslin?

§   Services at the Methodist Church Sunday.

§   Those suits at Earl's are real "nobby ones."

§   Miss May Ramey has returned to her home in Cornelia.

§   Dr. Henson is very sick at the residence of a Mr. Howell in North [Carolina].

§   You can get lumber on short notice from C. E. & W. R. Cannon, Tiger, Ga.

§   J. J. Wall, of Tiger was thrown from his horse last Friday and broke his collar bone.

§   If you have any rye straw for sale, confer with Taylor & Sweet, Tallulah Falls.

§   Mrs. J. C. Langston returned to her home in Walhalla to-day after a pleasant visit among relatives here.

§   Mr. Marvin Roane, of Atlanta, is spending this week with his parents Mr. and Mrs. W. F. Roane.

§   Mrs. R. A. Parker and Mrs. Turner Page are at the Langston Infirmary being treated by our local physicians.

§   Clerk J. S. Ramey moved to the country last Tuesday. We believe Spart will soon get tired of making the daily walk.

§   Thanks to Jesse W. Green, of Turnerville, John M. Moore, of Wolffork, Thos. J. Ritchie, of Dillard, for the $ $.

§   Mrs. Thomas Price, of the Valley, caught a red horse yesterday that weighed two and one half pounds and measured 19 inches in length.

§   We heard J. H. Coffee say that usually he gets done "laying by" corn by the fourth day of July, but as he got a late start it will take him until the fifth, this year.

§   Mr. W. C. Norton has a field of fine herds grass which will be ready for the mower in a few days.

§   The Rabun County Singing Convention will convene at Tallulah Academy on the first Friday in August next and continue until Sunday. President Gaston King hopes for a full representation from all the societies.

§   Mrs. M. L. Shirley has been making slight improvements for some days, though the road to recovery seems to have many breakers. Her condition yesterday, we were informed, was hardly so favorable as for a few days previous.

§   Mr. and Mrs. W. B. Freeman, of Athens, who have been the guests of the Wall House for the past month, expect to make a tour via Russell, S. C., Highlands, Franklin and other points of interest when they will return and spend the remainder of the summer here.

§   Dr. J. W. Oslin, of Gainesville, Ga., was the orator of the day at the Masonic Festival last Saturday. Dr. Oslin is well equipped for such occasions, having served the Grand Chapter of Royal Arch Masons of the state as grand high priest and has been worshipful master of subordinate lodges for thirty eight years. He spoke at the Baptist church which was filled to its utmost capacity with one of the most attentive congregations that ever convened in Clayton.

§   United States Deputies John Godfrey and Johnson passed through town Tuesday with Bartow Foster and Lester Blalock, of Persimmon, for violation of the United States Internal Revenue laws. These occurences are so frequent that you rarely hear any comment. Not only are these occurences frequent but such scenes have been witnessed for over a quarter of century...

§   Dillard.
    Mrs. Franks and three children of Franklin, are visiting Mrs. Lafayette Garland.
    Mr. and Mrs. Jesse Green, Mrs. Carrie Ayers and two children, of Turnerville, Ga., visited Mrs. B. R. Dillard last week.
    Miss Lillie Wall, of Clayton, visited Miss Zoe Godfrey last Saturday night.
    Claude Green was in the Valley last week.
    A. L. Dillard has gone to house keeping by himself. Look out, girls.
    Quite a crowd of our people at the festival at Clayton Saturday and report a nice time.
    Mr. and Mrs. Eugene Mozeley of Clayton visited her parents, Mr. and Mrs. Fuller, Saturday and Sunday.
    Luck Gibson has Typhoid fever.
    Mr. William Holbrooks, of Tiger visited his sister, Mrs. Emory Keener last Saturday.
    Mr. Dan Hoghed and wife, who have been in the Valley for some time, started for their home in Toccoa Tuesday.
    Mr. and Mrs. Emory Keener are spending this week in North Carolina.

Little Bessie Martin, the infant child of James Martin, died last Tuesday and was buried in the Baptist cemetery Wednesday evening.

§   Upper Warwoman
Little Howard Swafford has been real sick but is improving.
Misses Lula and Maud Holden and Mary Beck visited Josie Swafford Sunday.
Mr. Augustus Wall is just getting up after a spell of sickness.
Mr. S. M. Beck is in very feeble health now.
Eugene Swafford is suffering very much with sore eyes.
Jesse Green, of Turnerville, visited relatives on Warwoman last week.
Clint James, after a stay of three or four weeks among friends, returned to Walhalla last week.

§   Germany. Mr. W. S. Whitmire will begin a protracted meeting on Saturday before the 5th Sunday in July at the Baptist church at Mountain Grove.

§   Old Tiger
We were glad to have Mr. Harry Duncan and Miss May Ramey with us Sunday.
Mr. Clifton McCrackin is still on the sick list.
Mr. Dial D. Taylor was all smiles and sunshine with his ex-sweet heart Sunday.
We are glad to know that Mrs. Tom Williams is better.
Mrs. E. W. Morton has been real sick, but is improving.
There is to be an excursion from Atlanta to Tallulah Falls July 18th. J. Fred Cannon manager.

§   Below is the ordinance of the town governing tax payers. Read it and see if you have complied with the law. If you have not done so we are authorized to say you may save trouble by calling on J. C. Picket or J. I. Langston tax assessors...

§   Hon. T. C. Dickinson Here.
A telegram announces the safe arrival of Hon. T. C. Dickinson, financial agent of the Black Diamond Railway System, in New York last Saturday, as stated in the News he would... During the absence of Mr. Dickinson from London and while he is in this country waiting for the surveys in the South to be finished, Sir Thomas Tancreed is in Alaska on another inspection trip... –Dover News

§   All except eleven of the rights of way for the Black Diamond have been secured in this county and the agents are now working in Scott...—Cynthaniana Log Cabin.

§   We have never seen a more favored section in any country than here. To-day there stands corn all over the mountain sides, where it is in cultivation, over your head and as thick as it usually grows in the bottom lands. There is the best inducement to offer the emigrant we ever saw in any section or country. Cheap lands, so highly productive as the lands here, are not found in any other section where we have been, and we doubt if there are better opportunities for the man of moderate means in the United States. Many small tracts of land have not only the most productive soil, but it has the finest water that the earth can produce. It has a natural range for cattle, sheep and hogs, and has a natural money product—the chestnut tree.

There is scarcely a lot of land in Rabun county that does not contain a beautiful natural park. We say emphatically we never saw a section so favored naturally and we shall soon see an ingress of people here to help us enjoy this highly favored section.

§   Upper Tiger

There was a large attendance at preaching at Bethel Sunday. The church was badly crowded.

Mr. Jesse W. Green and family of Turnerville accompanied by his daughter, Mrs. Carrie Ayers, of Atlanta, passed by Monday on return to their homes.

We are glad to learn that D. P. Lacount's children are getting better.

Mr. Albert Lovell is having some nice work done on his dwelling house by the noted carpenter, Mr. George Donaldson.

Benton Cannon made a trip to Turnerville Monday.

Mr. Kimsey Pitts and wife visited the Polly house last Saturday and Sunday.

We are informed that Mr. Franklin, from Habersham, who taught a singing convention at Liberty last summer, is contemplating teaching a singing school at Bethel in a week or two.

We wonder what young man has gone to see his best girl, who lives two and one half miles from Clayton, every Sunday this summer and last Sunday she failed to talk to him because she was not there. He says he has a crop of every thing planted but goobers and he expects to plan a crop of them this fall.

Messrs. Jno. and Will McKay were up from the Falls visiting their folks Sunday.

§   Notice. We will pay highest market price for rye straw, either in trade or cash. Taylor and Sweet, Tallulah Falls, Ga.

§   Warwoman

Lee Blackwell while chopping wood Monday received a severe injury by a piece of wood striking him on the left eye.

Mrs. Fred Bowers has been seriously ill, but is recovering slowly.

Mr. S. L. Bleckley and family will start in a few days for Demorest.

Dan Teams[?] has moved [illegible] to Clarkesville[?].

§   Annual settlement between W. E. Thompson, County Treasurer and W. S. Long, Ordinary. June 20th 1899...

The Clayton Tribune, Volume 2, Number 24, Thursday, July 6, 1899

§   Harry Duncan took in the fourth at[?] Clarkesville.

§   Services at the Methodist church Sunday evening.

§   J. L. Hamby returned from Pine Mountain yesterday.

§   Col. And Mrs. Hamby visited Mr. Cadwell Hamby the first of the week.

§   Mr. Jessie Coffee, of Atlanta, is spending this week with home folks.

§   Friend W. D. Burch was here this week talking hardware and temperance.

§   Captain S. M. Beck has about 20 acres of land in herds grass now ready for the mowers.

§   Miss Georgia Donaldson, of Atlanta, is up on a visit to Mr. and Mrs. W. C. Donaldson.

§   Miss Manda Earl is spending a few days with her sister, Mrs. Langston, in Walhalla.

§   Misses Ruby and Bonnie Paris [illegible] their little friend, Mary Green[?] in Chechero [illegible].

§   Miss Nannie[?] Oliver, who has been visiting friends in North Carolina, returned home Sunday.

§   Misses Ida and Effie Duncan have returned from Clarkesville. They witnessed the celebration of the fourth.

§   Drummer Barnett and wife of Atlanta spent a few days with the latter's aunt, Mrs. Dover, this week.

§   Professor J. C. Howard is spending this week with his friends and scholars around Eppes.—Clarkesville Advertiser.

§   Misses Kate Bell and Bessie Strother, after a very pleasant visit to friends and relatives here, returned to their home in Walhalla last Tuesday.

§   Mrs. M. L. Shirley has made no material change since our last issue. Her physicians entertain hope for her recovery though as before the process is slow.

§   Commissioner W. J. Neville will be in his office in Clayton on Saturday, the 8th day of July, for the purpose of making contracts with the public school teachers of the county.

§   Mrs. Thurza Kerby, of Tiger, has spent the week in town the guest of Mrs. Dover. Mrs. Kerby has had a very painful ankle the result of a sprain, but is very much improved.

§   We heard John Godfrey say that he had been down to the "Bob" place and captured a large still riveted with iron brads, and that there were enough chicken feathers to make a feather bed in the still house.

§   Teachers will be paid on average attendance as follows: First grade to be paid 4 ½ cents per day; second grade 4 cents per day; third grade 3 ½ cents. Schools averaging less than twenty will be paid 4 ½ per day, regardless of grade.

§   On return of the Bald Mountain party last week, Mr. W. J. Neville, Jr., received a letter from home informing him that his father, Capt. Wm. J. Neville was dangerously ill. Will left Friday morning for his home at Walhalla, S. C.—Franklin Press

§   Mr. W. H. Greenwood sold out his interest in the drug store last week to Mr. Frank T. Smith who will continue the business at the old stand. Mr. Greenwood will go into business in Rabun county, Ga. he and his brother having bought out the mercantile business of Lee Ritchie.—Franklin Press

§   We learn from the Keowee Courier that Capt. William James Neville died at his home in Walhalla on Sunday morning, June 25th, 1899, at 5.20 o'clock, after a lingering illness from paralysis. His funeral services were conducted at the residence Monday morning and his body interred in the cemetery of the Baptist church.

§   Mr. A. J. Ritchie arrived home last week, crowned with diplomas from Harvard and our own honored State University at Athens. He comes home with honors from both schools. His brother, W. R. Ritchie, will graduate next year. He will remain in Athens this summer, having been given a position by the faculty until the opening of the next [illegible].

§   Sheriff Ritchie is over in Towns county after some offenders.

§   Miss Susie Long has been visiting her grandparents this week.

§   Mr. and Mrs. Everett Earl are spending this week with Mr. J. F. Earl.

§   We are informed that Mrs. John Butts, living four miles from Clarkesville, committed suicide by hanging herself last Saturday morning.

§   We have received a copy of the History and Conquest of the Philippines and our other island possessions, through agent E. F. Blalock and we are delighted with it.

§   At the recent examination held here, James Green, aged sixteen years, son of John W. Green, was given first grade license by the Board of Education. He made the highest per cent out of about thirty applicants. James is an exceedingly bright boy and some of the boys in this community should emulate him. We predict for "Jim" a bright future.

§   Mrs. Emiline Smith, wife of G. V. Smith, happened to a painful accident last Friday night about 8 clock. She and her husband reside on Wolfcreek and were on their way to Clayton, after crossing Scotch's Creek on a log and getting on a rock pile built to attach a water rack which is up a few feet above the ground, not being acquainted with the surroundings, she walked off and broke her arm in three places and dislocated it in four. She was brought to Mrs. W. C. Donaldson's and is doing well under treatment of local physicians.

§   From the Southern Record. Mr. Whitmire and wife of Rabun county, parents of Mr. W. S. Whitmire of Toccoa, are the guests of the latter on Bruce's Hights.

§   Bridge Creek
   Too late for last week.
   Martin and Frank Arrendale and James Crawford went to Clayton last week. James Crawford went to be examined by Drs. Green and Dover for pension disability contracted in Uncle Sam's army during the late civil war, as they have been appointed by the authorities at the capital for that purpose. This is the first examined the U. S. authorities have ever made in this county and James Crawford, we are informed, was the only officer Uncle Sam ever had during the civil war from Rabun county. He says he cannot speak too highly for the doctors for the kind treatment they gave him at the examination.
   We had a fine sermon preached at Rocky Grove Baptist church last Sunday by E. H. Baker.
   Mr. Logan Hunter and Miss Mary Arrendale, from Tiger, were at church Sunday.
   We think the girls ought to look after Billy Baker as he is one of the best boys on Bridge Creek.
   J. M. Arrendale, James Crawford and a lot of girls went fishing Friday.
   Mr. John Arrendale is going to teach the public school on Bridge Creek this year. He is one of the best voting men in this community.
   Mr. Lacounte's family is improving.

§   North Chechero
   Too late for last week.
   But few apples in this section.
   F. D. Price killed a large rattlesnake last week.
   We have two good Sunday schools at Chechero now. All are invited who will come sober.
   Mr. A. M. Williams, who has been sick for six weeks with grip, is improving some.
   M. L. Carver is quite sick at present.
   Miss Ada Green spent short time with us Monday.

§   Persimmon
   We are sorry to report the health of our community not so good as it was when last reported.
   John Moore, one of our young men, died last Friday and was buried Saturday. John was a good boy and we miss his presence in Sunday school and everywhere, but we trust his departure from us will be the means of many others turning to God.
   There is but little hope of Mrs. Albert Parker living.
   We were glad to see the old man James fill his seat in the Baptist church Saturday. He has not been able for some time to attend church.
   Miss Fannie Littleton has gone to Gaston King's to make her home awhile.

Mrs. M. V. York has returned home from Cornelia.

§   Below are the names of the applicants for teachers license and grades obtained at the recent examination: First grade: A. A. O'Kelly, James Green, Claude Green, Manda Earl, C. J. Crunkleton. Second grade: F. D. Singleton, J. M. Bleckley, R. N. Dover, Virgil Green, Ada Green, Bulah Green, Maybelle Coffee, Oscar Powell, Luther York, John Holden, W. F. Holden, Lena Bleckley, Paul Kimsey, Nin Ramey, Garnett Williams. Third grade: J. M. Hopper, Mary Bynum, Genela Bynum, Lillie Kimsey, Ina Coffee.

§   Rabun Gap
The farmers are as busy as bees trying to get done laying by corn.
The writer was on Persimmon last week and drank water 400 feet under the ground. It was in the tunnel at the mine.
Mrs. Curry, who has been visiting her son, Chas. W. Curry, left for her home Tuesday morning. She and her little daughter spent several days with us.
We had a good singing at the Baptist church Sunday.
Messrs. Andy and Will Ritchie are at home[?] on a visit. We are glad to see the boys.
Mr. Editor. You must hurry up the Black Diamond hands[.] We are nearly ready to go to work.

§   Tallulah Falls
We have had a fine week to work.
The new hotel will soon be finished. They are receiving guests now.
We had a good Sunday School Sunday.
Rev. Hughs preached a good sermon here Sunday. He expects to begin a protracted meeting on the first Sunday in August.
Mr. Harvey Hunnicutt was down [illegible] town the other day with a new [illegible].

§   The Franklin Press announced the opening of the dispensary at Franklin, N. C. in the following language:
Be it known that on Tuesday morning June 27th 1899, at 9.28 ½ o'clock, the dispensary was opened in Franklin, by W. R. Stallcup, manager.

§   We are now informed that John Earl will furnish the five dollars mentioned in the Tribune some time ago for the largest watermelon grown in Rabun county. It must be weighed and sworn to before our ordinary, W. S. Long and he will keep a record of all melons. There must be one reliable witness besides the grower for each melon brought in. Save your seeds from the best melons you will want them next year.

§   Wolf Creek
Crops are doing fine.
Mr. Oscar Powel, of the Valley, spent last Sunday and Monday with friends here.
Quite a crown went to Tiger last Sunday.
Miss Rachel Williams visited friends and relatives on Chechero last week.

Mr. Albert Cannon is suffering from the effects of a boil on his arm.

Several of the boys went to Tallulah Falls last week to commence work at the new hotel.

§   Wolffork

Some people are laying by their corn.

Several of the boys went to Nantahala Mt. this week.

Mr. M. L. Dickerson has gone to Clarkesville this week.

Mrs. Lafayette and Mrs. W. A. Keener are still on the sick list.

Uncle Ralph Keener is still able to carry a bushel of corn to mill, and Mr. Manly Johnson, who is in his ninetieth year, can still read without specks.

Mr. Reese Carter and Mr. Charlie Ritchie caught a wild cat Wednesday. While trying to shake the cat from the tree Mr. Parker fell and broke his leg. We hope he will nurse his leg patiently and soon be able to shake another one out.

§   An Entire Family Poisoned. From the Banks County Journal.

The family of Jack Andrews, consisting of himself, wife and seven children, was poisoned Sunday... Dr. Lothridge was summoned early Sunday afternoon, but it was too late to relieve the two that died...

§   Warwoman

We are having fine weather for farming.

A crowd of young people went fishing yesterday.

Mrs. Reever is seriously ill at present.

The friends of Miss Fanie Holden were glad to have her and her cousin with them Sunday.

Mr. Jeff Swofford and family visited the family of Mr. Fred Powers Saturday.

We are sorry to hear of the illness of Mrs. John Howard. Hope she is better ere this.

Jack McCall found a bee tree last week containing five gallons of pure honey.

The teachers on this side seem to be like Nin. Think some one told them wrong.

Mr. J. D. Hunter[?] is having his house furnished.

Mr. Sam Bowers has gone to Sapphire N. C.

There will be a baptizing at Mill Creek next Sunday.

Mr. W. C. Speed is improving.

§   Germany

Crops are looking fine.

Mr. Evans preached an interesting sermon here Sunday.

Mr. Gibralter York visited friends here Sunday.

Mr. and Mrs. Charlie Rogers spent Saturday night with Dock Justus.

Marvin and Grover Powell and Damascus Almond went to the Nantahala Mt. last week and report a good time.

Mr. and Mrs. Burnett passed through here Saturday on their way to Clayton.

Mr. L. M. Crane and Kerm Williams were in Jermany Sunday.

Mr. Virgil Green will commence his school the 17th. We hope he will have a good school.

§   Upper Tiger

Quite a crowd of young people attended the darkeys' meeting last Sunday.

Jno. Laprade of Burton, visited Walter and Jim Kerby Sunday.

Mr. [illegible] Wall and wife passed by Monday [illegible] from a visit to relatives and friends in Habersham.

We are glad to learn that Dr. Henson is going to have his house finished at this place.

Mr. Hill Williams passed by Tuesday enroute to Clayton.

W. J. McCrackin caught a fine mud turtle in a steel trap a few days ago.

Uncle Charlie Smith's family is on the sick list.

The Clayton Tribune, Volume 2, Number 25, Thursday, July 13, 1899

§   City Directory: J. L. Henson, Mayor. Councilmen: W. C. Donaldson, T. J. Coffee, J. A. Reynolds. Marshall G. M. Oliver. Regular meetings, first Tuesday.

§   A. J. Ritchie left for Atlanta yesterday.

§   J. I. Langston returned from a trip to Highlands yesterday.

§   Mr. John A. Earl is off on a business trip to Atlanta.

§   Quite a number of our citizens went to the Falls yesterday.

§   Mr. J. R. Godfrey, of Porter Mills, was in Clayton Friday.

§   J. F. Earl has made a large order for odd pants of extra lengths and assorted sizes.

§   Mr. A. J. Duncan brought to town today the first watermelon of the season, 16 ½ pounds.

§   J. B. McCrackin, of Clemson College, S. C., was in town yesterday shaking hands with friends.

§   A distinguished party of young ladies were the guests of Mr. and Mrs. A. J. Duncan, of Chechero.

§   Mr. Jesse Coffee, after a pleasant visit to home folks, returned to his home in Atlanta Wednesday.

§   There was no Justices' court held here last Friday, owing to the severe sickness of D. T. Duncan, Esq.

§   Walter Paris and Edgar Estes, of St. Augustine, Fla., and L. P. Mille, of Ocee, Ga., are the guests of Col. Paris.

§   We are delighted to see Mr. J. C. Picket running his mowing machine Monday. He mowed several acres of grass for W. C. Norton.

§   Mr. M. W. Swofford killed a white crane at his home on Chechero last Monday that measured 3 feet 2 inches from tip to tip and nearly 3 feet high.

§   Rev. A. J. Sears, of Lincolnton, Ga., spent a few days here the pat week. Mr. Sears was pastor here some years ago and has many friends and was warmly greeted by them.

§   J. F. Earl sold six suits of cloths last Saturday and one of our popular young men in town purchased a fine suit Monday...

§   We have three hundred dollars worth of lumber for sell which we will sell for cash, produce or your note and give you fifteen months time. Anyone wishing to purchase will please call at once on C. E. & W. R. Cannon, Tiger, Ga.

§   Sheriff Ritchie arrested Earnest Meece, six miles east of Blairsville, Union county, yesterday and lodged him in jail here. He is charged with burning benches and doing other mischief to a church on Dick's creek in this county.

§   Mrs. Shirley's condition is not materially changed since our last issue. Naturally from her prolonged confinement she is in a very weakened condition, and if there be no more breakers, it will require some time for her to regain her wonted[?] strength.

§   J. J. Strickland, Esq., of Athens, was honored with the election to the vice presidency of the Georgia Bar Association which was recently held at Warm Springs, Ga. Mr. Strickland, by his indomitable energy, has worked himself to the top round of the ladder in his profession.

§   Rev. Chas. Curry and Asberry Keener started Monday for the Conference at Dahlonega. A short distance below Tiger, Rev. Curry's horse was stung by a hornet or wasp and made a dash into the woods and damaged the buggy and bruised the boys considerably. They withed up the buggy and proceeded to the conference.

§   Sheriff Roane, of Macon County, N. C. and Dept. Sheriff J. H. Lewis, of Jackson county N. C., accompanied by H. L. Ramey of this county, captured Robert and Reuben Frady at the Berry Beck homestead on Warwoman last Thursday. The Fradys are wanted for the murder of Tylor Buchannon, of Jackson county N. C. The murder was, according to reports, a cold blooded one.

§   The Board of Education met last Tuesday for the purpose of investing charges against Miss Sibbie Bynum for cruel treatment during a school she taught at Ivy Hill last summer. L. C. Hollifield, Jr., was the prosecutor. Mr. Hollifield alleged that his child was unmercifully and unlawfully whipped by Miss Bynum. The Board listened patiently to the evidence and decided in favor of Miss Bynum.

§ Arrivals at the Blue Ridge Hotel for the past week: James Church, Dawsonville, N. J. Kelly and wife, Winder, C. T. Roane, Carl Crisp and G. N. McGee, of Franklin, N. C., J. H. Lewis, Dillsboro, N. C., John A. Wilson, county [*sic*], Boone Crawford, Gainesville, C. L. Vigal, L. D. Ewing, Clyde King and Chas. H. Tolbert, of Atlanta, W. D. Burch and L. D. Kinsey, of Cornelia, J. I. Woodall, Tallulah Falls, W. J. Kilby, Winston, N. C., Chas. McHan, Chattanooga, Tenn.

§ Bridge Creek

The farmers are all about done.

A large crowd from here went fishing Saturday.

W. B. Watts and Rush Dixon, of Tiger, were on Bridge Creek Sunday.

James Crawford went to Tiger last Monday.

M. L. Arrendale and wife went to Flat Creek Saturday and returned Sunday.

W. P. Nix returned home Saturday. He has been to the Falls working on the new hotel.

M. L. Arrendale says his fields are getting full of corn now instead of weeds.

Miss Lou Arrendale of Burton visited relatives on Bridge Creek Sunday.

John V. Arrendale will begin his school next Monday. We think he will have a large attendance.

§ Three Forks

Plenty of rain and every body says that they have the best corn crop this year they have had in years.

Jess Burrell and Thomas Wall went for a load of corn yesterday and came back in the afternoon without either corn or wagon. Suppose they had a break down.

We are glad J. M. Hopper is going to teach school again this year.

Meeting at Hale Ridge next Sunday.

§ North Chechero

The farmers are about through their work.

Our school will begin next Monday.

M. L. Carver is improving some.

A. R. Williams killed a pilot snake in his yard Sunday.

B. E. Ramey went to Mountain Rest last week.

Mrs. James Bell is improving some.

D. S. Williams found a bee tree last week.

Quite a crowd at preaching here Sunday.

Mr. Jesse Coffee is up on a visit to home folks.

Mr. Willie Duncan has gone to Atlanta.

§ Vandiver

Mr. John Bell McCrackin, Sargent of Guards of Convict Camps at Clemson College, S. C., is visiting his brother Clifton, who has typhoid fever. Mr. McCrackin has many friends here who are glad to see him.

Crops are looking well.

H. D. McCrackin and wife, of Cornelia, are visiting around here.

We had a delightful rain yesterday.

§   Wolffork

We had a good rain Thursday, it was much needed.

Meeting at Pleasant Grove today.

Mrs. Rufus Keener is visiting her son A. M. Keener.

Lafayete Keener had a corn hoeing this evening.

Luther Dickerson is making a table like he is going to house keeping. Lookout girls.

Mrs. E. A. Moore has been sick for a week but is improving.

Mr. Editor, tell us what has gone with Uncle Billy.

§   "Uncle Billy Smith is very sick at this writing," was the way the rural correspondent put it. "I am not surprise[d]," said the printer who set up the copy, "this writing is enough to make anyone sick."

§   Upper Tiger

We are having a very flourishing singing school at Bethel this week conducted by Mr. Franklin from Habersham.

Emory Blalock, of Burton, was with us Monday canvassing and delivering histories of the present war.

Will Hunter, who has been waiting on Mrs. Moses Shirley as nurse, is suffering very much with rheumatism.

Walter Rembert, who has been absent for some time in the west, has returned and is looking well.

Quite a crowd attended church at Ivy Hill Sunday.

Messrs. Henry Cannon and Bud Sington are off on a business trip to Toccoa.

We are informed that Jesse Dockins and Clifton McCrackin, who have fever, are improving.

§   All who owe me anything on notes or account which is due in this month or next had better look after them when due, for I will put them out for collection three days after. Don't fail to remember this. Your friend, S. S. Whitmire.

§   W. T. Daniel who is a graduate of Roanoke College, Roanoke, Ala., Moore's Business College, Atlanta, Ga., Peabody Normal College and the University of Nashville, Nashville, Tenn., has accepted Clayton school for the public term. He has had twelve years experience as a teacher, and comes to us highly recommended.

§   Rabun County Teacher's Association.

The public teachers of this county met on the 8th inst. for the purpose of organizing a Teachers' Association. On motion, Prof. A. A. O'Kelly was elected president and Chas. J. Crunkleton secretary.

Hon. R. E. A. Hamby addressed the audience.

On motion Hon. R. E. A. Hamby, Martin Chastain and Virgil McCrackin were appointed as a committee to draft by-laws and constitution for the regulation of the Association. Also to meet on the last Saturday in July and after this to the first Saturday in each month, in Clayton at 10 o'clock a. m. sharp.

C. J. Crunkleton, R. N. Dover and Garnett Williams were appointed a committee to see the editor of the Tribune asking him to give to the Teachers Association a column in his paper for the benefit of the association.

On motion the association adjourned until the last Saturday in July.

A. A. O'Kelly, Pres.

C. J. Crunkleton, Sec.

The program of the association will be given in the next issue of the Tribune.

§   Old Tiger

Rev. Harris preached at Eden church Sunday.

Andrew Watts died with typhoid fever a few days ago near the late residence of James Dockins and was buried at the Dockins' grave yard.

Two cases of fever in this section, Clifton McCrackin and Jesse Docikns.

We expect James Franklin to open a singing school at Tiger church July 17. Mr. Franklin is a popular singing teacher in this section of the county. He puts life into his schools.

Dr. W. J. Green is often seen in this part of the county, as he has several patients here just now.

Robert Denny and wife visited friends in Stonepile last Sunday.

Mr. Willard Taylor is teaching school near Jassieth bridge in Habersham county.

I. J. H. Hunnicutt was seen here Sunday. He wears his new suit at Tiger as well as at Tallulah. Honey looks like he is just sixteen.

Bart Stonecypher went to the Falls.

Walter Taylor has returned home.

J. B. McCrcakin, of Clemson College, South Carolina, and H. D. McCrackin, from Cornelia, are at their old home with their sick brother Clifton.

§   County To Be Divided Into School Districts.

The Board of Education passed an order last Tuesday to divide the county into school districts. The plan of districting the county is as follows:

One member of the board with the district trustees will define the lines. Dr. Green and trustees will [district] Clayton; M. W. Swafford and trustees, Chechero and Tiger; F. G. Holden and trustees, Moccasin and Warwoman (Moccasin has been divided); Cicero Blalock and trustees, Stonepile and Tallulah; Z. B. Dillard and trustees, Valley and Persimmon.

This committee is to have the work done by the first Tuesday in October next, and goes into effect [*Note: Paper torn here*].

§   When you want caskets or coffins call on S. W. Dover.

§   Condition of Georgia Crops. Comprehensive Analysis by Commissioner Stevens Showing by Carefully Compiled Figures Condition of Crops by Counties For Month of May... [*Note: Chart showing each county's production.*]

The Clayton Tribune, Volume 2, Number 27, Thursday, July 27, 1899

§   A New Railroad To Run From Knoxville To Port Royal.

The North Georgia Railroad Company, which was incorporated in 1890, is about to take a new lease on life, change its name and organize a system of lines connecting Knoxville, Tenn., with Port Royal, S. C...

The new company will be known as the Ohio, Knoxville and Port Royal Railway Company and one of the objects of the organization will be to connect Columbus, O., with Port Royal and the south Atlantic seaboard...

I. L. Tribble[?], secretary of the board of directors of the North Georgia Railway Company, called at the department of the secretary of state yesterday morning to file the petition for the amendments, but declined to give out any further information regarding the plans and purposes of the new road...

The president of the North Georgia Railway Company is P. K. McCully and the following were named as incorporators at the time charter was granted in 1890: C. D. Smith, William Scruggs, John McFall[?], Mark A. Hardin, W. C. Candler, W. J. Kirk, William R. McConnell, E. B. Murray, W. F. Parker, A. Trufuerman, J. E. Brazeale, P. K. McCully and A. Means.

§   Chamberlain's Cough Remedy... For sale by J. L. Hamby.

§   Grand and Traverse Jurors Drawn for August Term 1899.

Traverse Jurors: Rolin L. Whitmire, Julius M. Carver, Alexander Roane, Thomas J. Ritchie, Joseph M. Watts, James W. Derrick, Wm. T. Smith, David Garland, John B. Kell, John B. Jones, Joseph E. Beard, Geo. J. Hix, Wm. B. Watts, Ethel D. Swofford, John A. Reynolds, Wm. B. Parker, John Speed, Robert N. Dover, John Darnell, Geo. W. Eliot, Ephraim H. Williams, James Z. Hopper, John Nix, Monroe Turpin, John F. Ritchie, John W. Watts, Abel R. Williams, Jesse R. Jones, Tillman Ramey, Jonathon C. Ford, Major L. Scruggs, Jesse E. Singleton, John H. Collins, John C. Howard, James E. Bleckley, Drew Turpin.

Grand Jurors: Julius F. Thompson, Wm. R. L. Ritchie, John Talley, Jr., Marcus K. Allen, Wm. J. Ramey, Virgil M. Lovell, Sandy B. Wilbanks, John W. Green, E. N. Holden, James A. Wilson, Columbus F. Garland, Frazier A. Taylor, Horace R. Cannon, Willis A. Carver, Ransom G. Smith, Jno. L. Hamby, Thomas G. Winchester, Peter E. Thompson, Hiram A. Keener, Samuel Taylor, Sr., Marion H. James, Drew M. Green, Alford E. Dickerson, Allen S. Williams, James A. Turpen, Daniel Kell, Joseph L. Watts, James H. Shed, Thomas M. Wood.

§   Below is an extract from an editorial from the Gainesville Eagle in reference to the murder of [?]. S. Smith in Hall county jail...

Another thing which the sheriff should have done and which he did not do was to immediately notify Bud Smith, chief of police, who has a pack of bloodhounds who is a lightning calculator in catching criminals...

§   Georgia State Horticultural Society.

We are requested to publish the following letter: Augusta, Ga., July 18th, 1899. Mr. Davis, Cliff House, Tallulah Falls, Ga.

Dear sir: There will be fully 200 delegates to the meeting of this society at Tallulah, Aug. 2nd and 3rd, possibly the number will go to 225, a number of ladies in the delegation...

The society will send up a representative, Mr. Jas. Summers, July 31st who will make all arrangements as to halls for the meetings and exhibits...

I am, Very truly, L. A. Berckmans[?].

§   The Tragedy in Hall County Jail.

On Friday night, the fourteenth instant, a most uncalled-for and atrocious crime was committed in Hall county jail. It was the brutal killing of "Si" Smith by an unknown [?] mob...

In fact with the "peculiar" case with which the horrible work was done, it must have been accomplished by some of Sheriff Mundy's neighbors...

We doubted the wisdom of Judge Estes' action in ordering Smith to Gainesville jail at the time when it was done, and there is no one who doubts it now. Smith Would have been much safer at Clarksville or Clayton than at Gainesville. Feeling as we did at the time about the unwise step of removing Smith to Hall county jail instead of allowing the Sheriff of Habersham county to take charge of him, we greatly appreciated the sentiments of Col. George P. Erwin's letter, when he wrote his Honor advising against this course and saving that Smith had some rights in the matter...thank God, the law abiding element of old Rabun has alway prevented such a disgraceful affair as a lynching [at the jail]...

§   J. D. Hester[?], Pine Mountain. A nice stock of General Merchandise. When around Pine Mountain give us a call and save money.

§   J. M. York is still in the ring with a lot of Staple and Fancy Groceries Consisting of Flour, Oil, Candy, Canned Goods and other things as cheap as can be found. Call on him at Clayton, Ga.

§   The Blue Ridge Hotel. A lovely home for the commercial traveler. Table furnished with the best the market affords. Patronage Solicited.

§   Petition for Charter.

State of Georgia, Fanin County.

To the Hon. Phillip Cook, Secretary of State. The petition of C. J. Welborne, Jr., W. E. Candler, E. G. Welborne, of the county of Union; W. R. McConnell, John H. Davis, T. J. Hooper, O. C. Wyly and W. B. Pass, of the county of Towns; B. S. Holden, Leonard Higdon, of the county of Fannin, and Thomas F. Greer of the county of Gilmer and said State; and A. A. Cambell of the county of Cherokee and State of North Carolina, and Vauix[?] Gibbs, Nash H. Bart, W. L. Albright, of the county of Hamilton and State Tennessee respectfully shows:

1st – That they desire to form a railroad corporation pursuant to the laws of the State of Georgia.

2nd. – The name of the railroad company, for which petitioners this week incorporation is to be The Missing Link Railroad Company, the same not being the name of any existing railway corporation in the State of Georgia...

4th. – Said railroad to be constructed from a point on the Tennessee State Line in Catoosa county, Ga. near Chattanooga, Tennessee, to a point on the South [Carolina] line in the county of Rabun, in the State of Georgia near Walhalla, in the State of South Carolina, and to be constructed through the counties of Catoosa, Whitfield, Murray, Fannin, Union, Towns and Rabun, in said State of Georgia...

Wherefore they pray to be incorporated under the laws of this State.

Thomas F. Greer, Atty. for Petitioners.

Names of Petitioners: W. R. McConnell, John H. Davis, T. J. Hooper, O. C. Wyly, W. L. Albright, W. B. Pass, C. J. Welborn, Jr., W. E. Candler, E. C. Welborn, Thomas F. Greer, D. S. Holden, Leonard Higdon, Nash H. Burt, A. A. Campbell, Vauix Gibbs.

§   Bridge Creek

Good rains and crops are looking fine.

Elisha Carnes has returned from N. C.

A. J. Meece is very sick this week.

T. F. Arrendale and J. E. Beard carried two loads of fine rye straw to the Falls last week.

Jerry Burton and wife are visiting relatives in Gordon county this week.

Rev. E. H. Baker is successfully carrying on a protracted meeting at Rocky Grove this week.

The Sunday School here is booming.

§   Teachers Association Saturday.

§   G. V. Garrett is painting the town[?] red.

§   Superior Court will soon be here[?].

§   Mr. W. C. Norton is on the sick list[?].

§   [Illegible] Henson has returned from Clarkesville.

§   Mr. John A. Earl has returned from[?] Atlanta.

§   [Mrs.] Shirley is very much improved since Sunday.

§   [Illegible] Grady Langston has returned from Walhalla.

§   Marshall G. B. Dockens, of Tallulah Falls, was in town yesterday.

§   [Mr.] and Mrs. R. A. Whitmire [illegible] returned from a visit to [?]klin, Co.

§   [Missing] North Georgia Railroad is, [missing] reliably informed, the [missing] Diamond, in reality.

§   [Missing] B. Bleckley, of Anderson, S. [missing] in old Rabun for a week.

§   [Missing] you "Ben" for the wheel.

§   [Missing] Lucy Watts, who is stopping [missing] L. C. Hollifield's and be-[missing] by our physicians, is [missing].

§   Earnest Young, of Lavonia, left for his home yesterday after spending several days pleasantly in town.

§   Will Lee, colored, killed a coach whip snake seven feet long near the residence of J. C. Singleton's Sunday.

§   Our thanks are due Mrs. Emily Adams, of Highlands for a number of paid subscriptions to her North Carolina friends.

§   There will be religous services conducted by Rev. J. W. Hughes at Lipscomb church Sunday at 11 o'clock.

§   Messrs. Sandy Cunningham, E. M. Mitchel and Master Arthur Robinson have returned to their homes in Atlanta.

§   Mr. Fletcher Hughes, son of Rev. J. W. Hughes, of Novetta, Ga., will remain here with his father for several weeks.

§   Judge Logan E. Bleckley is visiting relatives...in the county. This is his native heath[?] and is alway welcomed by our people.

§   Mrs. Ada Martin, of Dixon, Ga., and Messrs. Dock and Pat Isbell, of Fairplay, S. C., have been the guests of Mr. and Mrs. J. I. Langston for the past few days.

§   Mr. Bry F. Phillips, of Chechero, was here Saturday and sold a drove of sheep to T. J. Ritchie. Mr. Phillips is one of those men that usually has something to sell.

§   Mr. and Mrs. Claud Estes and their four bright children have been the merry guests of the Blue Ridge for several days the past week. They leave for Franklin, N. C., today.

§   The Georgia State Horticultural society will be held at Tallulah Falls, Ga., August second and third next, and it is expected a large crowd will attend. Read L. A. Berkman's letter to Mr. Davis, in another column.

§   We are informed the small pox, the real genuine stuff, has broken out in White county near Cleveland, Ga. We are informed by private parties that Cornelia has quarantined, and trains are not allowed to stop there, at present.

§   Our thanks are due Mr. R. J. S. Dickson for some nice cabbage heads. One of them we consider a freak of nature, as it had, besides a main head, seven small ones that grew from the stalk growing out just above the stems of the leaf.

§   An attempt was made to burn W. C. Donaldson's wood shop last Monday night. The fire had gained considerable headway and had it not been discovered at the time Mr. Donaldson would have lost his entire layout of tools, lumber and wagon material. The parties who set it are not known.

§   Our entire community was shocked last Friday when it was known that Mr. M. L. Shirley's house was destroyed by fire. It caught about noon from a stove flew. The loss to Mr. Shirley is over one thousand dollars. No insurance. It is generally known that Mr. Shirley is confined in jail here which makes the unfortunate affair bear heavily on him. Most all valuables in the house were saved.

§   G. W. Donaldson is engaged building a nice residence for J. M. Wilkerson at the Wilkerson Mineral springs two miles southwest of town. These springs have been of local note for over half a century. Several analysis have been made of these springs and they contain valuable healing properties. Col. Kelsey, who built Highlands, N. C., negotiated for this property, but there was some hitch in the deal and failed of consummation. These springs are located on a lofty peak and will no doubt command the attention of capital in the future.

§   The following are registered at the Blue Ridge Hotel: W. C. Colwell, A. N. Robinson, Eugene Mitchel and A. M. Cunningham, of Atlanta, J. B. Johnson and J. W. Holmes, of Hiwasse, C. D. Stark, W. F. Stark, E. C. Stark, L. P. Shankle, L. L. Davis and J. D. Yarbrough, of Harmony Grove, W. V. Garrett, of Franklin, N. C., Earnest Young, of Lavonia, D. A. Thornton, of Hartwell, D. W. S. Fry, of Clarkesville, B. T. Palmer, of Gainesville, Claude Estes, Mrs. Claude Estes, Misses Lillian, Mamie, Evelyn and Claudia Estes, of Macon.

§   Rabun Gap
    Too late for last week.
    The drought still continues.
    Prof. O'Kelly's school began Monday with 99 students. The prospect is very promising for a good school.
    Dr. Garland is preparing to build him a cottage in the Valley.
    Mrs. John Howard is improving some.
    Miss Flora Cafe, of Toccoa, is spending the week in the Valley.
    A crowd of Valley boys went to Nantahala last week and caught two large wildcats and killed two large rattlesnakes.
    Mrs. J. A. Hopper, Amos Gillispie and family went to Toccoa last week.
    Mr. James Fuller and wife are visiting in Towns county this week.

§   Wolffork
    Hot and dry.
    We haven't as good crops as usual.
    Mr. Umphrey Pendergraw fell over a stump last Saturday and disjointed her hip.
    Miss Lillie Moore is visiting relatives on Persimmon.
    Lee Ritchie was in this section Wednesday.
    Mr. John Jusus was up on business this week.

W. R. Keener has the large corn in this community.

Glad to have J. M. Bleckley with us again.

§   Germany

We are having some fine weather.

Quite a crowd went to Persimmon Sunday.

Mr. Whitmire baptized Mr. Gates last Sunday.

Mrs. Colenback is still on the sick list.

Miss Mary Pitts and Dora Dickerson went to Wollfork Sunday.

Prof. Green spent Sunday night [with] James Almond.

Mr. Holcomb, the peddler, passed through here Monday.

Mr. Powell commissioner, was looking over his roads Monday.

Mr. Ed Almon and wife went to Clarkesville this week.

Mr. Whitmire will commence his meeting Saturday night at Germany.

§   Old Tiger

Prof. James Franklin closed a singing school here last Saturday. Mr. Franklin is liked here and considered a good teacher.

Nin Ramey opened the public school here last Monday with 30 enrolled.

Luther York is teaching school near Turnerville.

Rev. Logan Whitmire and D. D. Taylor closed a meeting here last Sunday. We hope much and lasting good was done.

J. B. McCrackin has [gone] home.

Clifton McCrackin and Jesse Dockins are rapidly improving.

§   Wolfcreek

We are all done laying by corn.

Crops are looking fine.

A. S. Williams has some grapes ready for market.

W. E. Jones made a bushel and a half of wheat from one seed in three year.

G. V. Smith can beat Mr. Dickerson on a cabbage. He raised one stalk with 23 heads on it.

John Martin and wife are visiting relatives here this week.

We are sorry that M. L. Shirley's house got burned.

§   Dillard

We are very glad to say Mrs. Howard, who has been very ill for some time, is improving.

Mr. John Moore and Miss Beulah Angil, of Franklin, N. C., are visiting relatives and friends in the Valley.

Mr. Brown, of Ashville, N. C. preached an interesting sermon at the Baptist church Sunday.

Miss Mamie Penland, of N. C., who has been visiting her sister, Mrs. Tom Ritchie, returned home Sunday.

Mr. Berrong and wife, of Towns Co., visited relatives in the Valley this week.

Fort Hill school began Monday morning with thirty students.

Rabun Gap school is progressing nicely.

Mrs. Holden and Mrs. Dr. Garland went to Toccoa last week.

A nice lot of goods arrived at Greenwoods store this week. The boys mean business.

Miss Mary Bynum was in the Valley Sunday.

Mr. Shaw, of Raleigh, N. C., was in the Valley this week.

§   Persimmon

Last Saturday was the Baptist meeting day on Persimmon and as the pastor was not present Rev. W. S. Whitmire preached in his place. On Saturday Elijah Philyaw joined by letter and on Sunday Mr. Samuel Gates a Presbyterian joined and was baptized.

E. B. Philyaw says he can beat R. J. S. Dickson on Tobacco. He has a patch of about three hundred plants most of them topped and some about ready to cut.

Mrs. Ledford, of the Valley, is visiting relatives around here.

Miss Lillie Moore, of the Valley, is visiting among us this week.

Jas. Justus, of Jermany, spent Sunday with John M. York.

W. E. Lindsey is very feeble.

Mrs. J. C. York is improving.

§   Dr. Cady's Condition Powders... For sale by J. L. Hamby.

§   Chechero

We are having some rain, which is needed.

Mrs. Malissa McWhorter is very sick at this writing.

J. R. Ramey visited relatives here last week.

B. E. Ramey will pay $3.00 per thousand pounds for ryestraw.

J. M. Bell and J. M. Dotson visited friends in this section Sunday.

W. M. Carver is improving from the fever.

Rev. R. Vinson will preach at the late A. C. Godfrey's residence Sunday.

§   I forbid anyone seining on my land. I do not care for hooking. Bry F. Phillips, Chechero.

§   Will They Come? Five Prospective Railroads... [Map.] Black Diamond. Missing Link Railway. Clayton R. R. Tallulah Falls Railway.

The Clayton Tribune, Volume 2, Number 28, Thursday, August 3, 1899

§   Vandiver

Too late for last week.

We are having good rains and good meetings.

Mr. J. B. McCrackin, after spending three weeks with his sick brother and many friends here, has returned to S. C. Come again Bell.

Clifton McCrackin is improving.

Mr. J. E. Bleckley has broken the record making rye in this part... Mr. Bleckley is also contemplating making a singing school teacher out of his son, Leon, who has just come out of singing school the champion base singer[?].

§   In the Mountains.
Atlanta Journal.
Mr. Eugene Mitchell has been spending a week at Clayton, in Rabun county...

Mr. Mitchell says that the speckled trout are not natives of the mountain streams of northeast Georgia. They were brought from beyond the Blue Ridge mountains many years ago and propagated in the streams on this side of those mountains...

Mr. Mitchell also says that the people of Clayton believe that the "Black Diamond railway" will yet be built. This line was projected before the war. The route extends from Port Royal, S. C., up through Walhalla, round through Clayton, and through Rabun Gap to Knoxville. Some of the masonry where the old road was worked can be seen near Clayton...

There is also talk up in Rabun about building a railroad from Walhalla, through Clayton, Rabun county, Towns, Union, Fannin, right on to Chattanooga.

Mr. Mitchell says Clayton is a beautiful little town of 300 people, nestling in a Valley, with Screamer towering 3,200 feet on one side and another giant whose name I have forgotten on the other... Clayton is 17 miles from Tallulah Falls, reached only by private conveyance over the roughest road in the world...

§   Dillard
Mr. Dock Dillard, of Greenville, S. C., Mr. Mac Dillard, wife and boy of Westminster, and Mr. George Dillard are in the Valley this week.

Mr. and Mrs. Wilke, of White county, and Mr. and Mrs. Berrong of Towns county, are visiting here this week.

Mr. Bismark Hogshed, of Toccoa, Ga., is in the Valley this week.

Mrs. Eugene Mozeley, of Clayton, visited her father and mother last week.

A crowd in the Nantahala mountains last week killed 11 eleven rattlesnakes, seven in one pile.

Miss Georgia Coffee visited Mr. Tom Coffee's family at Clayton Saturday and Sunday.

Mrs. Dr. Garland and Sarah Smith went to Franklin, N. C. Sunday.

Mr. Dred Swafford, of Warwoman, was in the Valley Tuesday.

§   Betty's Creek
We are glad to say that Mr. David Shope, who has been sick for two months, is improving some now.

Uncle Benny Grist of the Valley is visiting among us this week, getting new subscribers for the Tribune.

We had a very nice singing Sunday evening.

Mr. James Williams and family, of North Carolina, are visiting relatives this week.

Last Friday George Ledford killed eleven rattlesnakes, two large ones and nine small ones. The same day Joseph Rickman and James Shope killed three. We think they got them all.

Mr. Bill Darnell spent a portion of last week on Nantahala mountains hunting.

We were very glad to see Miss Julia Daily, who has been sick for some, at Sunday school Sunday.

Mr. Bryson, the sheep buyer, got near seventy head of sheep on Betty's creek last week.

§   Upper Warwoman

Rev. Curry preached a very interesting sermon at Antioch Sunday.

A. M. Holden killed a large rattlesnake the other day.

Mr. and Mrs. Roll Watkins and Mr. and Mrs. John Colins, of Westminister, S. C., spent several days with relatives on Warwoman last week.

Mr. S. Bowers and Clint James visited Jeff Swafford Sunday.

Eugene Beck and Luther Beck killed two large rattlesnakes in an old house Sunday.

Mrs. Mary Knox, who has been spending several months with Mrs. S. M. Beck, returned to her home at Westminster last week.

Eugene Swafford made a business trip to Tallulah Falls Monday.

§   A Wedding.

Dallas Smith and Miss Lena Williams were married last Friday morning in the court house by Judge Long. The couple live on Chechero and are of good families and we wish them great joy on the marital voyage of life.

§   Porter Green is up from Turnerville.

§   Three weeks till court from Monday next.

§   J. F. Earl received a shipment of pants yesterday.

§   A large crowd attended the services on Black Rock Sunday.

§   Roper Webb, of Hartwell, Ga., is registered at the Blue Ridge Inn.

§   The road commissioners of this district held a meeting here yesterday.

§   John B. Duncan, of Scaly, gave our office a pleasant visit last Friday.

§   Dr. and Mrs. Bell, of Walhalla, were in town several days the past week.

§   J. F. Earl went to the Falls yesterday.

§   J. A. Green has returned to Dixon, Ga., after a visit with home folks here.

§   Our popular townsmen L. M. and Jesse Robins are visiting for a few days at Seneca.

§   Mrs. J. L. Henson has been quite sick for several days.

§   Mr. "Bud" Allman, of Macon Co., N. C., is visiting relatives and acquaintances in town.

§   Mr. and Mrs. Logan White, of Warwoman, are visiting the latter's parents, Mr. and Mrs. Bell.

§   Lee Miller started for his home at Ocee, Ga., to-day after several weeks stay in town, the guest of Col. Paris. He made many friends while here.

§   The revenue officers have raided in the county this week and, we are told, have had success in their business.

§   Mrs. Ella Swafford sent to our office a pea pod that measured 33 inches in length. How is this for a pea pod?

§   We hear of many well attended and glorious times at the protracted meetings in different parts of the county.

§   Mr. M. W. Swafford brought a melon to town yesterday that weighed 30 [or 80?] pounds. He says he has better ones.

§   We are still agents for the daily Constitution...

§   Col. Paris tells us the Justice's court in the Valley tomorrow will be one of the most interesting and important of many years.

§   Dr. and Mrs. Bell, of Walhalla, S. C., and Dr. Dover and Miss Blanche Wall visited Tallulah Falls and Tallulah Lodge Monday.

§   T. N. Carter and Clarence Miller prominent business men of Westminister, came up yesterday and have gone to the Valley to-day.

§   Thanks to M. W. Swafford for some fine large tomatoes, the flesh of which is not surpassed and the shape of them was simply beautiful.

§   Mr. W. C. Norton had the misfortune to lose one of his mule yesterday. It is thought by some that it died from eating sneeze weed.

§   Mrs. James M. Bell, who has been in feeble health for some time and is now at the home of Squire Duncan under special treatment, is slightly improved.

§   Mr. B. B. Bleckley, of Anderson, S. C., killed on the wind during his visit here last week a blue crane that measured 6 feet from tip to tip and stood 5 feet high.

§   Sheriff J. R. Ritchie incarcerated in the county jail Jasper Blackwell, of Warwoman, Sunday morning on a charge of entering the dwelling house of S. P. Powell with intent to steal.

§   Mrs. J. C. Cannon and children, of Atlanta, have been the guests of Mr. and Mrs. J. W. Green since Sunday. They left yesterday for Highlands and will be there until about the first of September.

§   We greatly miss the presence of "Uncle Jeff" Duncan who is now a popular guide at Tallulah Falls. His friends are inquiring almost daily of him. Uncle Jeff, if they snub you down there come home.

§   While out in company with J. F. Earl on his farm a few days ago we counted 27 Irish potatoes from one hill. These potatoes are of a beautiful red color and a new variety in this section, and we believe are excellent.

§   Revs. Sanders, Evans, Taylor, Barrett, Maney, Dillingham, Pitts, and Allman are conducting a protracted meeting at Pleasant Grove this week. They are having great success in bringing sinners to repentance.

§   Protracted Services.
   Beginning Sunday, Aug. 6, 1899, we will continue the services at Clayton.
   Rev. A. A. Tilly, former pastor and ex-Chaplain of the 2nd Reg. Ga. V. will assist the pastor.
   At Wesley Chapel, Rev. Hinsy[?] B. Mays, of Jefferson, Ga., will assist...
   Chas. W. Curry, P. C.

§   B. T. Palmer, of Gainesville, special agent of the old Mutual Life Insurance Company of New York, has been among our people for several days talking insurance talk. He has written applications for quite a number of the best citizens of the county.

§   W. E. Thompson sent a wagon load of leather in the rough to Seneca yesterday. W. E. and Caney do more work and say the least about it of any men we ever saw. If we had these mountains filled to the tops with such men, what a country we would have!

§   It is a very common occurrence for old ladies to keep small articles of various kinds, but never did we hear of a cigar being kept 15 years. Fifteen years ago J. T. McConnell gave Mrs. Dr. Long a cigar and she kept it until a few days ago. She gave it to her grandson, J. M. Long, and he declares he never smoked a better one.

§   G. V. Garrett has painted the Blue Ridge Hotel, the store house and new dwelling house of W. H. Duncan and the residence of "Bud" York and will soon begin painting the court house. Now, if Pope Barrow and some others will follow suit our little mountain city will begin to compare with other progressive towns. Let the good work go on.

§   Mr. J. A. Swafford is at Cornelia running the Hotel Grant. The friends of B. W. Grant are sorry to know of his health failing him. There has never been a man of more push and energy in the hotel business nor one more popular. He has made for himself an enviable reputation. We hope he may soon be restored to his usual good health.

§ The contest for the five dollar premium for the largest melon raised in the county has begun. Last Saturday morning Mr. J. F. Earl asked us to witness the pulling of a melon that he wished to put in the contest. It weighed 35 ¼ pounds. This is the largest melon brought to town this season. We understand B. E. Ramey has one on the vine that weights 41 pounds and he expects it to weight by the time it matures 60 pounds.

§ Deputy John Godfrey brought to town yesterday Eve Reed, hand cuffed, for violating the internal revenue laws. Among the hundred men Dept. Godfrey has arrested in the county this man Reed is the third one has put the cuffs on. We doubt if there is in the state a more popular officer in the service among his home people. He is one of our best friends in the newspaper business...

§ A lively party from Anderson county, S. C., have been quartered in town in tents since last Friday. The names of the party are, Mr. and Mrs. A. S. Farmer and their little daughter, Alberta, S. B. Elrod, R. A. Buchanan, W. E. Buchanan, Miss Leila Buchanan, Burnice Farmer and Genie Harrison, colored, chief cook and bottle washer and general superintendent of the crowd...

§ Dept. Collectors Vigal and Bergstrom while on a raid in Moccasin district last Tuesday, were greatly inconvenienced by the loss of one of their buggy wheels. They had stopped Thursday night at the house of Mr. John Tally, near Pine Mountain, and next morning some one took from their buggy one of the front wheels. They went 8 miles to Highlands and borrowed a wheel and arrived two days later in Clayton and from here they went to Gainesville some what embarrassed. We think the boys tried to keep the joke, but it leaked out on them. H. L. Hawkins found the wheel in the woods last Tuesday near Mr. Talley's house and he will ship it to the owner at once. Mr. Hawkins says the parties had it hopelessly hid but he found it just the same.

§ From Southern Record.
Mr. Steve Whitmire is spending some time in Rabun, where he has some valuable property. A mica mine which he is having worked up there promises great things for Mr. Whitmire.

§ Program.
For Rabun County Teachers Association, to be held at Clayton, Saturday Sept. 2, 1899...
Aims and methods in teaching history by Nin Ramey and Virgil McCrackin...
Spelling—by Garnett Williams and Miss Susie Ramey...
Recitation—by Miss Belle York. Grammar—by J. C. and Virgil Green...
Writing—by Martin Chastain and M. S. Moore. Recitation—by Miss Lena Bleckley...
Methods in teaching arithmetic—by W. T. Daniel and Jackson Crunkleton...
Recitation—by Miss Ruth Smith...

The best method of teaching simple language independent of text books—by Misses Manda Earl and Beulah Green...

Value and methods of moral training in the schools—by A. A. O'Kelly and J. M. Bleckley. Miss Texie York, W. T. Daniel, Frank Singleton, Committe on Program.

§   What the Negro is Doing

Harve Penland has gone to Toccoa this week with a load of Irish potatoes, cider and apples.

Old Aunt Nerva Coffee, aged 75 years, and who has been sick since last winter, is somewhat improved in health. Aunt Nerva has been the trusted washer woman for this vicinity for many years and has never failed till last spring responding to the call from the people.

Leander Echols is seen on our streets occasionally selling honey and other products of the farm. He is seen at the jail often trying to buy land of Mr. M. L. Shirley. We are told that L[?] don't have to hunt the money to buy any thing [illegible].

§   We clip the following from an old copy of the Clayton Telegraph of July 8, 1898. The paper was a two column quarto and it's editor was A. B. Sams.

Office Rules. Below is Uncle Billy Bowers' rules to govern those that visit his printing office...

The Clayton Tribune, Volume 2, Number 29, Thursday, August 10, 1899

§   The Missing Link R'y.

Atlanta Constitution.

Ringgold, Ga., July 29—The Missing Link railroad, which is to be built from Chattanooga, Tenn., to Walhalla, S. C., is the main topic of conversation here...

Colonel Albright conducted his business affairs in such a quiet manner that but few knew the particulars until publication of same.

As previously stated in The Constitution, the road will be built from Chattanooga through Catoosa county by way of Chickamauga Park, crossing the Western and Atlantic at Ringgold...

The Missing Link railroad will open up a large area of undeveloped country, and it will pass through the great copper belt of north Georgia. In passing through Murray, Union, Towns, and Rabun, it gives connection to the outside world a large section of country vastly rich in agriculture, mineral and timber...

Colonel Albright says that had ex-Senator Brice, of Ohio, lived, the road would by this time have been in operation or under construction...

§   The Quarantine Line.

Washington, August 8.—The secretary of agriculture has issued an order permitting the removal of Union and Towns and part of the county of Rabun, all in Georgia, northward across the quarantine line, without the restrictions imposed by the quarantine regulations.

§   Judge Estes has the following card published in the Gainesville Eagle:

Mr. Editor: I desire to say that when I received a telegram from G. P. Erwin saying that "Habersham jail is safe—that J. S. Smith had employed counsel and has some rights," what I said was, "I do not know what rights he refers to. He certainly has not the right to say what jail he should be imprisoned in. He has the rights guaranteed to every person charged with crime, a speedy and impartial trial by a jury of his peers."

I said this and nothing more.

J. B. Estes.

§   We mixed with good people in the Valley at their Justices' court last Friday at Rabun Gap. Prof. O'Kelley still maintains his high reputation as an instructor and has a splendid school. He is ably assisted by Miss Ruth Smith. Justices of the Peace Grist and Beavert were at their post of duty and were arbeitrating friends for the small sum of one dollar and five cents for each case. Bailiff Smith was there waiting on the court at 35 cents a piece.

§   The Sad Death of Waller Bynum.

On last Friday, about 4 o'clock, near Pine Mountain, Waller Bynum, aged 18 years, was killed while being dragged nearly two miles by a mule.

Young Bynum, divested of nearly every [piece] of clothing by the long distance he was dragged over rocks and the hard road, was found hanging by his left foot to an iron stirrup, dead. The young man was going to school to Miss Thornton, who has charge of the school at Mount Pleasant, about two miles from the home of the Bynum family. On the morning of the fatal accident he took two mules from home for the purpose of going to the Glade school house where his sister, Miss Genelia, has been teaching. After school he [started] for his sister riding one mule and leading the other and when about a mile from the Mt. Pleasant school in some way the saddle became turned on one of the mules—this is presumed from the fact at this point the print of his head was seen in the sand along the road for 30 or 40 years and then for some little distance no sign was seen. This shows that he was making an effort to regain his position on the mule, but the remaining distance showed that his body was constantly on the ground for nearly the distance of two miles. From all signs the mule was going with all the speed that was in his power. Not far from the place where he had had a scuffle with the mules his hat was found and along the entire distance blood and small pieces of his clothing were found in the road and the print of the body and blood along presents a sad scene.

His collar bone was broken and the skin and flesh was torn from the back of his head to the skull, and otherwise bruised and flesh torn.

The peculiar circumstance under which young Bynum lost his life make it a very sad one.

The interment took place at Long Bottom cemetery at 4 o'clock Saturday, in the presence of a grief stricken family and a sorrowing community.

The family have the sympathy of the entire county.

§   Ordinary's Citations.

Georgia—Rabun County. All persons interested are hereby notified that, if no good cause be shown to the contrary, an order will be granted by the undersigned, on the 9th day of September, 1899, establishing a change on the public road leading from Clayton to Pine Mountain as marked out by the commissioners appointed for that purpose, commencing near the old Smash wagon ford at the old bridge place and running down the left bank of Warwoman creek, crossing Sarah's creek, through the lands of Mrs. Martha Bynum and C. C. Ledford, and intersecting with said old road near and on the east side of the ford on said Warwoman creek, southeast of C. C. Ledford's residence, in Warwoman district, a distance of about one half mile. W. S. Long, Ordinary. Aug. 7th, 1899.

§   Georgia—Rabun County. All persons interested are hereby notified that, if no good cause be shown to the contrary, an order will be granted by the undersigned, on the 9th day of September, 1899, establishing a change on the Race path's road as marked out by the commissioners appointed for that purpose, commencing near the branch, and near the residence of L. C. Hollifield in said county, and running to the right of the old road, through the lands of L. C. Hollifield and John Watts, and intersecting the old road near the residence of John Watts. W. S. Long, Ordinary. This August 7th, 1899.

§   Rabun Sheriff Sales.
   Will be sold, on the first Tuesday in September next, at public outcry, at the court house in said county, within the legal hours of sale, to the highest bidder for cash, the following described lands to wit: A part of lot of land No. thirty-two (32) in the 5th land district of Rabun county and bounded as follows: On the north by the lands of H. C. Ramey, on the east by the lands of Mart Swafford, on the south by lands of John Dotson, and on the west by lands of D. Worly, containing fifty acres more or less. Levied on and to be sold as the property of E. G. Lacounte to satisfy an execution issued form the justices court of the 1275th district G. M. of said county in favor of Andy Worley as agent for Sabina Worley against M. L. Lacounte and E. G. Lacount as principal and J. E. Bleckly as security on replevy[?] bond, fi fa proceedings for the benefit of J. E. Bleckley, security. Levy made and returned to me by Loma Gibson, lawful constable. Written notice given in terms of the law. This August 9th, 1899. J. R. Ritchie, Sheriff.

§   Also, parts of lots of land Nos. twenty eight (28) and twenty nine (29) in the 13th district, of formerly Habersham county, now Rabun county Georgia containing one hundred and ninety (190) acres more or less, and bounded as follows: On the north and east by the lands of William Fincannon, on the south by lands of J. J. Wilson and J. L. Fincannon and on the west by lands of T. P. Wilson and others. Levied on as the property of G. R. Ledford to satisfy an execution issued from the Superior court of Habersham county Georgia, in favor of C. T. Wilbanks against G. R. and D. J. Ledford. Written notice of said levy posted on said land, there being no person in actual possession. This the 7th day of August 1899. J. R. Ritchie, Sheriff.

§   Also at the same time and place and on the same terms, will be sold part of land lot No. 19 in the second land district of Rabun Co. Ga., and bounded as follows: Commencing on the original line between J. C. Pickett and J. B. Dockins formerly between W. M. Pickett and W. S. Moseley where said line crosses the public road leading from Clayton to Hiwassee, thence a northwest course to a big rock on the little branch just above the spring, thence up the hollow to the end of a flat ridge between a flat hollow on the south and a branch on the north, a blazed line to the conditional line between said J. B. Dockins and John York where said line crosses the ridge, thence south said conditional line to the public road, thence on south [illegible] conditional line to the east and west original line to the Southeast corner of said lot No. 19, thence north the original line to the beginning corner, the place where Martin A. Hopkins now resides, containing eighty acres more or less. Levied on as the property of Martin A. Hopkins by virtue of two executions issued from the Justice's court of the 587th district G. M. of said county in favor of John B. Dockins against Martin A. Hopkins for a balance of purchase money due on said lands.

Tenant in possession and defendant in executions notified of said levies in terms of law. This Aug. 9th, 1899. J. R. Ritchie, Sheriff.

§   John A. Earl made a trip to the Falls Tuesday.

§   John B. Murray has been up from Toccoa several days.

§   A. J. Kell was over from Scaly Monday and remembered us with the stuff.

§   H. K. Cannon returned from marketing "down the country" Monday night.

§   W. L. Morgan, of Prathers, N. C., in company with F. G. Holden was here last Monday.

§   Mr. T. L. Bynum is spending the week with his grief stricken mother at his home near Pine Mountain.

§   Mrs. Amos McCurry, of Greenville, S. C., will visit friends and relatives in the county for several days.

§   Dr. B. F. Smith, of Elberton, Ga., and a former citizen of this county was here Tuesday on business.

§   M. B. Darnell, of Dillard, was in town Tuesday evening and greased our palm to help the Tribune glide along.

§   Mr. Layfayette Wall, of Clara, Ga., came up Sunday night and is stopping several days with home folks and friends.

§   Mrs. W. F. Roane has returned home after a two weeks visit among her children, T. E., Marvin and Willie Roane, of Atlanta.

§   Mrs. Mary Watts, of Tiger, who has been staying with Mr. and Mrs. J. E. Derrick for about two weeks to be treated by our local physicians, is improving in health.

§ Mr. and Mrs. Walter D. Smith, Misses Mary Santley and Jennie Morse, of Atlanta, were at the Wall House part of last week. They were enroute to Highlands.

§ Coroner Uncle Billie Wheeler was in town Tuesday and he invited me out to see the lightning bugs in the corn at high noon. We don't doubt Uncle Billie's word. We know he has a fine crop.

§ The melon contest is quite lively now. Bring your melons in and when the contest is over the names of the contestants and the weight of the melons will be published. Ordinary W. S. Long is keeping a complete record. The contest will close Tuesday, August 29th at 10 a. m. The five dollars has been deposited by John A. Earl, who offered the premium, with W. S. Long.

§ We learn from the Constitution that Tom Bryson, and a man by the name of Tanner, of Gainesville, Ga., and a man by the name of Hamilton of Maysvile, Ga., have been arrested for the murder of J. S. Smith in Hall county jail. The parties are in Atlanta jail. Bryson and Tanner deny the charge, but Hamilton has acknowledged and implicated others in the horrible crime.

§ While masons were engaged tearing down a brick chimney for Judge Long yesterday they came across a brick that had a deer's track indented into it after [illegible]. No one here not even the oldest living inhabitants know at what date the chimney was built, but they say the building is one of the oldest in town. It must have been built over seventy five years ago when the deers were in great number. The oldest citizens here say they can remember where they went in gangs here.

§ Old Tiger

Miss Laura Dotson died unexpectedly last Thursday evening and buried at the old Cannon graveyard Friday. Revs. W. H. Hughes and D. D. Taylor conducted the funeral services. The bereaved family have the entire sympathy of their community.

Rev. Logan Whitmire preached at the home of D. D. Taylor last Saturday night.

Church conference day at Tiger last Saturday. Babe Lacount was restored to fellowship of the church and lettered out with his wife, son and mother. Mrs. Lacount is one of the oldest members of the church at that place.

We learn that Dud Dockins attended the protracted meeting at Bethel. It is said it had been seven years since he had been to church.

Rev. Huges is running a protracted meeting at Tallulah Falls.

Mr. Clifton McCrackin and Jesse Dockins will soon be up from a spell of fever.

Tom Hunnicutt, of N. C., is visiting his home people here.

Mr. Charlie Derrick was amongst the boys here last week.

§ J. I. Langston and children, Charlie and Miss Stella, have been unwell for several days.

§ Vandiver

Road working is the order of the day.

Mr. Harison Rholetter spent Sunday with his girl.

Mr. Clifton McCrackin has gone to the Falls today.

Will Stancil is moving his shingle mill on the lands of Walter Smith which is a great help to this section.

J. E. Bleckley has the best corn in this community.

§　Bettys Creek

Miss May Garland is sick with sore throat.

Charley Ritchie and Lex Darnell returned home Saturday.

Miss May Wall has been visiting relatives here this week.

Uncle Benny Grist is still on Betty's Creek.

Asberry Darnell visited us Saturday.

A. Ledford has been visiting in North Carolina.

Miss Maybel Coffee is teaching school on Betty's Creek.

§　Three Forks

We are having plenty of rain in this settlement now and have had for the last six weeks and prospects are good for more.

We are having a good school over here this fall, the average is about thirty-five and Mr. J. M. Hopper, of Macon county is our teacher.

A number of our people went to Clear Creek, N. C., to preaching Saturday and Sunday last and got disappointed as usual. There was meeting but no preaching.

Mr. Lester Kell and John Duncan, of this settlement, went to Highlands, N. C., last Sunday morning and with a lively crowd from there went out on top of Satulah, a noted mountain of Macon county. Whe had a nice time and obtained a fine view of the surrounding country.

Mr. Len[?] Kell is going now to have his horse shod.

Miss Hasie Talley is visiting relatives in the settlement.

Garfield Duncan has been gone from home since Saturday morning. Lookout girls, he may come to see you.

John Duncan and father are making preparations to make a trip to Seneca.

Don't forget the Devil's court house—if you want to see it come over to Duncan's and John will be glad to take you over there. It is worth going to see.

§　State of Georgia—Rabun County. Constitution and By Laws of Rabun County Teachers' Association... Committee on Constitution and By-laws. Virgil McCrackin, W. T. Daniel, R. N. Dover.

The Clayton Tribune, Volume 2, Number 30, Thursday, August 17, 1899

§　Arrested for the Si Smith Murder.

The latest development in the Si Smith murder case was the arrest of Taylor Hamilton of Mayesville by Detective Looney Monday afternoon. Sheriff Munday went to Mayesville with Looney to identify Hamilton, but this he did not do. Hamilton is said to have confessed that he was the man who acted the part of the "prisoner" on the night of the murder, and also implicated others.

Looney telegraphed Chief of Police Smith, giving the names of the parties implicated, whereupon Charles H. Tanner and Tom L. Bryson were immediately arrested and lodged in jail here. Hamilton was carried to Atlanta jail from Mayesville...

Col. Howard Thompson has been engaged to defend Tanner and Bryson.

Mr. Thompson brought his clients Tanner and Bryson before Ordinary Rudolph this morning on a writ of habeas corpus to secure their discharge from the custody of the sheriff. Detective Looney and the prosecutor, Mr. Hill, of Habersham county, were absent from the city, there fore could not show cause why the prisoners should be held...—Gainesville Eagle

§   "Five Minutes to Surrender."
Keowee Courier:--
Greenville, August 5—J. D. M. Dillard, who has been leading contractor and builder in Greenville, was arrested tonight by Sheriff Gilreath, charged with assault and attempt to kill. The assault was committed some time ago and a warrant was issued, but Dillard left town and returned last night.

Late tonight Sheriff Gilreath learned of his presence and went to his house to make the arrest. It is said Dillard defied the officer and got into the cupola on the top of the house, armed with a revolver. The sheriff gave him five minutes to surrender. He decided to come down and was taken to jail. He will give bail tomorrow. The assault was made on a young man with a knife. He was severely cut in several places, but is now out and about.

§   Persimmon
Weather is pleasant and showers frequent. Katydids are making the forest ring.
Corn crops are excellent in this community...
We are glad to see V. V. Justus among us again.
Mr. Normon and Miss Tula, Lillie and Lena have been visiting in this community during the past week.
About twenty-eight of Persimmon's inhabitants went to the convention at Burton Saturday and Sunday. They all report a fine time.
J. C. York brought back a fine melon with him from the convention. Go again, J. C.
L. T. Teems is gone to Highlands, N. C.

§   John Neville, Tom Price, James Collins, John Lamb and Gus McCurry of the Valley were out last night taking a moonlight drive and their wagon ran up on the bank of the road and turned over among the rocks and some of them were horribly mangled about the face. Some of them were literally covered with blood, and we are told Price is not expected to live and that Collier [sic] is in very serious condition. The others escaped serious injury. We are unable to get the particulars as we are on the eve of going to press.

§   A Word to Our Readers. Court week will soon be here...

§   Special Term of Hall Court to Try Men Charged With Lynching Si Smith.
From the Constitution.

Gainesville, Ga., August 14. Judge J. B. Estes, of the Northeastern circuit, has called a special term of Hall superior court to try Taylor Hamilton, Tom Bryson and Charley Tanner, who were arrested one week ago today, charged with being in the mob which entered the Hall jail July 14th and shot to death Si Smith, who killed Judge W. B. Bell, of Habersham county, April 2d. last... Judge Estes returned Saturday from Dawson superior court, and when the question of a special term was presented to him he issued an order calling on the grand jury to assemble Wednesday [morning]...

Solicitor General W. A. Charters will be assisted in the prosecution by Judge J. B. Jones, of Toccoa, and Colonel George P. Erwin, of Clarkesville. Colonel Howard Thompson has been retained by the defense...

§   A new store in town.

§   Miss Effie Duncan is visiting at Cornelia.

§   Sugar at 15 pounds to the dollar at Henson['s].

§   J. E. Derrick has new fodder for sale. Call on him.

§   Judge F. A. Bleckley is able to visit among friends now.

§   Lamar Wilbanks, of Clarkesville, spent Tuesday night in town.

§   Dr. Dover is off for a short visit to Walhalla. He is expected home to-day.

§   Miss Carrie Shroder, of Mt. Airy, Ga., is the guest of the Misses Duncan.

§   W. C. Donaldson is making a nice improvement on the dwelling [illegible] Judge Long.

§   Lafayett Wall, of Clara, Ga., is spending sometime here among friends and relatives.

§   [Missing] to Rev. Ode Evans for a [missing] melon set up to the editor [missing] of this office.

§   [Missing] friends of Mr. S. W. Dover [missing] pleased to know that he is [missing] out on his farm.

§   [Missing] comes to us from a reliable [missing] that A. J. Munday, sheriff [missing] county, has disappeared.

§   [Missing] Ida Duncan says she has [missing] her wedding until she [missing] some one to have her.

§ [Missing] John Williams, of Texas, [missing] visiting relatives here, was [missing] lightning on the 9th [missing].

§ Mr. Willie Duncan, son of A. J. Duncan, is dangerously ill in Atlanta. The family has our sympathy.

§ Thanks to Mrs. H. A. Burdick and L. V. Littleton, of Cullasaja, N. C., for paid subscription sent us by mail.

§ J. F. Earl has sold over five hundred dollar's worth of clothing within the last few weeks—he advertises.

§ Mrs. E. A. Bell, of Walhalla, S. C., will be the guest of Mrs. Emily Wall and Miss Blanche for a couple of weeks.

§ Sheriff Ritchie moved his family to town [yesterday]. He will live in the jail and will hereafter act as sheriff and jailor.

§ D. J. Carter, the general representative of the Southern Newspaper Union, Charlotte, N. C., made our office a pleasant call Tuesday.

§ Cicero York has in his garden a cabbage that measures four feet in diameter. We do not mean the cabbage head but the leaves.

§ Miss Fannie Robins and Misses Fannie and Annie Crisp, of Walhalla, have been the guests of Mr. and Mrs. L. N. Robins this week.

§ I do not want any shooting, hunting or fruit gathering done on my lands or trespassing in any way on my premises. Mrs. E. A. Bell.

§ E. M. Wilborn was here Saturday and tells us he killed a rattlesnake a few days ago nearly four feet long and had 15 rattles and the usual button.

§ Mr. B. S. Barnwell and son, of Abbeville, S. C., were here last week. Mr. Barnwell has a landed interest in this county and was up looking after it.

§ Col. Tribble, Capt. P. K. McCully, Mr. Feasley Tribble, of Anderson, S. C., and Capt. Dick Strother, of Walhalla, were guests of the Wall House Wednesday night.

§ Ex-clerk L. C. Hollifield requests us to say that he has a number of deeds lying in the clerk's office that have been recorded and he will be pleased if parties will call for them during court.

§ J. S. Harkins, of the Valley, while returning from a trip to Toccoa a few days ago, received a severe shock by lightning while stopping at Walkin's lime kiln, in Habersham county.

§ Cols. Geo. P. Erwin, of Clarkesville, and J. B. Jones, of Toccoa, have been employed in the prosecution of Taylor Hamilton, Tom Bryson and Charles Tanner, who are implicated in the murder of Si Smith in the Hall county jail.

§ Rev. Henry B. Mays, of Jefferson, Ga., is spending some time with our pastor, Rev. Chas. W. Curry. They are engaged in a meeting in the Tennessee Valley. Rev. Mays is a clear and forcible speaker and talks interestingly in regard to his travels abroad.

§ James M. Bell, J. M. Wilkerson and W. B. Watts, road commissioners of the Clayton district, met here last Thursday after looking over the public roads within their charge, and they report the roads in reasonable good condition except in a few instances which were ordered put in repair at once.

§ One dollar premium is offered for the largest turnip grown in the county this year. The party offering the premium is entitled to the turnip. Also a premium of fifty cents is offered for the largest Irish potato grown in the county and left at this office. Contest closes Jan'y. 1st, 00.

§ Frank Brinecha, of Walhalla, fell from a cliff of rocks about 40 feet high on Black Rock mountain last Sunday. His front teeth were broken and otherwise bruised up. His boy comrades came to town for a conveyance to bring him in, but he recuperated and was met pacing into town a wiser boy.

§ Local attorneys have received notice that three of the most important cases in our Superior court is not likely to come up at this term, consequently the Aug. term will be cut short. The cases referred to are: The noted Chapple-Moss and Child and the Cannon-Young and the Cannon-White cases.

§ It was announced in our last issue that the contest for the five dollar premium for the largest watermelon raised in the county would end August 27th, but Mr. J. A. Earl, who pays the premium, asks us to state that the contest will be continued for the season. So bring your melons on till frost.

§ Mr. W. A. Martin of the Valley was here Saturday last and told us that he had gathered about 20 tons of hay on his farm in the Flats. Mr. Martin raised this hay on about seven acres of land. Hay is worth twenty dollars per ton, which make the neat little sum of four hundred dollars off seven acres and with very little work. He says there are many hundred acres in the Flats that will produce equally as well as his.

§ Mr. W. M. Darnell, a highly respected citizen of the Valley, was found in an unconscious condition on the side of the road near the residence of Dock Burrell last Sunday about 2 o'clock and died in a few minutes after being carried by friends to an empty house nearby. His wife preceded him to the great beyond about four years ago. He leaves four children to mourn his departure. Three sons, one of whom is in the west, and one daughter.

§　Jasper Blackwell Escapes Jail.

Last Sunday at noon Jasper Blackwell escaped from jail. Mr. J. I. Langston, who has charge of the jail in the absence of Sheriff Ritchie, went upstairs of the jail to feed the prisoners and just as he had entered the second door Blackwell, who was secreted behind the first door ran out and made his escape. Quite a little crowd with dogs chased him east of town quite a distance, but a thunder storm rose and stopped the search for some time, which enabled him to gain quite a headway. We learn that Blackwell passed a man the same evening on Warwoman intoxicated and took from him a pair of suspenders and a hat. Blackwell is charged with grand larceny.

§　Old Tiger

Law day at Tiger last Saturday. Cols. W. S. Paris and Calaway Edwards were the council. The biggest day in fifteen years. The most important case was Miss Allie Stone versus the town of Tallulah.

Mrs. Hannah McCrackin is low with typhoid fever.

Preaching at Eden last Sunday. Willard Taylor was baptized and received in church.

H. K. Cannon and wife from Clayton visited Ben Ellard on Stonepile, last Sunday.

Misses Martha Jenkins and Reed Bleckley were at Eden Sunday.

Mr. L. P. Wall, of Chechero, visited his daughter, Mrs. Williams, who has sick for some time, last week.

Misses Ellie and Bertie Allia[?] visited their sister at Tallulah this week.

Road working is the order of business—getting ready for Judge Estes.

Lonie Gipson's daughter, of Stonepile district, has typhoid fever.

Mr. Tom Dotson is very feeble from cancer.

Dave Nations and wife are in North Carolina on a visit. They are not in W. T. York's condition—their kin people are not in the county.

§　Upper Warwoman

Mr. Emory and Berry Beck returned home last week.

Mr. T. E. Carver, Misses Dovie and Clara Carver, of Chechero, visited friends on Warwoman Sunday.

Marlor Swafford killed a large rattlesnake Monday.

Miss Rosa Billingsley, of Pine Mt., is attending school here.

Mr. Sam Bowers and Miss Gussie Bleckley were married last week. We wish them a long and happy life.

§　Wolfcreek

Crops look well in our section. School is prosperous in our locality.

Mr. G. W. Alison and wife, of N. C., are visiting their people this week.

A. S. Williams had a nice peach pie for dinner Saturday.

Mrs. G. V. Smith's arm is slightly improved.

§　Code of Ethics for [missing section] Teachers' Association [missing] T. Daniels...

§   Dillard

Mr. Riley Garland and wife, of Toccoa, Ga., are visiting relatives in the Valley this week.

Mr. William Darnell, aged sixty four years, died Sunday morning and was buried Monday afternoon at the Baptist cemetery. He was one of the Valley's oldest and highest respected citizens.

Willie Dillard, who has fever, is improving slowly.

Love Beavert is very sick.

Mr. Mangal and wife, of South Carolina, visited Mr. George Darnell's this week.

The Clayton Tribune, Volume 2, Number 31, Thursday, August 24, 1899

§   In Memory of Waller Bynum...

Waller Bynum, after a career of usefulness and satisfaction to his friends and family, has gone from us...

Lois Thornton, Griffin, Ga. Teacher, Mt. Pleasant School, Rabun County.

§   Below is a letter from a Rabun county boy who is in the Philipine army:

Co. E, 28th U. S. Infantry, Manila, June 19th, 1899, Mr. Garnett Williams.

Dear cousin:

It is with pleasure I write you a few lines that leave me well and hope you are the same. At this writing I am 40 miles from Manila at Morong, on Lazuna de bay. My regiment has gone to Jolo, eight or nine hundred miles from here. I am on a gun boat. Well, Garnett since I came to this country you can bet I have seen some hard fighting and have heard many a bullet whiz, still I am plugging away at them. It is a snap on this boat, for we have fine guns. We have two 6 pounder rapid firing cannons, 2 gatling guns, 10 barrels each, that sing a song for Filipinos that makes many of them fall to sleep to wake no more. To give you an idea of how they work I will relate an incident that happened a few days ago. We got into a bunch of negroes. In 30 minutes we had fired 1500 rounds out of the two gatling guns and 150 out of the 6 pounders. We have a Colt's automatic which fired so many I won't mention them. It fires 400 shots per minute. There are 25 of us on here from Co. E and when all the guns are going the old boy himself would not stay in front of us long. I will give you a description of the country in my next letter. It has been quite a while since we were at Manila. You can bet the boys have been killing them off the last few days. At one place we killed so many negroes they had to throw them over the trenches so others could take their place and they were laid out also. I have seen quite a lot of the world since I left here...

Your cousin, Robt. F. Williams.

§   Hamilton Confesses.

The Grand Jury of Hall county was called together Wednesday of last week and we print the following from the Georgia Cracker: The Grand Jury adjourned yesterday afternoon at 4:30 o'clock. True bills were returned against Mark Bell, Ollie Bell, Tom Bryson, Charlie Tanner, Henry Towery and Taylor Hamilton, charging them with murder.

The Grand Jury made a few presentments... Also that it was the sense of that body that it was inadvisable to hold a special term of court before about the middle of November. Judge Estes stated that he thought this best but would think the matter over and announce later when the special term to try these cases would be held.

Taylor Hamilton is said to have made a full confession before the Grand Jury... However, he told to an Atlanta Journal reporter Thursday what purpoted to be the confession he made here before the Grand Jury.

He says that Tom Bryson came to Maysville the day before Si Smith was killed and told him, and several others, that there was going to be a lynching in Gainesville that night and he wanted Hamilton, Freeman and John Campbell, of Maysville, to go with him and be in the mob... Hamilton then goes on to relate how he was induced to come here...how Sheriff Munday was awakened and was told the sheriff of Gilmer county had a prisoner to be locked up...

About the arrest by Detective Looney, Hamilton says: "The first I saw of Captain Looney was when he came to Maysville..."

§   It is our pleasure to call the attention of our readers to the advertisement of the Cornelia Institute. We specially commend Prof. Booth, principal of this institute, as a scholar of rare attainments. He is a christian gentleman and will teach your children the great lessons of morality as well as the languages.

There was an enrollment of 200 last year, twenty-two of whom were from our county. The school building is an ideal one, the location the very best, and the people of the town are generous, kind and progressive.

§   Highlands.

The long continued hot weather is fast filling Highlands' lonely boarding houses. Among the late arrivals at the Davis House are Judge Day and wife, of Canton, Ohio. The late Secretary of State expresses great admiration of Highlands and surroundings, and our people are equally pleased with the eminent statesman.

§   Persimmon

A good rain fell today.

J. C. York has returned home from Cornelia, where he has been doing some carpenter work.

Dr. D. A. York's children are up with their grandparents. They say they wish their papa would move up here.

C. J. Crunkleton's condition is very serious. We trust he will be able for the schoolroom again soon.

T. M. Justus and Virgil Nichols have opened a store on the creek.

We are glad the daily mail is in operation now.

The road work will be finished up this week.

Commissioner Neville is on his round visiting the schools.

Rev. Hughes' son preached Saturday night and Sunday last. Rev. Hughes is a fine young man.

§   Court next Monday.

§   Our jail has no inmates.

§   Mrs. Shirley continues to improve.

§   Mr. D. T. Duncan is quite sick to-day.

§   Marshal Oliver is suffering from a mashed foot.

§   Our temple of justice has received a coat of white.

§   John A. Earl made Russel, S. C., a visit Saturday.

§   Mrs. E. A. Bell will return to Walhalla to-morrow.

§   Mrs. Henson says it pays her to advertise in the Tribune.

§   Dr. Green left for Atlanta this morning for a few days.

§   Eddie Norton has been threatened with fever for a several days.

§   Mrs. Huntington, of Atlanta, is the guest of Dr. and Mrs. Green.

§   Sheriff Ritchie is officialy serving witnesses on Tallulah to-day.

§   Dr. J. C. Dover made a professional trip to South Carolina yesterday.

§   Mrs. Amanda Green, of Turnerville, is visiting her son, Dr. Green, for a few days.

§   Rev. R. S. Sanders is having fine success at a protracted meeting at Tallulah church.

§   We do not remember ever hearing of as many mashed feet and skinned heads before.

§   John Godfrey arrested Peter Leal yesterday for violating the internal revenue laws.

§   W. C. Donaldson is making a nice improvement on the property of W. A. Matheson.

§   Our hotels are making preparations for court and the fair sex are preparing for courting.

§   W. C. Farmer, of Leatherwood, Ga., returned home Monday after a visit here of a few days.

§   B. C. Reynolds, of Tallapoosa, Ga., was the guest of relatives a few days during the past week.

§   Religious services are being protracted at Rabun Gap by Rev. C. W. Curry with good results.

§   J. T. Church, representing John B. Daniel, druggist, of Atlanta, was here yesterday talking drugs.

§   The chestnut crop is a failure this year. We do not believe old Screamer mountain will produce one bushel.

§   Why not have your house painted? Mr. M. V. Garrett is here now in the business and will do your work on short notice.

§   Marion Long and Will Bruce went out hunting yesterday and came in with a string of squirrells and a large groundhog that weighed ten pounds.

§   I will pay cash 12 ½ cents per pound for nice fresh butter and 10 cents per dozen for fresh eggs. Mrs. D. A. Henson.

§   John Qualls, of Whetstone, S. C., had the misfortune to get his foot badly shot on last Monday. The affair was an accident.

§   Mr. Walter Dickson, of Fair Play, S. C., has been up among his friends and relatives. He returned to his place of business Monday.

§   Mrs. W. B. Grant, of Jacksonville, Fla., will be the guest of the Wall House for the season. Mr. Grant will join Mrs. Grant here in a few days.

§   Lafayette Dickson presented us yesterday with a beet of the turnip variety that weighed five and half pounds and measured 23 inches in circumference. Can you beat this beet?

§   A large party of pleasure seekers from Harmony Grove, Ga., passed through town last Friday en route to the Nantahala river. They were all smiling and seemed to be enjoying themselves.

§   Babe Lacounte, Judge Long and W. C. Donaldson have knocked a bit of the monotonous dull and hot days in town by the sound of the hammer, saw and the ring of the steel dressing granite.

§   Thomas Price, one of the party who was mangled in the moonlight ride about a week ago, is still in very critical condition. His recovery both physically and mentally is a matter of doubt.

§   Henry Cannon opened the contest for the largest Irish potato grown in the county this year by bringing three large fine ones to our office last Saturday.

§   Mr. C. F. Potter, of New York, who has mining in this county, will be the guest of Mr. S. S. Hall for some time. Mr. Potter has many friends in this section.

§   Willie Duncan is still at the Grady hospital in Atlanta very sick. His father, Mr. A. J. Duncan, is at his bedside and writes home that Willie is delirious and his condition is discouraging. Since writing the above we learn that there are no hopes of his recovery.

§   Charlie Williams, son of E. H. Williams, of Wolfcreek, was in town yesterday to have a toe amputated. A cow stepped on his foot and severely bruising it, so as to have his toe taken off.

§   We want to attend court at Clayton, Ga., next Monday and Tuesday, and request that all our patrons who may be there be prepared to settle what is due on their accounts and we will be under obligations.—Franklin Press

§   The Southern Record comes to us this week with a two page advertisement of Cornelia Institute and Cornelia's business men. Cornelia is a town of destiny and it has more natural born merchants than any town in North East Georgia, and the Southern Record knows exactly how to present men and things to the public...

§   Dr. Henson showed us two gold nuggets that were taken from the mines in California in the fifties by Mr. James M. Ritchie of the Valley. The two weighed one half ounce and Dr. Henson paid ten dollars for them. Dr. Henson will take pleasure in showing them.

§   Mr. H. A. Kilby of Quartz, who was bitten by a rattle snake pilate the first of July last, was in town Friday with his arm in a swing. Mr. Kelby was unconscious from 4 o'clock on the morning he was bitten until thirty hours later. He is not a well man yet and suffers much pain.

§   An old pherotype[?] picture was found in tearing an old chimney from the residence of Ordinary Long Monday. The face of the image was nearly perfect and the film was about all that was left, the tin having almost entirely corroded. No one here has the least idea whom the picture is the likeness.

§   An Old Landmark Gone.
Mr. William Stonecypher, of Burton, an aged and highly respected citizen of this county, died at his home Tuesday night about midnight, from the effects of a fall from a ladder the same day. Mr. Stonecypher has been troubled with something like paralytic strokes for some time past and it is thought he was so affected at the time he fell. Mr. Stonecypher is a native of the county, having been born near his home place and spent his long and useful life near the place of his birth. The deceased had many relatives in the county. He is an Uncle of Senator W. J. Green and our Clerk of

Superior Court J. S. Ramey. The bereaved have the sympathy of the entire community.

§   This is to notify all parties not to tresspass on my land Nos. 28 and 82 in the fifth land district. Any persons trespassing by hunting, fishing or taking fruit or any other property will be prosecuted to the full extent of the law. D. A. Henson.

§   Mr. J. L. Henson showed us some tomatoes, one of which weighed 14 ounces after being taken from the vine twenty-four hours. They were grown by Greenwood of Dillard. They are a new variety to us and a beautiful one. Tomatoes like almost every thing in the vegetable line, grows with great profusion here.

§   Mr. J. N. Crunkleton, of Persimmon, happened to a painful and what may prove to be a fatal accident a few days ago. He had trimed his pencil and had his knife on his knee and some papers started to drop fro his hand and making a quick grab for them stuck the blade of the knife into his wrist joint, from which he is suffering greatly.

§   M. L. Shirley, who has been confined in jail here since last day of May, charged with shooting his wife, has made bond in the sum of eight hundred dollars for his appearance at the August term of the superior court. His bondsmen are L. N. Shirley, James E. Bleckley, H. B. Stonecypher and J. L. Watts. Mr. Shirley was a proud man when he was given his liberty.

§   Cornelia Institute, Cornelia, GA.
Stands as the most successful and thoroughly equipped school of the kind in the state. Location, in Habersham county, which has the lowest death rate of any county in the U. S. Health pure air and the finest mountain scenery make Cornelia an ideal location for such a school.
Two railroads, Southern and Tallulah Falls. Building brick, large modern and well furnished. Heated by hot air furnace which is perfect. Faculty composed of young progressive, christia men and women. Dormitories for boys and girls under care of teachers.
First term's enrollment, 200, 22 of whom were from Rabun Co. No shoddy out of date methods, but everything up to date. Expenses reduced to the minimum. Confer with the President.
A. E. Booth, Cornelia, Ga.

§   Col. S. C. Dunlap has been made manager of the Tallulah Falls Railway, which runs from Cornelia to Tallulah Falls, a distance of 25 miles. President George Lewis Prentiss of the road was here a few days ago and closed up the deal with Colonel Dunlap, who assumed control of the property last Saturday morning.
Col. Dunlap's successful management of the Gainesville, Jefferson and Southern railroad attracted the attention of President Prentiss, who has been negotiating with him for some time. Col. Dunlap remains receiver of the C. J. & S. railroad, and will divide his time between the two lines. Everybody feels confident Col. Dunlap will push the Tallulah Falls line and make it a profit to the owners.

§ Betty's Creek

Miss May Garland is still on the sick list.

Misses Laura and Texie Hopper, of Persimmon, are visiting relatives today.

The boys and girls are attending the protracted meeting and we hope are doing much good.

Mr. Sam Cary and wife of North Carolina, were the guests of J. P. Norton Saturday and Sunday.

A crowd of the Betty's Creek and Persimmon folks went to a bee tree cutting near Isaac Ramey's and got two gallons of honey.

Persimmon need not brag so big. Betty's Creek has corn so big that lightning bugs never know when the daylight comes. The stalks are like mill logs and the grains will soon be like iron wedges.

Mr. Syney Bradley and wife visited their son J. M. Bradley Sunday.

L. M. Brooks, L. L. Long, J. J. P. Norton attendend the association last week at Hamburg, N. C.

§ Germany

We are having some fine weather.

People are all visiting.

We had a fine quilting at Cal York's Saturday.

Clerk J. S. Ramey was shaking hands with friends here yesterday.

J. M. Justus, who has been visiting on Germany, will return home soon.

Virgil and Miss Deska Justus went to Wolffork Sunday.

Marvin Powell says if he had a dollar and a half he would take it to the ordinary.

The Clayton Tribune, Volume 2, Number 34, Thursday, September 14, 1899

§ Young Harris News.

We believe in helping the sick and needy and think everybody should look after their welfare...

§ Clarksville Advertiser.

Rev. James F. West, of Mossy Creek district, was elected Representative of White county last Wednesday, to fill the unexpired term of Hon. Watson Fain, deceased. Mr. West was opposed by Messers. Benton West, J. H. Lumsden, and Fain, a son of Hon. Watson Fain, but was elected by a good majority.

Capt. S. H. Mosely, of Toccoa, died at his home there Sunday afternoon. Capt. Mosely was one of the most prominent men in the county. He had been a man active in public affairs and was a powerful factor in building up Toccoa city. He leaves a wife and several children. The funeral took place Sunday afternoon.

§ Wolffork

Hot and dry but have some prospects of a shower.

The men and boys are busy engaged in saving fodder and melons and our good housewives and daughters are busy picking, pickling and drying beans.

Mr. John Keener, who spent the summer with relatives in Alabama, is at home again.

We missed J. M. Bleckley at Sunday School Sunday.

Mr. Rockaway Keener gives a quilting tomorrow.

Uncle Rufus Keener is nearly eighty years old and says he has never taken any medicine and he can still work.

James Pendergrass returned from Lavonia Monday.

Miss Lula Justus has gone home.

§   Program for Rabun County Teachers Association to be held at Clayton Oct. 7th 1899...

Address of Welcome.—W. T. Daniel...

Teaching reading.—C. J. Crunkleton and Nin Ramey...

Essay—Rabun County's Public School.—Miss Manda Earl...

Recitation—Miss Lena Bleckley...

Writing—L. M. Chastain and M. S. Moore...

Personal habits of teacher—J. M. Bleckley...

Conducting recitation—Miss Ruth Smith, Virgil McCrackin and Claude Green...

Recitation—Miss Belle York...

Art of questioning—W. T. Daniel...

How to interest pupils in map-drawing—W. S. Dickson and F. D. Singleton...

Recitation—Miss Sibbie Bynum...

[Illegible] and home help, or hinder each other—Oscar Powell and James Green...

Inter-relation of parent and teacher—A. A. O'Kelley, R. N. Dover and Garnett Williams...

Essay—Value of a teachers association—Miss Susie Ramey...

School laws of Georgia and progress of the schools of Rabun county—W. J. Neville, C. S. C.

Miss Texie York, W. T. Daniel, Franklin Singleton, Committee on Program.

§   Persimmon

We are glad to have some cool nights. It will be good for the health of our community.

C. J. Crunkleton is confined to his bed again, but we hope he will soon be up.

Quite a number of sick children in this vicinity.

We are glad the men are in hurting[?] sheep, for they are sure to leave some money.

Rev. Worlie, of Jackson, N. C. is preaching at Boiling Springs. He [is] among the best preachers that has preached to us for some time.

J. C. York has been doing some carpenter work at Tallulah.

T. E. King is preparing to build a new store house. Hurrah for Persimmon, four stores and all doing well.

§   If a sufficient number, to justify us going to the extra expense, will pay us, during the months of October, November and December, one dollar for the Tribune, we will print a county map showing land lots and fractions of land districts, water courses, post offices, towns, etc. and make those paying the dollar a present of one of these maps. Persons desiring a map will please let us know by Oct. 1st.

§   We sold a load of cabbage a few days ago to a party who was going to Toccoa to market them and we thought of Bro. Fowler of the Record, and here is the caper he cuts over it:

The editor of the Record returns thanks to that prince of good fellows, John A. Reynolds, of Clayton, Rabun county, for one of the largest and finest heads of cabbage we have seen this season. We knew John was a good editor, surveyor, etc., but did not know that he was a good gardner as this cabbage shows him to be—provided the children or Mrs. Reynolds did not do the gardening. That's all right, John, we will give you credit for it until we hear from your family to the contrary. We are satisfied some editors can do other things beside cuss delinquent subscribers.

§   All persons indebted to me by account that will pay me without process of law are especially requested to pay off or settle by note by Oct. 1st. Yours Respectfully, W. R. L. Ritchie.

§   Rabun Sheriff Sales.

Will be sold on the first Tuesday in October next, at the court house in said county, within the legal hours of sale to the highest bidder for cash, the following property to-wit:

A certain town lot in the town of Clayton in Rabun county, Georgia, and known as the W. S. Whitmire store house lot and the one on which the W. S. Whitmire old store house now stands and described as follows, to wit: Commencing at a point three feet north of the north west corner of the front plaza of said store house, thence east and paralel with the north wall of said store house sixty five feet, thence south paralel with the east end or wall of said store house sixty eight feet, thence west paralel with the south wall of said house sixty five feet, thence north sixty eight feet to the beginning corner, containing one ninth of an acre more or less, together with all the rights and privileges thereunto belonging.

Said property levied on as the property of J. L. Hamby by virtue of two fi fas issued from the Superior court of Rabun county, one in favor of Yow and Maritt and one in favor of Oppenheimer & Company both against said J. L. Hamby. Written notice given defendant in the executions and tenant in possession in the terms of the law.

§   Also at the same time and place, and on the same terms, a three eights undivided interest in lots of land Nos. 155, 181 and 182 in the second land district of Rabun county, Georgia. Said land lying on the waters of Patterson creek, west of the Harrison Darnell estate.

Levied on as the property of T. B. Carter by virtue of a mortgage execution in favor of R. B. Ritchie and W. A. Martin as executors of the last will and testament of A. J. Martin, deceased, against said T. B. Carter issued from the superior court of Rabun county. Written notice of said levy given in terms of law.

This Sept. 6, 1899. J. R. Ritchie, Sheriff.

§   Ordinary's Citations.

Georgia—Rabun County. Notice is hereby given that the undersigned has applied to the ordinary of said county for leave to sell lands belonging to the estate of Wm. T. Dickerson for the purpose of distribution. Said application will be heard at the regular term of the Court of Ordinary for said county to be held on the first Monday in October, 1899. M. L. Dickerson, Administrator upon the estate of W. T. Dickerson.

§   Georgia—Rabun county. All persons interested are hereby notified that if no good cause be shown to the contrary, an order will be granted by the undersigned on the 9th day of October 1899 establishing a new road, as marked out by the road commissioners appointed for that purpose, commencing about [illegible] fourth of a mile north of W. H. York's residence; thence up popcorn creek by the residences of W. E. Burton and J. J. Burton in said county, through the lands of W. H. York, D. G. Burton, M. C. Canup, S. J. Burton and William Mincalf, and intersecting with the Hiawassee road at Coward Gap on the Towns county line. This Sept. 6th, 1899. W. S. Long, Ordinary.

§   H. J. Ramey, administrator of the estate of James Dockins, deceased, has in due form applied to the undersigned for leave to sell the lands belonging to the estate of said deceased, and said application will be heard on the first Monday in October next. This the 6th day of September, 1899. W. S. Long, Ordinary.

§   Georgia—Rabun county. To all whom it may concern: A. A. Darnell, of said state, having applied to me for letters of administration de bonis non, on the estate of Harrison Darnell of said county, this is to cite all and singular the heirs and [creditors] of Harrison Darnell, to be and appear at the October term, 1899, of said court, and show cause, if any they can, why letters of administration de bonis non, should not be granted on estate of Harrison Darnell. Witness my official signature. This 28th day of August, 1899. W. S. Long, Ordinary, Rabun county.

§   Georgia—Rabun County. Notice is hereby given that the undersigned has applied to the ordinary of said county for leave to sell land belonging to the estate of L. N. Jones for payment of debts and for the purpose of distribution among the heirs of said deceased. Said application will be heard at the regular term of the court of Ordinary for said county to be held on the first Monday in October, 1899. This 31st day of August, 1899. James F. Smith, Administrator upon the estate of L. N. Jones.

§   Ordinary Long is feeling badly.

§   J. T. Long is still receiving new goods.

§   Claude Green visited home folks last week.

§   J. L. Hamby visited the Falls Tuesday.

§   We will pay one dollar per bushel for chinquapins.

§   Joseph B. Murray is putting up a residence on his farm.

§   The chinquapin season is here to the delight of the small boys.

§   That prince of drummers, W. D. Burch, was among us Monday.

§   Miss Toccoa Prather, of Tugalo, is registered at the Blue Ridge Hotel.

§   Bring us your beets, irish potatoes and turnips and get the premium.

§   Miss Elsie Ramey, of Cornelia, is visiting friends and relatives here.

§   J. R. Ritchie has taken the contract of carrying the mail to and from Tallulah Falls.

§   Rev. W. A. Simmons will preach at the Methodist church next Sunday night at 7 o'clock.

§   Mrs. Emily Wall has been in feeble health for several days but is improved.

§   Capt. Beck tells us that Jeff Beck raised a stalk of corn with five ears on it, good ones too.

§   Representative R. E. A. Hamby left Monday morning for Atlanta. He is expected home today.

§   There will [be] religious services at the Baptist church next Saturday at 11 o'clock, by Rev. Geo. Seay.

§   We made an error in publishing the presentments last week by leaving out the name of H. A. Keener.

§   Our people will thank the Hon. Pope Barrow if he will have his house on the public square painted.

§   Capt. Beck has saved about 15 tons of hay up to date and will save as much more. How is this for Rabun?

§   Mrs. D. T. Duncan spent several days the past week at the Falls, the guest of her daughter, Mrs. H. R. Cannon.

§   Drs. Green and Dover received a nice lot of furniture in the way of chairs, lounges and etc. for their office yesterday.

§   Mrs. W. A. Simmons and children, of Acworth, Ga., will spend two weeks with parents, Mr. and Mrs. S. W. Dover.

§   Marion Long has severed his connection with the mercantile firm of J. T. Long & Son and has moved to the farm.

§   The Revenue officials have been raiding in portions of the county but the boys are foddering and the officers are disappointed.

§   A very small per cent of our patrons paid us during court week. We are grateful to those who did and will thank those in arrears to come and settle.

§   Uncle Billie Wheeler says the wind has blown his corn over and let the light in so he can see to gather beans without the aid of a lantern.

§   The committee appointed by the last grand jury to examine certain books were in session three days. They finished their work last Saturday.

§   Eddie Norton, who has been confined to his home for some time with a case of Typhoid fever, is not improved, though his condition is not serious.

§   The marshall has in his possession one of Roosevelts rough riding saddles. He captured it last Monday night after the rough rider had been thrown.

§   John Scott, who was confined in jail here some time ago for refusing to work on the public road at Tallulah Falls, was given his liberty last Tuesday morning.

§   Miss Eliza Duncan threatens to discontinue her paper if her name is not put in it. We certainly do not want you to discontinue, Miss Liza, and here is your name, MISS ELIZA JANE DUNCAN.

§   Mr. J. S. Chambers and Mr. John D. Hill, of Homer, Ga., left Monday for their home after spending several days pleasantly in town. Mr. Chambers speaks highly of this section. Rabun may lose one of her fair daughters.

§   Rev. W. A. Simmons, of Acworth, Ga., after having arranged to have his appointments filled, joined Mrs. Simmons and children here last evening and will remain here for a week or two, to the delight of many friends.

§   Col. A. J. Ritchie left Monday for Athens, Ga., where he will remain during the winter. He has about recovered from the wounds infected by Williams during court week. Mr. Ritchie has many friends who wish him great success.

§   Last Saturday during a trial in the council room, Mr. D. T. Duncan made one of the best little talks to the boys and some of the older ones that has been our pleasure to hear in many days, we are glad he made it. He said in essence that a man who would not help support law and order in the town in which he lives ought to leave it. It is to every man's interest and to the interest of his children to help punish violators of the law.

§   Capt. William Berry, who is connected with the Tallulah Falls Railroad, was here Tuesday en route to Franklin, N. C. and other points, in the interest of the road. He is looking up the resources along the proposed line of the extension of the road and is meeting with encouragement.

§   Old Tiger

Fodder pulling, syrup making and rye sowing is the order of business in this community.

Miss Ada Green and James were guests of Jess Green last Sunday.

Our Sunday school is progressing nicely. Mr. Clifton McCrackin delivered an address last Sunday to the school which was enjoyed by all. Clifton has gone to enter school at Cornelia. We wish him much success. He is one of Rabun['s] best young men.

George Stancil is very low with consumption. He is not expected to live long.

Miss Martha Jenkins is expected to go into the shingle mill business soon.

It is reported that Lip Ramey from Pine Mountain will make the next race for sheriff of the county in this section.

Col. W. S. Paris passed through on his way to the Falls last week.

Law day at Tiger last Saturday. Most of the cases were continued on account of absent witnesses and lawyers.

Miss Elsie Taylor is visiting friends and relatives on Chechero.

§   Tennessee Valley

Mrs. Fannie Whitmire and Miss Mary Scruggs visited Clayton Sunday.

Rev. Yoder of Macon county North Carolina, visited the family of A. G. Dillard Monday.

Mr. Wm. Roane, of Clayton and his son Marvin, of Atlanta, visited friends in the Valley Monday.

W. H. Greenwood went to Atlanta on business this week.

Col. A. J. Ritchie left for Athens this week where he goes to accept a position.

Nearly all of our farmers are going it heavy on pea vine hay this year and we think it a good plan. So far we think Messrs. Ira Holden and Lee Ritchie are ahead on hay minus the pea vine.

Schools have closed for fodder pulling to open again in two weeks. But not with as full an attendance as before for it seems people forget about school after fodder.

Mrs. Octa Greenwood, who has been sick, is improving.

Rev. Chas. W. Curry preached to a full house at Wesley Chapel Sunday morning and also at the Ridge in the afternoon.

Mr. and Mrs. W. J. Grist visited the latter's relatives in Macon county N. C. this week.

Jovial Tom Ritchie left for Richmond, Va., Monday with a drove of cattle and sheep.

Miss Beulah Green has vacated her school and is at home again.

§   Religious Education by W. T. Daniel. Perhaps in no other age has the intellectual life of the race reached such an astonishing momentum, or, at least, has taken in the material universe in such comprehensive generalizations...

<u>The Clayton Tribune, Volume 2, Number 35, Thursday, September 21, 1899</u>

§   To the People of Persimmon.

Dear Brethren and Friends:

By a combination of circumstances over which I had no control, I was prevented from reaching our quarterly conference on Thursday Sept. 14th. It was a great disappointment to me as I was very anxious to meet the good people of this section of Rabun county.

That I may yet have this priviledge I have so arranged my round as to preach at Boiling Springs school house Sunday, Oct. 22nd, and if it suit the people I will preach a series of services the week following. At the close of the Sunday services with the assistance of Rev. J. W. Hughes I will administer the sacrament of the Lord's supper, and during the week we will present the destinctive doctrines of the Methodist church, which we believe to be the fundamental doctrines of the Bible...

Ellison R. Cook, P. E., Dahlonega District.

§   Tennessee Valley

Col. Sam Kelly, a rising young lawyer of Franklin, N. C., visited his sister, Mrs. W. H. Greenwood Monday.

Prof. A. A. O'Kelly visited Clayton this week.

Miss Annie Gibson, a charming young lady who has been visiting her sister, Mrs. Fisher, left for her home in Betor, N. C., last Saturday.

Miss Bertha Scruggs, one of our nicest young ladies, left Monday for Gillsville where she expects to visit her sister.

Several from the valley attended the quarterly meeting Saturday and Sunday. Among those who attended were Messrs. H. A. Keener, David Garland, John Ritchie, John Holden, George Kelly and Malcolm Moore and Mattie Holden.

Jim Martin has been quite sick for the past week.

Misses Ruth Smith and Mabelle Coffee are visiting the former's parents at Hartwell this week.

§   Ordinary's Citation.

Georgia—Rabun County.

Court of Ordinary for said County.

Settling for county purposes.

It is ordered that a tax of sixty nine and four-tenths cents...be levied on all the taxable property of said county to-wit:

1st To pay the legal indebtedness of the county, due or to become due. 19 cts on each $100.

2nd To repair court-house, jail, bridges or any other public improvement, 6 cts on each $100.

3rd To pay sheriffs, jailors, or any other officer that may be legally entitled. 12 cts on each $100.

4th To pay Coroners all fees that may be due them for holding inquests and etc. 1 ct on each $100.

5th To pay the expenses of the county for bailiffs at courts, non resident witness fees, stationary and etc. 3c on each $100.

6th To pay Jurors per diem compensation. .164 on each $100.

7th To pay the expense of the county in supporting the poor. 9 cts on each $100.

8th To pay any other lawful charge against the county, such as election managers, Jury Commissioners, registers and etc. 3 cts on each $100.

Making in the aggregate the said sum of sixty nine and four tenth (.694) on the one hundred dollars on the taxable property of said county.

This Sept. 19th[?] 1899. W. S. Long, Ordinary.

§   Henry Cannon is off to Anderson this[?] week.

§   Rev. W. A. Simmons will preach [missing] Methodist church tonight.

§   Judge F. A. Bleckley attended [missing] Masonic Lodge here last Friday[?].

§   The mountain wagons are beginning[?] to move down the country [missing].

§   Col. W. S. Paris attended Superior[?] court at Clarkesville last week[?].

§   [Missing] R. Smith and family, of [missing] are the guests of Mr. and [missing] Langston.

§   Mr.[?] J. S. Harkins left Friday for [missing] with a load of fine apples [missing] and cabbage.

§   [Missing] E. Thompson and Caney [missing] made a business trip to [missing or illegible].

§   Misses Kate Bell and Carrie Keith of Walhalla are the guests of Miss Blanche Wall.

§   W. C. Donaldson is absent from home making some improvements on Willie Watts' mill machinery.

§   The past few weeks have been unusually fine for saving hay and fodder and our farmers have made good use of the time.

§   J. R. Ritchie will carry passengers to and fro from Tallulah Falls. Rates. $1 each way. Will furnish hack upon one day's notice. Mail schedule.

§   Mr. T. B. Carter, who has been mentally deranged and confined in the asylum at Millidgeville for some time, came home Tuesday very much improved.

§   Uncle Henry Winters says he has made a new discovery in the way of hornets. He says he found a nest of regular hornet in size but they are yellow.

§   Mr. and Mrs. W. T. York, of the Valley, have at their beautiful home a number of boarders from Hartwell, Ga. They will remain until the approach of winter.

§ The Black Diamond surveyors are in camp at M. V. Beck's, on Warwoman, and within the next week they will be camped near town. Capt. Kirk will be in Clayton Saturday.

§ Mr. S. S. Whitmire has returned from a trip to Ashville, N. C., and other points where he has been in interest of his mica mine. He reports things lively there and says the only thing that sells at high prices is mica.

§ G. B. Dockins, aged 24 years, died at Tallulah Falls, on the 15th inst. at 11.50 o'clock. He leaves a wife and a large number of relatives to mourn his departure. The funeral services were conducted by Rev. Julius McGath.

§ Senator W. J. Green is spending this week in Athens as a member of the special committee appointed by the Legislature at its last session to investigate the affairs of the North Eastern Railroad. He is not expected home till Monday next.

§ Hon. Chas. L. Bass, of Toccoa, and Miss Mattie Bass, of Clarkesville and associate editor of the Clarkesville Advertiser, and T. F. Green, of Athens, have been the guests of the Wall House since Saturday last. Charlie and Miss Mattie feel kindly towards old Rabun, among other reasons the county was named for one of their ancestors.

§ This is to notify all parties in interest that there will be an act introduced at the next sitting of the Legislature, entitled an act to regulate and maintain the price of corn in Rabun county at one dollar per bushel the year around and for other purposes. J. L. Hamby, chief promoter.

§ I have in range the following cattle, and when last seen was on the Rainey mountains on Chechero: One muly steer, one brindle muly steer, and one white frosty colored steer, horned, all marked two smooth crops. Address, D. M. Green, Rabun Gap.

§ We see from our exchanges that candidates for the various county officers are in the field. We think it is quite early for announcements, as the general election is about a year from now, but if anyone wants to offer for office in Rabun the Tribune will gladly announce for you. However, we have heard of no one aspiring to office in the county yet.

§ W. V. Garret is about done waving the paint brush on the court house and jail.

§ Last week we announced that Rev. W. A. Simmons would preach at the Methodist church at 7 o'clock and at that hour the church was filled with people from town and country. Rev. Simmons' theme was: "Men reap what they sow."

§ We have it authentically that there are three children in Chechero district who bear the following somewhat rain-bow names:
   William Eugene Thomas Andrew Augustus Balus Lafayette Russley Carver.
   Martha Arminda Manda Sarah Mariah Melinda Lucinda Lizziebeth Carver.

Mary Nancy Savannah Lucreasa Rosanna Jeneila Corretta Carver.

§   Notice This Please. I am now needing what you are due me, and now ask that all persons who are indebted to me either by note or account come at once and make settlement or I shall not hesitate to [commence?] suit. Now I think this is a fair warning [illegible]. Yours, J. L. Hamby.

§   R. C. T. A. Column.
   To the Teachers.
   I am glad of this opportunity. If I can not have the pleasure of meeting the teachers of Rabun county face to face, I can have the opportunity to exchange ideas on methods of teaching, through a column of our kind editor's paper. This is written especially to our brother and sister teachers who have not visited or joined The Teachers' Association, which is proving a success.
   I would have been very glad if every teacher of Rabun county had been present at our last meeting. Had you, no doubt, you would have treasured up some good ideas on teaching for future use, explained by Prof. W. T. Daniel and other accomplished teachers...
   Texie York

§   Old Tiger
   The farmers in this section are moving lively just now and saving their fodder.
   George Dockins died suddenly at Tallulah last Friday night. He leaves a wife, relatives and friends to mourn his loss.
   Dr. Green has gone to Athens on business.
   Ray Cannon, from Clayton, visited Tom and Leon Bleckley last week.
   Marven Turepn and wife went to Camp creek to church last Sunday.
   Prof. Nin Ramey and Johnnie Jenkins have formed a copartnership and selling mountain produce in Athens.
   Mr. F. A. Bleckley and wife spent Saturday night with their son, J. E. Bleckley, at this place.
   Dud Dockins has been in this community horse trading.
   Bart Stonecypher and wife visited relatives at Turnerville last week.
   Jesse W. Green was in our midst a few days ago looking after his farm.
   The people in this section are elated over the extension of the railroad from Tallulah Falls to Clayton.

§   Persimmon
   The health of our community is not so good at present. It seems to be a throat trouble generally.
   Miss Nora Justus is having serious time with her throat.
   C. J. Crunkleton is improving some.
   The protracted meeting is still going on at Boiling Springs.
   M. B. York came up from Cornelia Saturday and carried Miss Texie York back with him Sunday. She will fill a position as teacher in the Cornelia Institute for a while when she will return home and take charge of her school at Cross Roads.

For the past week I. P. Coleman has been sowing wheat, and he is getting a fine chance in the ground.

Mr. Ed Powell and wife, of the Valley, were the guests of T. M. Justus Sunday.

It is said that if a man has faith as to a grain of mustard he can remove mountains. I don't suppose a girl would have to have as much to move a Hill from Habersham to Rabun.

§   C. C. York and wife attended the quarterly meeting at Bethel last week. Mrs. York staid over until Monday.

§   Rabun county Georgia. The Easiest Place to Make a Living on earth. The production Of the soil is Phenominal. Can Make a Living with a Few Month's Work in the Year. Best Home Market in the United States for every Product. It is unsurpassed As A Corn Producing Section. Can sell your products to wagoners at your door.

The Clayton Tribune, Volume 2, Number 37, Thursday, October 5, 1899

§   Capt. Albright passed through town Thursday enroute to Hiawassee to look after his copper mine at that place. He says surveying for the Missing Link Railroad will begin this week.—Young Harris News.

§   The Supremacy of Thought by W. T. Daniel...

§   Ordinary's Citations.
Georgia—Rabun County. All persons interested are hereby notified that, if no good cause be shown to the contrary an order will be granted by the undersigned on the 31st day of October, 1899, establishing a change on the road leading from Tallulah Academy to Plum Orchard church, said change commencing at H. C. Blalock's store in Tallulah District and running to the left of the old road, through the lands of H. C. Blalock and J. H. Derrick and intersecting the old road at the Raper Gap. This Sept. 26th 1899. W. S. Long, Ordinary.

§   Georgia—Rabun County. V. T. Stonecypher having made application in due form to be appointed permanent administrator upon the estate of Wm. Stonecypher, late of said county, notice is hereby given that said application will be heard at the regular term of the court of ordinary for said county, to be held on the first Monday in November, 1899. Witness my hand and official signature this 25th day of September, 1899. W. S. Long, Ordinary.

§   Georgia—Rabun County. John Howard, Administrator de-bonis non, of Thomas Carter, deceased, has in due form applied to the undersigned for leave to sell the lands belonging to the estate of said deceased, and said application will be heard on the first Monday in November next. This 2nd day of October, 1899. W. S. Long, Ordinary.

§   Col. Hamby is in Atlanta attending the United States court.

§   J. C. York tells us he killed 20 squirrels off one tree.

§   Mrs. M. E. Davis, of Tallulah Falls, is visiting relatives in town.

§   The Board of education met in regular session here last Tuesday.

§   J. C. Singleton returned Monday night after a 12 day's trip down in Georgia.

§   There were quite a crowd of representative men of the county in town Tuesday.

§   J. A. Almon has dug 31 bushels of Irish potatoes and he is not near done.

§   Next Saturday is the regular session of the teacher's association [illegible].

§   Mr. Calvin Speed, of Victoria, N. C. made our office a pleasant call Friday last.

§   A number of arrests have been made by the marshall this week, but few convictions.

§   Mr. H. M. Hopper, of Rabun county, was in town Saturday.—Franklin (N. C.) Press.

§   Sam Mitchell and his son, Tom, have returned from a prosperous trip down the country.

§   H. M. Munday, rodman[?] of the Black Diamond surveying party, has been sick for several days.

§   D. C. Brown and wife, of Winston, Ga., spent several days among friends here the past week.

§   Mr. W. P. Wilson has moved to Victoria, N. C., and we unsterstand he is doing well. Good luck to you W. P.

§   J. L. Hamby had the misfortune to get dog bitten. Fortunately the dog was not mad, but we can't say as much for Hamby.

§   John Godfrey passed through town yesterday with Lester Queen. Queen is charged with violating the United States revenue law.

§   Esq. J. E. Derrick and J. H. Ramey, of the Flats, are tied on the Irish potato contest. Bring your potatoes along and get the premium.

§   D. J. Duncan, after about two month's stay at the Falls, returned to Clayton Monday evening. Mr. Duncan is always welcomed and greeted by his friends.

§ Deputy Collectors Crawford and Bergstrom cut two distilleries on Timpson Creek and in Moccason the past week. They also cut down beer at three other places.

§ A. B. Chastain of Scaly, N. C., has moved in the Robins cottage on the Valley road. He is here temporarily. His wife is being treated by local physicians.

§ Mr. A. J. Duncan was in town to-day. He says he wants the stock law or the gates pulled down on the public roads as he has to get out of his buggy and open seven gates in the rain.

§ Mrs. Maggie Brown returned to her home, Spartanburgh, S. C., today after a pleasant visit with Mr. and Mrs. John W. Godfrey of Tennessee Valley.

§ The following are registered at the Blue Ridge: E. L. Bergstrom, Boone Crawford, L. H. Moore, D. W. S. Fry, Clarkesville. S. L. McKinny, Blue Ridge. H. W. Gleason, Atlanta.

§ H. W. Gleason, representing the reliable medical concern of Chamberlain Medicine Co., Des Moines, Iowa, was here Tuesday. He renewed advertising contract for the Co. with us for another year.

§ Mr. J. A. Swofford, after spending about two months at Cornelia assisting B. W. Grant, proprietor of the Grant House, returned home Monday. Mr. Grant has improved so as to be able to look after his business personally.

§ Lafayete Watts began building a wagon twelve year ago and completed it yesterday when Sheriff Ritchie purchased it and drove into town with it last evening. If this is not correct, Mr. Watts, get after the sheriff, he is our authority.

§ Mr. H. R. Cannon, of Tallulah Falls, is in town to-day. Mr. Cannon paid us his second year's subscription, gave us an ad, which will appear in our next issue, and otherwise cheered us up. He is a fine business man and we are glad he has had a prosperous year.

§ This is to notify any and all persons indebted to us if you do not settle with us either by note or payment by the 15th day of Oct. 1899 we will put your account out immediately for collection. Please bear this in mind as we mean just exactly what we say. Yours Truly, C. E. and W. R. Cannon.

§ The watermelon contest which has been advertised since last spring began July 31st by J. F. Earl bringing three weighing 35 ¼, 39 ¼ and 44 ½. At different dates, the following entered the contest: M. W. Swafford 35 lbs. and 15 oz., L. P. Wall 40 lbs. and oz., W. S. Price 39 and 42, W. A. Swafford 40 lbs. and 15 ½ oz. and 47 and 15 oz., J. H. Coffee 39 ½, W. P. Smith 43 ½. As you will see, W. A. Swafford raised the largest, it weighing 47 pounds and 15 ounces. Mr. J. A. Earl offered the premium of $5 which was paid Mr. Swafford last Tuesday by Judge Long, to whom the money had been deposited.

§   Notice of Local Legislation.

Notice is hereby given that a Bill with the following title will be introduced at the next session of the General Assembly of Georgia, to wit: "A bill to be entitled, an act to prevent the driving of cattle from any point south of Blue Ridge into the counties of Rabun, Towns, Union in said state to prescribe penalties for violating the same and for other purposes."

W. J. Green, Senator 40th Dist.

§   Notice is hereby given that a tax of five tenths of one percent is levied on all the taxable property within the incorporate limits of the town of Clayton, Ga., to pay the expenses and indebtedness of said town for the year 1899 and that the final date of payment of said taxes closes on the 25th day of Dec. 1899 and that executions be issued against all[?] delinquent tax payers immediately after said date. By order of the town council in regular meeting. This Sept. 25th 1899.

J. L. Henson, Mayor. J. A. Reynolds, Clerk of Council.

§   Three Children Burned.

Last Saturday night about 10 o'clock three children were burned to death near Tallulah Lodge. Fan[?] Scott, the mother of the children, left the house about 8 o'clock to attend a dance at the lodge and left her little children, aged from five to ten, fastened in the house alone, when the house caught on fire, or set as some think, and the children were burned beyond recognition.

The building belongs to Fletcher Robinson and was occupied by a Mr. Brookey[?], who was at the dance with the [illegible] was burned.

§   Betty's Creek

The people are all bout through their fodder.

Making syrup and going to candy pullings is the general occupation now.

Mrs. Lush Garland fell last Wednesday and hurt herself pretty bad. She is improving now.

Mr. George Hopper went to Macon, N. C., Sunday to see his best girl.

Uncle Benny Grist is up to see us again. He is working in the interest of the Tribune.

Capt. L. M. Beavert and wife were the guests of A. A. Darnell and family Sunday.

Chinquapins are about gone but chestnuts will soon be in if there are any.

Mrs. Georgia Darnell visited L. L. Long and family Sunday.

Mr. Alfred Ledford is suffering a great deal from a boil.

Mr. A. A. Darnell went to Clayton Monday on business.

§   I am tired of accounts. I now want money, notes or fi fas. Settle by the 15th and your name will not be called at the white oak nor will your dog try to bite the bailiff. If you mean to pay me without being sued don't fail to settle by that time. I want all that are good to settle by the 15th. Yours, very truly, W. R. L. Ritchie.

§   Notice is hereby given that I do not want any shooting, hunting or sruit gathering done on my lands, or trespassing in any way on my premises, nor on Lafayete Wall's farm and premises, at or near Clayton, as I am controlling that place now. S. W. Dover.

§   The fourth Quarterly Conference for the Rabun mission charge will be held at Ivy Hill on Thursday Oct. 26th. All are cordially invited. The members of the Quarterly Conference will be expected to attend without fail. J. W. Hughes, P. C.

The Clayton Tribune, Volume 2, Number 38, Thursday, October 12, 1899

§   Missing Link Sure to Come.

On September 21st the Chattanooga (Tenn.) News printed a map of the proposed Missing Link railroad. In the same issue that paper gives the following prospectus the road.

Let us examine the map of Georgia and see. Let us take Blue Ridge as a nucleus, and from there examine the country about. From Blue Ridge west lie the counties of Fannin, Union, Rabun and Towns, a territory of 100 miles and 70 miles in width, which has no railroad. The mineral wealth of this district is unsurpassed by any in known world, and so declared by the greatest scientist of the present day. It is not only the abundance of gold that has been found and mined fifty years before California had been discovered... And, for the purpose of [further] showing what may be relied upon for traffic besides mineral and timber, it may be stated that thousands of sheep and cattle are yearly shipped from Union, Towns and Rabun counties, and which are either driven to Murphy N. C., a distance of thirty and fifty miles, or across the Blue Ridge to Gainesville Ga., a distance of fifty miles... Thousands of people come from all parts of the South Atlantic and Gulf States to spend the summer season in the mountains of North Georgia...from Augusta, Ga., Port Royal and Columbia, S. C., would come this way...

§   Three Forks

People are generally done foddering on this side and those who are not done are trying their best to get done. The frost didn't get much fodder over here, but I think it got some on the Blue Ridge.

Meeting at Hail Ridge last Saturday and Sunday. Miss Genela Kell joined the church and was baptized Sunday. Mr. Thos. Ford was the preacher.

Mr. Isaace Duncan and wife, of Seneca, S. C., have been visiting relatives and friends in Rabun and part of Macon, N. C., for the past two weeks.

Mr. J. M. Hopper went down on the river somewhere last Saturday and came back Sunday. Girls, you had better lookout down there or he'll be trying to get some of you off over to Macon county.

Some of the boys caught a kitten coon one morning last week and think there is more where they caught it.

Bead picking, pulling and drying is the order of the day and has been for some time.

There are no apples to speak of in this settlement and the cabbage are all rotting on the stalk.

§   Tennessee Valley

Too late for last week.

Mr. Paul Martin, a bright young man of Clay Co., N. C., is visiting relatives in the Valley.

Mr. Lee Ritchie, one of our best citizens, visited Pine Mountain on business this week.

Mr. Geo. Greenwood visited Clayton Tuesday.

Mr. Noah Garland, an enterprising livery stable man, of Toccoa, with his wife and children visited his mother this week.

Messrs. W. J. Neville and Z. B. Dillard attended the regular meeting of the board of Education at Clayton Tuesday.

Misse Estelle and Lizzie Gillispie have both been quite sick the past week, but are better at this writing.

Ethel and Margie Powell, who have been sick diptheria, are improving rapidly.

Mr. John Carter and wife, of Toccoa, have been visiting Mrs. Lee Ritchie.

Miss Ruth Smith, the accomplished assistant teacher at the academy, has been sick this week.

Mr. Moore, traveling salesman for Beck and Greggs, was in the Valley Monday.

Oscar Powell, who has been spending his vacation with his home folks, left Sunday for Tallulah river to resume his duties in the school room training the young ideas to shoot.

Mrs. Dr. Garland and her little son Claud, returned from Franklin Sunday, after spending a week her father.

§   A daily mail route from Clayton to Pine Mountain has been established by the Government. The first mail left here last Monday morning and is being carried by A. M. Wall. On this route a new post office, seven miles east of Clayton, has been established. The name of the new office is Warwoman and Mrs. A. M. Wall is postmistress. This route was badly needed and we are glad the government has established the route. Now we are in daily communication with Pine Mountain, Highlands, Victoria, N. C., Walhalla, Russell and other parts of South Carolina. Before this route was established it required about a week's time to get an answer from Pine Mountain, a distance of sixteen miles.

§   We are requested to publish the game law as now in force in this state and as the law is quite voluminous on the subject, we publish an extract which will suffice for this county...

The act of which the above is an extract superceeds all previous laws on the subject of game, and was passed by the Legislature of 1896. The Journal shows that our Representative R. E. A. Hamby voted against the bill.

§   R. C. T. A. Column. A Successful Man by W. T. Daniel...

§   Old Tiger

Mrs. Wallie Norton visited relatives in [Habersham] last week.

Mr. George Brendle and wife of N. C., have just returned from a visit to friends and relatives here.

We are sorry to hear that Johnnie Jenkins has fever but hope he will soon recover.

Mr. Granville Dixon was with his girl last Sunday.

Mr. Shug Ramey has just returned from market.

Mr. H. R. Cannon from Tallulah Falls was up on business the first of this week.

§   Ordinary's Citations.

Georgia—Rabun County. All persons interested are hereby notified that, if no good cause be shown to the contrary, an order will be granted by the undersigned, on the 13th day of November, 1899, establishing a change on the road leading from Clayton to Walhalla, said change commencing at or near the corner of C. C. Ledford's fence in Warwoman district, thence the old Smash wagon road, crossing the creek at the old ford through the lands of C. C. Ledford and Martha Bynum, and intersecting the old road at the old bridge place. Oct. 11th 1899. W. S. Long, Ordinary.

§   Betty's Creek

Mr. Mack Hopper, who has been in Tennesse for some time, is visiting friends here this week.

A. A. Darnell went to Macon, N. C., Sunday.

Mr. David Shope, who has dropsy, is not improved, but is getting worse.

Mrs. Thomas Garland is not improved.

Miss May Garland had a new sweetheart Sunday. Charlie, why didn't you go?

We have a new superintendent, J. M. Brooks, and we hope our Sunday School will prove a success and also our prayer meeting.

The people on Betty's Creek will now have a vacation as they are about [through] making sirup and drying pumpkins.

Miss Fannie Norton has been very sick but is better at this writing.

Miss Lena Hopper, of Quartz, was with us Tuesday night. She was on her way to W. H. Greenwood's.

George Daily says it will be hard times before he quits the Tribune.

Mr. Henry Daily is building a new grist mill.

Mr. L. D. Garland has added a back room to his house.

§   Miss Lisa Duncan[?] is visiting at Tallulah Falls.

§   Heman Earl[?] [missing] a fine ground hog Wednesday.

§   S. S. Whitmire[?] returned from Seneca, S. C., Saturday.

§   Miss Stella Langston[?] is visiting in Walhalla [missing].

§   Miss Ida Duncan[?] is feeling better after seven[?] days of bad feeling.

§   The Georgia[?] Legislature convenes Wednesday the 25th of this month.

§   Aunt Mary [missing or illegible].

§   Every one who are due me any thing and not paid within five days will be sued. S. S. Whitmire.

§   Mrs. D. T. Duncan has growing in her front yard a horned cucumber. This variety is a new one to us.

§   Representative Hamby has been feeling badly since his return from Atlanta but is now so as to be in his office.

§   Eddie Norton after fifty days confinement with Typhoid fever is now able to be out in town.

§   Mrs. J. S. Ramey left this morning for Cornelia where she will be the guest of relatives for eight or ten days.

§   Among those who remembered us this week were J. M. York, of Persimmon, and A. M. Holden of Warwoman.

§   We had a pleasant time hunting Tuesday with Mr. J. A. Earl. We bagged a number of squirrells and had a lot of fun.

§   Mrs. W. B. Grant, who has been at the Wall House for the summer, returned to her home in Jacksonville, Fla., last week.

§   I will preach at Wolf Fork school house next Sunday p. m. at 2:30. All are invited. Chas. W. Curry.

§   Mrs. W. B. Grant and Miss Blanche Wall, of Clayton, spent last Saturday at the home of Mrs. E. A. Bell.—Keowee Courier.

§   Hon. Howard Thompson, of Gainesville, Ga., spent a short time in town the latter part of last week. He has many friends here.

§   We errored in a former issue when we said Mrs. W. P. Rembert was the guest of John B. Donaldson. She was the guest of Mrs. J. B. Murray.

§   J. F. Earl has made a number of nice improvements about the home. Among other things he has graveled the walks which aids very much to the appearance.

§   The Blue Ridge Hotel received a coat of paint on the outside some time ago. Now painter W. V. Garrett is giving the inside a thorough and beautiful coating.

§   The Black Diamond surveying corps is camped in town and with the exceptions of a day or two the weather has been very fine and they are progressing rapidly with the work.

§ Uncle Jeff Duncan is quartered with D. G. Dover on Black Rock mountain and spending these pleasant days shooting squirrells. Uncle Jeff is a professional squirrell hunter.

§ The Blue Ridge Hotel was serenaded Tuesday night by the col. people of the Black Diamond survey. They sang some of the old time darkey airs and this occasion was much enjoyed by the guests.

§ Notice is hereby given that the Rabun County Teacher's Association will meet at Clayton Saturday Oct. 21 1899, for the purpose of carrving out the program prepared for Oct. 7th, and such other business as may come before the Association. By order of the president. This Oct. 11, 1899. A. A. O'Kelley, Pres.

§ All who are indebted to me will please call and see me by the first of November and settle by cash or make me a good note as I cannot let my books stand over. So prompt settlements make long friends. J. T. Long.

§ Tennessee Valley
The many friends of Jim Martin will be pained to learn that he is quite sick at present.
Mr. Sam Holden, of Pine Mountain visited in the Valley Saturday and Sunday.
Mr. Alf Whitmire, one of Rabun's best citizens was in the Valley last week on business.
Mr. Frank Smith, of Franklin, visited W. H. Greenwood Friday and Saturday.
Mr. W. H. Greenwood went to Franklin Thursday.
Mr. George Mann, of North Carolina, filled Rev. C. W. Curry's pulpit last Sunday and Sunday night.
Miss Stella Langston, a beautiful young lady of Clayton, passed through the Valley Saturday on her way to N. C.
Mr. N. F. Howard, of North Carolina, was in the Valley his week surveying land.

§ Notice.
I will be at the following named places for the purpose of collecting the State and county taxes for the year 1899.
Clayton, Oct. 19th from 9 o'clock a. m. till 8 p. m.
Valley, Oct. 20 from 9 a. m. till 8 p. m.
Persimmon, Oct. 21 from 9 a. m. till 8 p. m.
Tallulah Oct. 23 from 9 o'clock a. m. till 3 p. m.
Stonepile, Oct. 24 from 9 o'clock a. m. till 8 p. m.
Tiger, Oct. 25 from 9 a. m. till 3 p. m.
Chechero, Oct. 26 from 9 a. m. till 8 p. m.
Warwoman, Oct. 27 from 9 a. m. till 8 p. m.
Moccasin, Oct. 28 from 9 a. m. till 8 p. m.
Joseph Dickerson, T. C.

§ Notice.
All persons are hereby notified that trespassing on my premises by hunting,

taking fruit or otherwise will be prosecuted. You are specially notified hereby to keep out of my turnip patch. W. C. Norton.

§ Some hounds were chasing a wolf all around Franklin through the whole of Sunday night. It had been started on Shooting creek in Clay county Saturday and the last heard of it was at Mr. W. C. Allman's place where it was seen early Monday Morning.—Franklin Press.

The same night a wolf captured a 20 pounds turkey gobler for us and had the audacity to devour him within 30 yards of our door.

The Clayton Tribune, Volume 2, Number 39, Thursday, October 19, 1899

§ Cornelia Institute.

Cornelia, Georgia, Oct. 10, 1899.

If space permits, I would like to speak a word commendatory of the Cornelia Institution of learning now flourishing under the capable management of Prof. A. E. Booth and his corps of faithful co-adjutors... A. L. M.

§ Little Orphan Girl. We publish the following by request of J. C. Powell. The author is unknown to us...

§ We heard of certain ones (and we know they are few) speaking lightly of the Tribune because of so much local talk in its columns. We want to say that the Tribune is nearing its 700th mark because of this feature of the paper, and we may safely add that their understandings of things is very limited... Now since we began writing this short article our little daughter brings to us a card from Col. A. J. Ritchie, a Rabun boy, now of Cambridge, Mass., asking us to send the Tribune to his address there, and she hands us 25c and says, send the Tribune to Miss Carrie Edwards to Victoria, N. C. and what for?... Any person who would belittle his own town, county or county paper is not worthy of notice.

The Tribune will however continue to notice and give notice of Spokendike visiting Mr. and Mrs. Lewallen, and if any of our readers object, and such things are distasteful to them, their paper will be discontinued upon payment of dues. We want it distinctly understood the Tribune is a LOCAL paper and will continue to be run as such.

§ We have received a copy of "Echoes from Tallulah Falls," Vol. 1, No. 1, edited by Walter Hunnicut and managed by William Berry. It is full of general news and neatly printed. We hope it's life will not be short and full of trouble.

§ The committee appointed by the last Grand Jury to investigate the books of the Ordinary, County Treasurer and sheriff met here last Friday and completed their work Saturday. The committee are: H. A. Keener, C. F. Garland and John W. Green, we persume their work is a part of the court and their acts will not be made public until the next term of the court.

§   Persimmon

Mr. Editor, I will ask your pardon as I have not appeared for some time.

T. E. King has a new store house which speaks well for Persimmon.

Rev. Hughes preached at Bethel Sunday but the attendance was under average as some of our citizens are attending Habersham's singing convention held at Providence.

M. V. York has returned from Cornelia.

Tom Justus is having his dam put back in order to overflow his land.

The Boiling Spring school is not as good as before fodder.

The health of our community is tolerable good at present.

§   Wolfcseek

We have a nice rain after some dry weather. Syrup making is the order of the day. Are about done gathering apples and the crop is short.

J. H. Williams and wife is visiting friends and relatives on Wolfcreek this week.

Will Stancil is setting up a saw mill near Camp Creek.

We understand there is a bill pending in the legislature to set the price of corn to one dollar. If the members want to fall to rise no more let them try something like that.

§   Tennessee Valley

Messrs. W. J. Neville and Logan Dickerson returned Sunday from Grantsville where they went to attend the Dairyman Association.

Dr. Henson, the clever dentist from Clayton, did some work in the Valley this week.

Rev. C. W. Curry, after spending a month with his home folk at Griffin, was with us Sunday and filled his appointment.

Dr. D. L. Garland's new house is about complete and he expects to move next week.

Mr. W. H. Greenwood left for Atlanta Wednesday where he goes to accept a position with Lamar & Rankin Drug Company.

Mr. Kendly and party from Fort Madison, S. C., spent two days this week in the Valley looking at Estatoah Falls and other places of interest.

Uncle Mack Neville is sick this week but his friends hope to see him out soon.

Messrs. Ben Greenwood and Malcalm Moore went hunting the other day and caught a fine ground hog.

Mr. Frank Ritchie has returned from Athens this week.

§   The coming of Dewey will be a great thing for the State Fair.

§   R. E. A. Hamby spent this week in Atlanta.

§   Miss Lillie Wall is attending the fair this week.

§   The town boys are having much sport these days flying kites.

§   Dr. J. C. Dover is spending a few days in Atlanta on business.

§   The Blue Ridge Hotel will engage in quilting this winter.

§   Lafayette Wall, of Clara, Ga., made a hurried trip here a few days ago.

§   Col. Paris[?] [illegible] court last Saturday [illegible].

§   R[?]. L. Moss[?], Jr., of Athens[?], Ga., [illegible] business trip here first of the week.

§   S. S. Whitmire will manage the mercantile firm of T. N. Carter at this place.

§   Tax collector Joseph L. Dickerson is in town today on his first round.

§   Miss Blanche Wall is visiting at Anderson, S. C. and Clarkesville, Ga.

§   Dr. Henson has gone to Nacoochee Valley, White county for a few days.

§   John W. Godfrey and daughter, Miss Zoie, are spending this week in Atlanta.

§   W. P. Rembert, of Blairsville, is spending some time among home people here.

§   J. A. Swofford left last Friday for Atlanta where he has accepted a position with the Hotel Wine Meister.

§   Col. Fred W. Eliot[?], of Toccoa, Ga., was here Monday. He was here in the interest of some of the projected railroads.

§   It is "hard times," but not so hard that a large number of our citizens are and will take in the State fair in Atlanta.

§   Rev. C. W. Curry will make Clayton his home the remainder of the conference year and will be the guest of the Wall House.

§   Our townsman Warren Dunlap was convicted in the United States court Monday and was sentenced to two months imprisonment.

§   It is reported that the raccoons have destroyed the corn crop of corn, root and branch, of Pechin Smith who lives on Cliff creek, this county.

§   Mrs. Alander Parker, who has been stoping[?] at Squire Derrick's for the purpose of receiving treatments for physicians, has returned to her home at Persimmon.

§   The Black Diamond surveyors have moved from here to the Valley. They are camped near John Scruggs[?]. The survey will be [illegible] for the next ten miles compared to the last ten miles.

§   J. C. York caught a fox...last night after a thirty minutes' race and J. I. Langston and a party from town caught one this morning within the incorporate limits.

§   There was a wedding at the Blue Ridge Hotel last night. The contracting parties were: Mr. S. O. Littleton and Miss Octie Watkins, of Cullasaja, N. C. Esq. D. T. Duncan performed the ceremony.

§   Mrs. Paris raised in her garden this year three California bean stalks, the berry of which is said to be a very good substitute for coffee. The plant is very prolific. We counted one hundred and three pods that grew on one limb.

§   By the first of next month T. N. Carter will have a complete line of general merchandise at the Hamby stand. Mr. Carter will run a wagon from here to Westminster and he will buy everthing from the farmers that is merchantable. We welcome him to our town with his indomitable energy and a man of affairs.

§   Major York and D. M. Turpen passed through town Tuesday with a pair of millstones, cut from the noted W. C. Scruggs' query. The millstones were cut for George Watkins of South Carolina. The weight of the runner stone is estimated to weigh two thousand pounds.

§   Mr. John A. Wilson brought the news here yesterday that Rafe Whitmire was stabbed by a negro last Monday evening near Hartwell, Ga., and died Tuesday morning at 2 o'clock. The murdered man is a native of this county. He was the son of Mr. William Whitmire our townsman and brother of W. S. and R. A. Whitmire. The family have the sympathy of the community.

§   Dr. Green has a peach tree in his orchard in full bloom and the Doctor says if the frost does not come to soon he will have a full crop of peaches, at least on one tree. The sight is an odd one at this season of the year and should you succeed in getting a crop, we would be pleased to have an invitation to help devour them but we shall look for icicles instead of peaches.

§   One of the social events of the week was the marriage of C. E. Cannon to Miss Nannie Oliver, at the home of the bride's father, two miles south of Clayton. Mr. Cannon is on[?] the firm of C. E. and W. R. Cannon, prominent merchants of Tiger, Ga., and son of [illegible] Representative R. C[?]. Cannon. He is a sober and industrious young man and the woman he weds is a bright and lovely young lady. We wish the couple a happy future.

§   It was suggested by a prominent gentleman of Athens a few days ago that certain of young ladies in town might meet with success matrimonially were it known that the justice of the peace and the ordinary of the county are in the same family. We will say in the way of inducement further[?], that the ceremony and license are free and to help the matter along a conveyance may be obtained free of charge by the head of the family.

§   T. J. Ritchie passed through town yesterday on his way to Richmond, Va., with 31 head of fine cattle and one hundred and twenty eight head of sheep. Since the prohibitary[?] laws passed by North Carolina making it a penalty to drive cattle from the State through that state, Mr. Ritchie drives to Westminster, S. C., and ships on the Southern Railway to points north. Raise cattle boys and if we cannot ship one way we can another. Cattle will always sell for the cash.

§   Wolffork
The people are busily engaged in corn gathering and syrup making.
Ed Page is off to market.
Rev. Chas. W. Curry preached an interesting sermon Sunday last.
Miss Ella Moore was all smiles Sunday as her best fellow was on Wolffork.
Ask Mr. Lester Hopper if he is not tired of hunting and catching nothing.
Mr. James Powell and wife were on Wolffork last week.
Ask Marcus Bleckley and James Green why they go to the post office so often.
Mr. W. R. Keener says he has made a large crop of beans and pumpkins.
Mr. Joseph Dickerson has gone to Tallulah Falls.

§   Three Forks
We are having some rainy weather over here now, just enough to keep the market wagons at home, though there is one out now that we wish it would rain back.
The two Mr. Burrels went to Clear Creek to meeting last Sunday and report a good meeting.
Mr. I. R. Duncan is now gone to Mr. S. James' to help make some wagons.
J. M. Hopper and J. B. Duncan went coon hunting the other night and caught all the bad luck they were looking for.
Chestnuts are scarce here and worth $2 per bushel.
Don't know yet when the picnic will be at the D. C. H.

§   A party from Toccoa has written here asking for store room. They will come at an early date if a room satisfactory can be had. Come on, the more the better.

§   For some time there have been a number of lawless acts committed in town by unknown parties, but the climax was reached Sunday night last when a crowd did considerable damage to the Baptist church and public school house. A few warrants have been issued we understand, but no arrests have been made.

The Clayton Tribune, Volume 2, Number 40, Thursday, October 26, 1899

§   In the Phillipines.
Jolo, P. I., August 20th, '99.
For the convenience of kindred and friends that I have not had the opportunity to write to, I will write a few lines which I hope will reach the Tribune and through it reach many of you. I lived in Rabun county two years near Wolfcreek church, where my father was raised. Ten years ago I left there and went to Texas where my father lives now. Two years ago I thought nothing would suit me better than to be a soldier,

so I enlisted in the 23rd United States Infantry, desiring to see some of the world. I was soldering at Fort Clark, Texas, near the line of Mexico when on the fifteenth day of February the battleship Maine was sunk. Then there was not a soldier that did not want to scrap with the Spaniards. So on the 17th day of April we packed our knapsacks and boarded the train for New Orleans, Louisiana...

Respectfully, Robt. F. Williams.

§   A New Thing in Georgia.

The Prohibitionists of Georgia have set apart a day to be observed as "Prohibition Day" over the entire State. The day set apart is the 5th Sunday in this month—Oct. 29th.

Appropriate programs are being furnished to all the churches, Sunday schools, Epworth Leauges, Young People's Societies, etc., of the state, with an earnest appeal that temperance exercises be held in every church in the State on that day.

The Monday following Prohibition Day (Oct. 30th) is to be known as "Prohibition Work Day." Every man, woman and child in Georgia, who is interested in the cause of temperance and who would free the State from the liquor traffic, is asked to contribute the earnings of this day to the temperance cause. These contributions would be sent to Rev. A. J. Hughes, Supt. Georgia Prohibition Association, Watkinsville, Ga., to be used in the fight now being waged against the liquor traffic in Georgia, under the direction of the finance comittee: Messrs. Walter B. Hill, C. B. Willingham and Jno. H. Reynolds... –Athens Sentinel.

§   The Idealist in Literature by W. T. Daniel...

§   Tennessee Valley

Mr. George Wikle and wife, of White county, visited the family of Mr. Ed Powell two days last week. Mr. Wikle likes our county and he says he expects to move up here next year.

Mrs. Carrie Ayers, of Turnerville, spent several days with Mrs. R. B. Dillard this week.

W. J. Neville took a drove of hogs to Walhalla Monday.

Rev. A. B. Thomas, of Sylva, N. C., who has had charge of the Baptist church here for the past two[?] years, preached his farewell sermon here to a large audience Sunday. Mr. Thomas has a host of friends who hate to see him leave. The church has called Rev. Sims to take his place.

Lee Dillard caught two very large wildcats last week.

Messrs. J. J. and B. H. Greenwood, Willie Grist, R. B. Dillard, Frank Ritchie and Malcom Moore all took in the fair Thursday so as to get a peep at the nation's hero— George Dewey.

Mr. D. J. Crump, of Habersham county spent Monday night with Ben Greenwood.

Messrs. W. C. Scruggs and G. W. Greenwood, two of Rabun's solid citizens, went to Atlanta Tuesday to take in the fair.

Mr. Jim Powell and wife, of Germany, attended preaching in the Valley Sunday.

Mrs. W. A. Curtis and her son Will, of Franklin, visited friends in here Saturday.

Sam Franks, of Franklin, N. C., is visiting his sister, Mrs. Dr. Garland here.

Mr. Chas. Langston and Miss Lillie Wall were the guests of Miss Zoe Godfrey Sunday.

§   Administrator's Sale.
Georgia—Rabun County.

By virtue of an order of the court of Ordinary of said county, will be sold at public outcry, on the first Tuesday in December next, within the legal hours of sale, the following real estate situated in Rabun county to-wit:

Lot of land No. 7 in the first district. This lot is valuable for its gold deposits. Gold miners who slight the opportunity of attending this sale will live to regret it.

Also parts of Lots of land No. 90 and 100 in the second land District, it being all of said lots north of the public road leading from Rabun Gap to Burton, known as the Persimmon road, except that part of said lots owned by R. M. Keener, this tract of [land] being bounded on the north by lands of R. M. Keener and on the south by said Persimmon road containing one hundred acres more or less.

Also parts of lots of land Nos. 97, 99, and 100 in 2nd land district of said county. This includes all of the lands of the Dickerson estate in said lots south of the Persimmon road except 3 acres more or less where H. L. Dickerson now resides and includes all the lands on the places where W. L. Dickerson and H. L. Dickerson now reside[?] except the 3 acres above excepted and is bounded on the north by the Persimmon road, on the east by lands of Nancy Keener and R. M. Keener, on the south by lands of Ed Pitts and on the west by lands of H. L. Dickerson and the District line containing [illegible] acres more or less.

The aforesaid [illegible] Persimmon road are unimproved and in original forest; those south of the road are partially cleared and in cultivation, having erected thereon two dwelling houses and suitable [illegible] buildings.

Also at the same time and place parts of lots Nos. 102 and 103 in 2nd land district of said county containing fifty acres more or less, the place where John Parker now resides.

To be sold as[?] the property of the estate of W. T. Dickerson, late of said county, deceased, for the purpose of paying debts and making distribution among the heirs.

Terms of sale, one half cash and note with interest at eight per cent per annum with good security due twelve months from date of sale, for remainder.

M. L. Dickerson, Administrator of W. T. Dickerson.

§   Old Tiger

Miss Mouth[?] Kendrix died suddenly at her home Saturday night.

Henry Brindle and son, of Swain, N. C., were among friends here this week.

Capt. L. M. Beavert, of the Valley, passed through this week enroute to the fair in Atlanta.

The public school at this place is progressing nicely at this place. An entertainment is expected at the close of school.

John W. Green and son Ray was in this community a few days ago looking after business.

Jesse Green is the boss horse swapper in this section. We don't want Mr. Mitchell to be offended with Jesse.

Johnie Jenkins is improving[?] with a severe spell of Typhoid fever.

A lively debate is expected at Eden church next Friday night. The Tiger boys against Flat creek boys.

Prof. Cobb, of Royston, Ga., is expected to make the race for the State senate of his district which is the 31st. Prof. Cobb is a worthy man for the place and we bid him God speed in his undertaking.

C. E. and W. R. Cannon have enlarged their store room and have two nice clerks and are ready to accommodate the people.

Grantville Dixon is a regular visitor at John Jenkin's.

§   Editor Tribune:

Departed this life, Oct. 20th, in Atlanta, Ga., Rev. Clayton Quillian. Many people in Rabun county will be sorry to hear of the death of Bro. Quillian, as many homes were brought out of darkness through the instrumentality of Clayton Quillian. Having served near two years with him in your county and knowing his tireless work for the good of the people we may say "a good man has gone" for a more consecrated christian I never knew than the subject of this sketch...after a hard year helping his brethren his worn body gave way to Typhoid fever... A wife and two little girls are left to mourn for this Godly man...

W. A. Simmons, Oct. 21st, 1899.

§   Thad Bynum is taking in the fair.

§   G. M. Oliver is placed on the sick list.

§   John A. Earl is taking in the State Fair.

§   Dr. Green is having his beautiful home painted.

§   We are almost tired writing Atlanta this week.

§   Mr. D. T. Duncan has become a regular horse jockey.

§   J. M. York is combining business with pleasure in Atlanta.

§   Presiding Elder E. R. Cook, of Dahlonega, will be here to-morrow.

§   Squirrells, squirrels, and they are being slaughtered by the hundreds.

§   Mrs. Hamby's condition has [illegible] yesterday for the [illegible].

§   Ordinary W. S. Long and Mrs. Long and the little folks left this morning for the fair.

§   Mr. Ed Henry and wife, of Highlands, are the guests of Mr. and Mrs. Robins.

§   We will take corn on subscription. Now you have no excuse, you have plenty of it.

§   Misses Ida and Effie Duncan are gone where nearly all our citizens are gone—to Atlanta.

§   The Black Diamond surveying party have taken a vacation for ten days. They left Monday morning.

§   Last Sunday the revenue officers destroyed four distilleries on Tallulah river and captured a son of Thomas Coleman.

§   We want it distinctly understood that a large portion of the reading matter of our paper is the "tale told as it is told to us."

§   Mr. Langston has in his yard an apple tree full of young apples. It bloomed some time ago and now the young fruit is well developed.

§   We are in receipt of a letter from Will Holbrooks, who is in Atlanta jail. He orders the Tribune and says "the way of the transgresser is hard."

§   We are informed the United States authority has stationed a Deputy collector here and that he is expected at any time to take up his abode.

§   Services here at the Methodist church Sunday night. Also at Blue Ridge school house Sunday at 3 o'clock p. m. C. W. Curry, P. C.

§   Rev. Chas. W. Curry has been endeavoring to perfect plans to which the Sunday School children of Rabun county can have a part in the Dewey-Brumby celebration.

§   County School Commissioner Neville paid off the school teachers Monday. They are paid only 87% of contract as this exhausts the school funds available for the last quarter.

§   Brock-Brock.
   E. R. Brock and Miss Abble[?] Brock, of Habersham county, were married in the parlor of the Blue Ridge Hotel last Thursday night. D. T. Duncan, Esq., officiating.

§   T. L. Bryson, who has been at home for a month nursing his sick child, was carried back to Atlanta Saturday and lodged in jail to wait his trial at the next term of the superior court here.—Gainesville Eagle.

§   W. E. Thompson, induced by the alluring accounts of squirrel hunters, took an outing with his gun Monday, but his natural inclination for business and duty presenting its self to him and burning his conscience he returned after a few hours hunt with a lovely squirrell.

§   Uncle Henry Winters, colored, sprung a new one on us Sunday. While strolling in company with Mr. James Bell, we called at uncle Henry's and he was sound asleep. When aroused he said that he had hunted all night before and we saw simmering in a pot what we thought to be an O'possum, but we were told that it was a pole-cat and after a silence we asked him if he intended eating it, and he said no, he was boiling it to get[?] the oil, and he stated to us that the oil of a polecat is good for rheumatism.

§   Bud Dachus Shot by His Own Pistol.

Last Friday evening Bud Dachus of Walhalla, a native of Anderson county, S. C., was accidentally killed by a pistol shot from his own pistol. He was in company with his friend Lawrence Donthit, son of Ex-sheriff of Oconee county, at the sandy ford on Chattooga river, just on the Georgia side. Dachus and Donthit crossed the river in a batteau and just as they crossed Mr. Dachus unbuckled his belt and went to lay his pistol on the ground and evidence showed that his pistol slipped from his hand and struck a rock and fired, the ball entering his breast, and death came within a minute after the shot, never speaking except to call to his companion. An inquest was held and the verdict was that the deceased came to his death by accident.

§   Missionary Rally at Mt. Pleasant.

Sunday Oct. 22nd, 1899, will be one long to be remembered by many and especially those attending the Missionary Rally at Mt. Pleasant.

Mt. Pleasant is a very small church, in membership, though far exceeds any other of its kind in the county.

Several months ago the pastor, Rev. Chas. W. Curry, gave out, to a committee of four, missionary pyramids and Sunday was the day in which the committee would report.

After Sunday School and a short song service led by Miss Thornton the pastor asked J. B. Jolly and Miss Thornton to assist in the opening of the pyramids.

They reported as follows: Miss Roxie Russell $9.91. Miss Pearl Whitmire $3.20. Miss Fannie Holden $1.40. Prof. W. Holden $.85. Total $14.92.

Rev. Mr. Curry gave to the one receiving the largest contribution an elegant Oxford Bible. Miss Russell being the successful party...

One Who Was Present. Mt. Pleasant, Oct. 23, 1899.

§   Senator W. J. Green left Monday morning to be present at the meeting of the Georgia Legislature which convened the 25th. Representative R. E. A. Hamby is detained at home on account of the sickness of Mrs. Hamby who has been critically ill at her home for the past week. She was slightly improved yesterday.

§   Rabun Gap

Indian summer is on hand earlier than common. People are beginning to gather corn.

The engineers have surveyed and located the Black Diamond Railroad to the North Carolina line and gone back.

James A. Hopper will soon begin a new house for A. A. Darnell.

James Martin is very sick. It is thought he will not live long.

The Clayton Tribune, Volume 2, Number 44, Thursday, November 23, 1899

§   W. C. Norton returned from a trip to Walhalla Saturday.

§   Our thanks are due to Mrs. D. [missing] Duncan for a two pound winter radish.

§   Henry Cannon, of Long Creek, [missing] C., was here Monday looking hale[?] and hearty. We decided Mr. Cannon is a hustler.

§   H. A. Keener raised a sweet pumpkin[?] this year that weighed 80 pounds[?]. How would this one [missing] in the State fair.

§   Senator Green and Representative Hamby spent Sunday with [missing] families here and returned Sunday[?] to Atlanta.

§   P. G. Presley moved up from Winterville[?], Ga., last week and [missing] make Rabun his future home. [Missing] Presley was raised here and [missing] here four years ago and says [missing] Rabun beats all other places to make[?] a living easy.

§   It is with profound sorrow we learn[?] that our friend Charlie Grant [missing] Walhalla, is now confined with Typhoid[?] fever at the home of Mr. [missing] Langston. Only a few days [missing] the infant child died of Typhoid at their home.

§   Dept[?]. Marshal Stanley had quite [missing] a few days ago while out [missing]. He was chasing a man [missing] distillery and was in close [missing or illegible] Bamboo briar became wrapped[?] around his neck and a [missing] dog at the same time hold of [missing] legs[?].

§   Echoes from Tallulah Falls
    Uncle[?] Jeff Duncan, the faithful [missing] who has shown so many people[?] [missing] beauties of Tallulah, passed[?] through town last Thursday. [Missing] Jeff was from Atlanta, [missing] he had been taking in the [missing].
    John Scruggs was with us Friday[?]. Mr. Scruggs is one [missing] Rabun's[?] best citizens. We are [missing] glad to welcome him.

§   [Missing or illegible] young steers and [missing] one to two years old. [Illegible.] Address, T. E. Carver, Chechero, Ga.

§   Blue Hights
    Well, Mr. Editor, I guess some of your readers think your correspondent from Blue Hights is dead or gone west, but it is not so.
    Corn gathering, shucking, pumpkin piling, hog killing and cussing is all the go.
    Mr. W. M. Edwards and son Andrew was in our midst last week delivering fruit trees. Mr. Edwards is an energetic business man.
    Dr. Moore and family, of Hartwell, Ga., who have spent the summer here, the guest of W. T. York, has moved into our midst and now occupy the Conly House.

Hervey Cathey died at the home of his parents Nov. 8th, of fever. It is sad that one so young and just bursting into the bloom of manhood should be taken from this world. It is impossible for us to comprehend the mysterious workings of the Divine Providence but this should be a warning to all old and young. He was a kind and affectionate son, and was loved by all who knew him.

§   Dream of Judgement.

I learned the following beautiful poem from the venerable Horace W. Cannon, deceased, an old and respected citizen and publish the same by request. R. S. Sanders...

§   The Dog Law.

We extend our hearty congratulations to Hon. W. W. Dews, of Randolph county, for his untiring and recent successful efforts in having passed in the house of representatives a bill for taxing of dogs...

§   There Are Others.

From the Keowee (S. C.) Courier.

On last Friday morning, 10th instant, between one and three o'clock, eleven of the new street lamps in Walhalla were smashed by licks struck with a stick and utterly destroyed. The private lamps of Dr. J. W. Bell and C. W. Pitchford Co. were also destroyed thus making thirteen in all, an unlucky number for the offender or offenders.

The work of destruction began at the West end of Main street and one lamp after another was knocked out. It was not long, however, until Marshal J. W. Beck [illegible] were on the lookout for the offender. Finally the lamp at the intersection of Tugaloo and [illegible] streets near the Episcopal church, was smashed... [Illegible section] sworn out before Mayor S. F. Holleman charging Tench C. Hunsinger with disorderly conduct, also before W. O. White, Magistrate, for malicious trespass in breaking lamps. On Monday morning warrants were taken for Bob Williams, a young negro man who works for Hunsinger, for the same offenses. The cases against them were called for trial Tuesday morning at 11 o'clock before Mayor Holleman...

§   All owners of valuable dogs around Clayton say they will pay the tax of $1.00 willingly. This law if ratified by the Grand Jury will swell the school fund no doubt several thousand dollars in the county. We spent about five minutes taking the dog census in town and we found even sixty in this short time, and Mr. M. L. Shirley came to town at the time and reported, in his immediate neighborhood, 20 dogs.

§   There is much excitement in the Legislature just now over the Willingham temperance bill. There are friends on both sides and the fight promises to be a lively one. We are in favor of temperance, but for many years we have been made to doubt that prohibition prohibits. The plans of suppressing the liquor trafic in the main have failed and in our humble opinion will continue to fail.

§   Ordinary's Citations.

Georgia—Rabun county. All persons interested are hereby notified that, if no good cause be shown to the contrary, an order will be granted by the undersigned, on the 21st day of Dec. 1899, establishing two changes on the road leading from Rabun Gap to the Persimmon district.

1st change commencing near H. M. Hopper's residence and running through the lands of H. M. Hopper, L. C. Whitmire, J. L. Dickerson, J. B. Moore and I. M. Keener, and intersecting the old road at old schoolhouse place. 2nd change commencing on top of the hill east of I. M. Keener, and running through the lands of I. M. Keener and H. A. Dickerson intersecting the old road on top of the hill near H. A. Dickerson's as marked out by the commissioners appointed for that purpose. W. S. Long, Ordinary. Nov. 18th, 1899.

Notice. I will receive sealed bids up to 12 o'clock, Monday, Dec. 4th 1899, for the contract to blast the rock out of Smash wagon ford, and out of the road on the east side of said ford. Said contractor will be required to give bond for the faithful performance of said work.

Hammers, drills, powder and fuse furnished by the county. I reserve the right to reject any and all bids. Plans and specifications on file in my office. Terms cash, when completed and received. Nov. 20th 1899 W. S. Long, Ordinary, Rabun Co., Ga.

§ Georgia—Rabun county. All persons interested are hereby notified that, if no good cause be shown to the contrary, an order will be granted by the undersigned, on the 29th day of December, 1899, establishing a new road as marked out by the road commissioners appointed for that purpose, commencing at the S. W. corner of R. J. S. Dickson's field in said county, and running in a northern direction up She Creek, through the David Green Gap, through the lands of R. J. S. Dickson, Sylvester Ramey, W. J. Ramey, E. L. McConnell, J. W. Smith, A. M. Williams, A. L. Carver, F. A. Bleckley, B[?]. E. Ramey and John W. Green, and intersecting the Warwoman road near the residence of John W. Green. W. S. Long, Ordinary, November 22nd, 1899.

§ Notices to Debtors and Creditors. Georgia—Rabun County. All persons having demands against the estate of William Stonecypher, late of Rabun county, deceased, are hereby notified to tender in their demands to the undersigned according to law, and all persons indebted to said estate are required to make immediate payment. Nov. 9th, 1899. V. T. Stonecypher, Administrator.

§ Administrator's Sale of Personal Property. Will be sold, at the late residence of Wm. Stonecypher, on Tuesday, the 28th day of November, 1899, at public outcry, to the highest bidder, the following property to-wit: One mule, 15 head of hogs, 200 bushels of corn, 1500 bundles of tops and fodder, one buggy, one wagon, one set of smith tools, farming tools, sorghum mill, 3 bee hives, household and kitchen furniture, one new organ and a singer sewing machine and various other articles.

Terms of sale. All amounts of five dollars and upwards on eleven months time with note and approved security at 7 per cent interest. All sums under five dollars cash on day of sale. V. T. Stonecypher, Administrator.

§ Ed McConnell of Chechero was very sick Monday, but is now able to be out.

§ Thanks to D. M. Smith and J. F. Godfrey for substantial favors this week.

§ E. C. Jackson, of Athens, was in town to-day talking hardware to our merchants.

§ Rev. Saunders, wife and children, are visiting parents at Alto, Ga. for several days.

§ M. L. Shirley is rebuilding a residence where his splendid home was burned last summer.

§ A drove of hogs belonging to Robt. Ritchie passed through town to-day en route to Toccoa.

§ W. C. Donaldson and Jno. H. Donaldson are at work on Dr. Henson's residence at Tiger.

§ Miss Fanie Manley of Aid , Ga., will be the guest of her sister, Mrs. R. A. Whitmire for some time.

§ Nelson Tilly will locate his saw mill plant in a few days east of town on the land of J. F. Earls.

§ Mr. J. F. Earl is putting in a line of wood pipe from a spring on spur of Screamer mountain to his residence.

§ If you want to buy your goods cheap, go to S. S. Whitmire, Manager for T. N. Carter, at the J. L. Hamby old stand.

§ We extend to our down the country sports a cordial invitation to come up and hunt squirrels and have a good time.

§ W. D. Burch of Cornelia, was here Monday. Mr. Burch has traveled this section for many years and is very popular.

§ The revenue officials have taken a recess for a few days. They captured a number of coppers within the last two weeks.

§ W. S. Long says he has decided to retire after a long service as barber for the town. He thanks his friends for past patronage.

§ Old Mrs. Crawford, an estimable woman of Black's Creek community, sustained a fall early this morning resulting in serious injury to her hip-joint.

§ If you want to sell your corn, chicks, eggs, butter and sweet potatoes and etc., bring to Whitmire. Corn 45 cents, meat 7 cents, sugar 16 & 20 pounds wet.

§ Dr. Henson has been down at Tiger for the past week working on his house and by the way, he will have one of the finest houses in the county when completed.

§   Messrs T. B. Carter and Gus McCurry, of Rabun county, spent Wednesday night with the editor. Carter was on his way to Jackson county.—Franklin Press

§   One and all are requested to come and settle their accounts by January 1st 1900. Come with good note or the money and begin on the new. J. T. Long.

§   John W. Lindsey of Wilkerson county, has been appointed to succeed Richard Johnson as commissioner of pensions. The appointment was made by Gov. Candler.

§   About 50 men are engaged in grading the change on the public road near the residence of J. E. Bleckley. The change will be of great benefit to the traveling public.

§   We have a freak in our office of the briar tribe. The briar is about three inches wide and the thickness of pasteboard and about four feet long and is corrugated, has different beautiful colors.

§   Beginning next issue we shall print the gold bulletin of Rabun county issued by our state geologist, W. S. Yates. We think they will prove interesting, especially to home readers.

§   Marinda J. Ramey, aged fity-seven, died on the 14th inst., at her home on Chechero after an illness of over four years. She leaves many relatives in the county to mourn her departure.

§   One of the biggest fires we ever saw was on west Black Rock last Tuesday. The fire was put out at the base of a very steep part of the mountain and the fire ascended so rapidly that seemed the whole mountain was on fire at the same time.

§   Mr. John A. Burrell of Persimmon is in town today, accompanied by Bexter Ellmore, of Macon county, N. C. They were here examining the record of deeds. Mr. Burrell reports some serious sickness in his community and several deaths from throat affection.

§   And again we took an outing for squirrels, with our devil and little fice[?] Dodger, and killed nineteen, we think the finest squirrels we ever saw. Some of the sports around town suggest that a little proof would be nice in the matter. The fact is we have the proof and can produce it any time.

§   We print the following from a letter to J. M. York, from W. P. Carnes, of Iva, S. C.: "I will ask you to do a favor for me. Step over to the office of the Tribune and tell him to continue my paper, and I will hand him the money if I come soon, or I will send it by Christmas, as I prize it more than any paper I take and I take five."

§   We hope the legislature will pass that part of the Comptroller General's recommendations as relates to the early enforcement of the collection of taxes. That part of the controler's recommendations should pass, would legally remove from tax collectors of the state favorisms so often asked and proves very embarrassing to the collectors and others, and costs the state large sums of money.

§   We are reliably informed that Cornelia, Ga., is on the eave of a substantial boom. There is a flouring mill being constructed now, and there will soon be constructed a fifty thousand dollar cotton factory. With other prosperous industries already established there and having one of the best schools in North East Georgia, and one of the best equipped school building in faculty and otherwise, in this section, good hotel accomadations, and a wide awake citizenship, with two railroads, we see nothing to hinder that town from becoming, at an early day, an important commercial and education center. The success of towns is like the success of individuals, it comes only by effort and it seems that the citizens of Cornelia are combined and are a unit in this direction.

§   Georgia—Rabun County.
    By virtue of an order of the court of ordinary of said county, will be sold at public outcry at the courthouse in said county on the first Tuesday in December next, within the legal hours of sale, the following real estate situated in Rabun county, to wit:
    Part of lot of land number one hundred and eighty one (181) in the second land district of said county, and bounded as follows: On the north by land lot number one hundred and eighty four (184), on the east by lands of Henry Daily, on the south by land lot number one hundred and fifty six (156), on the west by land of J. M. Brooks.
    The above is mountain land and contains eighty three and one third (83 1/3) acres, more or less and house on same.
    Also part of lot number one hundred and thirty four (134) in the second land district of said county bounded on north by land of H. A. Keener, and on the west by land of Ritchie and on the south by land of W. J. Neville.
    The above tract contains thirty one and one fourth (31 ¼) acres, more or less and is valuable bottom land in cultivation.
    Also part of lot number eighty one (81) in the first land district of said county, and bounded on the east by land of T. B. Carter, on the south by land of Henry Daily, and on the west by lot number eighty two (82), and contains sixty one (61) acres more or less and unimproved.
    The above tracts are more fully described by a report of commissioners to the Ordinary of this county, to be sold as the property of the estate of Thomas Carter, late of said county, deceased, for the purpose of paying debts and making distribution among the heirs. Terms of sale cash. This Nov. 7th, 1899.
    John Howard, Administrator de bonis non on the estate of Thomas Carter.

§   Georgia, Rabun County.
    By virtue of an order of the Court of Ordinary of said county, will be sold at public outcry, on the first Tuesday in December, 1899, at the court-house in said county, between the usual hours of sale, the following real estate situate in Rabun county, to wit: Parts of land lots no. thirty (30) and thirty one (31) in the fifth land district of said county, and bounded as follows: On the north by land of John Dotson and on the east by Tallulah river, on the south by Tallulah river and Watts' land and on the

west by lands of F. A. Taylor and Hiram Moore. Much of this land is improved with good bottom land and has good farm buildings on it. Sold as the property of the estate of James Dockins, deceased, for the purpose of paying debts and making distribution among the heirs. Terms of sale, one third in 30[?] days, one third November 1st, 1900, one third March 1st, 1901. Note with [illegible] security[?]. This Nov. [illegible] 1899. [Illegible], Administrator.

§   Attention Travelers. Four hundred and fifty bushels of fine corn cribbed at the Wall House. Am prepared to amply care for teams of travelers at moderate prices.

§   Rabun Gap Extra
James Martin, who has been lingering for many months with that dreaded disease consumption, died last Saturday night, at his father's home, Wm. Martin. The funeral occured at the Baptist church at the head of Tennessee Valley, Monday last. Services were conducted by Rev. Brown.
Our citizens are obligated to B. B. Bleckley, John Dillingham and James Dillingham, of Anderson, S. C., for contribution of one dollar each for the parsonage at our town.
Prof. A. A. O'Kelly closes his school here by giving an entertainment to-morrow night.
Rev. Chas. W. Curry preached his farewell sermon at Rabun Gap church last Sunday, and is now gone to the annual conference at Lagrange, Ga. We hope he will be returned to the work here.
The work is being pushed on the parsonage and the building will be ready by 1900 for occupancy.

§   Col. Albert A. Boone, of Black Diamond fame, has been arrested at the instance of Samuel W. Stairs, editor of the Dover (Ky.) News. The charge against Col. Boone is taking valuable papers from the office of the board of directors of the Black Diamond. Boone claims he had a right to the papers, but having no connection with the board, we fail to see his right to take from this office.

§   Notice. Parties will be prosecuted if they remove timber or otherwise tresspass upon my premises. Mell Crisp.

The Clayton Tribune, Volume 2, Number 45, Thursday, November 30, 1899

§   Dr. G. W. Long is not improved in health.

§   J. I. Langston went to Tallulah Falls Monday.

§   We have been having some cold damp weather.

§   Our coroner, Wm. Wheeler, is improving slowly.

§   Caney Thompson is suffering from a felon on his finger.

§   Capt. S. S. Hall has been very sick for the past several days.

§   Miss Liza Duncan has been on the sick list for some time past.

§   Albert Dillard of Westminster spent Sunday with home folks in the Valley.

§   A party of five from Atlanta with seven dogs are up on a hunt. They are quartered at the Blue Ridge Hotel.

§   E. L. McConnell is serving as special deputy sheriff under J. R. Ritchie. Ed is an old hand in the office and makes a good officer.

§   The snow birds are seen on the Nantahalla Bald the year round. Their nests and young are seen the entire summer. They build their nest near the ground among the laurels.

§   It is salesday next Tuesday and some fine farms will be sold, besides gold mining property. Do not fail to attend: you may miss a bargain of your life. On some of this property you get time to pay for same.

§   The prohibition party has been for years abusing the democratic party, and has accused it of being friendly to whiskey trusts. Now, we want to hear what it has to say against the lower house of representatives of the state of Georgia.

§   C. J. Crunkleton of Persimmon was in town Saturday. Our readers will remember that about August his knife pierced his right arm while catching a falling pencil. He has not done any manual labor since and is far from being well yet.

§   The Willingham Bill.
   Following is house bill 221, providing for absolute prohibition in Georgia, which passed the house yesterday after being perfected by the amendment offered by its author, Mr. Willingham...

§   Mr. W. A. Swafford presents us with a couple of turnips of the Bon Air variety. It is really the Rutabaga turnip. One of them weighed 4 pounds. They are a good winter turnip and grow well here. Thanks Mr. Swafford, will turnup our plate before that turnip.

§   Rabun County by S. W. McCallie, Assistant Geologist.
   The gold deposits of Rabun county may be described, as belonging to two different auriferous belts, one lying in the extreme western, and the other, in the extreme eastern, part of the county. The former belongs to what is known as the Dahlonega gold belt, while the latter appears to be the northeastern extension of the Hall county belt...

§   The United States officials were summoning witnesses to attend the United States court on the 29th in Gainesville to testify in the conspiracy case against J. B. and Lafayette Dockins, M. V. Beck and Jeff Swafford, the first part of this week.

§   We learn from the Southern Record that Toccoa's prospects for the future are very flattering. There are two cotton mills highly prospective and one in operation and has been for about two years, which has been prosperous, and its prosperity, no doubt, has induced capitol that way. We, however, give the Record credit for a good share of the prosperity of this growing city.

§   I will buy all the fur hides brought to me and pay the highest prices for them. James M. Bell[?].

§   We are told that when the new penitentiary is built in Atlanta that persons convicted of illicit distilling will be put to hard labor from six months to two years for each offense. Our authority for the above comes direct from a United States officer of high standing in the department, and the penitentiary will likely be build within two years. All persons now engaged in the work of illicit distilling are subject to be arrested in the future and suffer the heavy penalties. With a standing crew of officers located here, and the future pending danger of sure penalty, we think it our duty to let our people know something of the situation, present and future.

§   It is thought the Willingham temperance bill will fail to pass in the Senate.

§   A New Industry.
    C. J. Harris, of Dilsboro, N. C. has located a locust pin factory at Dillard, this county.
    Mr. Harris deals extensively in this business having a number of factories in Macon and other counties of North Carolina.
    We understand that if proper encouragement is given the pins will be shipped via Tallulah Falls.
    The factory at Dillard is under the supervision of Messers J. N. Sherrill and M. E. Addington, of Franklin, N. C.

§   Persimmon [blank]

§   Rabun Gap [blank]

§   Upper Tiger [blank]

§   Upper Warwoman [blank]

§   And Others [blank]

§   Wolfcreek
    Corn gathering and rye-sowing is about done in this section and reasonable crops were gathered.

The tax collector was around getting all the surplus money this week.

G. W. M. Chappell bought a large ox the other day, for a beef. This shows he is going to have something to eat.

The people are in their usual health in our section.

§   To-day is thanksgiving and we have no turkey.

§   Mrs. J. M. York has been feeble several days.

§   Mrs. J. E. Derrick has been sick several days.

§   Jesse[?] McCurry is down on Tiger [missing] buying cattle.

§   Quite a number of citizens of the [missing] were here yesterday.

§   Mr. W. T. York made a business[?] trip on Tiger Monday.

§   [Missing] J. H. Hunnicut, of Vandiver, [missing] up among friends yesterday.

§   [Missing] F. Earls has a large force of [missing] cutting saw logs on his farm.

§   The[?] shingle mill is heard at W. [missing] Thompson's plant north of [missing].

§   Thanks[?] to Harve Penland, colored[?], for a load of wood on subscription[?].

§   [Missing] Mitchell is gone to Haywood[?] N. C. [illegible].

§   Little Ray Swofford is trying to hold down a case of type at the Tribune office.

§   P. G. Presley is gone down to Athens after the remainder of his household furniture.

§   Mr. and Mrs. Calvin York are the guests of Mr. and Mrs. J. M. York to-day.

§   Jesse Robins, who has been in bad health for nearly a year, is now looking robust and is actively at work all the time.

§   Mr. and Mrs. D. D. Duncan, of Chechero, are the guests of Mrs. Ella Swofford to-day.

§   Miss Manda Earl has closed her school on Chechero with an entertainment and is now at home.

§   Judge Long killed six British birds off a wild locust tree in front of our office Monday at one shot.

§ Bergstrom and Stanley captured a still on Chechero yesterday and the proprietress, Miss Lillie Beck.

§ Frank Curtis, of the Franklin Press, Franklin, N. C., was a pleasant caller at our office Tuesday.

§ Charley Grant, while he has a high fever is not suffering any [illegible], is rational and is considered as doing very nicely.

§ Thanks to Mr. S. H. Robinson, of Tiger, for some corn on subscription. Also to Mr. H. A. Keener, of Rabun Gap.

§ Found—By J. E. Derrick. A pocket-book containing money. Owner can have the same by calling at this office and describing the contents.

§ News reached us as we go to press that Benj. Dockins, a highly respected and well known citizen of the county, was dying last night at his home near Pine Mountain.

§ Marion Long makes the sad report to us that the whortlleberries are in full bloom. No one regrets more we, for this is a sure sign there will be no berry crop next year.

§ The road change near the residence of James E. Bleckley is completed with the exception of some blasting. We are told the grade is splendid and the chane[?] is a great improvement.

§ Mr. A. J. Duncan has been engaged several days assisting J. F. Earl in laying a wood pipe, which conveys pure spring water to Mr. Earl's door. He completed the work yesterday.

§ As we go to press we learn that Dr. Long's condition is very critical, so much so his children have been called to his bedside. His sudden change for the worse is suffocation.

§ Mr. W. J. Neville, County School Commissioners, Rabun Gap, has been employed to assist S. S. Whitmire in the store of Tom Carter of Westminister, S. C. The stock will be increased largely, and we predict for this firm a complete success.

§ County Surveyor W. E. Jones came up yesterday with a load of the best sweet potatoes we ever tested and brought along three turnips weighing in the aggregate 21 pounds, and asks us to turn up our plate to them. We turn up our hat to you also, W. E.

§ Mr. W. B. Grant, of Jacksonville, Fla., arrived here Monday night. He will be here for several days looking after his mining interests. Mr. Grant has made many friends in the county who are always loath to see him leave. Mr. Grant is the guest of the Wall House.

§   Old Tiger

Wedding bells are ringing.

Mr. William Williams, of Timpson, and Rev. David Ramey's daughter, Miss Bettie, were married at Vandiver last Sunday, Esq. Verge Kerby officiating. A merry party accompanied Mr. Williams from Germany, among them was our old friend Calvin York.

Col. W. S. Paris passed through this section last Sunday enroute for Gainesville.

Col. Hamby and Doctor Green returned to their post of duty Monday.

School will close here Friday and we hope for a good time. Prof. O'Kelley is expected to deliver an address.

Miss Carrie Green attended Miss Manda Earl's entertainment on Chechero last Friday.

Jackson Scott has been very sick, but is improving.

William Shaw, of Vandiver, has moved near Toccoa. Mr. Shaw is a substantial citizen and we regret to give him up.

Messers Frank and Clifton McCrackin attended Mr. Virgil McCrackin's entertainment on Wolf Creek and both delivered an address. They are both nice young men and deserve the praise of the community.

The Clayton Tribune, Volume 2, Number 46, Thursday, December ~~30~~ 28, 1899

Note: While this issue has the number "28" written in above the crossed-out 30, from the news given within it is clear that it was published before the 28th. Given the issue number (46), it was most likely published on Thursday, December 7, and is included here as such.

§   Gold Bulletins of Rabun county. By S. W. McCallie, Assistant Geologist (Continued from Last Week.)...

§   Cotton Factories.

An exchange says: The South is working up to her incomparable inherent advantages, and during the year no less than 68 new factories have been erected as monuments to the enterprise of the section. These mills operate a million spindles...

§   The Road is Doing Well.

Some of the Gainesville people have visited Tallulah Falls recently and they say that Mr. Dunlap has put the Tallulah Falls railroad in good condition since he has assumed control of it.

Mr. Dunlap is certainly one of the best railroad men in the country. His management of the G. J. & S. Railroad has demonstrated the fact.

Tallulah Falls is a great place to go for a day's outing, but for the past several years people have been afraid to risk the road from Cornelia to the Falls, hence the travel in the past has not been what it will be in the future.—Gainesville Eagle.

§   We will pay 75 cents for cow peas. Tom Carter.

§   Jas. Langston and Chub Wall chased a fox over and around Screamer mountain last Friday.

§   Mr. and Mrs. W. D. Grant were up from Clarkesville the latter part of last week to see their son, Charlie, who has fever here.

§   W. J. Neville is smiling behind the counters of Tom Carter.

§   The columns of our paper are for rent at reasonable rates.

§   It is highly probable that Atlanta will have a National Park. There are many circumstances connected with the battles fought near Atlanta during the civil war that, in our opinion, makes it assured. Personally we want Atlanta to have the National Park and it would please us if she should get the National Capitol.

§   There will be a total eclipse of the sun May 28, 1900...

§   Last Call.
Notice.
I will be at Clayton court house on the 16, 18, and 19th of December, 1899, for the purpose of collecting the State and county taxes for the year 1899.
This Nov. 20, 1899.
Joseph L. Dickerson, T. C.

§   Old Tiger
Rev. D. D. Taylor and R. L. Whitmire preaced to a crowded house last Sunday. Rev. R. L. Whitmire was unamiously elected to supply the Baptist church at Tiger last Saturday and I. J. H. Hunnicut church clerk for the year 1900.
Prof. Nin Ramey's school closed here last Friday. An entertainment was given and enjoyed by all present. Prof. A. O'Kelly delivered an address to the school. He was the star entertainer of the occasion.
Miss Carrie, Lela, Ray and Iabel Cannon were the guests of Reed, Tom and Lean Bleckly last Sunday.
We think the time has come when the people of Rabun county ought to build a high school at Clayton, Tennessee Valley or Burton. Clayton is the place, but if Clayton won't act, go somewhere else. We ought to educate our boys and girls at home and build up our own county and patronize our own boys and girls. We earnestly ask the school authorities to use their influence to build a high school in Rabun county.
Look at the high schools in Habersham county—why not Rabun county build a good school? We must stand together if we succeed and we think this is a question the people of Rabun ought to write on.
Mr. David Prime, of Clemson College, S. C., has been in this section prospecting for a future home.
The young people of this community had a good singing at J. E. Bleckley's last Sunday.

§   Work begun on the Missing Link R. R.

A special from Chattanooga to the Atlanta Journal of the 17th inst. says:

Surveyors started work yesterday making the preliminary survey for the Missing Link railroad which runs from this city to Walhalla, S. C., through the northern part of Georgia.

One corps in charge of Henry Hamilton, of Dalton, Ga., started at Ringgold, and the other charge of J. H. Harrison, of Walhalla, started from that place.

Col. Albright, the president of the company in an interview here today states that he has all the money necessary to build the road and that Massachusetts and New capitalists are putting it up.

§   North Chechero

Freezing weather now.

Little Carrie York is very sick at this writing.

Miss Leila and Texie Turpen are visiting Miss Lizzie York.

The health of our community is very good now.

Hiram Coffee started to S. C. yesterday with a load of apples.

Mr. J. L. York returned from N. C. yesterday.

Miss Ida and Sallie York are visiting friends.

Mr. Willie Carver was with his best girl at Miss Manda Earl's entertainment Saturday.

Mr. J. C. Pickett visited J. L. York Saturday.

§   Will Bradley Fatally Shot.

News reached us late to-day that Will Bradley was fatally shot this afternoon near a distillery on Dick's creek, in the eastern portion of this county. The U. S. officers report they were cooking a lunch at the distillery when they heard distant shots. We are unable to get at any facts beyond the above. Bradley lives here and great anxiety is felt as to his condition. The ball entered his back near the left kidney and from reports he will not survive. Bradley walked some distance after he was shot and no doubt the party who did the shooting is known there, but we are unable to give our readers anything reliable more than he is fatally shot, and the revenue officials are accused of the crime. The people are aroused over the matter and are bold in condeming the act as the nature of the wound shows a cowardly act and say it is parallel case to the one "over the ridge" and out of sight. Personally we entertain no opinion but we give our readers the opinion of those who have expressed themselves in the matter.

But it does not seem to us as reasonable that the officers would intentionally shoot any one engaged in the illicit business. It certainly is not policy from any standpoint. We will give our readers a history of the affair in our next issue.

§   Germany

Cold weather has come.

Rev. Lon Dillingham preached at Germany Saturday and Sunday.

Clerk J. S. Ramey and Prof. Green made a flying trip here Sunday.

Marcus Keener and wife visited home folks Sunday.

Edgar York and Jeffie Holcomb spent Sunday night with their best girls.

We are sorry to learn the illness of Will Martin.
Little Della Moore, of Wolffork, spent last week with her sister Mrs. J. C. Justus.
Mr. A. E. Dickerson has bought him a new buggy.
Logan Rogers spent Saturday night with home folks.

§   Hog killing.

§   "Vig" Arrendale, of Burton, was in town Monday.

§   Col. W. T. Crane, of Clarkesville, was here Tuesday.

§   Thanks to B. E. Ramey for a fine load of pine knots.

§   Charlie Grant's condition is only medium, but not alarming.

§   Born—To Senator and Mrs. Green Tuesday night, a son.

§   The Revenue officials continue their work of destruction in this county.

§   On account of receiving legal advertisements late we are delayed in [missing] our paper.

§   Hon. Horace[?] C. Blalock of Burton was here[?] attending Ordinary [missing or illegible] Monday.

§   Carl Colwell, of Ivy Log, the drummer of the mountains was here Tuesday.

§   M. H. James of Persimmon was among the pleasant [illegible] at our office Tuesday.

§   Five cents per pound paid for old copper at T. M. Carter's at the Hamby old stand.

§   Thanks to Mrs. L. C. Hollifield for some fine turnips. Such acts of kindness are remembered by us.

§   Joseph A. Erwin, the popular clerk of the Superior court of Habersham co., was here Tuesday.

§   Mr. and Mrs. W. D. Grant were up from Clarkesville the latter part of last week to see their son, Charlie, who has fever here.

§   John Godfrey and Stanley carried to Gainesville yesterday Sidney Bradley and his son, who live near the Ridge Pole mountains.

§   We especially mention among those who favored us substantially on subscription this week John A. Earl and Ex-tax collector James F. Smith.

§   Call at Henson's for your Xmas goods...

§   Benj. Dockins died at his home last Thursday night after a continued illness since last summer. He leaves a large number of relatives in the county.

§   Representative R. E. A. Hamby spent the adjourned days of the legislature last week with friends and home people here. He answered the roll call Monday.

§   Ex sheriff J. B. Dockins, Lafayette Dockins, Jeff Swofford and M. V. Beck, who were tried for conspiracy at Gainesville the 27th, were honorably discharged after a close examination of the testimony.

§   Mrs. Reynolds joins us in expressions of gratitude to those good ladies in town who have kindly called on her since her confined critical illness. Your calls are cheering to her and kindly remembered by us.

§   John Howard, of Quartz, is prominently spoken of as a man well equipped for the office of County School Commissioner of this county. Mr. Howard is well qualified and is very popular among his people.

§   For Sale.
   One yoke of oxen, one milk cow, 100 bushels of corn, 1,000 bundles of fodder and one wagon. Also for rent one four room dwelling house, garden and stables. Call on Mrs. J. B. Murray, Clayton, Ga.

§   Col. W. S. Paris returnd home last night in the chilly hours of eve from a trip to Newton and Gwinette counties where he has been about ten days among old friends and home people. He has had a royal good time to the displeasure of a number us[?] here who occasionally want free advice on 'pints' legally.

§   Quite a crowd of Warwoman citizens were here Monday. Among them was Peter Speed who [illegible] on the [illegible] and public road west of the ford. Mr. Speed was the high bidder and the contract for making the improvement calls for [illegible]. Mr. Speed promises [illegible] people a good ford.

§   Senator Green was here during the adjourned days of the legislature and was detained from going to Atlanta Monday and Tuesday on account of the illness of Mrs. Green.

§   Last Tuesday was salesday and not in our two years stay here has there been as much property sold in any one day. The familiar voice of ex-sheriff J. B. Dockins began crying off the property sometime before noon and for a long time he stood at the court house [illegible] selling tract after tract till all that was advertised was sold. The first property sold was that of the estate of Thomas Carter and was bought by the following parties: C. F. Garland, W. J. Neville and J. W. Wilborne. The next property sold was the land of James Dockins, deceased, and was purchased by J. A. Erwin, of Clarkesville, Ga., and the price paid was $530 dollars. The next put for sale was the lands of the Dickerson estate and was bid off as follows: That part of the estate known as the Parker place brought $340 and was knocked off to Turner Page. The mining lot was bought by W. H. (Hilyer) York and the price paid was 455 dollars. Parts of lots 99 and 100 was bid on by Jefferson L. Dickerson. The price paid was 71 ½ dollars. Parts of lots 17 and 100 were knocked off to H. L. Dickerson for the sum of 99 dollars.

§   Betty's Creek
    Winter has made its appearance at last.
    Mr. John Baker went west last Sunday and returned home before dinner.
    Mrs. Albert Cragg is very sick at this writing.
    There was preaching at Powell Gap Sunday.
    Mrs. T. E. Arrendale's health is much better at this writing.
    John V. Arrendale visited relatives near Burton last Saturday night.
    James Crawford visited relatives on Scott's Creek Saturday.
    Mr. John Baker and Miss Harriet West were married at the home of the bride's father Sunday morning last J. F. Philyaw officiating.
    Mr. Bent Cannon was on Bridge Creek last Saturday night. We don't think he is coming so often for nothing.
    Mr. and Mrs. M. Arrendale went to Flat Creek Sunday.

§   Bridge Creek
    Cold weather.
    A. A. Darnell is burning his brick this week.
    The Revenues visited Betty's Creek Monday and got Andrew Bradley.
    J. Z. Hopper has gone to see his father-in-law who is not expected to live long.
    Mrs. Laura Martin is moving back in the house with her father, L. D. Garland, this week.
    Mr. George Daily expects to move to his farm this week.
    George Ledford, Charles Hopper and G. N. Garland took a drove of hogs to Toccoa last week.
    James A. Hopper is working on A. A. Darnell's new dwelling this week.
    Betty's Creek is ahead of any creek for grist mills. She has three.

The Clayton Tribune, Volume 2, Number 48, Thursday, December 21, 1899

§   To Our Readers:
    Owing to the advance in paper we are forced to cut off many of our delinquent subscribers and hereafter the Tribune will be run on a cash basis. We are informed by paper dealers that it will be a difficult matter to get paper at any price the coming year. The cause assigned for the advancement is the unprecedented prosperity and increasing demand for paper and the inability of the mills to furnish it. We ask those who are due us to call and settle their dues or they will be presented to them by agencies.

§ Our good readers will please excuse us for defects, half-sheets and one-sidedness, when they know we have misfortunes in our home. Since last June we have devoted much time by the side of a devoted wife, who is in very feeble health and now her condition is such that requires the best help of our office. Trouble of like character comes and will come to all. We feel we are among a noble and grateful people, and sympathy will take the place of condemnation.

§ An order has been issued from the Southern Railway headquarters forbidding its employees from smoking cigarettes while on duty...—Greenville Daily Times, Dec. 7.

§ Parents you are greatly responsible for the welfare of your children. Morally we should be very watchful. Are you doing your duty?

§ Old Tiger

Candy drawings and stock law is the order of the day in this community. We understand Deep Creek district is going to hold an election soon on the fence law in Habersham county. Then Tiger and Stonepile will have to vote for it unless they can get some relief.

Miss Ada Green, from Warwoman, has been the guest of her Bro. Jesse this week.

Misses Anda Smith and Russell Cannon have moved near Toccoa from this place.

Mr. Marcus Turpen had returned from Hartwell, Ga.

Mr. Baskins from Royston, Ga., is in this section prospecting for a good mill. We bid him God speed in his business.

Prof. Clifton McCrackin and Nin Ramey were out at Sunday School last Sunday and we had a good time.

Sug Ramey is very sick at this writing. We hope for a speedy recovery.

We want to say a little more on the school subject in reference to the government. Since the schools are divided into school districts we think it proper to appoint school trustees for each district.

H. K. Cannon and Ray passed down this way enroute to Cornelia.

§ Chechero

Christmas is nearly here and we have no turkey.

The health of Mr. J. L. York's family is slightly improved.

We are having some cold weather.

Mrs. F. A. Bleckley is in feeble health.

Our old friend Bill Wall and son Hilton paid us a short visit last week.

Mr. J. H. Coffee and son have returned home from market.

Miss Maggie Woodall spent Saturday night and Sunday with Miss Lizzie York.

Mr. Jim Ramey and wife and his son David and family passed through this section Tuesday en route to Anderson.

Little Lester York chased a rabbit Sunday and killed it with an ax.

§ Burton

Warm weather continues with fine rains.

Tax Collector Dickerson will be with us to-morrow and the people are hustling for their receipts to come [illegible] of the book before the bailiffs get them.

Professor L. M. Chastain is spoken of for the next County School Commissioner. Chastain is a fine man whose marvels cannot be excelled in this county and his qualifications cannot be doubted. If[?] the people wants a commissioner who will deal with all fairly and honestly Chastain is the man beyond a doubt.

Christmas will soon be here and will we honor the day as we should?

§   Rabun Gap (Intended for last week.)

One of the worst rain and wind[?] storms we have had in a long time closed[?] last Monday night.

Elic Garland has brought out R. E. L. Ritchie's interest in the mercantile business of Rabun Gap.

John Howard and Mrs. D. Garland are on the sick list this week.

Your writer and a party went to the Nantahalas last week coon hunting.

W. J. Neville is in business with T. N. Carter at Clayton.

§   Wolf [illegible]

Nothing of interest here this week.

Yes, I agree with the Tiger correspondent in regard to building a High School in Rabun. "Charity begins at home" is a true saying and we might add education begins at home. I see no reason why we should not have a High School in Rabun. We could build a school that would rival any in the state. We have material in abundance to build with. It has been said by some able writers that the mountains develop the strongest minds. And here we are, in the midst of one of the most mountainous parts of the state, without a school for higher intellectual training. Every year our young men and ladies have to go beyond the boundaries of Rabun to obtain a higher education, which could be given to them at home.

The correspondent referred to Habersham Co. That county is keeping abreast of educational opportunities. Her educational interests are thriving and she is keeping the monster, ignorance, surpressed under her feet. Now, if we don't want to be a "back number, let us throw off the yoke of oppression[?] and build a school that will be an honor to our county and to the state.

Mr. Frank Justus and several others are preparing to visit relatives in Transylvania Co., N. C., next week.

§   Salt at 85 cents per sack at Carter's.

§   We will sale for cash until after holidays. Tom Carter.

§   Mrs. C. C. Wall is building an addition to her residence.

§   Our jail this year has been very little expense to the county.

§   Sheriff Ritchie made an official trip to Toccoa last Saturday.

§   Judge J. B[?]. Gaston, of Gainesville, Ga., was up Tuesday.

§   Mr. Fred Cannon, of Atlanta, made our office a call Tuesday.

§ Col. Paris bagged 17 partridges, one hawk and two rabbits to-day.

§ Sandy Cunningham, of Atlanta, is registered at the Blue Ridge Hotel.

§ Prof. A. A. O'Kelley, of the Valley, was down among friends the past week.

§ Mr. and Mrs. J. C. Jackson of [illegible], Ga., are the guests of the editor's[?] family.

§ Our representatives, Hamby and Green, are home to the delight of their many friends.

§ William Wall, of Clarkesville, [illegible] his father's family, Mr. T[?]. W[?]. Wall, last week.

§ Coroner Wheeler was in town Saturday after being confined to his home for some two months.

§ Judge F. A. Bleckley leads all of us in porkers. He killed one today that weighed 858 pounds, net.

§ Next week is Christmas week and we will print only advertisements. Our devil is determined to take Xmas.

§ We thank J. J. Greenwood, James F. Smith and M. L. Dickerson for their kind assistance to us this week.

§ If people do not know you have goods to sell, how in the name of common sense do you expect to sell them?

§ The friends of Charlie Grant will be pleased to learn that he is up after several weeks confinement with Typhoid fever.

§ Joseph L. Dickerson, tax collector, has piled up the shekels this week. The people bear the heavy burden of taxes unmurmuringly.

§ O. E. Kennemer, representing the M. E. Kiser Co., wholesale dealer in shoes, Atlanta, Ga., was here Saturday last talking to our merchants.

§ Will Bradley, the man who was wounded some two weeks ago by the United States officers is reported to be resting comfortably with fair chance of recovery.

§ F. B. Dover, of Burton, died at his home last Sunday morning. The cause of Mr. Dover's death was due to abcess from teeth. He was one of our best citizens.

§ Drew Green had the misfortune to lose a fine horse last week. Miss Beulah Green rode the animal down to Judge F. A. Bleckley's where it was taken sick and died.

§   It is important that every land owner in the county has the proper number of the land lot entered on [illegible] tax digest as it may be sold for taxes and complications may arise.

§   Rev. Chas. W. Curry, former pastor of this circuit, is spending a few days with friends here. Mr. Curry has many friends here who regret very much to part with him.

§   The trial against John Godfrey, C. L. Vigal and Boone Crawford charged with shooting Will Bradley a few weeks ago, was postponed from last Tuesday till the 25th of January, 1960.

§   Dr. N. M. Rogers, of Shooting Creek, Clay Co., N. C., who is largely interested and actively engaged in the mineral developments of this section, was here Saturday examining records of deeds.

§   By courtesy of Joseph L. Dickerson he will be here on the 25th inst. and will receive money for[?] taxes on that day. The time by law has expired but Mr. Dickerson desiring to favor will be here on the day mentioned.

§   Mr. J. C. Dickson, of Turnerville, Ga., informs us that the school house at that place burned at 8 o'clock last Saturday. There was a singing school being carried on at the school building and it is supposed the fire caught from a defective flue.

§   I am no more in company with W. C. Scruggs in the millstone quarry business. I am to myself and will cut millstones for the public on short notice. D. P[?]. Lacounte.

§   Ain[?] Seay was captured with about 30 gallons of...whiskey here yesterday. A splendid team of horses and [illegible] wagon[?] was confiscated. [Illegible].

§   All persons who are indebted to the undersigned are hereby notified to come and settle at once if they want to save cost. This is fair warning. W. F. Roane, A. L. Roane.

§   Leave to Sell.
Georgia—Rabun county. H. C. Blalock, administrator of W. L. Arrendale, deceased, has in due form applied to the undersigned for leave to sell the lands belonging to the estate of said deceased and said application will be heard on the first Monday in January next. This 4th day of Dec. 1899. W. S. Long, Ordinary.

§   Leave to Sell.
Georgia—Rabun County. V. T. Stonecypher, administrator of William Stonecypher, deceased, has in due form applied to the undersigned for leave to sell the lands belonging to the estate of said deceased and said application will be heard on the first Monday in January next. This 4th day of Dec. 1899. W. S. Long, Ordinary.

§   Rabun Sheriff's Sale.

Georgia—Rabun county. Will be sold on the first Tuesday in January next at the court house in said county within[?] the legal hours of sale, to the highest bidder for cash, the following described property, to wit: Part of land lot no. fifty (50) in the second land district of said county, and containing eight acres and bounded as follows: On the south by land of Drew Wall, on the east by the old right of way of the Blue Ridge railroad, on the west by the Clayton and Franklin public road, on the north by land of N. A. Hunnicutt. There is a good mill shoal on this land with a right to back water and more [illegible] described by a deed from Z. Sweatman to W. H. Hughes, dated Oct. 14, 1889 and recorded in book K on pages 75 and 76 record of deeds of the clerk of superior court of said county. Levied on by virtue of a mortgage fi fa issued from the superior court of said county in favor of J. H. Hicks against W. H. Hughes. Notice of levy posted on this land in terms of law. This December 6th, 1899. J. R. Ritchie, Sheriff.

§   By virtue of an order of the court of Ordinary of said county, will be sold at public outcry, at the court house in said county, on the first Tuesday in January next, within the legal hours of sale, the following real estate situated in Rabun county to wit:

Part of lot of land no. thirty six (36) in the second land district of said county, and bounded on the north by lands of R. A. Coffee, on the east by Clayton and Franklin public road, on the south and west by lands of Peter Coffee and containing thirty (30) acres, more or less. This land lies in the town of Clayton and is valuable as town property.

Also parts of lots of land Nos. twenty one (21) and twenty-two in the fifth and district of said county and bounded as follows: On the north by the district line dividing the fifth and second land districts of said county and on the wes by lands of Lemuel Wilkerson, Lafayette Walls[?] and A. J. Keener, on the south by lands of Joseph Watts and on the east by lands of [illegible] and H. V. Murray and containing 75[?] acres more or less. The above described land [illegible] among the heirs. Terms of sale, one half cash and one half six months from the date of sale with note and approved security.

This Dec. 6th, 1899. James M. Smith, Administrator of L. N. Jones, deceased.

§   Administrator's Sale.

Georgia—Rabun County.

Will be sold in said county on the 28th day of December, 1899, between the hours of 10 o'clock a. m. and 4 o'clock p. m. at public outcry at the late residence of Benjiman Dockins, deceased, to the highest bidder, all of the perishable property of said Benjiman Dockins, embracing all his stoc to wit:

One fine jack five years old, one [illegible] six months old, one mare eight years old, two milk cows, and[?] a lot of other stock, such as hogs, sheep and cattle. Terms of sale all over five dollars on nine months note and approved security. All under five dollars cash. This Dec. 14th, 1899.

J. B. Dockins, Temporary Administrator.

I will also sell at the same time and place 4 [illegible] two years old past as my own property—on above stated terms. J. B. Dockins.

§ Martin-Page.

H[?]. R. Martin and Lizzie Page of the Tennessee Valley, were married to-day, at the house of the bride's father, Mr. Turner Page. Rev. J. S. Dickson performed the ceremony. Mr. Martin is one of the most industrious young men in the county, sober and good man. Miss Lizzie is a worthy and charming young lady, and we hope for them much prosperity and happiness.

§ Carter's. Eight hundred pounds of candy at Carter's...

§ Henson's. Fine Xmas candies at Henson's...

§ Earl. Friends and patrons: I want to induce you with low prices and good quality to come and see my stock of overcoats and ready-made clothing...

The Clayton Tribune, Volume 2, Number 49, Thursday, December 28, 1899

Note: Only one extant page for this issue.

§ Charlie Grist[?] is among home folks at Clarkesville.

§ More business firms will likely be established here soon. Let 'em come.

§ It is expected that A. A. O'Kelly will begin school here next Wednesday.

§ Mr. Stribling and Mr. Miller, of Westminster, were here several days this week.

§ Jasper C. Langston and family of Walhalla, S. C., have been the guest of relatives and returned [illegible].

§ Mr. Ned Shirley, of Stonepile, happened to the misfortune of fracturing his leg on the 26th inst.

§ I will fill my appointment at Lipscomb next Sunday at 11 o'clock.

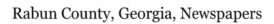

This page intentionally left blank.

INDEX

Items are indexed only once per page on which they appear.

agriculture (cont.)

hay 183, 195, 197, 199

hens, sitting 107

hogs 19, 48, 56, 68, 72, 82, 83, 97, 151, 216, 221, 223, 224, 235, 237, 242

honey 140, 156, 174, 191

horses 6, 15, 19, 27, 38, 58, 59, 66, 67, 70, 75, 77, 78, 80, 86, 116, 129, 141, 143, 146, 148, 158, 179, 201, 217, 218, 240, 241

jack 242

lumber 42, 112, 123, 135, 147, 148, 158, 166

mare 67, 242

market 4, 46, 68, 102, 104, 112, 117, 127, 208, 215, 238

melons 4, 155, 171, 173, 178, 180, 181, 191

mules 15, 54, 66, 68, 73, 76, 77, 92, 97, 171, 175, 223

oats 23, 117

onions 38, 41, 134

oxen 43, 54, 230, 236

peas 171

peaches 29, 94, 95, 108, 184, 214

pine knots 79, 235

plums 108

porkers 240

potatoes 38

Irish 41, 172, 174, 183, 189, 195, 203

sweet 224, 231

poultry 50

produce 42, 43, 201

pumpkin[?] 221

pumpkins 208, 215, 221

radish, winter 221

rooster, wild 67

rye 8, 80, 144, 169, 197, 229

rye straw 33, 148, 151, 164, 168

sheep 73, 114, 126, 129, 144, 151, 165, 170, 192, 197, 206, 215, 242

sorghum 223

steer 42, 221

sugar 181, 224

syrup 197, 205, 208, 212, 215

tanbark 16, 23, 33

thresher 1, 5, 8

timber 1, 24, 27, 29, 83, 100, 107, 133, 174, 206, 227

tobacco 107, 168

tomatoes 2, 171, 190

tops 80, 223

turnips 183, 188, 195, 211, 228, 231, 235

vegetables 37

watermelons 29, 88, 155, 157

wheat 167, 202

agriculture (cont.)

whortlleberries 231

wool 129

yearling 68

Alabama 64, 79, 192

Birmingham 71

Roanoke 160

Alaska 150

Klondike 31, 42

Albright

Capt. 202

Colonel 174, 234

W. L. 163, 164

Alerton, G. T. 17

Alford, W. J. 24

Algary, Henry 104

Alison, G. W. 184

Allen

Americus K. 21

Marcus K. 162

Miss 130

Mr. 131

Mrs. 131

Thomas 112

Toma[?] 96

Alley, Peril 73

Allia[?]

Bertie 184

Ellie 184

Allman

"Bud" 171

Rev. 172

W. C. 211

Almon

Ed 167

J. A. 203

Jim 7

Almond

C. 13

Damascus 156

J. A., Rev. 142

James 167

Altonah Hills 130

Ammoin, Alfred 82

Amonds, Alford 61

Anderson, J. R. 13

Andrews, Jack 156

Angel

Mrs. 117

Will 111

Angell, W. T. 90

Angil, Beulah 167

Anthony, E. R. 113

Arendale, W. L. 1

Arkansas 73

Bleckley (cont.)
    F. A., Hon. 56
    F. A., Judge 29, 98, 140, 181, 199, 240
    F. A., Mrs. 3, 7, 20, 238
    Gussie 184
    J. E. 73, 90, 104, 110, 147, 176, 179, 201,
        225, 231, 233
    J. M. 72, 145, 155, 167, 169, 174, 192
    J. M. Jr. 59
    James E. 74, 84, 85, 87, 101, 146, 162,
        190
    Joe, Mrs. 72, 142
    John 7, 29, 34
    John, Mrs. 29, 34
    Judge 2, 7
    L. E., Mrs. 125
    Leila 19
    Lela 100
    Lena 4, 89, 142, 155, 173, 192
    Leon 169, 201
    Logan 62
    Logan E., Judge 110, 122, 125, 165
    Marcus 78, 142, 215
    Marshal 107
    Mrs. 110
    Reed 67, 95, 146, 184
    S. L. 72, 151
    S. M., Capt. 69
    Savannah 67, 80, 140
    Sylvester 7
    Tom 59, 78, 80, 201
    Tom, Mrs. 59
    Zoa 38
Blecklie, F. A. 4
Bleckly
    Frank A., Hon. 9
    J. E. 176
    Lean 233
    Reed 233
    Tom 233
Bledkley, Messr. 93
Blue Mountains 130
Blue Ridge (mountains) 36
Boon, General 42
Boone
    Albert A., Col. 227
    Albert E. 92
    Albert E., Col. 101
    Albert E., Gen. 70
    Col. 120
    E. A., Col. 92
Booth
    A. E. 190
    A. E., Prof. 211
    Prof. 186
Boutell, J. M. 13

Boutelle, J. J. 2
Bowden, Colonel 33
Bowers
    Billy, Uncle 174
    Fred 89, 127
    Fred, Mrs. 151
    George 128
    Mr. 104
    Mrs. 104, 133
    S. 170
    Sam 156, 184
    Samuel 62
Boyd, James N. 101
Bradley
    Andrew 237
    J. M. 191
    James 123, 139
    James, Mrs. 123
    Jeff 90
    Sidney 72, 235
    Syney 191
    Will 234, 240, 241
    Willie 94
Bradshaw, J. T. 89, 90
Bradwell
    Prof. 25
    S. D., Capt. 27
Brady, S. D. 71
Bramblet
    J. C. 89
    James B. 21
Bramlet, Polly, Mrs. 72
Brawnson, Mr. 137
Brazeale, J. E. 162
Brendle, George 208
Brewe, Emily 76
Brice, ex-Senator 174
Bright, Mr. 78
Brindle, Henry 217
Brindles, William 90
Brinecha, Frank 183
Brinkley, Mary J. 13
Brock
    Abble[?] 219
    E. R. 219
    Pearl 125
Brocket, Geo. A. 71
Brocket Bridge Co. 71
Brookey[?], Mr. 205
Brooks
    J. M. 208, 226
    L. M. 191
Brown
    D. C. 129, 203
    D. C., Mrs. 129
    D. C., Rev. 11, 38

Canup (cont.)
    Miles C. 10, 74
Carnes
    Elisha 164
    John B. 90
    Mrs. 127
    W. P. 225
Carpenter, Carrie 117
Carrel, George, Rev. 66
Carter[?], John, Uncle 139
Carter
    D. C., Rev. 11
    D. F. 91
    D. J. 182
    D. L., Rev. 38
    Dave, Rev. 36, 47
    Dept. Collector 70
    J. C., Mrs. 126
    J. M. 16
    James W. 103
    John 207
    Mr. 78
    Reese 156
    T. B. 27, 90, 97, 193, 199, 225, 226
    T. M. 235
    T. N. 16, 46, 147, 171, 213, 214, 224, 239
    Thomas 202, 226, 236
    Tom 231, 232, 233, 239
Carter's 239, 243
Cartey, Wm. "Bill" 5
Cartledge, James M. 18
Carven, Thos., Prof. 30
Carver
    A. L. 223
    Addie 127
    Amanda 136
    Clara 184
    Crese[?] 127
    Dovie 184
    John 126
    Julius 111
    Julius, Mrs. 111
    Julius M. 87, 162
    Julius W. 22
    M. L. 154, 159
    Martha Arminda Manda Sarah Mariah
      Melinda Lucinda Lizziebeth 200
    Martin C. 74
    Mary Nancy Savannah Lucreasa Rosanna
      Jeneila Corretta 201
    T. E. 184, 221
    Thomas 126
    W. L. 68
    W. M. 168
    William Eugene Thomas Andrew Augustus
      Balus Lafayette Russley 200

Carver (cont.)
    Willie 234
    Willis A. 162
Carves, John 104
Cary, Sam 191
Cathey, Hervey 222
cats
    black house 45
    house 54
    wild 54, 112, 156, 166, 216
Chamberlain Cough Remedy 78
Chamberlain Medicine Co. 204
Chamberlain's Cough Remedy 162
Chamberlain's Colic, Cholera and Diarrhoea
    Remedy 142
Chamberlain's Pain Balm 138
Chambers, J. S. 196
Chandler, A. D., Gov. 57
Chappel, C. C. 17
Chappell, G. W. M. 230
Chapple 183
Charters, W. A. 85, 103, 143, 181
Chase National Bank 2
Chastain
    A. B. 204
    L. M. 73, 83, 192
    L. M., Professor 239
    Martin 160, 173
Chastine, L. M., Prof. 145
chataquas
    Gainesville 147
    Northeast Georgia Chataqua Association
      6 – 7
Chattahoochee (River) 130
checkers 1
Cheek
    Reuben 67, 74
    Rube 68
    Rube, Mrs. 146
    Ruben 95
Chickamauga Park (GA) 174
Children's Day 126, 138, 144
China 100
Christmas (Xmas) 41, 45, 46, 47, 54,
    56 – 57, 59, 75, 225, 236, 238, 239,
    240, 243
    eve 47, 54, 56
    hats 57
    questions about 56 – 57, 62
    serenaders 46
    serenading 56
    stockings 57, 62
    tree 45, 46, 47
Church
    Drummer 128
    J. T. 188

Cragg (cont.)
  Kinnie 74
  William T. 74
Crain, Col. 67
Crane
  Asbury 23
  Colonel 33
  Ella 23
  Franklin 23
  Jane 23
  John 59
  L. M. 156
  P. A. 23
  W. T., Col. 235
crane 158, 171
Crawford
  Boone 159, 204, 241
  Deputy Collector 204
  James 89, 154, 159, 237
  M. M. 10
  Mary 59
  Mrs. 224
Crenshaw
  L. W., Col. 123
  W. B. 119
Crisp
  Annie 182
  Carl 159
  Fannie 182
  J. M. 58
  John M. 22
  Mell 227
crochet 141
Croft, Geo. H. 71
Crone, Lewis M. 74
Crumley, H. C. 23
Crump, D. J. 216
Crumpleton, John W. 22
Crunkleton
  C. J. 25, 138, 155, 161, 186, 192, 201,
    228
  Chas. J. 160
  J. N. 86, 89, 190
  Jack 145
  Jackson 145, 173
  Sarah 122
Cuba
  Nuevitas 77, 79
  Porto de Nuevitas 77
Cuban soldier, ex 99
Cunningham
  A. M. 166
  Sandy 19, 165, 240
Curry
  C. W. 219
  C. W., Rev. 58, 94, 188, 210, 212, 213

Curry (cont.)
  Charles W., Rev. 121
  Chas., Rev. 158
  Chas. W. 95, 135, 143, 155, 172, 209
  Chas. W., Rev. 125, 128, 138, 183, 197,
    215, 219, 220, 227, 241
  Leila 138
  Mr. 126
  Mrs. 155
  Rev. 111, 117, 121, 133, 142, 170
Curtis
  Bro. 116
  Frank 231
  W. A. 138
  W. A., Mrs. 216
  Wesley 70
  Will 216
D. J. Starkweather and Co. 6
Daboeay, Percy Nide, Dr. 120
Dachus, Bud 220
Dailey, Henry 90
Daily
  Belle 136
  George 208, 237
  Henry 208, 226
  Julia 170
Dairyman Association 212
Dallrimple, George 94
Damascus church (SC) 37
dancing 55 – 56
Daniel
  John B. 128, 188
  W. T. 160, 173, 174, 179, 192, 197, 202,
    207, 216
  W. T., Prof. 201
Daniels, [missing] T. 184
Darnell
  A. A. 101, 194, 205, 208, 220, 237
  A. A., Mrs. 112
  Albert A. 21
  Asbery 123
  Asberry 179
  Asbury 139
  Bill 169
  Bry, little 123
  Bud 112
  Docia 123
  Effie 112, 123
  George 185
  Georgia 205
  Harrison 4, 123, 193, 194
  Harrison, Mrs. 79
  John 87, 162
  Lex 123, 179
  M. B. 90, 97, 177
  W. M. 4, 183

Dillard (cont.)
B. R., Mrs. 149
Dock 169
Eula 47
Frank 138
Geo. M. 29
George 112, 139, 169
Hiram 74, 90
J. B. 40
J. D. M. 180
J. H. 147
James H. 85
John 90
Lee 216
Lizzie 138
R. B. 10, 216
R. B., Mrs. 216
Rachel 47, 90
Rachel M. 29
Robert L. 29, 36
Sheriff 9
Willie 185
Z. B. 103, 118, 143, 161, 207
Zac 75
Dillars, B. R. 47
Dillingham
Capt. 8
E. C. 90
James 227
John 227
Lon, Rev. 234
Rev. 172
W. R. "Rush" 8
disease 1
boil 205
cancer 66, 116, 184
chronic 6
consumption 74, 80, 95, 197, 227
diarrhoea 61
diptheria 207
dropsy 208
earache 119
eye 116, 150
feeble 63, 64, 98, 105, 112, 114, 119, 126,
127, 136, 142, 150, 168, 171, 195,
230, 238
felon 227
fever 30, 40, 82, 126, 146, 160, 161, 168,
178, 185, 187, 208, 222, 231, 233,
235
grip 66, 88, 89, 90, 91, 96, 98, 104, 105,
108, 110, 111, 112, 154
headache 126
health, failing 172
heart 70
illness 66, 83, 94, 105, 129, 142, 151,

disease, illness (cont.)
156, 167, 182, 235, 236
inflammation 63
lingering 70, 135
liver complaint 81
malaria 81
measles 114
mumps 107
neuralgia 111
paralysis 153
rheumatism 61, 65, 106, 111, 160, 220
inflamationary 96
roseola 128
scarlatina 49
sickness 2, 8, 17, 20, 25, 32, 33, 36,
38, 42, 45, 46, 47, 49, 56, 57, 58,
59, 60, 63, 64, 67, 68, 69, 72, 73,
74, 75, 76, 78, 79, 80, 82, 83, 88,
89, 94, 96, 97, 102, 104, 106, 109,
110, 111, 112, 114, 115, 117, 118,
119, 120, 121, 122, 125, 126, 127,
128, 129, 132, 134, 135, 136, 139,
140, 141, 143, 146, 148, 150, 154,
156, 157, 160, 161, 164, 167, 168,
169, 170, 174, 184, 185, 187, 189,
191, 192, 197, 198, 207, 208, 210,
212, 218, 219, 220, 223, 228, 230,
232, 234, 237, 238, 239
smallpox 51, 107, 165
strokes, paralytic 189
teeth, absess 240
throat 201
affection 225
affliction 114, 117
sore 179
Typhoid fever 41, 47, 58, 149, 159, 161,
184, 196, 209, 217, 218, 221, 240
yellow jack 36
divorce 33
Dixon
Granville 208, 218
Jeff 64
Rush 159
Docikns, Jesse 161
Dockens, G. B., Marshall 164
Docking, George W. 32
Dockins
Benj. 231, 236
Benjiman 242
Clayton M. 77, 79
Dud 178, 201
Fannie 74, 111
G. B. 36, 200
G. B., Mrs. 36
George 201
H. D. 67, 146

Dockins (cont.)
 Henry 32, 33
 J. B. 40, 50, 60, 176, 177, 229, 236, 242
 James 146, 161, 194, 227, 236
 James, Mrs. 36
 Jess 80
 Jesse 73, 160, 167, 178
 John B. 74, 177
 Lafayette 142, 229, 236
 Mr. 36
 Nancy 111
Dodson, Laura 32, 38
Dog Law 222
dogs 68, 73, 77, 97, 116, 132, 137, 144, 145,
  184, 203, 221, 222, 228
 hounds 211
Donaldson
 G. W. 166
 George 151
 Georgia 152
 Jno. H. 224
 John 5, 209
 Mayor pro tem 119
 W. C. 89, 94, 105, 152, 157, 166, 181,
  187, 188, 199, 224
 W. C., Mrs. 98, 152, 154
Donalson
 John H. 114
 Mayor pro tem 124
 W. C. 119, 128
 W. C., Mrs. 105
Donthit, Lawrence 220
Dorsey
 E. A. 38, 46
 George 123
 Sallie 59, 70
Dotson
 H. B. 56, 97
 J. M. 168
 John 176, 226
 Laura 178
 Paul 56, 95
 Tom 100, 184
Dover[?], D. G. 72
Dover
 D. G. 74, 210
 D. G. "Dan" 85 – 87
 Dan 89
 Dr. 140, 154, 171, 181, 195
 F. B. 240
 J. C. 110
 J. C., Dr. 109, 113, 187, 212
 Jesse C. 39
 Jesse C., Dr. 88
 Mrs. 152
 R. N. 155, 161, 179, 192

Dover (cont.)
 R. N., Prof. 49
 Robert N. 87, 162
 S. W. 64, 89, 110, 161, 181, 195, 206
 S. W., Mrs. 110, 195
 W. S. 28
 W. S., Mrs. 28
Doyer, D. G. 63
Dr. Cady's Condition Powders 168
Dr. J. H. McLean's Liver and Kidney Balm
  45
Dr. J. H. McLean's Volcanic Oil Liniment 51
Dr. King's New Life Pills 81
Dream of Judgment (poem) 222
DuBoeay, P. N., Dr. 129
Duncan[?]
 Ida 208
 Lisa 208
Duncan
 A. J. 18, 84, 89, 157, 182, 189, 204, 231
 A. J. "Dev" 2
 A. J., Mrs. 157
 Andrew J. 22, 74, 85
 Brer' 38
 D. [missing]., Mrs. 221
 D. D. 230
 D. D., Mrs. 230
 D. J. 203
 D. T. 8, 12, 15, 18, 20, 29, 49, 58, 69, 86,
  93, 103, 109, 110, 143, 187, 196,
  214, 218
 D. T., Esq. 105, 157, 219
 D. T., Mrs. 35, 78, 195, 209
 Devero 100
 Effie 20, 29, 127, 152, 181, 219
 Eliza 65
 Eliza Jane 196
 Eppee 35
 Esq. 61, 66
 Garfield 179
 Harry 20, 83, 90, 95, 134, 150, 151
 I. R. 215
 Ida 63, 132, 152, 181, 219
 Isaace 206
 J. B. 215
 Jeff 135
 Jeff, Uncle 132, 210, 221
 John 179
 John B. 170
 Liza 143, 228
 Lizzie 40, 141, 144
 Misses 181
 Squire 171
 "Uncle Jeff" 172
 W. H. 32, 33, 58, 172
 Will 57

Godfrey (cont.)
   J. W., Marshal 38
   Joe 109
   John 75, 116, 149, 152, 187, 203, 235,
      241
   John, Dept. 63, 72
   John, Deputy 173
   John W. 42, 67, 70, 204, 213
   John W., Mrs. 204
   Joseph 74
   Zoe 149, 217
   Zoie 213
Godfry
   John, Marshal 7
   John Wes 29
   Marshal 3
gold fever 31
gold standard 33
Gomer, Bob 76
Grady hospital 189
Gramling, Spaulding & Co. 9, 101
Grand Bazar 44
Grand Hotel 100
Grand Lodge 42
Grant
   B. W. 172, 204
   C. E. 1
   Charley 231
   Charlie 110, 221, 233, 235, 240
   Charlie, Mrs. 110
   Mr. 188
   W. B. 231
   W. B., Mrs. 188, 209
   W. D. 233, 235
   W. D., Mrs. 233, 235
Grant House 204
Green[?], Mary 152
Green
   Ada 66, 73, 145, 154, 155, 197, 238
   Amanda 187
   Beulah 42, 127, 143, 145, 174, 197, 240
   Bulah 155
   Carrie 232
   Claude 71, 72, 89, 127, 134, 145, 146,
      149, 155, 192, 194
   D. M. 46, 90, 105, 200
   D. M., Dr. 20
   Dr. 40, 58, 74, 86, 94, 97, 112, 116, 117,
      119, 132, 134, 135, 140, 154, 161,
      187, 195, 201, 214, 218, 232
   Drew 240
   Drew M. 21, 162
   J. A. 170
   J. C. 89, 173
   J. C., Mrs. 146
   J. W. 14, 15, 172, 223

Green (cont.)
   J. W., Hon. 8
   J. W., Mrs. 118, 172
   James 66, 145, 155, 192, 197, 215
   James "Jim" 153
   Jess 197
   Jess, Mrs. 67
   Jesse 67, 72, 149, 150, 217, 238
   Jesse, Mrs. 149
   Jesse W. 67, 85, 148, 151, 201
   Jno. 91
   John A. 8, 90
   John A., Prof. 3
   John Sr. 37
   John W. 66, 73, 129, 153, 162, 211, 217
   Mrs. 187, 235, 236
   Porter 67, 71, 99, 134, 170
   Prof. 167, 234
   Ray 217
   representative 240
   Senator 221, 235, 236
   Susie 67
   T. F. 200
   Virgil 66, 73, 134, 139, 145, 155, 156, 173
   W. J. 60, 85, 89, 97, 103, 135, 143
   W. J. "Doc" 80
   W. J., Dr. 49, 146, 161
   W. J., Mrs. 135
   W. J., Senator 189, 200, 205, 220
Greenville (SC) jail 180
Greenwood 168, 190
   B. H. 64, 119, 216
   Ben 139, 212, 216
   G. W. 90, 216
   Geo. 207
   Geo. W. 142
   Geo. W., Mrs. 142
   J. J. 94, 216, 240
   James, Mrs. 142
   James J. 22
   Octa 197
   W. H. 142, 153, 197, 208, 210, 212
   W. H., Mrs. 142, 198
   Will 139
   Will, Mrs. 139
Greenwood & York 14, 15, 16
Greer, Thomas F. 163, 164
Gresham, Messr. 39
Griggs, M. P., Mrs. 17
Grist[?], Charlie 243
Grist
   A. J. 89
   Andrew J. 22
   Benny 125
   Benny, Uncle 169, 179, 205
   Judson 64

McCrackin (cont.)
  H. C. 50
  H. C., Prof. 51
  H. D. 160, 161
  Hannah 73, 184
  Hiram 40, 68
  Hiram, Mrs. 80
  J. B. 89 – 90, 157, 167
  J. B. "Bell" 168
  J. F. 89
  Jeff 73
  John Bell 159
  Laura 67
  M. V. 57, 89
  Virgil 160, 173, 179, 192, 232
  W. J. 157
  W. P. 82
  William P. 21
McCrakin, Martin V. 74
McCrcakin, J. B. 161
McCully
  P. K. 162
  P. K., Capt. 118, 182
McCurry
  Amos 34
  Amos, Mrs. 177
  Gus 180, 225
  I. A. 36, 46, 90, 145
  Isaac 132
  Jess 125
  Jesse 47, 119, 230
  Texie 126
  W. J. 27, 42, 145
  William J. 22
McElwain, Messr. 24
McFall[?], John 162
McGath, Julius, Rev. 200
McGee, G. N. 159
McGuire, J. M. 65
McHan, Chas. 159
McIntyre[?], Barney 48
McKay
  Charlie 100
  Jno. 151
  Joe 73
  Will 151
McKinley Administration 41
McKinney, S. L. 115
McKinny, S. L. 204
McNutt, William 101
McWharter, W. M. 111
McWhorter, Malissa 168
Means, A. 162
Meece
  A. J. 164
  Earnest 158

Merrimac 54
Merritt
  Lory 57
  Messr. 24
Merritte, Dr. 25
Metcalf, Cloy 84
Meyers, R. C. V. 36
Mexico 215
Michigan
  Grand Rapids 82
Middlebrook
  Mr. 29
  Mrs. 29
Mille, L. P. 157
Miller
  Clarence 171
  Lee 171
  Mr. 243
Mincalf, William 194
mink 45
Mitchel
  E. M. 165
  Eugene 166
Mitchell 230
  Austin 117
  Eugene 169
  Mr. 32, 80, 217
  Sam 38, 78, 90, 203
  Tom 203
Mongold, Thomas 4
Montgomery, E. S. 101
moonshine 75 – 76
  See also: beverages, illicit, making
moonshiners 92 – 93
Moore 31, 46, 101, 102
  Dela, Little 235
  Dr. 221
  E. A., Mrs. 160
  Edhriam H. 74
  Ella 215
  George 76
  H. V. 89, 122
  Hiram 80, 227
  J. B. 223
  James 58
  John 108, 154, 167
  John M. 115, 148
  L. H. 204
  Leila 70
  Lillie 108, 166, 168
  Lizzie 108
  M. M. 90, 99
  M. S. 173, 192
  Malcalm 212
  Malcolm 198
  Malcom 216

Railroads (cont.)
    Southern 147, 190, 215, 238
    station
        Demorest 6
        Tallulah Falls 17
    Tallulah Falls 60, 93, 168, 190, 197, 232
    Tallulah Falls to Clayton 201
    Vicennis, Vevay and South Atlantic 70
    Western and Atlantic 174
Rainey, Susie 47
Ramburn, Henry F. 145
Ramey
    [Illegible] 72
    A. J. 68
    B[?]. E. 223
    B. E. 56, 63, 68, 85, 95, 97, 107, 159, 168,
        173, 235
    Banjo Dave 90
    Benjamin "Bennie" 79
    Bettie 232
    David 238
    David, Rev. 232
    Eliza 107
    Ella 104, 145
    Elsie 51, 195
    H. C. 50, 176
    H. J. 146, 194
    H. L. 97, 158
    Isaac 191
    J. B. 143
    J. H. 90, 203
    J. J. 83, 125
    J. M. 92, 104
    J. M., little 97
    J. R. 129, 168
    J. S. 57, 63, 81, 103, 115, 117, 125, 143
    J. S. "Spart", Clerk 148
    J. S., Clerk 189 – 190, 191, 234
    J. S., Mrs. 128, 134, 141, 209
    J. S., Prof. 3
    J. W. 56
    James 73, 95
    James H. 74, 85
    James M. 67, 74
    Jim 238
    L. M. 133
    Leander M. 90
    Lip 197
    Lizzie 74
    Lula 136
    M. B. 129
    Marinda 97, 129
    Marinda J. 225
    Martin 75
    Marvin 57
    Mary 95

Ramey (cont.)
    May 143, 148, 150
    Nin 1, 144, 146, 155, 167, 173, 192, 238
    Nin, Prof. 201, 233
    R. C. 145
    R. M., Miss 109
    Rebecca 111
    Shug 208
    Sug 238
    Susie 32, 48, 115, 173, 192
    Sylvester 223
    Tillman 72, 87, 162
    Tillman, Mrs. 72
    Virgal 112
    W. H. L. 90
    W. J. 68, 223
    W. P. 92
    William 68
    William J. 21
    Wm. J. 162
Ramie
    Sport 51
    Susie 51
Ramsey, Mr. 68
Ramy, Susie 43
Rathell, F. D. 91
Ray
    Mary 28
    Mr. 17
Redwine, J. E. 145
Reed
    Eve 173
    George W. 74
    George W. Sr. 21
Reever, Mrs. 156
Rembert
    Lelah 37
    M. L. 37
    W. P. 213
    W. P., Mrs. 209
    Walter 160
Renner, Chas. F. 102
revenue stamps 78
revenuers
    revenue men 27
    revenue officers 48, 49, 69, 75 – 76, 83,
        132, 171, 196, 219
    revenue officials 29, 33 – 34, 224, 235
    revenues (officers) 65, 72 – 73, 126, 142,
        237
Reynolds
    B. C. 188
    J. A. 56, 157, 205
    Jimmie 143
    Jno. H. 216
    John A. 17, 87, 162, 193

skunk 54
Sloan 79
Smith
  [?]. S. 162
  A. P. 67
  Albert 89
  Anda 238
  Andrew 90
  Andy 67, 80
  B. F. 45
  B. F., Dr. 177
  Bailiff 175
  Billy, Uncle 160
  Bud 162
  C. D. 162
  Charles 51
  Charlie, Uncle 157
  Chief of Police 180
  Cife 112
  D. M. 125, 224
  Dallas 170
  David, Mrs. 125
  Drew 59
  Emanual 74
  Emiline 153 – 154
  Emily, Aunt 95
  Frank 210
  Frank T. 153
  G. [?]. 46
  G. V. 153, 167
  G. V., Mrs. 184
  George 133
  J. B. 89, 90
  J. D. 107
  J. F. 50
  J. J. 90
  J. S. 175, 178
  J. T. 63
  J. W. 4, 68, 223
  J. W., Prof. 27
  James, Mrs. 118
  James F. 21, 60, 89, 106, 194, 235, 240
  James M. 242
  Jane 124, 129
  Jesse W. 22
  Jessie 144
  Jim 107
  John 71, 125
  John B. 74
  John W. 73
  L. D. 104
  Leander 95
  M. J., Mrs. 133
  Milo 66
  Milo M. 67
  Mrs. 129

Smith (cont.)
  Pechin 213
  R. 199
  Ransom 76
  Ransom G. 162
  Rocky Bottom, Uncle 75
  Ruth 173, 175, 192, 198, 207
  Sarah 169
  Si 121, 141, 144, 163, 179, 180 – 181, 183, 186
  W. P. 204
  Walter 74, 101, 179
  Walter D. 178
  Walter D., Mrs. 178
  Wm. T. 87, 162
snakes 146
  coach whip 165
  pilot 159
  rattle snake pilate 189
  rattlesnakes 7, 132, 137, 142, 154, 166, 169, 170, 182, 184
Sons of Rest, The 8
Soukee[?] River 130
South, the 232
South Carolina 30, 32, 50, 51, 68, 72, 79, 91, 100, 106, 142, 146, 164, 168, 185, 187, 207, 214, 222, 234
  Abbeville 182
  Anderson 7, 8, 34, 38, 42, 58, 91, 118, 119, 123, 164, 171, 182, 199, 213, 220, 227, 238
  Anderson County 173
  Charleston 92, 99, 120, 130
  Clemson College 32, 33, 36, 67, 90, 157, 159, 161, 233
  Columbia 206
  Damascus 37
  Double Springs 96
  Fairplay 57, 69, 165, 188
  Fort Hill 68, 128
  Fort Madison 212
  Greenville 34, 169, 177, 180, 238
  Hampton 123
  Hardensville 26
  Iva 225
  Long Creek 68, 73, 78, 81, 111, 129, 133, 221
  Mount Rest 30
  Mountain Rest 89, 159
  Oakway 57, 65, 89
  Oconee County 37, 39, 96, 220
  Pendleton 79
  Piedmont 102
  Port Royal 42, 69, 92, 100, 103, 118, 120, 162, 169, 206
  Russel(l) 148, 187, 207

Sweat, William R. 22
Sweatman
    Susan 124
    Z. 21, 242
Sweet 41
    Mayor 31, 43
    Messr. 27
    W. B. 29
    W. R. 16, 32, 36
Sweet & Taylor 51
    See also: Taylor & Sweet
Switzerland of America, The 24
Swofford
    Charles 129
    Charles C. 120
    Ella 230
    Ethel D. 162
    J. A. 204, 213
    Jeff 156, 235
    Luther 126
    M. J. 60
    M. W. 89, 103, 143, 158
    Marlor 107
    Ray, Little 230
    W. A. 90, 120, 129
    William A. 74, 85
Sylvester Bleckley Mercantile Co. 7
T. N. Carter & Co. 46, 147, 213
Talley
    Hasie 179
    John 173
    John Jr. 162
    Mr. 173
Tallulah Falls, guide 30
Tallulah Falls Hall 25
Tally, John 173
Tancred
    Thomas 100
    Thomas, Sir 118
Tancreed, Thomas, Sir 150
Tanner
    Charles 183
    Charles H. 180
    Charley 181
    Charlie 185
    J. S. 103
    John 18 – 19, 64, 126, 136
    John, Mrs. 102
    Minnie 60
    (Mr.) 178
Tate, Carter, Hon. 35
Taylor
    Cincinatus 13
    Clint 74
    D. D., Rev. 74, 80, 139, 167, 178, 233
    Dancie 38

Taylor (cont.)
    Dial D. 150
    Drucie 38
    Elsie 197
    F. A. 227
    Frazier A. 162
    Henry J. 74
    J. R. 29, 35, 41, 45
    Jane 13
    Jeptha 90, 107
    Jeptha H. 74, 85
    Jesse 13, 90
    John 13
    Messr. 27
    Mr. 121
    Radway 32
    Rev. 95, 172
    S. T., Prof. 30, 38
    Samuel 13, 90
    Samuel, Rev. 108, 142
    Samuel Sr. 21, 162
    Tatum 140
    V. C. 32
    Walter 51, 161
    Willard 161, 184
Taylor & Sweet 14, 45, 48, 50, 148, 151
Teague
    Jim 89
    Liceny 84
    Minnie 89
Teams[?], Dan 151
Teams, Alph 86
Teems
    Daniel 142
    L. T. 89, 180
    Lee T. 101
temperance 152, 216, 222
ten-pin alley 24
Tennessee 70, 125, 164, 208
    Chattanooga 71, 159, 164, 169, 174, 206,
        234
    Hamilton County 163
    Knoxville 12, 92, 101, 162, 169
    Nashville 101, 136, 160
Texas 20, 47, 117, 182, 215, 216
    Climax 90
    Fort Clark 216
Thanksgiving 230
Thomas
    A. B., Rev. 89, 121, 136, 216
    Benn 37
    Phil 29
    Rev. 139
    W. H. 101
Thomason, F. H. 143

Made in the USA
Middletown, DE
15 February 2023